Politics
1964

WADSWORTH CONTINUING EDUCATION SERIES
Leonard Freedman, General Editor

Contemporary Communism: Theory and Practice
*edited by Howard R. Swearer
and Richard P. Longaker
University of California, Los Angeles*

Contemporary Moral Issues
*edited by Harry K. Girvetz
University of California, Santa Barbara*

Issues of the Sixties
*edited by Leonard Freedman
University Extension
University of California at Los Angeles
and Cornelius P. Cotter
Stanford University*

Metropolis: Values in Conflict
*edited by C. E. Elias, Jr.,
James Gillies, and Svend Riemer
University of California, Los Angeles*

Politics 1964
*edited by Francis M. Carney
and H. Frank Way, Jr.
University of California, Riverside*

N

Politics 1964

EDITED BY FRANCIS M. CARNEY
AND H. FRANK WAY, JR.

University of California, Riverside

WADSWORTH PUBLISHING COMPANY, INC.

Belmont, California

L.C. Cat. Card No.: 64-13518

Printed in the United States of America

PREFACE

POLITICS 1964 presents the major economic, social, and international issues confronting both the nation and the voter in a presidential election year. This collection from the writings of the leading statesmen and political analysts in recent and current American politics has been prepared for the use of every responsible citizen who is—or should be—vitally concerned with the national and international politics that will play such a decisive part in choosing the next President of the United States. Even more than in recent presidential elections, the 1964 Republican and Democratic candidates, as well as the public, must be aware of their increasing responsibilities. The voter cannot analyze a candidate's awareness of his responsibilities without knowing what is going to be demanded of the next President. It has, therefore, been our objective to present various views of these responsibilities for the information and guidance of the voter, who will, of course, choose the next President.

Part One, "The Processes," presents a many-faceted analysis of our political system, especially as it operates in a presidential year and as it will influence and persuade the voter. Accordingly, the articles in this part focus attention on political parties and political pressure groups; the Presidency is also closely examined in some of its many dimensions. The emphasis changes in Part Two, "The Issues," to a presentation of conflicting views of the most important issues confronting the public and the government today. Regardless of which party the next President represents, he must have made his position on these vital issues sufficiently clear to have won the confidence of the majority of the American voters. Certainly, other important issues, such as agriculture and the problem of surpluses, will confront the voter in 1964. We do feel, however, that the issues presented are major issues: whether they are debated in the campaign on a partisan basis or not, they are part of the political climate of our time and thus deserve thoughtful consideration.

Since many of the selections included in this collection have been excerpted, we have taken the liberty of giving some of them titles to indicate the nature of their content as presented in this book. We have transcribed the articles as faithfully as possible—correcting only obvious misprints, eliminating footnotes where feasible, and renumbering footnotes that remain.

We wish to extend our appreciation to the numerous individuals and organizations that have contributed to this publication. In particular, we thank the various authors whose articles appear here. We should also like to express our appreciation to University Extension of the University of California for its assistance. Our special thanks go to Leonard Freedman, Head of the Department of Social Sciences, University Extension, University of California. Our gratitude is also extended to Carolyn Kirkpatrick, James Bell, and Michael Philips, who assisted in the preparation of the manuscript.

Francis M. Carney
H. Frank Way, Jr.

University of California
Riverside

The senseless and brutal assassination of President John F. Kennedy on November 22, 1963, shocked and grieved men of good will the world over. At the same time, however, our sorrowing nation witnessed the strength and stability of its constitutional system in the immediate transfer of the office of the Presidency to Lyndon B. Johnson. Clearly, the framers of the Constitution did not fashion an office that would draw its strength and effectiveness entirely from the personal qualities of any incumbent. Until his death, the office of President of the United States seemed to belong uniquely to John Fitzgerald Kennedy. Still, President Johnson was able to draw upon that reserve of power and majesty which the office instantly confers upon an incumbent. While that reserve of power and the stability and continuity it symbolizes is testimony to the wisdom of the framers and to the durability of our constitutional order, it is to the personal quality of the institution—the fact that there is a *Presidency* and a *President*—that we wish here to direct our attention.

In evaluating the succession of President Johnson, we should recognize that the New Frontier was not the program of Mr. Kennedy alone but that of the Kennedy administration—an administration that included Lyndon B. Johnson. In matters of taxing and spending, education, employment, national defense, space exploration, and foreign-trade policy, the Kennedy position reflected a broad administration and Democratic Party consensus about the nature of the national problems and the needed solutions to these problems. Thus there was a large measure of continuity in policy and little or no change in the policy issues (covered in Part Two of this book) that the electorate would face in 1964.

Then, too, as President Johnson discovered, there are relentless and almost intractable objective realities in the modern world which limit and define the ambit within which policy is made. In his last months, President Kennedy spoke often of the limits on his power, of his rising consciousness that he was simply not able to do all the things that he wanted to do. Those limiting realities—the great and inscrutable power of the adversaries, the restlessness and pride of the allies, poverty and the hunger for modernity in the uncommitted world, the salience and persistence of particular and local interests in this nation, and the power and will of proud men in the states and Congress who represent those interests— yield no more readily to the commanding tones of President Johnson than they did to the eloquency and energy of President Kennedy. The very limitations on the nation's freedom of action ensure a measure of continuity of policy and public issues.

But it would be wrong to conclude that the Vice Presidency is merely the *alter ego* of the Presidency, or that the party bond implies that Democratic politicians are so many interchangeable parts, or that the objective limits on action leave no margin for the impact of the differing personal capacities of men. If the history of the Presidency has taught us anything, it is that this great office has been shaped by men as well as by events. As Professor Edward S. Corwin noted years ago, the modern Presidency is the product of the interaction of crisis and personality. Each great President leaves the stamp of his personality on the office, and all Presidents leave their personal mark on their own times. We have witnessed in a moving way the remarkable extent to which the Presidency is personalized. When the nation learned that President Kennedy had been slain, its sorrow for the man and his family and for its own loss was mingled with a noticeable mood of anxiety and fear. Men and women and young people seemed to feel as though the *Presidency* had been slain, as though the wounds in the body of the man were like so many wounds in the body politic. That such anxiety was misplaced or unjustified in no way refutes the fact that for Americans the office of our chief magistrate is inextricably linked with the person of its occupant.

With his death, the Kennedy Era began to end. Despite the continuity of the office, change is inevitable. As President Johnson took office, the following areas were those in which change was expected to occur.

RELATIONS BETWEEN THE PRESIDENT AND CONGRESS. All Presidents enjoy, upon entering their tenure, a "honeymoon" with Congress during which the normal tensions between the executive and legislative branches are abated somewhat and Congress is inclined to be generous to the Presidential requests. President Kennedy had his honeymoon in 1961, but by 1963 his legislative requests were being severely mauled in Congress. The normal honeymoon, the extra good will enjoyed by Presidents suddenly thrust by tragic circumstance into the White House, and a possible wish by the captains of Congress to pay their respects to the fallen President by acceding, posthumously for him, to a portion of his program, seem likely to allow President Johnson to reap a larger harvest of the legislative program sown by President Kennedy than the latter could reasonably have expected to harvest himself. However, very real interests opposed to the Kennedy program are powerfully entrenched and represented in

Congress. President Johnson's ultimate success in working with Congress depends not only on his skill and commitment, but also on the extent of his willingness to trim that program.

PARTY STRATEGIES FOR 1964. A Johnson Presidency and candidacy to succeed himself may impair the attractiveness of the southern strategy for the Republicans. The latter strategy was based upon a perception of deep and widespread southern antipathy to President Kennedy. It is not clear that the same antipathy has been directed against Mr. Johnson. He may be a more formidable candidate in the South than Mr. Kennedy would have been, thus changing the basis of the southern strategy. On the other hand, southern antipathy toward Mr. Johnson may develop to a strength equal to the antipathy directed toward Mr. Kennedy. White supremacists of the South may indeed feel that Johnson's sin in embracing the Kennedy civil-rights program is even greater than Mr. Kennedy's because Johnson, by standing for the full civil-rights program, "betrays his southern birthright."

The Democrats, for their part, may feel that Mr. Johnson does not have, and as President does not have the time to develop, the appeal to the urban, labor, and liberal constituencies that Mr. Kennedy so definitely did have. We may expect a distinct but ineffective attempt on the part of some liberal Democrats to deny the nomination to Mr. Johnson. Most likely, however, the Democrats will choose as Vice-Presidential nominee a candidate from the North and with strong appeal for the urban, labor, and liberal components of the Democratic Party.

FOREIGN AFFAIRS. In no field of the President's responsibilities are his personal style and his personal capacities more important than in the field of foreign affairs. Under the Constitution the President is uniquely responsible for the conduct of the nation's foreign policy. In the years of the Cold War, moreover, personal diplomacy among heads of state has become a normal procedure. President Kennedy, in addition, was, as no President since Franklin D. Roosevelt had been, his own Secretary of State. He kept the formation and execution of foreign policy very firmly in his own hands. His own chief interest, the bent of his talent, and his prior training all bespoke a primary interest in foreign policy. His own marked personal grace and even the cosmopolitan charm of his wife were not the least conspicuous instruments of his personal diplomacy. The change of men necessarily brings with it some change in the *style* of conduct of the nation's foreign policy.

The matter of change in the *substance* of our foreign policy is not so clear-cut. Those realities that limit our margins for decision and action are most relentless in the field of foreign affairs. Yet Mr. Kennedy had succeeded in marking out a personal position in foreign affairs that did not have the support of all the elements of his own party and which brought upon his head some of the severest criticism he had to bear. By September of 1963, Mr. Kennedy had clearly come to stand for *détente* in our mutual relations with the Soviet Union, for a thaw in the Cold War, for negotiation rather than the risk of provocative action. He dared a measure of guarded optimism for the prospect that the two great power blocs might one day live in fruitful mutual interaction in an atmosphere of peace and good will. The sober retreat from the brink of nuclear war over the Soviet missiles in Cuba, the nuclear test-ban agreement, the agreement to sell surplus United States wheat to the Soviet Union, and the offer to the U.S.S.R. to engage in cooperative efforts in the conquest of space were the personal initiatives of Mr. Kennedy. As we have said, it is not clear that all Americans support them or the spirit in which they were made. President Johnson may not share the perspective of Mr. Kennedy. In the field of foreign affairs, then, we cannot ignore the possibility of some changes as a result of the death of Mr. Kennedy.

CIVIL RIGHTS. In his every word and action as Vice President, Mr. Johnson lent his full support to the civil-rights objectives and achievements of President Kennedy. He has spoken pridefully, moreover, of his own achievements as Chairman of the President's Commission on Equal Opportunity. As a Senator, his votes in 1957 and 1958 on civil-rights roll calls were virtually identical with the votes of the then Senator Kennedy. Yet, because he is a son of the Southwest and because as Majority Leader he was a celebrated mediator between the pro-civil rights and southern wings of his own party, many men and groups wonder about the intensity of his commitment to the Kennedy civil-rights program. He is being watched closely for signs that he is prepared to jettison portions of the civil-rights program, to salvage other pieces of domestic and foreign-policy legislation, or to preserve a measure of unity in his party and to dampen down the flames of controversy over that agitated question.

These, then, are the areas in which the greatest amount of change may come, owing to the murder of Mr. Kennedy. From this brief postscript, it is clear, however, that we believe that *continuity* best characterizes the succession of Lyndon Johnson to the Presidency. Just as have so many Americans, we too express wonder as we contemplate the uninterrupted chain of Presidential successions from 1789 to 1963. Finally, we express our personal sorrow that the evil events of November 22, 1963, took from us that vibrant, gifted, and gallant man. If it is not too great an impertinence, we should like to dedicate this volume to the memory of John Fitzgerald Kennedy.

CONTENTS

PART ONE: THE PROCESSES

PART TWO: THE ISSUES

PART ONE

THE PROCESSES

CHAPTER ONE

The Retreat From Politics

The Editors

In *Politics 1960,* we embraced the view that politics refers to all things pertaining to the public life of a community, to all the ways the people of a community go about arranging for the general interest. We also held that in a representative democracy politics is the legitimate concern of all of the people, and that the vitality of a democracy is measurable by the extent and quality of popular participation in government. We suggested, moreover, that there was some evidence that the American people were in the midst of a flight from politics, that both the extent and the quality of our participation had become impaired, and that there were serious questions about the vitality of our democratic institutions.

Now, four years later, we find that the questions remain, and that the retreat from politics may be gathering momentum. It is true that voting in the 1960 presidential election was up nearly 5 percent over that of 1956. It is also true that the extraordinary public interest in President Kennedy, his family, and his social circles has lent to politics a certain "chic" or glamor. It is entirely possible that the curve of participation for the 1964 election may rise again, if President Kennedy is challenged by a forceful and attractive Republican, and if the campaign managers and the mass media do well their job of dramatizing the contest. But we must emphasize that quantity alone is not sufficient evidence of the democratic vitality of a people. The quality of the vote is as important as its size. And it is in the quality of our voting that recent research has uncovered signs of pathology. If there is a long-term enfeeblement of our democratic nerve, it cannot be reversed by such short-run forces as an exciting or close presidential race or the appearance on the stage of a personally attractive politician.

What, then, is the evidence that supports the fear that we are in a retreat from politics? The quantitative evidence is alarming enough. In each of the last three presidential elections, less than two thirds of the eligible citizens voted. In some recent congressional elections, the voter turnout dipped below half of those eligible, and in many municipal and county elections, turnouts under a quarter of those eligible are common. Upon reflection, these seemingly simple facts are staggering. Professor V. O. Key, Jr., has said that if an electorate loses "the capacity to bestir itself to high levels of activity when the occasion warrants, the chances are that a basic alteration in the location and responsiveness of authority within the society has occurred." When a third of the citizens do not participate in the choosing of the President, when half do not help to choose the Congress, and when local officials are named by less than a third of the constituency, what can we say of the "location and responsiveness of authority within the society"?

Voting, obviously, is the most elementary act of citizenship. When we look at participation beyond the simple act of voting, the findings are yet more dismal. The University of Michigan Survey Research Center found that in 1956 only 3 percent of the eligible electorate belonged to any political club or organization, only 10 percent had given money or bought tickets to help one or the other of the parties, 7 percent had attended any meeting or rally, and only 3 percent had done any "other work" for a party or candidate. So we may assume that at best 10 percent of the electorate is overtly "active" on behalf of a party or candidate.

That political activity for most people consists solely of voting is not in itself cause for concern. What haunts the imagination is the nearly unanimous finding of the scholarly studies of electoral behavior that even among the voters there is a large measure of indifference to the outcome of elections and a widespread feeling that one's vote really does not amount to very much—that it will have little effect on government or "the way things are." Professor William Buchanan speaks for the scholars when he notes that evidence of awareness among citizens of any personal influence on the policy-determining process and of any accompanying determination to make this influence felt is "not very impressive." Buchanan further observes that even those whom he classifies as "purposive voters" do not prefer political to social techniques for shaping the environment, nor do they show any particular optimism about the results that can be achieved with the vote.

The emergent portrait of the American voter has instigated a flourishing literature that attempts to re-examine traditional democratic theory in the light of the changed picture of the voter. We find this debate over democratic theory in itself a striking fact and, insofar as many of its participants seem reconciled with a diminished role for the citizen, further evidence of a decline in our political vitality.

We cannot examine exhaustively here that literature which, relying primarily on the evidence of the scholarly voting studies, either embraces eagerly or resigns itself to a significantly diminished role for the democratic electorate. Most of the minimalist democrats place equal emphases on the incapacity of the individual voters—on their lack of information, their lack of interest, their hostility to ambiguity and complexity, their fecklessness, and their lack of analytical sophistication—and on the complexity and technicality of the issues themselves, a complexity and technicality that in the opinion of the minimalists taxes the capacities of even the informed and interested citizen.

Arthur M. Schlesinger, Jr., distinguished historian of "heroic" ages of our national history and now an adviser to a President whom he plainly hopes may be cast in the same heroic mold of Jackson and Franklin D. Roosevelt, calls for a modification of traditional democratic theory. Mr. Schlesinger argues that the citizen clearly can no longer play the role envisioned for him by that theory, not only because of the citizen's imperfections of mind and will, but also because the issues have become so deep and so obscure and the machinery for their resolution so complex that ordinary men are helpless and cowed. What is worse, continues Mr. Schlesinger, recognition of his helplessness and of his failure in the role that theory sets for him sickens modern democratic man, turns him from the practice of politics, and estranges him from the political order. Schlesinger rightly characterizes this divorcement as a morbid and dangerous condition, yet one which we invite and indeed chain ourselves to, so long as our belief system demands a major role for the citizen and simultaneously limits leadership severely by binding it with the thongs of constant popular approval and constitutional disabilities. We must, Mr. Schlesinger concludes, learn to live with—to be comfortable with, in fact—a citizen role confined to the selection of "heroic leaders" who must be left free to cope in superior fashion with the grotesquely difficult problems of our time. Mr. Schlesinger, let it be stressed, professes adherence to the democratic way, and feels that his system of heroic leadership meets the requirements of a reasonable democratic order.

Walter Lippmann, who characterizes himself as a liberal democrat, placed himself in the ranks of the minimalists with the publication in 1955 of his troubled *The Public Philosophy*. Mr. Lippmann did not need the evidence of the voting studies. For him, the history of modern times— specifically from World War I to the present—is sufficient evidence of the "catastrophic" nature of the "intrusion" of the people as voters into the policy-making processes of democracies. To Lippmann, the ability of the masses to have their way, to force a close responsiveness upon elected officials, represents a "derangement" of the proper powers and relations of government. In *The Public Philosophy*, Mr. Lippmann called for a return to "the tradition of civility" with a stricter ordering of public power. An appropriate arrangement of power would leave the people as voters with a still vital though limited role—a role not dissimilar from that envisioned for them by Mr. Schlesinger, a role that is essentially passive. For Lippmann stated that in the tradition of civility, the special political competence of the people is to give their consent to being governed, to grant or withhold approval of the measures taken by leadership. But, he insisted, it is not within their competence to do more, to participate actively, to direct or guide the leadership with an affirmative voice.

Perhaps the most celebrated of revisionist statements comes from the authors of *Voting,* one of the most important of the scholarly studies of the electorate. After an initially somber confrontation with the implications of their own data—derived from a panel study in depth of the citizens of Elmira, New York, during the 1948 presidential election—these authors concluded that apathy, ignorance, irrationality, and general lack of civic sense in a large part of the electorate may actually function to produce a system that "not only works on the most difficult and complex questions but often works with distinction." In order to establish their variation on an old liberal theme derived from Bernard Mandeville, namely that "private vice equals public virtue," the authors of *Voting* first defined a healthy society as one that holds steadily to a balance between cleavage and consensus. They found the healthy American balance between cleavage and consensus to rest first of all on the well-demonstrated heterogeneity of American society, a property of our collective character rather than of our separate individual characters or qualities. Our heterogeneity—they call it "pluralism"—"makes for enough consensus to hold the system together and enough cleavage to make it move." Our political health, then, emerges as a by-product of our social life rather than as a product of our virtue, of our will, or of our determination together to seek out the common interest. What might appear as defective citizenship in the light of classical democratic theory actually may contribute to our political health. Disinterestedness or apathy keeps down the level of political excitement and allows change to take place quietly. Nonvoting or nonparticipation in politics allows decisions to be made by those who are interested and informed. This self-selective nonparticipation results in a species of "specialization of function" in which some citizens perform the political tasks of the society and others serve their country by remaining out of politics.

We cannot here make any point by point rebuttal of the various arguments of those whom we have called "democratic minimalists." Certainly the minimalists have their critics. Eugene Burdick, V. O. Key, S. M. Lipset, and Walter Berns, among others, have produced penetrating critiques of the tentative theory offered by the authors of *Voting.* What strikes us as significant about the efflorescence of democratic revisionist literature is that such literature should appear at all and that it comes from writers and scholars who are wholly committed to democracy. If it is true, as Mr. Schlesinger declares, that ". . . the people can no longer govern," then our society has become something different from what it was and from what it still pretends to be.

We do not agree with those who would accept as democratic a greatly reduced role for the citizens. We do not think that one can characterize as "healthy," "rather superior," or "distinguished" a political system in which large fractions of the citizenry do not participate at all and when many of those citizens who do participate have little or no sense of the efficacy of their acts, little or no confidence that their political life is of any importance to themselves or to society. Such an electorate may be fitted for no more active a role than the occasional selection of leaders who are free to govern without direction or inspiration from the people. Alexis de Tocqueville feared that individual powerlessness before the state was a menace overhanging all democratic societies. In a brooding passage, he predicted that in the condition of individual isolation and powerlessness, "the people shake off their state of dependence just long enough to select their master, and then relapse into it again."

But we do not think that the citizens must be isolated and powerless. We think that there can be widespread citizen participation in policy making, that there can be more discussion of issues and more dissemination of information about policy problems. If the official policy-making labyrinth that winds through and around the parties, the major interest groups, and the recesses of Capitol Hill, and if the layered complexity of the executive establishment is too obscure for the citizen to see how he can affect it—then the institutional machinery can be changed, and be made more accessible. Even when the normal machinery of politics has become inaccessible to the citizens, there still are ways to influence official policy. Can anyone doubt that government is responding with concern to the promptings of the young Negro demonstrators in the South and elsewhere? It is not heroic leaders but heroic people who have propelled civil rights to the very center of our public concerns.

We do not believe that the revisionists have fully understood classical democratic theory. Theorists of democracy from Aristotle to John Stuart Mill have expressed the faith that ordinary citizens can know their own interests and the general interest as well, and furthermore, that ordinary citizens can make wise or good political decisions. But the classical theorists did not account democracy a good form of government solely because men can make good decisions. From the Greeks to Mill, the advocates of democracy have held it to be good because it makes men better. The democrats of Periclean Athens held one to be a man only if he participated in government. Aristotle believed that to engage in governance was to complete or to fulfill one's human nature whereas to be walled off from government was to be forever stunted in one's development. And if the authors of *The Federalist* feared the "unruly passions" of men in politics, they also expressed their conviction that responsibility tempers the passions and makes men sober and prudent. J. S. Mill argued that nonparticipating publics were stunted not only in their intelligence but in their "moral capacities" as well, and he valued representative government less for the quality of its decisions than for its role in promoting individual excellence. Indeed, almost everywhere one turns in an examination of the older advocacies of the democratic way, he finds thinkers who valued democracy mainly for what democracy does for men rather than for what democratic men do for their societies. Certainly, Rousseau believed that to be citizens, participating members of a self-governed community ennobled men—made them better, helped them to become what all men have it in their nature to become. The natural-rights thinkers valued popular government because it alone vouchsafed to men their birthright: the right to govern themselves that belonged to them by nature and which their nature required for completion. To say that classical democratic theory consists mainly of a set of expectations about the rationality, interest, and knowledgeability of men is to imply that the only classical democratic theorists were the Utilitarians or Philosophical Radicals and that there was no democratic theory before or after Jeremy Bentham and James Mill.

Manifestly, most of the theorists of democracy believed that democratic men would be interested, rational, informed, and would act in part by principle. And we think that is exactly the point: they believed that *democratic* men would so act, not that all men would. Is the voter in the scholarly studies a bad democrat because he is irrational, disinterested, lacking knowledge, and devoid of principle? Might it not be as just to say that he is apathetic, irrational, and uninformed *because* he no longer participates, no longer cares to participate, and feels deep in the bone that it is no longer possible for him to have a role in his own government? If modern social science has taught us anything, it has taught us that character develops in a cultural and social matrix. It does not surprise us that the sex, family, and work practices and institutions of a people do much to mold their character. We acknowledge that the distribution and exercise of authority within a society also affects character or personality. It should not take an act of faith to believe that a population that confidently and with zest governs itself would differ from one that in political matters is supine or inert. We think, then, that the poor showing of Americans in the scholarly voting studies is a function of the loss of will and belief in the capacity to govern, a function of a changed perspective toward the institutions that enable the people to govern or that frustrate the will to self-government.

We come finally to the thorny problem of the capacity of even interested and informed democratic men to deal with the incredibly and agonizingly complex issues of today. For the issues of today are complex, their resolution fateful, and the margin for error almost nonexistent. There are students of modern government who believe that only the experts and those who can talk with the experts should be permitted to play leading or creating roles in national public-policy making. Former Secretary of State Dean Acheson, for example, in speaking of the role of the Congress in major national policy formation, stated that the inexpert and not wholly informed gentlemen of the legislature must yield primacy in policy initiation to the executive branch, which branch has its corps of specialists and its means of gathering and organizing expert, technical, and competent opinion on the complex matters of defense and foreign policy, and national and international monetary policy. Acheson was not contending that the people are not ultimately sovereign or that they ought not to concern themselves with policy matters. He was arguing rather that not even Congress is sufficiently expert and informed to play the leading role in policy formation.

What role, then, could the people play? What would be the value of public discussion and debate, assuming that we had public debate, if it is debate only amongst the incompetent, the uninformed, and the inexpert? What would be the policy value of the opinion rising from such a discussion? Acheson's austere scorn for incompetent opinion, it seems to us, leads to the democratic minimalism of Schlesinger: the people cannot govern; they can but choose their governors.

There are two aspects of the crucial relationship between expert knowledge and democratic policy making that must be discussed here. The first concerns the function of the expert in a democracy; the second concerns the meaning one chooses to give to the concept of popular participation or self-government. Democrats have not always been hospitable to the notion that expert knowledge or special abilities are important adjuncts of wise government. Even in our contemporary culture, in which the expert has come into his own, we leaven our respect of him with some suspicion of the "egghead," the "bigdome," the "brain trust," and the "bright young man." Yet it was democracy's handmaiden, liberalism, which, in Charles Frankel's words, practically "invented the idea that there are social problems," to which expert knowledge and intelligence might be applied for the solutions thereof. But, for the liberal democrat, the expert's role was always a subsidiary one. He was to advise the policy maker, not to make policy himself. The popular leader of democratic thought has not appeared as a scientist of the commonweal, as a calculator of probabilities or estimator of quantities relentlessly fed to him by disinterested experts. The decision of the democratic leader has always had to be a judgment of what is right, or what conduces in the long run to the general good, with his judgment intersected by what he understands to be the popular will. Hence, his decision is a judgment about what ought to be done, as well as an estimate of consequences. Naturally, he must balance estimates of consequences (which estimates he gets from his own knowledge or from the advice of experts), his perception of the popular will, and his own intimations of what ought to be done. The core of the decision, however, is ethical; and it is the faith of the democrat that there are no ethical experts: the political decision with its ultimately moral core can be reached by ordinary men after full discussion, complete airing of views, and free access to relevant information.

Let us look at an example. President Kennedy is obviously a very bright, very well-educated man. His breadth of knowledge and grasp of complex matters are by now known to everyone. Yet he is not a nuclear physicist, nor a specialist in the technology of bomb testing and its detection. Similarly, he must be accounted an amateur in such fields as military tactics and monetary policy. For all of the President's undoubted intellectual capacity, he stands closer to the average man than he does to the genuine specialist in these varied fields. Yet the President had to decide whether to enter into a nuclear test-ban agreement with the U.S.S.R. The technical specialists could not make the decision for him. And it is apparent that the President's decision to make the treaty was made not on technical grounds alone; nor, obviously, was it made on military grounds alone. The decision was based on Kennedy's judgment of what ought to be done, with some discount, of course, for the technical or material probabilities. In other words, it was a political decision, and in essence, not beyond the grasp of the ordinary citizen who might take the trouble to examine it. Simultaneously, of the chief critics of the test-ban agreement, Senators Thurmond and Goldwater objected to the test ban not on grounds on which the experts stood unanimously, but because the two Senators thought that there ought to be no slackening of our effort in the cold war with the Soviet Union. In congressional hearings on the treaty, much press attention was paid to Dr. Edward Teller's opposition to a test ban, with the implication left for a not-too-careful public that Dr. Teller, the scientist and the father of the H-bomb, was speaking from a position of scientific knowledge. But Dr. Teller's main grounds of opposition were not scientific at all. Rather, they issued from his conviction that the Russians were untrustworthy and would cheat on the treaty. Those scientists who favored the treaty did so on essentially nonscientific grounds also. In other words, the scientists, Senators Goldwater and Thurmond, and the President himself were making judgments no different in kind from those that we are called upon to make as citizens and voters. The differences in degree of knowledgeability stem from the fact that the President and the Senators have more information on the problem, have spent more time in studying and thinking about it, and have had the advantage of almost incessant exchanges of views with experts and colleagues.

That brings us to the question of what is meant by popular participation or self-government. Obviously, no one can seriously contend that every major decision of government should be made the subject of a referendum, that we the people constitute ourselves as a permanently sitting town meeting. We are a representative democracy and our representatives must act for us. We elect leaders, and we expect also that they will lead and not simply follow popular opinion. But if the democratic minimalists argue that the citizens today can but issue a blank check to the electoral victors among competing politicians, the maximalist democrat insists that there be a dialogue between leaders and citizens, a true process of interaction in which leaders and citizens learn from one another, challenge one another, and both goad and restrain one another. This means that there ought to be more rather than less public discussion, a more generous outpouring of information about questions of public policy, more education, and more serious exposition of issues by candidates. Popular participation requires that there be an electoral system in which the electors speak meaningfully to the elected—and to the defeated, as well. The maximal democrat does not demand that the electoral decision function as a fetter on the heroic leader. But he does ask that the electoral decision function as a guide to the democratic leader—as a warning or rebuke or encouragement or reward, yes—but also as clear information about what most citizens believe are the pathways to the realization of the general interest.

We think, then, that the present democratic dialogue in the nation is scanty in volume and inadequate in quality, and that it requires extension and improvement if self-government is to amount to anything more than the periodic selection of our governors. Moreover, millions of our citizens *feel* powerless. We think it not unlikely that persons who feel politically powerless have begun to respond to politics in the dull, brutish way of the powerless in all times and places. We suggest that the feelings of powerlessness and remoteness—rather than any innate defectiveness of the human material—account for the depressing statistics of the scholarly voting studies.

Is self-government possible for us today? Is the retreat from politics justified? It is our belief that the means of self-government are at hand, or at least within our grasp, if we have the will to use them. We also recognize that we may be too optimistic. The evidence of the voting studies is sobering. It is possible that the issues of public policy have become so huge, so complex, and so technical as to be beyond the capacity of the ordinary citizen to understand them. Perhaps we are so close to nuclear catastrophe that we cannot gamble on the wisdom and capacity of the average man. Perhaps, also, the machinery of our political system has become so complicated and incoherent that the citizen is in fact kept from the levers of public policy. It is our hope that these questions will be illuminated by the materials we present in this volume, and that further thought and discussion will be stimulated. In Part One, we offer several perspectives on some of the key processes of democracy as they come together in the election of a President. In Part Two, we present differing and often conflicting perspectives on some of the main issues of 1964. That we do this, we think, bears witness of our own conviction that the democratic dialogue is still a vital one.

CHAPTER TWO

The Profile of the Electorate

For over twenty-five years, scholars have been studying the American citizens, as voters, with the most advanced of the ever improving techniques of social science. Many of the "discoveries" of the voting studies have turned out only to be confirmations of things long known or suspected about the voting behavior of Americans. On the other hand, some of the new information has called into serious question several old assumptions about political behavior, and has brought us a clearer, if in some ways an alarming, profile of the electorate.

We know that about one third of the eligible population does not vote at all, not even in presidential elections. This one third of our citizens lives essentially outside the political order. Who are they? The biggest part are the chronic nonvoters, the folk who constitute what we might call the substratum of American life: the very poor, the long-term unemployed, the marginally employed, the migrant workers, and the least educated, most deprived, and most discriminated against segments of our people—Indians, Negroes, Mexican-Americans, Puerto Ricans, and other unassimilated ethnic minorities. These are not the only nonvoters, of course, and we may well expect that Negroes, for instance, though undereducated, underemployed, comparatively deprived, and discriminated against, will nevertheless display an awakened political consciousness, and therefore will move increasingly into the ranks of the voters.

But aside from the substratum, there are other demographic categories inclined toward nonvoting. We may denote them in comparative terms: rural dwellers, as opposed to urbanites and suburbanites; the very young and the very old, as opposed to the middle-aged; newcomers to an area, as opposed to long-time residents; women, as opposed to men; Protestants, as opposed to Catholics and Jews; workers who are not union members, as opposed to trade unionists; the poorly educated, as opposed to the highly educated. Persons with weak or nonexistent attachments to a political party are less apt to vote than are strong partisans, and most of the major

13

voter studies show that persons who are "cross-pressured"—pulled by their various predispositions or other influences in *opposite* directions of choice —tend to resolve the conflict simply by not voting. We must remember, however, that nationwide participation statistics are biased by two built-in features: (1) voting in general elections in the South has usually been significantly lower than elsewhere because the one-party system there has made most election results a foregone conclusion (the Democrats win) and because Negroes, the very poor, and the illiterate have been kept away from the polls by any number of devices; (2) the confusing variety of registration laws in the states, most of which rest upon some specification of residence in a locality and therefore keep thousands of our highly mobile population off the voter rolls.

To speak of cross-pressured voters brings to mind another conclusion widely held by scholars of voting behavior: most people's choice between a Republican and a Democratic candidate tends to be a function of the voter's various social characteristics—principally, his income, occupation, class, ethnic group, religion, urban or rural residence, and section of the country. To a lesser extent, age and sex also seem to be influential. Of course, all such characteristics intersect and overlap in both individuals and groups. While it is far too strong to say that social characteristics determine political preference, we can note certain rough correspondences between social characteristics and party preference. Low-income groups, wage-earners, members of most ethnic and national minority groups, Catholics and Jews, urban residents, Southerners, and young voters all incline markedly toward the Democratic Party. Conversely, upper-income groups, white-collar and managerial workers, Anglo-Saxons and other "Old Americans," Protestants, rural and suburban residents, and older voters all incline toward the Republican Party. In the 1940s and 1950s, there was a slight tendency for women to prefer the Republican Party.

It must be emphasized that political choice is not an automatic function of group membership. Most Americans inherit their political party choice, and apparently this colors or influences all our subsequent political perceptions. Most of us first perceive politics through the lens of our parents' partisan choice, and we proceed to organize or interpret the events of the political world with it. Most of us, therefore, are partisans, and we do not easily give up our original party choice. Of course, there are switchers and independents. These may be people in whom the party pull was originally weak. They may have been strong partisans, who in mid-career switched loyalty in response to some major event; as, for instance, perhaps millions of life-long Republicans became Democrats during the depression and New Deal. Very often, independents are people who are cross-pressured. Thus, a well-to-do Irish-Catholic corporation executive might be pulled toward the Republicans by his economic associations, whereas the national and religious chords of memory pull him toward the Democrats. For this hypothetical voter, either independency or non-voting might best express his irresolution. Some of us are ticket splitters, voting for an appealing candidate of one party for President but sticking with our original-party candidates for all or most of the lower offices. This undoubtedly accounts for the fact that in the 1950s, General Eisenhower won office by large pluralities while the Democrats in three successive elections won majorities in both houses of Congress. For obvious reasons, it is easier to "vote for the man" in presidential elections, but to "vote for the party" in lesser races when neither candidate is well known to most voters.

Since most of us vote the party most of the time, how do we distribute ourselves between the parties? One cannot give perfectly accurate figures, but apparently a little under 50 percent of us are more or less regular Democratic voters, slightly more than 30 percent prefer the Republicans, and the remainder of us are some variety of independent voter, or are wholly unpolitical. Some students of politics have felt—because our electoral choices fairly steadily follow party loyalty, and our party choice in turn seems to be fixed by our social characteristics—that most of us vote "irrationally," that is, blindly, automatically, or unthinkingly. But such a conclusion does not necessarily follow. To vote for the party and not for the man may be wholly rational, if one knows something about the parties and very little about the men. No one, moreover, can say certainly that there are not correspondences between the objective interests of a group aligned with a party and the party's positions on issues. Most voters evidently do see differences between the parties on policy matters, and characterize those differences in terms not too removed from the objective reality. What is more disturbing than party voting and group alignment with parties is the vagueness or imprecision so many voters bring to politics, the choosing of a candidate for seemingly irrelevant personal characteristics, the lack of concern about the outcome, the feeling that one's vote "doesn't mean very much," and the lack of knowledge about the issues.

In this chapter we present two striking studies that illustrate (in the selection by the Survey Research Center scholars) the startlingly low level of conceptual power our electorate displays when looking at political life, and (in the study by the University of Minnesota scholars) that despite significant differences on issues between the parties at the leadership level, differences flatten out and get blurred among the electorate.

THE FORMATION OF POLITICAL CONCEPTS*

Angus Campbell, Philip E. Converse,
Warren E. Miller, and Donald E. Stokes

Smith, Bruner, and White, in their volume *Opinions and Personality*, report an intensive analysis of the political attitudes of ten relatively well-informed and intelligent subjects. Nine of the ten, on the basis of their performance in a standardized test, ranked within the top 10 per cent of the national population in intellectual capacity. Of the tenth, the authors write:

Many of the verbal coins used in the exchange of opinions were unfamiliar to him, so that we had to learn his views without relying on such standard pieces as "Socialism," "Liberalism," "veto," and "isolationism." . . . At a concrete level he functioned effectively, showing good common sense and practical judgment. It was in the realm of abstraction that his limitations were most marked. . . . He never read books, rarely listened to the radio, and did little more than scan such newspapers and magazines as came his way. Both his information and his opinions were arrived at almost wholly through channels of conversation.

Now "Sam Hodder," as this anonymous subject is called, was not a person of meager intelligence. He was *well above the average* in basic intellectual capacity, standing in the top twenty per cent of a cross-section population. But limited to a grade school education and subsequent life as a factory employee, events had not conspired to foster those habits of abstract concept formation taken for granted in intellectual strata of the society. Despite substantial innate capacity, then, even Sam Hodder did not in practice measure up to the expectations of political concept formation that often seem assumed for the bulk of the electorate. . . .

We would imagine that if we asked Sam Hodder what he liked and disliked about the major parties, his predominant opinion would be that he liked the Democratic Party because "it is the party of the working man." If his political world was largely undifferentiated, he might have few perceptions beyond this. If there were further differentiation, he would perhaps indicate that the Republican Party had shown him it was

* From *The American Voter* by Angus Campbell, Philip E. Converse, Warren E. Miller, and Donald E. Stokes. New York: John Wiley & Sons, Inc., 1960. Pp. 218–250. Reprinted by permission. Messrs. Campbell, Converse, Miller, and Stokes are on the staff of the Survey Research Center at the University of Michigan.

actively against labor or the worker, or actively for big business, management, or one of the "natural" antagonists of the working man. He might
be able, also, to document his impressions by reference to specific events
or policy debates: the role of the parties in the Depression, or the cham-
pioning of legislation such as Taft-Hartley or social security. His view
of partisan politics might be more or less differentiated, but his evaluations
would revolve around the perception that one of the parties took special
pains to look after the day-to-day interests of a significant grouping in the
population with which he identified.

This is not ideology in a programmatic sense. There is little comprehen-
sion here of the basic problems that lead to the need for political protection; nor is there, as we have said, any interest in "long-range plans" that
would aim at resolution of these problems. In fact, there is little that requires abstract thinking at all: the most significant elements of this sort
implied are the quasi-abstractions "group" and "interest." As the authors
note, "because of his concrete thinking he could not [attribute evil to]
an abstract construct such as the economic order." He is concerned with
politics to the degree that he feels that political change might rob him
and others like him of their jobs or of concrete benefits involving wages,
working conditions, and the like. He has no conception of the modes
whereby political power secures or protects interests—these are the concerns of group leadership, whether that leadership be of union or of party.
Having perceived some correlation between group success and the emergence of concrete benefits, he is willing to put his faith in any leadership
that has shown enough interest in his group to figure out what must be
done to maintain its welfare. He partakes of ideology by endorsing a
leadership that has ideology. He engages, so to speak, in an "ideology
by proxy."

This is not to say that Sam Hodder could never be jarred loose from
these loyalties. Quite to the contrary, we must suppose that he remains a
perceiving, evaluating individual with a healthy capacity for suspicion.
If he were to suffer economic distress under circumstances in which the
union appeared impotent or indifferent, or if the party stopped doing
things that he felt made his lot a better one, he would undoubtedly cast
about for new loyalties, new leadership.

But the difference between ideology and "ideology by proxy" is more
than academic. For at points of political change the concepts employed
by Sam Hodder in his evaluations make for critical differences in attitude
and behavior. Let us suppose that union and party are committed to long-
range economic, political, and social change toward the general end of
improving the lot of many Sam Hodders; that is, we will suppose that
union and party are, in ideological terms, "of the left." Now suppose that
over a period of time union and party leadership swing back toward the

center or even come to collude with the right, although by one mechanism or another the day-to-day security of Sam's economic position is maintained. If Sam were ideologically inclined he might become disturbed and disillusioned at the forsaking of broader goals. Sensitive to ideological matters, he would behave as the analyst would presume: the changed relationship between his own position and that of the group on an underlying ideological continuum would change the values that the group held for him. He might participate in moves to change the leadership, or he might seek more promising agents further to the left. . . .

Favorable or unfavorable reactions to the political parties or candidates often consist of beliefs that they are agents that will aid or ignore this or that grouping in the population. In some of our protocols these perceptions are connected tightly with other comments more clearly ideological in character. But often it is apparent under probing by the interviewer that the respondent does not fit these notions of group benefit into any broader or more abstract frame of reference. They are, of course, self-sufficient without it: there is nothing logically incomplete in the belief that a leader or party is sensitive to problems unique to a social grouping.

However simple these conceptions of politics may appear, there are many people in the American electorate whose modes of conceptualizing the political world and its social or economic consequences are a good deal less complex still and who appear even more remote from the type of thinking presumed by "ideology." In a diffuse way "times are good" or "times are bad"—there is war or peace, depression or prosperity. If some pattern can be perceived linking the nature of the times with a particular party in power, this pattern may come to be considered a causal sequence. Once again, however, after such perceptions have been volunteered, further probing usually seems to indicate that most political issue content has thereby been exhausted.

There are many citizens whose issue perceptions are even more impoverished. Some of these people are staunch adherents of one of the political parties, although they freely admit it is simply a matter of family tradition and they personally have no idea what the parties "stand for." Others ignore the parties despite direct questioning, and focus their political evaluations upon the personal characteristics of the current candidates themselves—their sincerity, their religious beliefs, their family life, their "popularity." And, finally, there are those who lack the interest or background to differentiate successfully between either the candidates or the parties.

It seems important to estimate the incidence of these various modes of conceptualizing issue controversy in a cross section of the adult population. . . . Toward this end we attempted to assign our 1956 respondents to various "levels" of conceptualization on the basis of their discursive responses in evaluating the good and bad points of the two parties and the two candidates . . . Despite the inevitable crudities of the categories employed, these levels seemed to provide a clear ordering in terms of conceptual sophistication. The expected ordering turned out to receive striking confirmation in other characteristics of the occupants at successive levels. And the classification system was sufficiently clear to insure satisfactory inter-rater reliability.

The nature of the categories used has been foreshadowed above. A fairly flexible view of ideology was taken as a point of departure, and lower levels involved an increasing remoteness in content and in level of conceptualization from this "ideal." Each respondent was assigned to the highest level warranted by any portion of his commentary. Although some finer differentiations were employed in the actual coding process, we shall focus most of our attention upon four major levels.

The first of these (to be denoted Level A) embraces all respondents whose evaluations of the candidates and the parties have any suggestion of the abstract conception one would associate with ideology. We did not wish to be bound to familiar content in assessing this level of issue conceptualization. However, it rapidly became apparent that virtually all high-order abstractions used were familiar from current political commentary. This seems to mean simply that insights as to basic new ordering dimensions are not likely to be forthcoming in a restricted sample of the population. Even our most sophisticated respondents were no more than alert consumers of the refined content of the political culture. They might express original viewpoints, but they were totally dependent on the standard abstractions for their basic conceptual tools. We did encounter one or two respondents who might be suspected of seeking unfamiliar dimensions of high abstraction. These people were included in Level A. Otherwise, persons placed here talked in terms of the liberal-conservative continuum, or one of the narrower domains of abstract content involved in current ideological controversy: trends in the relationship between federal power and local autonomy, the fate of individual incentive under government "dole," and the like.

The second grouping (Level B) was reserved for persons whose issue comment revolved around fairly concrete and short-term group interest, or what we have already described in some detail as "ideology by proxy." In the next category (Level C) were persons engrossed in simplistic associations between the "goodness" and "badness" of the times and the identity of the party in power, or who appeared to have exhausted their view of the situation with mention of some rather isolated and specific issue. The final level (Level D) thereby contains individuals who evaluated the political objects without recourse to issues that might fairly be related to debates over domestic public policy. Excluded as true issue content, for example, were observations concerning mudslinging, charges of graft, comments on the personal attributes of the candidates, or references to their age, health, or past experience. . . .

LEVEL A, IDEOLOGY AND NEAR-IDEOLOGY. We shall consider two categories of respondents distinguished within Level A. The first was reserved for persons whose comments imply the kinds of conception of politics assumed by ideological interpretations of political behavior and political change. We shall refer to these individuals as "ideologues." The second category within Level A includes people who employ concepts of some ideological flavor but who, for one reason or another, do not apply them in a manner that seems to qualify them as "ideologues."

Some people clearly perceived a fundamental liberal-conservative continuum on which various of the political objects might be located and along which these objects might shift relative positions over time. Although we were more interested in the fact of this conception than in the manner in which the individual related himself to it, in most cases such respondents clearly located themselves at one or another point on the continuum and evaluated the parties or factions within parties from this position. These ideologues are not, from a sophisticated point of view, exceptional observers. Their commentary is neither profound, stimulating, nor creative. But they have absorbed some of the ideological abstractions of our day, and are able to put them to use in their political evaluations. In brief, they are the persons who fulfill most clearly the assumptions about political perceptions discussed at the beginning of the chapter.

It should not be inferred that mastery of the terms "liberal" or "conservative" was necessary for inclusion in this upper "ideologue" grouping of Level A. The category was open to respondents who might deal in rather unorthodox modes of organization, although only a case or two of this variety was recruited. Similarly, some respondents who appeared unaware of the sophisticated terms banked their evaluations of the parties on perceptions that the Democrats "rushed into things too fast" or were willing "to work on problems right when they came up, not hanging back like the Republicans." Comments of this sort, although very rare, cut so directly to the heart of the liberal-conservative distinction that there was no question of their classification in the upper grouping of Level A. These are clearly people whose conceptions are subsumed in the descriptions of the "liberal" or "conservative" temper of the public mind.

The first interview drawn from this upper category within Level A is somewhat unusual in the degree of content pertaining to state politics, but otherwise is quite representative of the responses that received this classification. The respondent is a woman residing in the suburbs of Chicago.

(Like about Democrats?) No. *(Is there anything at all you like about the Demo-cratic Party?)* No, nothing at all.

(Dislike about Democrats?) From being raised in a notoriously Republican section—a small town downstate—there were things I didn't like. There was family influence that way. *(What in particular was there you didn't like about the Democratic Party?)* Well, the Democratic Party tends to favor socialized medicine—and I'm being influenced in that because I came from a doctor's family.

(Like about Republicans?) Well, I think they're more middle-of-the-road—more conservative. *(How do you mean, "conservative"?)* They are not so subject to radical change. *(Is there anything else in particular that you like about the Republican Party?)* Oh, I like their foreign policy—and the segregation busi-ness, that's a middle-of-the-road policy. You can't push it too fast. You can instigate things, but you have to let them take their course slowly. *(Is there anything else?)* I don't like Mr. Hodge. *(Is there anything else?)* The labor unions telling workers how to vote—they know which side their bread is but-tered on so they have to vote the way they are told to!

(Dislike about Republicans?) Mr. Hodge! *(Is there anything else?)* I can't think of anything.

This respondent operates with a fairly clear sense of the liberal-con-servative distinction and uses it to locate both the major parties and the more specific policy positions espoused.

(Like about Democrats?) Well, that depends on what you are thinking of—historically or here lately. I think they are supposed to be more interested in the small businessman and low tariffs. *(Is there anything in particular that you like about the Democratic Party?)* Nothing except it being a more liberal party, and I think of the Republicans as being more conservative and interested in big business.

(Dislike about Democrats?) I think extravagance, primarily. *(Is there anything else?)* Nothing that occurs to me offhand.

(Like about Republicans?) Well, I never thought so. I have been a Republican the last several years because of the personalities involved, I guess.

(Dislike about Republicans?) This again is traditional—just that they give too much support to big business and monopoly concerns. *(Any other things you don't like about the Republican Party?)* No. . . .

It is striking, then, that responses of only 2½ per cent of our cross-section sample warranted inclusion in this top category. Since people placed here are much more likely to take a fuller role in politics than are persons lower on the scale, they bulk somewhat larger in the active electorate. But these ideologues still represent no more than 3½ per cent of our actual voters in 1956. In view of the fact that the partisan division of the national vote for federal office often shifts by as much as five or ten per cent within the biennial or quadrennial period, it is clear that this group alone could account for only a tiny portion of such short-term change, either by switching party or by staying at home.

There is, however, a more substantial group of respondents who have some claim to ideological perception. We have segregated them from the upper layer of ideologues because we are somewhat less confident that they fulfill the assumptions that we are examining. These people displaying "near-ideology" consist of three general types.

The first type is most similar to the full "ideologue." Frequently these people employ the liberal-conservative distinction, but their use of these concepts has little of the dynamic or highly relativistic quality found in the ideologue. "Liberalism" or "conservatism" is a status attribute of a party: there is less sense here of a continuum embracing many shadings of position, with objects shifting inward toward the center or outward toward extremes over time. Others give no explicit recognition to the liberal-conservative distinction, but employ organizing concepts of a sufficiently high order of abstraction to cut some swath through areas of ideological controversy. One interview drawn to exemplify this type of "near-ideology" comes from a man in southern Ohio:

(Like about Democrats?) Yes, I like their platform. *(What is that?)* They're more inclined to help the working class of people, and that is the majority in our country. And I like the idea of stopping the hydrogen bomb tests. It would make for more friendly feelings toward other countries, and they would be more friendly to us. I think the Democratic Party wants peace as much as the Republican Party.

(Dislike about Democrats?) Yeah, there's a lot of things. One thing is they're too much for federal control of utilities. *(Is there anything else you don't like about the Democratic Party?)* Well, it seems they don't always run the best men there are for their offices. *(For example?)* There's several I could mention that don't have the best reputation in the world.

(Like about Republicans?) Well, they play up to individual rights, which is good. That's good—it makes a person feel more independent.

(Dislike about Republicans?) They believe in big industry, utilities, etc. *(Anything else you don't like?)* They've passed a lot of labor bills I don't approve of.

This respondent does not introduce the liberal-conservative distinction explicitly. His opening comment about Democratic interest in the working class is of the group-interest type that will form the broad criterion for Level B. But he also includes commentary about the problem of federal control over utilities and the value of individual rights. Both of these observations involve abstractions common to the ideological disputes of our era. The respondent's own position concerning the role of government toward utilities is left rather unclear: he resents tendencies of the Democrats toward federal control, yet appears to dislike the Republican position as well. Here as elsewhere, however, we restrict our attention to the nature of the concepts employed rather than become involved in judgments of the coherence of ideological positions. . . .

A second type of interview considered "near-ideology" included persons who used one or another of the labels common to ideological discussion, but in a context rather bare of supporting perceptions, so that we must take it on faith that the term had the normal connotations for the user. Generally the flavor of the context is not one to cast great doubt on the appropriateness of the meaning, but the lack of supporting material usually indicates that other simpler concepts are equally or more prominent in the individual's thinking about politics. . . . The respondent drawn to exemplify the second type is a man from Texas:

(Like about Democrats?) (After a long delay.) I think the Democrats are more concerned with all the people. *(How do you mean?)* They put out more liberal legislation for all the people.

(Dislike about Democrats?) They have a sordid history over the past 20 years, though no worse than the Republican Administrations. *(How do you mean?)* Oh, things like deep freezes and corruption in government.

(Like about Republicans?) No!

(Dislike about Republicans?) Oh, they're more for a moneyed group.

Here the bulk of the content follows the lines of group benefit concepts that are generally classified at a lower level. Nevertheless, the term "liberal" is employed in a context of some reasonable meaning, and it is possible that fuller probing would have developed a more explicit indication of more abstract ideological conceptions. . . .

The final type of interview classified as near-ideology within Level A was in one sense the inverse of the preceding type. Persons were classified here who had highly differentiated images relevant to one or another ideological content domain, yet failed to introduce the generalized concepts that are normally used to summarize and order these perceptions in sophisticated debate. Whereas respondents of the preceding type had absorbed labels but had difficulty bringing appropriate specific information to them, individuals here were laden with information but showed no tendency to distill such detail to a higher level of abstraction.

In some of these cases, it was conceivable that the failure to indicate an awareness of more generalized organizing dimensions was accidental. Nevertheless, we find among these people, as well as those of the preceding type, an increasing tendency to depend upon party and group concepts as organizing focuses for issue content, rather than ideological positions. Thus responses of these types are already merging with the concept usages of individuals in Level B.

The interview drawn to represent this final type of near-ideology was contributed by a man in southern California:

(Like about Democrats?) The Democratic Party is more for higher social security. They're more for old age pensions and better working conditions for the working man. They want a higher standard of living for all people, not just a few. The promises that are made by the Democrats are kept if at all possible. The facts are told to the American people.

(Dislike about Democrats?) It seems to me they could handle their campaign better. *(How do you mean?)* Well, for instance, they could do a little better job of selling to the public. They should try and quiet Truman down so he will not pull a boner as in the Democratic convention. *(Do you have any other dislikes for the Democratic Party?)* No.

(Like about Republicans?) Not one thing! *(In general, is there anything that you like about the Republican Party?)* No!

(Dislike about Republicans?) I dislike everything about the Republican Party. *(Could you explain what you mean?)* I was growing up at the time of the Hoover Administration. What a time I had, too. There was barely enough to eat. I don't think the Republicans wanted that, but they did nothing to stop it. Not until Roosevelt came along and made things start to happen. Now the Republican Party still stands for big business, at the expense of the farmer and the working man. Promises made are not kept—ask the poor farmer, if no one else.

Over the course of these remarks there are points at which summary constructs familiar in ideological discussion would be highly appropriate. However, the recital of specific measures supported by the Democrats is not generalized to such a level of abstraction. Instead, the "standard of living" is used to sum up the direction of party policy, and this matter is treated as a benefit linked to a group, albeit a large group, within the population. Similarly, a perception of Republican passivity in the face of the Depression is vividly contrasted in the subject's mind with initiatives taken by Roosevelt. Yet this is not seen as a special case of a general posture toward change. Rather, it is left as a concrete vignette, developed once again into a proposition about group interest. . . .

If the reader has been struck by this generosity of assignment, he should hold this fact in mind as we measure our progress across the electorate. For despite our attempts at generous estimates, we find that with all the ideologues and near-ideologues of Level A cumulated we have only covered about 12 per cent of all subjects interviewed, and 15 per cent of our 1956 voters. In other words, about 85 per cent of the 1956 electorate brought simpler conceptual tools to bear on their issue concerns.

LEVEL B, GROUP BENEFITS. In the last interviews to be cited from Level A, we noted an increasing tendency to evaluate the political objects in terms of their response to interests of visible groupings in the population. Such perceptions are the dominant themes characterizing Level B, and constitute what we have described earlier as "ideology by proxy." . . .

As was the case with Level A, several types might be distinguished within Level B. One major content distinction had to do with the degree to which perceptions of group interest were elaborated. Some respondents tended to perceive politics in terms of a competition of these group interests, with the political parties arraying themselves in favor of one group and in opposition to another. However, many respondents did not develop the discussion of group benefit beyond the context of a single group, nor did they express a feeling that the party or candidate not seen as favorable was actively pursuing a threatening policy, either by ignoring or seeking to harm the group, or by supporting another group seen as a natural antagonist. Individuals who perceived a conflict of group interests in the political arena seemed to give more sophisticated interviews than those whose perceptions were bound up in the sympathy that one of the parties or candidates might be expected to show toward a single group. In terms of numbers, Level B was fairly evenly split between these two types. . . .

People having relatively substantial perceptions of a competition of group interests make up the first category of any size that we have encountered. Fourteen per cent of our sample received this classification. Although the perception of group interest provides a tangible criterion for inclusion at this level, the reader is urged to compare the illustrative interviews drawn randomly from this group with those of the higher level in terms of the more general grasp of politics that is represented. The first illustrative responses come from an Iowa man:

(*Like about Democrats?*) I don't know of anything. (*Is there anything you like about the Democratic Party?*) No, I wouldn't say there is.

(*Dislike about Democrats?*) I don't particularly agree how they have passed out the money and increased the taxes.

(*Like about Republicans?*) I think they try to run the country without running in debt and keep us out of wars. (*Anything else that you like about the Republican Party?*) No.

(*Dislike about Republicans?*) They are more for big business. (*Anything else?*) No. (*What do you mean by "big business"?*) Well, the little man gets crowded out. They cater to the big men.

(*Now I'd like to ask you about the good and bad points of the two candidates for President. Is there anything in particular about Stevenson that might make you want to vote for him?*) No, I don't believe so.

(*Is there anything in particular about Eisenhower that might make you want to vote for him?*) He has been a good leader all of his life. (*Anything else?*) No.

(Is there anything in particular about Eisenhower that might make you want to vote against him?) The only thing is whether or not his health would permit him to finish his term.

The second illustration of category B-I comes from an Ohio farm woman.

(Like about Democrats?) I think they have always helped the farmers. To tell you the truth, I don't see how any farmer could vote for Mr. Eisenhower. *(Is there anything else you like about the Democratic Party?)* We have always had good times under their Adminstration. They are more for the working class of people. Any farmer would be a fool to vote for Eisenhower.

(Dislike about Democrats?) No, I can't say there is.

(Like about Republicans?) No.

(Dislike about Republicans?) About everything. *(What are you thinking of?)* They promise so much but they don't do anything. *(Anything else?)* I think the Republicans favor the richer folks. I never did think much of the Republicans for putting into office a military man.

(Like about Stevenson?) I think he is a *very smart* man. *(Is there anything else?)* I think he will do what he says, will help the farmer. We will have higher prices. *(Anything else?)* No.

(Dislike about Stevenson?) No. But I have this against Stevenson, but I wouldn't vote against him. In the Illinois National Guards he had Negroes and Whites together. They ate and slept together. I don't like that. I think Negroes should have their own place. I don't see why they would want to mix.

(Like about Eisenhower?) No.

(Dislike about Eisenhower?) Yes. He favors Wall Street. I don't think he is physically able, and he will step aside and that Richard Nixon will be president. *(Anything else?)* To tell the truth, I never thought he knew enough about politics to be a President. He is a military man. He takes too many vacations and I don't see how he can do the job. . . .

With the interview involving perceptions of conflicting group interest added to those of Level A, we have now accounted for about one quarter of our sample and slightly less than one third of the voters. Another 17 per cent of the respondents talked of benefits accruing to a single group through the aid of a single party. The first interview drawn to illustrate this type comes from a man in Texas:

(Like about Democrats?) Well, I don't know. I've just always before been a Democrat. My daddy before me always was. *(Can you name any good things that you like about the party?)* Well, no, I guess not.

(Dislike about Democrats?) I don't know of anything.

(Like about Republicans?) No.

(Dislike about Republicans?) Well, I just don't believe they are for the common people. *(Anything else that you don't like about the Republican Party?)* No, I don't think so.

(Like about Stevenson?) No, ma'am.

(Dislike about Stevenson?) Well, I wouldn't know hardly how to put that. I just don't hardly think he's the man for President.

(Like about Eisenhower?) Well, his past is all. *(Is there anything else that might make you want to vote for him?)* No.

(Dislike about Eisenhower?) Nothing but the right man in the Democratic Party.

A woman in South Carolina responds:

(Like about Democrats?) They're more interested in small businessmen and farms. *(Can you tell me any more about that?)* No, but I've always heard this.

(Dislike about Democrats?) The race problem. (Its stand on the race problem.)

(Like about Republicans?) No.

(Dislike about Republicans?) Race problem.

(Like about Stevenson?) No.

(Dislike about Stevenson?) He's divorced.

(Like about Eisenhower?) I don't know of anything in particular but in general he's a good man.

(Dislike about Eisenhower?) His health. (Respondent is a nurse.)

These interviews, chosen randomly from among the more capable responses falling in Level B, serve to represent the conflict-of-interest and the single-group interest responses. As we have suggested, some interviews of rather low calibre with group-benefit mentions were separated to form a lower category within Level B. By and large, the quality of responses here is close to what we shall later encounter in Level C, despite the group references. These poorer interviews of Level B, making up another 11 per cent of the sample include responses similar to that of this wife of a machinist in Louisville, Kentucky:

(Like about Democrats?) That's Stevenson, ain't it?

(Yes, that's his party.) No, I don't know anything about Stevenson, but I do like the party. *(What is it that you like about the Democratic Party?)* There's always been more Democrats running for President than there has been for the other party, and they've got in more. *(Is there anything else you like about the Democratic Party?)* No.

(Dislike about Democrats?) I don't know anything about the Democratic Party. (Respondent was thinking so awfully hard and getting nowhere at all.) Well,

for one thing, they were hard on the farmers. (I explained that we were talking about the Democratic Party and repeated the question.) No, I always liked it until Truman was in. He said he was going to do things for the farmers and he backed out.

(*Like about Republicans?*) That's Stevenson, ain't it? I get them mixed up. (*No, that's Eisenhower's party.*) Well, one thing, I heard he lowered taxes. (*Is there anything else you like about the Republican Party?*) And he's a good man—I hope he gets in this time.

(*Dislike about Republicans?*) No, I can't think of anything.

(*Like about Stevenson?*) No, I just don't like Stevenson.

(*Dislike about Stevenson?*) No, there's no faults. I just don't like him.

(*Like about Eisenhower?*) I don't know of any.

(*Dislike about Eisenhower?*) No, I don't have anything against Ike.

As we complete our survey of the range of interviews included in Level B, it seems undeniable that we have moved to levels of conceptualization remote from those presumed by ideological interpretations of political behavior. Yet Levels A and B taken together account for little more than half of the total sample, and for only some sixty per cent of the 1956 respondents who voted.

LEVEL C, THE "GOODNESS" AND "BADNESS" OF THE TIMES. The third level coincides closely with the third quartile of our sample. In some ways interviews classified here are most effectively defined in negative terms. On the one hand, these responses do not include perceptions of group interest, and they lack as well any sense of a structure of concepts that might be conceived to border on ideology. On the other hand, these interviews escape classification in Level D by virtue of some reference, however nebulous or fragmentary, to a subject of controversy over public policy. . . .

Level C houses the extremes of the global, nebulous mood and the isolated specific perception. It was assumed on *a priori* grounds that such concept formation represented less sophistication than did perceptions of group interest, which involve minimally a discrimination of a group or groups in the society and group goals for which political power is relevant. Neither the global sense of the "goodness" or "badness" of the times, nor the limitation of cognitions to isolated policy measures seemed to indicate conceptualization of equal breadth or differentiation.

Several characteristics not used as criteria for assignment had great incidence in these Level C interviews. We have already pointed to the focus that emerges here on promises made or broken. There is a vastly increased tendency as well for the respondent to plead great ignorance of anything political. Now and again there is some apparent element of modesty underlying this confession; in the great majority of the cases, however, it is easy to see what the individual means. Although more than two thirds of the people in Level C voted in 1956, there is a pervasive recognition of inadequate information among these respondents.

Furthermore, there seems to be an increasingly moral cast to evaluations at this level. Irritation and concern over matters of graft and campaign "mudslinging" are given frequent vent. Such observations are not absent from responses at higher levels; but in Levels C and D they come to form the main thrust of the individual's perceptions with monotonous regularity. As one might expect, the strong partisan often tends to lay charges of mudslinging entirely on the ledger of the opposition. Sometimes indignation is lodged in a definitive statement that the opposing party or candidate has said "things"—often the person cannot specify further under probing—that have been "proved false." But such allegations do not begin to exhaust the references to mudslinging. An impressive proportion of individuals at these lower levels roundly condemns both parties for "running each other down so." These people seem genuinely depressed by any cross-party criticism of policy and platform. When a person has just watched or listened to some of the campaign speeches, these reactions often remain much more salient than the content of the criticism itself.

Let us present some sample interviews from Level C. The first interview drawn is that of a Philadelphia woman:

(*Like about Democrats?*) This is a very hard ground—a lot of promises were made that weren't kept. (*What ones do you mean?*) It confuses the public and it confuses me. A person don't know who to vote for. All the same, both parties are guilty in some instances of breaking campaign promises.

(*Dislike about Democrats?*) No.

(*Like about Republicans?*) No particular thing as long as they do good for the people.

(*Dislike about Republicans?*) Just what I said before. (Respondent very vague, difficult to pin down to a particular question.) More should be done for human beings, for the good of the people. Those who take responsibility should worry about all the people of the world. We had bloodshed and we don't want it any more.

(*Like about Stevenson?*) I think he's a very smart man as far as he's concerned. (*Anything else?*) I think he's very ambitious.

(*Dislike about Stevenson?*) No.

(Like about Eisenhower?) The only reason that I would want to vote for him is that he is a former Army man and saw the horrors of war and therefore would want to keep the peace. That's the main concern in the world today.

(Dislike about Eisenhower?) No.

The second interview comes from a white woman in North Carolina:

(Like about Democrats?) They's a lot of nice Democrats. They's not too much difference in the parties.

(Dislike about Democrats?) Nothing in particular. Politics is something I don't study on much.

(Like about Republicans?) Seems like they helped a lot to stop the war.

(Dislike about Republicans?) The only thing is they's a lot of Republicans seems like they can be bought over—seems like they say they're Republicans, but they'll vote Democratic for money.

(Like about Stevenson?) I don't know much about the man. Our radio's tore up and I ain't heard any news lately.

(Dislike about Stevenson?) I don't know much about the man. I don't know what to say.

(Like about Eisenhower?) Seems like he's done pretty well this time, but I don't know. We could of had a better President than he is, I guess.

(Dislike about Eisenhower?) Well, no. I don't know whether I'll even vote or not. Sometimes I say I don't never intend to vote again. . . .

LEVEL D, ABSENCE OF ISSUE CONTENT. The remaining quarter of the sample failed to comment upon any issues of political debate in their responses to the unstructured questions. While vote turnout is relatively low within this group, these people still account for 17 per cent of our voters in 1956, and hence by themselves outnumber our ideologues in the active electorate by a 5–1 ratio.

To the degree that occupants of Level D have perceptions of the parties at all, they are bound up in moralistic themes like mudslinging and chicanery. More often the parties are poorly discriminated, and comment is devoted almost entirely to the personal characteristics of the candidates—their popularity, their sincerity, their religious practice, or home life.

Although we have encountered occasional bizarre conceptions in the previous interviews, these are more intrusive in Level D responses. Sometimes these oddities betray rather unorthodox conceptions of fundamental aspects of American political process. A few respondents, for example, confess to little understanding of what is going on but have a feeling that "it's a critical time, all right." An occasional individual appears to fear that the nation may emerge from the campaign without any president at all. "I don't know much about either of them, but just so long as one of them wins it will be all right."

In other cases there are factual inaccuracies that often have come to loom large in the respondent's thinking. One man was pleased with Eisenhower because he was the first American President who had ever gone to church. Another man appeared deeply angered because he had heard a speech in which Stevenson pronounced that there was no God. A woman who reported that she had become entranced by the Republican convention on television and had watched every minute of it came away without visible issue content but some perplexity at the fact that Nixon had received the vice-presidential nomination. "He's a foreigner, isn't he?" she asked the interviewer. . . .

The party or candidate types in Level D are not unique in the sample from the point of view of basic partisan motivations. In numerous interviews at higher levels it seems patent that issue perceptions are no more than garnish for a deep sense of partisanship, and throughout the sample generally, party loyalty exerts a substantial influence on perceptions of more specific events. Similarly, there are individuals at higher levels who disavow interest in parties and claim to attend primarily to the candidates. But at higher levels there are large numbers of respondents who could not be classified clearly in either camp. In Level D, where all else is shorn away, these primitive modes of approach to politics become most clearly differentiated, and seem to be of great analytic significance.

Since Level D comprised one quarter of the sample it was feasible to return to the interviews and subdivide respondents into these types. The distribution that emerged within Level D was as follows:

	Proportion of Level D
Simple Party Orientation	⅕
Simple Candidate Orientation	⅖
No Political Perceptions	⅕
Unclassified (mixed types)	⅕

. . . A California woman was drawn from the [first] category [party-oriented]:

(*Like about Democrats?*) I'm a Democrat. (*Is there anything you like about the Democratic Party?*) I don't know.

(*Dislike about Democrats?*) I'm a Democrat, that's all I know. My husband's dead now—he was a Democrat. *(Is there anything you don't like about the party?)* I don't know.

(Like about Republicans?) I don't know.

(Dislike about Republicans?) I don't know.

(Like about Stevenson?) Stevenson is a good Democrat. *(Is there anything else about him that might make you want to vote for him?)* No, nothing.

(Dislike about Stevenson?) I don't know. *(Is there anything about him that might make you want to vote against him?)* No.

(Like about Eisenhower?) I don't know. *(Is there anything about Eisenhower that might make you want to vote for him?)* I don't know.

(Dislike about Eisenhower?) I don't know. *(Is there anything about him that might make you want to vote against him?)* No. . . .

A Texas woman serves as an example [of candidate orientation]:

(Like about Democrats?) No, I don't know anything about political parties. I'm not interested in them at all.

(Dislike about Democrats?) No, nothing.

(Like about Republicans?) No, I don't know about the party. I like Ike.

(Dislike about Republicans?) No, nothing I can put my finger on.

(Like about Stevenson?) Right now I can't think of anything I like well enough to vote for him.

(Dislike about Stevenson?) No, I just have my choice and it is not Stevenson. It is Ike.

(Like about Eisenhower?) I just like him, the way things have gone. *(How do you mean?)* That's really all I know.

(Dislike about Eisenhower?) No.

The final illustration of the candidate type within Level D comes from a Massachusetts man.

(Like about Democrats?) I haven't heard too much. I don't get any great likes or dislikes.

(Dislike about Democrats?) I hate the darned backbiting.

(Like about Republicans?) No.

(Dislike about Republicans?) No.

(Like about Stevenson?) No, I don't like him at all.

(Dislike about Stevenson?) I have no use for Stevenson whatsoever. I had enough of him at the last election. I don't like the cut-throat business—condemn another man and then shake hands with him five minutes later.

(Like about Eisenhower?) As a man I like Eisenhower better. Not particularly for the job of President, but he is not so apt to cut your throat.

(Dislike about Eisenhower?) No.

The interviews that had virtually nothing to say may be rapidly disposed of. The following interview from this group came from a Missouri woman:

(Like about Democrats?) No—I don't know as there is.

(Dislike about Democrats?) No.

(Like about Republicans?) No, it's the same way I am about the other party.

(Dislike about Republicans?) No. Parties are all about the same to me.

(Like about Stevenson?) No, I don't think so.

(Dislike about Stevenson?) No.

(Like about Eisenhower?) I really don't care which man is best or otherwise. I don't know about either one of the men enough to give an opinion.

(Dislike about Eisenhower?) No.

We have now accounted for our total sample. This profile of an electorate is not calculated to increase our confidence in interpretations of elections that presume widespread ideological concerns in the adult population. To be sure, we have been able to assess only those aspects of political conceptualization that are revealed in conscious verbal materials. It might be argued for example that poorly educated people would have difficulty expressing a sense of apprehension at aggressive leadership of the "left," at a time when no need is felt for aggressive action. Such ineffable sentiment might, for the inarticulate, come to focus on reactions to personal attributes of the candidate. This is a possibility, yet one which we are not inclined to credit highly. If there were strong links between elements of the "deeper self" and reactions to ideological position that do bypass conscious concept formation and evaluation, we might have expected a stronger association between our measurement of conservatism and partisan decisions. Many of the people who reacted with dismay to the possibility of change suggested by the scale items undoubtedly failed to think of themselves, at a conscious level, as "conservative," if for no other reason than the fact the concept is not part of their cognitive tool chest.

But the fact remains that both the structured approach and the analysis of free answers lead to precisely the same conclusions: the concepts important to ideological analysis are useful only for that small segment of the population that is equipped to approach political decisions at a rarefied level.

TABLE 1. *Summary of the Distribution of the Total Sample and of 1956 Voters in Levels of Conceptualization*

	Proportion of Total Sample	Proportion of Voters
A. Ideology		
I. Ideology	2½%	3½%
II. Near-ideology	9	12
B. Group Benefits		
I. Perception of conflict	14	16
Single-group interest	17	18
II. Shallow group benefit responses	11	11
C. Nature of the times	24	23
D. No issue content		
I. Party orientation	4	3½
II. Candidate orientation	9	7
III. No content	5	3
IV. Unclassified	4½	4
	100%	100%

ISSUE CONFLICT AND CONSENSUS*

Herbert McClosky, Paul J. Hoffmann, and Rosemary O'Hara

American political parties are often regarded as "brokerage" organizations, weak in principle, devoid of ideology, and inclined to differ chiefly over unimportant questions. In contrast to the "ideological" parties of Europe—which supposedly appeal to their followers through sharply defined, coherent, and logically related doctrines—the American parties are thought to fit their convictions to the changing demands of the political

---

* From "Issue Conflict and Consensus among Party Leaders and Followers," by Herbert McClosky, Paul J. Hoffmann, and Rosemary O'Hara. *American Political Science Review*, LIV (June 1960), 406–427. Reprinted by permission. Mr. McClosky is Professor of Political Science at the University of California, Berkeley. Mr. Hoffmann and Miss O'Hara are at the University of Minnesota.

contest. According to this view, each set of American party leaders is satisfied to play Tweedledee to the other's Tweedledum.

Pressures Toward Uniformity and Cleavage

Although these "conclusions" are mainly derived from a priori analysis or from casual observations of "anecdotal" data (little systematic effort having been made so far to verify or refute them), they are often taken as confirmed—largely, one imagines, because they are compatible with certain conspicuous features of American politics. Among these features is the entrenchment of a two-party system which, by affording both parties a genuine opportunity to win elections, tempts them to appeal to as many diverse elements in the electorate as are needed to put together a majority. Since both parties want to attract support from the centrist and moderate segments of the electorate, their views on basic issues will, it is thought, tend to converge. Like giant business enterprises competing for the same market, they will be led to offer commodities that are in many respects identical. It is one thing for a small party in a multi-party system to preserve its ideological purity, quite another for a mass party in a two-party system to do so. The one has little hope of becoming a majority, and can most easily survive by remaining identified with the narrow audience from which it draws its chief supporters; the other can succeed only by accommodating the conflicting claims of many diverse groups—only, in short, by blunting ideological distinctions. . . .

The research reported here was designed not to refute these observations but to test the accuracy of the claim that they are sufficient to prevent differences in outlook from taking root in the American party system. We believed that the homogenizing tendencies referred to are strongly offset by contrary influences, and that voters are preponderantly led to support the party whose opinions they share. We further thought that the competition for office, though giving rise to similarities between the parties, also impels them to diverge from each other in order to sharpen their respective appeals. For this and other reasons, we expected to find that the leaders of the two parties, instead of ignoring differences alleged to exist within the electorate, would differ on issues more sharply than their followers would. We believed further that even in a brokerage system the parties would serve as independent reference groups, developing norms, values, and self-images to which their supporters could readily respond. Their influence, we felt, would frequently exceed that of ethnic, occupational, residential and other reference groups. In sum, we proceeded on the belief that the parties are not simply spokesmen for other interest groups, but are in their own right agencies for formulating, transmitting, and anchoring political opinions, that they attract adherents who in general share those opinions, and that through a feedback process of mutual reinforcement between the organization and its typical supporters, the parties develop integrated and stable political tendencies. Other hypotheses will be specified as we present and analyze our findings.

Procedures

The questions considered in this paper were part of a large field study made in 1957–1958 on the nature, sources, and correlates of political affiliation, activity, and belief in the American party system (hereafter referred to as the PAB study). Pilot studies on Minnesota samples had led us to suspect that many "settled" notions about party affiliation and belief in America would not stand up under careful empirical scrutiny; further, we felt that little progress would be made in the exploration of this subject until a comprehensive portrait of party membership in America had been drawn. Accordingly, a nationwide study was launched to acquire a detailed description of party leaders and supporters, gathering data on their backgrounds, political experiences, personality characteristics, values, motivations, social and political attitudes, outlooks on key issues, and related matters.

For our samples of party "leaders" we turned to the Democratic and Republican national conventions, largely because they are the leading and most representative of the party organs, their delegates coming from every part of the United States and from every level of party and government activity. Our samples ranged from governors, senators, and national committeemen at the one end to precinct workers and local officials at the other. In the absence of comprehensive information about the characteristics of the party elites in America, no one can say how closely the convention delegates mirror the total party leadership. We felt it fair to assume, nevertheless, that the delegates represented as faithful a cross section of American party leadership as could be had without an extraordinary expenditure of money and labor. Using convention delegates as our universe of leaders also held some obvious advantages for research, since the composition of this universe (by name, address, party, state, sex, place of residence, and party or public office) can usually be ascertained from the convention calls. Of the 6,848 delegates and alternates available to be sampled, 3,193 actually participated; 3,020 (1,788 Democrats and 1,232 Republicans) completed and returned questionnaires that were usable in all respects. The proportion of returns was roughly equivalent for both sets of party leaders.

The rank and file sample, which we wanted both for its intrinsic value and for its utility as a control group, was obtained by special arrangement with the American Institute of Public Opinion. In January 1958, Gallup interviewers personally distributed our questionnaire to 2,917 adult voters in two successive national cross-section surveys. Some 1,610 questionnaires were filled out and returned, of which 1,484 were completely usable. This sample closely matched the national population on such characteristics as sex, age, region, size of city, and party affiliation, and, though it somewhat oversampled the upper educational levels, we considered it sufficiently large and representative for most of our purposes. Of the 1,484 respondents, 821 were Democratic supporters (629 "pure" Democrats, plus 192 whom we classified as "independent" Democrats) and 623 were Republican supporters (479 "pure" Republicans, plus 144 "independent" Republicans). Forty respondents could not be identified as adherents of either party. . . .

Findings: Comparisons Between Leaders

No more conclusive findings emerge from our study of party issues than those growing out of the comparisons between the two sets of party leaders. Despite the brokerage tendency of the American parties, their active members are obviously separated by large and important differences. The differences, moreover, conform with the popular image in which the Democratic party is seen as the more "progressive" or "radical," the Republican as the more "moderate" or "conservative" of the two. In addition, the disagreements are remarkably consistent, a function not of chance but of systematic points of view, whereby the responses to any one of the issues could reasonably have been predicted from knowledge of the responses to the other issues.

Examination of Tables I-A-E shows that the leaders differ significantly on 23 of the 24 issues listed and that they are separated on 15 of these issues by .18 or more ratio points—in short, by differences that are in absolute magnitude very large. The two samples are furthest apart in their attitudes toward public ownership and are especially divided on the question of government ownership of natural resources, the Democrats strongly favoring it, the Republicans just as strongly wanting it cut back. The difference of .39 in the ratio scores is the largest for any of the issues tested. In percentages, the differences are 58 per cent (D) vs. 13 per cent (R) in favor of increasing support, and 19 per cent (D) vs. 52 per cent (R) in favor of decreasing support. Both parties preponderantly support public control and development of atomic energy, but the Democrats do so more uniformly.

TABLE I–A. *Comparison of party leaders and followers on "public ownership" issues, by percentages and ratios of support*

	Leaders		Followers	
	Dem.	Repub.	Dem.	Repub.
Issues	N = 1,788	N = 1,232	N = 821	N = 623
		(%s down)		
Public Ownership of Natural Resources				
% favoring: Increase	57.5	12.9	35.3	31.1
Decrease	18.6	51.9	15.0	19.9
Same, n.c.*	23.8	35.2	49.7	49.0
Support Ratio	.69	.30	.60	.56
Public Control of Atomic Energy				
% favoring: Increase	73.2	45.0	64.2	59.4
Decrease	7.2	15.3	7.1	10.0
Same, n.c.	19.6	39.7	28.7	30.6
Support Ratio	.83	.65	.79	.75
Mean Support Ratios for the Public Ownership Category	.76	.48	.70	.66

* n.c. = no code.

V. O. Key, among others, has observed that the Republican party is especially responsive to the "financial and manufacturing community," reflecting the view that government should intervene as little as possible to burden or restrain prevailing business interests. The validity of this observation is evident throughout all our data, and is most clearly seen in the responses to the issues listed under Government Regulation of the Economy, Equalitarianism and Human Welfare, Tax Policy. Democratic leaders are far more eager than Republican leaders to strengthen enforcement of anti-monopoly laws and to increase regulation of public utilities and business. Indeed, the solidarity of Republican opposition to the regulation of business is rather overwhelming: 84 per cent want to decrease such regulation and fewer than 0.6 per cent say they want to increase it. Although the Democrats, on balance, also feel that government controls on business should not be expanded further, the differences between the two samples on this issue are nevertheless substantial.

The two sets of leaders are also far apart on the farm issue, the Democrats preferring slightly to increase farm supports, the Republicans wanting strongly to reduce them. . . . The Republican desire to reduce government expenditures and to promote independence from "government handouts" prevails on the farm question as it does on other issues, while the Democratic preference for a more regulated economy in which government intervenes to reduce economic risk and to stabilize prosperity is equally evident on the other side. Party attitudes on this issue appear to

TABLE I–B. Comparison of party leaders and followers on "government regulation of the economy" issues, by percentages and ratios of support

Issues	Leaders		Followers	
	Dem. N = 1,788	Repub. N = 1,232	Dem. N = 821	Repub. N = 623
	(%s down)			
Level of Farm Price Supports				
% favoring: Increase	43.4	6.7	39.0	23.0
Decrease	28.1	67.4	27.6	40.3
Same, n.c.	28.5	25.8	33.4	36.7
Support Ratio	.58	.20	.56	.41
Government Regulation of Business				
% favoring: Increase	20.2	0.6	18.6	7.4
Decrease	38.5	84.1	33.4	46.2
Same, n.c.	41.3	15.3	48.0	46.4
Support Ratio	.41	.08	.43	.31
Regulation of Public Utilities				
% favoring: Increase	59.0	17.9	39.3	26.0
Decrease	6.4	17.6	11.1	12.0
Same, n.c.	34.6	64.5	49.6	62.0
Support Ratio	.76	.50	.64	.57
Enforcement of Anti-Monopoly Laws				
% favoring: Increase	78.0	44.9	53.2	51.0
Decrease	2.9	9.0	7.9	6.6
Same, n.c.	19.1	46.1	38.9	42.4
Support Ratio	.88	.68	.73	.72
Regulation of Trade Unions				
% favoring: Increase	59.3	86.4	46.6	57.8
Decrease	12.4	4.5	8.9	10.6
Same, n.c.	28.3	9.2	44.5	31.6
Support Ratio	.73	.91	.69	.74
Level of Tariffs				
% favoring: Increase	13.0	19.2	16.6	15.2
Decrease	43.0	26.3	25.3	21.3
Same, n.c.	43.9	54.5	58.1	63.4
Support Ratio	.35	.46	.46	.47
Restrictions on Credit				
% favoring: Increase	24.8	20.6	26.1	25.7
Decrease	39.3	20.6	22.2	23.8
Same, n.c.	35.9	58.8	51.8	50.5
Support Ratio	.43	.50	.52	.51
Mean Support Ratios for "Government Regulation of the Economy" Category	.59	.48	.58	.53

TABLE I–C. *Comparison of party leaders and followers on "equalitarian and human welfare" issues, by percentages and ratios of support*

Issues	Leaders		Followers	
	Dem. N = 1,788	Repub. N = 1,232	Dem. N = 821	Repub. N = 623
		(%s down)		
Federal Aid to Education				
% favoring: Increase	66.2	22.3	74.9	64.8
Decrease	13.4	43.2	5.6	8.3
Same, n.c.	20.4	34.5	19.5	26.8
Support Ratio	.76	.40	.85	.78
Slum Clearance and Public Housing				
% favoring: Increase	78.4	40.1	79.5	72.5
Decrease	5.6	21.6	5.8	7.9
Same, n.c.	16.0	38.3	14.6	19.6
Support Ratio	.86	.59	.87	.82
Social Security Benefits				
% favoring: Increase	60.0	22.5	69.4	57.0
Decrease	3.9	13.1	3.0	3.8
Same, n.c.	36.1	64.4	27.5	39.2
Support Ratio	.78	.55	.83	.77
Minimum Wages				
% favoring: Increase	50.0	15.5	59.0	43.5
Decrease	4.7	12.5	2.9	5.0
Same, n.c.	45.2	72.0	38.1	51.5
Support Ratio	.73	.52	.78	.69
Enforcement of Integration				
% favoring: Increase	43.8	25.5	41.9	40.8
Decrease	26.6	31.7	27.4	23.6
Same, n.c.	29.5	42.8	30.7	35.6
Support Ratio	.59	.47	.57	.59
Immigration into United States				
% favoring: Increase	36.1	18.4	10.4	8.0
Decrease	27.0	29.9	52.0	44.6
Same, n.c.	36.9	51.7	37.6	47.4
Support Ratio	.54	.44	.29	.32
Mean Support Ratios for "Equalitarian and Human Welfare" Category	.71	.50	.70	.66

be determined as much by ideological tendencies as by deliberate calculation of the political advantages to be gained by favoring or opposing subsidies to farmers. . . .

Having implied that agricultural policies partly result from principle, we must note that on three other issues in this category (trade unions, credit, and tariffs), principle seems to be overweighed by old-fashioned economic considerations. In spite of their distaste for government interference in economic affairs, the Republicans almost unanimously favor

TABLE I–D. *Comparison of party leaders and followers on "tax policy" issues, by percentages and ratios of support*

	Leaders		Followers	
	Dem.	Repub.	Dem.	Repub.
Issues	N = 1,788	N = 1,232	N = 821	N = 623
		(%s down)		
Corporate Income Tax				
% favoring: Increase	32.3	4.0	32.0	23.3
Decrease	23.3	61.5	20.5	25.7
Same, n.c.	44.4	34.5	47.5	51.0
Support Ratio	.54	.21	.56	.49
Tax on Large Incomes				
% favoring: Increase	27.0	5.4	46.6	34.7
Decrease	23.1	56.9	13.8	21.7
Same, n.c.	49.9	37.7	39.6	43.6
Support Ratio	.52	.24	.66	.56
Tax on Business				
% favoring: Increase	12.6	1.0	24.6	15.9
Decrease	38.3	71.1	24.1	32.6
Same, n.c.	49.1	27.8	51.3	51.5
Support Ratio	.37	.15	.50	.42
Tax on Middle Incomes				
% favoring: Increase	2.7	0.8	4.5	3.0
Decrease	50.2	63.9	49.3	44.3
Same, n.c.	47.1	35.3	46.2	52.6
Support Ratio	.26	.18	.28	.29
Tax on Small Incomes				
% favoring: Increase	1.4	2.9	1.6	2.1
Decrease	79.2	65.0	77.5	69.6
Same, n.c.	19.4	32.1	20.9	28.3
Support Ratio	.11	.19	.12	.16
Mean Support Ratios for "Tax Policy" Category	.36	.19	.42	.38

greater regulation of trade unions and they are more strongly disposed than the Democrats toward government intervention to restrict credit and to raise tariffs. Of course, party cleavages over the credit and tariff issues have a long history, which may by now have endowed them with ideological force beyond immediate economic considerations. The preponderant Democratic preference for greater regulation of trade unions is doubtless a response to recent "exposures" of corrupt labor practices, though it may also signify that the party's perspective toward the trade unions is shifting somewhat. . . .

Our fourth category, Tax Policy, divides the parties almost as severely as do the other categories. The mean difference for the category as a whole is .20, and it would doubtless have been larger but for the universal

TABLE I–E. *Comparison of party leaders and followers on "foreign policy" issues, by percentages and ratios of support*

	Leaders		Followers	
Issues	Dem. N = 1,788	Repub. N = 1,232	Dem. N = 821	Repub. N = 623
		(%s down)		
Reliance on the United Nations				
% favoring: Increase	48.9	24.4	34.7	33.4
Decrease	17.6	34.8	17.3	19.3
Same, n.c.	33.5	40.7	48.0	47.3
Support Ratio	.66	.45	.59	.57
American Participation in Military Alliances				
% favoring: Increase	41.5	22.7	39.1	32.3
Decrease	17.6	25.7	14.0	15.4
Same, n.c.	40.9	51.6	46.9	52.3
Support Ratio	.62	.48	.62	.58
Foreign Aid				
% favoring: Increase	17.8	7.6	10.1	10.1
Decrease	51.0	61.7	58.6	57.3
Same, n.c.	31.1	30.7	31.3	32.6
Support Ratio	.33	.23	.26	.26
Defense Spending				
% favoring: Increase	20.7	13.6	50.5	45.7
Decrease	34.4	33.6	16.4	15.4
Same, n.c.	44.8	52.8	33.0	38.8
Support Ratio	.43	.40	.67	.65
Mean Support Ratios for "Foreign Policy" Category (excl. Defense Spending)	.54	.39	.49	.47

unpopularity of proposals to increase taxes on small and middle income groups. Table I-D shows that the differences between the parties on the tax issues follow the patterns previously observed and that tax policy is for the Democrats a device for redistributing income and promoting social equality. Neither party, however, is keen about raising taxes for *any* group: even the Democrats have little enthusiasm for new taxes on upper income groups or on business and corporate enterprises. The Republican leaders are overwhelmingly opposed to increased taxes for *any* group, rich *or* poor. This can be seen in their low ratio scores on the tax issues, which range from only .15 to .24. . . .

Of the five categories considered, Foreign Policy shows the smallest average difference, but even on these issues the divergence between Democratic and Republican leader attitudes is significant. Except for defense spending the Democrats turn out to be more internationalist than the Republicans, as evidenced in their greater commitment to the United Nations and to American participation in international military alliances like NATO. Twice as many Democrats as Republicans want the United States to rely more heavily upon such organizations, while many more Republicans want to reduce our international involvements. . . .

Nevertheless, it would be incorrect to conclude that one party believes in internationalism and the other in isolationism. The differences are far too small to warrant any such inference. . . .

Comparisons Between Followers

So far we have addressed ourselves to the differences between Democratic and Republican *leaders*. In each of the tables presented, however, data are included from which the two sets of party *followers* may also be compared.

The observation most clearly warranted from these data is that the rank and file members of the two parties are far less divided than their leaders. Not only do they diverge significantly on fewer issues—seven as compared with 23 for the leader samples—but the magnitudes of the differences in their ratio scores are substantially smaller for every one of the 24 issues. No difference is larger than .14, and on the majority of the issues the disparity is smaller than .05. Insofar as they differ at all, however, the followers tend to divide in a pattern similar to that shown by the leaders, the correlation between their rank orders being .72. All the issues on which the followers significantly disagree are of the "bread and butter" variety, the more symbolic issues being so remotely experienced and so vaguely grasped that rank and file voters are often unable to identify them with either party. Policies affecting farm prices, business regulation, taxes, or minimum wages, by contrast, are quickly felt by the groups to whom they are addressed and are therefore more capable of arousing partisan identifications. It should also be noted that while the average differences are small for all five categories, they are smallest of all for foreign policy—the most removed and least well understood group of issues in the entire array. . . .

These findings give little support to the claim that the "natural divisions" of the electorate are being smothered by party leaders. Not only do the leaders disagree more sharply than their respective followers, but the level of consensus among the electorate (with or without regard to party) is fairly high. Inspection of the "increase" and "decrease" percentage scores (Tables I-A-E) shows that substantial differences of opinion exist among the electorate on only five of the 24 issues (credit restrictions, farm supports, segregation, and corporate and business taxes). Of course, voters may divide more sharply on issues at election time, since campaigns intensify party feeling and may also intensify opinions on issues. Available data from election studies allow no unequivocal conclusion on this point, but even the party-linked differences found among voters during elections may largely be echoes of the opinions announced by the candidates— transient sentiments developed for the occasion and quickly forgotten. . . .

Summary and Conclusions

1. Although it has received wide currency, especially among Europeans, the belief that the two American parties are identical in principle and doctrine has little foundation in fact. Examination of the opinions of Democratic and Republican leaders shows them to be distinct communities of co-believers who diverge sharply on many important issues. Their disagreements, furthermore, conform to an image familiar to many observers and are generally consistent with differences turned up by studies of Congressional roll calls. The unpopularity of many of the positions held by Republican leaders suggests also that the parties submit to the demands of their constituents less slavishly than is commonly supposed.

2. Republican and Democratic leaders stand furthest apart on the issues that grow out of their group identification and support—out of the managerial, proprietary, and high-status connections of the one, and the labor, minority, low-status, and intellectual connections of the other. The opinions of each party elite are linked less by chance than by membership in a common ideological domain. Democratic leaders typically display the stronger urge to elevate the lowborn, the uneducated, the deprived minorities, and the poor in general; they are also more disposed to employ the nation's collective power to advance humanitarian and social welfare goals (e.g., social security, immigration, racial integration, a higher minimum wage, and public education). They are more critical of wealth and big business and more eager to bring them under regulation. Theirs is the greater faith in the wisdom of using legislation for redistributing the national product and for furnishing social services on a wide scale. Of the two groups of leaders, the Democrats are the more "progressively" oriented toward social reform and experimentation. The Republican leaders, while not uniformly differentiated from their opponents, subscribe in greater measure to the symbols and practices of individualism, laissez-faire, and national independence. They prefer to overcome humanity's misfortunes by relying upon personal effort, private incentives, frugality, hard work, responsibility, self-denial (for both men and government), and the strengthening rather than the diminution of the economic and status distinctions that are the "natural" rewards of the differences in human character and fortunes. Were it not for the hackneyed nature of

the designation and the danger of forcing traits into a mold they fit only imperfectly, we might be tempted to describe the Republicans as the chief upholders of what Max Weber has called the "Protestant Ethic." Not that the Democrats are insensible to the "virtues" of the Protestant-capitalistic ethos, but they embrace them less firmly or uniformly. The differences between the two elites have probably been intensified by the rise of the New Deal and by the shift of former radicals into the Democratic party following the decline of socialist and other left-wing movements during and after the war.

CHAPTER THREE

The Role of the Parties

In any of several ways, the electoral result in a democracy usually implies some species of advice to the government. In an extreme or plebiscitary form of democracy, the election is a mandate to the victors to put into effect a specific policy or program. The vote is thus a direct order to the government. The voters are understood to have weighed the alternative specific policies presented to them in the campaign and through the voice of the majority to have made their binding choice. At the other end of the democratic spectrum, the election is simply a choice of a set of men to legislate and to administer the government—men not tied to any set of specific policies, perhaps not even identified with a distinct approach to the problems of the day, but chosen on the basis of their past performances in government, their excellence in other walks of life, their appeal in the campaign, or sometimes simply by the aversion of the voters to their opponents.

Most people would not say that in the United States we simply choose men who are then set free to choose in turn such governmental policies as they will. There is a manifest issue content to our national election. The candidates and their parties have past records as government or as opposition. The parties adopt "platforms" at their national conventions, platforms which point pridefully to past performance and offer promises of performances to come. The national candidates discuss issues in the campaigns and somehow manage to convey the impression to the voters that each has a program of governmental policy, and that if elected he will proceed to enact it. For their part, the voters, even if they do not understand specific policies or proposals, have widespread expectations of an approach to policy from the competing candidates and parties. Yet, clearly, American elections are not mandates for specific policies; or at least the elections are not so treated by the holders of public office. Somehow, the meaning of the election or the intent of the electorate is difficult to interpret, difficult to translate into public policy. If the voters expect that they have spoken with a clear voice about public policy, it must be said that the voice is heard differently by the men in the various centers of power in the national government.

Close to the center of any effort to understand the multifold processes between the election results and the emergence of public policy stand those remarkable organizations, the American major political parties. Of course, there are other factors contributing to the subtlety and elusiveness of our system—the separation of powers in the national government, the persistent vitality of the federal system, in which the states jealously guard their particular identities and their particular interests, the complex inner organization of the Congress itself, and the existence of a great multitude of differing interests scattered throughout the society. It is indeed difficult to believe that there could possibly be a single majority united behind some set of specific policies—but all of these interests intersect in the parties, and all of them influence and are influenced by the party system.

Among scholars and among the men in public life, the debate over the merits of the existing party system has been continuous. The critics of the parties advocate what is called "responsible party government." Under responsible party government, political parties would be capable of generating serious programs of public policy, conceived in the national interest and actuated by a set of principles to which all members of the parties would be committed. Not only would the parties be capable of generating alternative programs of public policy, they would also be skilled in taking their cases to the electorate in a way that would make a national campaign a great public dialogue on the issues. Finally, responsible parties are conceived of as having sufficient coherence and internal discipline to be able to enact their programs in the event that a majority of voters gives its approval at the polls. Advocates of responsible parties, thus, tend to favor the view that the election result is a more or less clear policy mandate. Responsible party advocates argue that the huge but complex and interlocking social-economic order of today requires energetic and positive government action—but that present governments are not certain of where they want to go. And even when leadership does propose action it is hampered and frustrated by delay, inaction, obstruction, and a querulous parochialism from Congress and the various interest groups. Many of the responsible party advocates also believe that meaningful elections and the clear location of responsibility in a party (a closer correspondence between elections and government) would go a long way toward reducing the apathy, hopelessness, and estrangement that many fear is growing more and more characteristic of the electorate.

Defenders of the present party system, and they appear to be more numerous than the critics, insist that the critics do not understand the nature of American society. They argue that this society is far too diverse in its interests ever to be satisfactorily assimilated into just two coherent, disciplined, and strongly programmatic—not to say ideological—political parties. The alternatives to the present decentralized and compromise-oriented parties, they say, is either a multiparty system of the European model—with all of its attendant disadvantages—or the division of the population into two competing, mutually distrustful, and increasingly bitter camps with a consequent threat to the fragile bonds of unity, and the possibility of ultimate civil war. What we require, they feel, are parties with broad popular appeal—broad enough to offer something to all important groups and all segments of popular opinion. In that way, the defenders say, no groups ever become wholly estranged from power, none is wholly cut off from access to government and, hence, none becomes bitter, extremist, inflamed, or alienated from the political order. If that achievement requires that parties be loosely organized, undisciplined, and oriented toward the winning of elections rather than the creation and achievement of policy goals, if it means election campaigns that are peculiarly bland and sometimes bafflingly vague with respect to actual differences between the parties and the candidates, then so be it. The price is not too high to pay.

In this chapter, we offer examples of the principal divergent viewpoints about the adequacy of our party system. Austin Ranney and Willmoore Kendall stand up for the party system roughly as it is. They argue that the parties do afford a good means of popular consultation between the government and the people, and that greater policy divergences between the parties, more policy-oriented parties, and parties with greater centralization and discipline over their members in government would lead to multipartyism and to rupture of the thread of unity.

James MacGregor Burns believes that there are really four parties, not two. For Burns, there are *Presidential* Democratic and Republican Parties and *Congressional* Democratic and Republican Parties. There are differences of approach and emphasis between the two Presidential Parties, but each is more or less urban-based and oriented toward positive government action to meet social problems at home, and toward an enlightened, multifaceted approach to the problems of the cold war. The Congressional Parties are essentially rural-based and inattentive to social problems that beset the majority of the population. Concomitantly, the Congressional Parties are oriented toward a rather narrow nationalism in meeting foreign-policy problems. There is, then, for Burns, no real majority in the Congress or in the government as a whole. Instead, he feels, our politics follow a model derived from James Madison, in which various local and particular interests, entrenched in posts of power in Congress, are able to frustrate majority-sanctioned government action intended to cope with immense common problems. In the selection offered here, Burns indicts the present party system and offers his own prescription for improvement.

In the concluding section, the late C. Wright Mills offers a more bitter perspective. Mills alleges that the parties and politics, in the conventional senses of the terms, are already trivial, and that real power over major questions lies outside Congress and the parties in the hands of a loose coalition of big business and the military. We hope that the materials presented in the chapter will not only help to illuminate some of the vital processes of democracy but will also stimulate the public to enter the debate over the effectiveness of those processes.

THE AMERICAN PARTY SYSTEM
AND DEMOCRACY*

Austin Ranney and Willmoore Kendall

The American party system, when measured against the conception of popular consultation, . . . gets very high marks indeed. By sustaining and refreshing the consensus on which our society and governmental system are based, it makes possible our characteristic brand of pluralistic bargaining-compromising discussion of public issues, which is probably about as close to the model of creative democratic discussion in the nation-state as a community like the United States can hope to get. Moreover, the party system usually produces clear popular mandates on the issue of *who* shall rule, although, like every other traditional institution for popular consultation except perhaps the town meeting, it rarely produces clear popular mandates on the issue of *what* the government shall do on this or that matter of public policy. Finally, the parties, more than any other aspect of our governing system, do see to it that law-making and law-enforcing go forward under a loose sort of majority control, the essence of which we do not understand unless we think of the relevant majority as usually cutting across party lines, and in such a way as to create no irreconcilable minorities that will divide the nation into warring camps.

* Abridged from Chapter 22 of *Democracy and the American Party System* by Austin Ranney and Willmoore Kendall, © 1956, by Harcourt, Brace & World, Inc., and reprinted with their permission. Austin Ranney is Professor of Political Science at the University of Wisconsin. Willmoore Kendall has taught political science at Yale University and at Stanford University.

For these reasons, therefore, few persons today would argue that American government would be more democratic with *no* party system at all than with the one it has; and few would quarrel with the proposition that the party system is one of the most powerful forces, if not *the* most powerful, operating to "democratize" our formal-governmental system, which, be it remembered, was not intended to be democratic and which, if permitted to operate in its "pure" form, would probably provide a far less democratic system of popular consultation and majority rule than that which we actually have.

In pondering the role and appraising the value of the present system, accordingly, the fruitful question is not whether it is more democratic than *no* party system at all, but where some *other* kind of party system would be more democratic than our present one. A number of eminent and thoughtful commentators, including Woodrow Wilson, Henry Jones Ford, Frank J. Goodnow, E. E. Schattschneider, James M. Burns, and the members of the Committee on Political Parties of the American Political Science Association, have answered the latter question in the affirmative by arguing that a more "responsible" party system would be more "democratic" than our present one. And other writers, including Pendleton Herring, Herbert Agar, Ernest S. Griffith, and [Ranney and Kendall] take the contrary position that a more "responsible" party system would probably be *less* "democratic" than our present system, given the nature of the American community.

We cannot hope to settle this controversy once and for all . . . We can, however, [summarize] in some detail the position of each group of writers, so that the areas of agreement and disagreement between them can be clearly understood by the reader as a basis for making up his own mind as to what kind of party system he wants. . . .

The Doctrine of Responsible Party Government

THE NEED FOR IMPROVED GOVERNMENTAL ACTION. The advocates of responsible party government argue that the government of the United States today faces domestic and foreign problems of such magnitude that they can be solved only by comprehensive, internally consistent, and expertly designed programs of public policy that are consistently supported both by a majority of federal officeholders and by a majority of the people throughout the nation. Anything less than such programs risks national disaster. We do not, however, want such programs *any* way we can get them; rather we want them to be developed, adopted, and executed *democratically*. In other words, we want not *action* alone, but *democratic* action as well.

THE CRUCIAL ROLE OF THE PARTIES. The national political parties, according to these writers, are the only agencies that can conceivably provide us with the kind of governmental action just described. They are comprehensive and representative in their membership and leadership, while their only possible rivals, the pressure groups, are limited and narrow in both respects. The parties are concerned with the *national* interest, while each pressure group is concerned only with its particular *special* interest. The parties operate in the open and deal directly with the voters, while the pressure groups operate largely in secret and deal for the most part only with governmental officials. If we are to have democratic and comprehensive programs for the national interest, then, only the national parties can provide them.

THE INADEQUACY OF OUR PRESENT PARTY SYSTEM. The responsible-party-government writers are convinced that our present national parties are incapable of furnishing the nation with the kind of governmental action described above. The argument runs as follows. The parties' lack of cohesion both inside and outside the government makes it impossible for them to draw up or execute sense-making programs of public policy. And this same lack of cohesion also prevents the voters from holding *either* party "responsible" in any meaningful sense for whatever the government does or does not do. Our present system of decentralized and loose parties and the pluralistic "concurrent-majority" kind of policy-making process they foster makes for *in*action rather than action; and it therefore simply cannot handle such problems as resisting Communist aggression without bringing on thermonuclear war, or stabilizing the economy without stagnating it—problems that by their very nature demand vigorous, coherent, and *national* action. Consequently, the present party system breaks down in time of crisis and in the face of such problems, and policy is made by "presidential dictatorship." We therefore cannot escape the conclusion that the present parties are incapable of sustaining democratic government at such times. . . .

The Defense of the Present Party System

The case against making our parties more centralized and disciplined may be briefly summarized as follows.

QUESTIONS ABOUT THE BRITISH MODEL. The advocates of more "responsible" parties regard the British party system—or rather an idealized version of it—as a working model of the kind of party system they want to see the United States adopt. British parties, they feel, actually do put forth internally consistent, sense-making, *and* clearly distinguishable programs arrived at in each party by a process of intraparty discussion and decision. Accordingly, British parties present the voters with a clear choice at each election. Moreover, the high party cohesion and discipline that result from the national party leaders' power to approve or disapprove local candidates for Parliament mean that the majority party is always clearly and unequivocally responsible for how the government is run. Hence, if someone objects, "But the kind of party system you advocate simply cannot work," these writers can (and often do) reply, "Of course it can: look at the British system!"

Some writers, however, have raised questions about the British model and its applicability to American conditions. For one thing, they say, the British party system does not in fact operate as its idealizers believe. And they have received impressive support for this argument from a recent article by David Butler, Fellow of Nuffield College, Oxford, and one of the leading British writers on the British party system, in which he explodes two "American myths about British parties." The first of these "myths" is that British parties offer the voters distinct and sharply differentiated programs. The fact is, says Butler, that the Conservative and Labor parties have clearly disagreed with each other on only one issue since 1945, that of the nationalization of certain industries; and even that issue has become very minor, since Labor now makes few demands for more nationalization and the Tories are willing to accept what nationalization now exists. The main differences between the parties now are merely those between the "ins" and the "outs." Butler even argues that "the fate of Britain ten years hence will be far less affected by whether the Conservatives or the Labour Party win the next election, than the fate of the United States will be affected by the decision it will have to take in 1956 between a Republican and a Democrat [for president]." The second "myth" is that party policy is made by the rank and file via "intra-party democracy." Here, Butler says, Americans should not mistake the form for the reality; for the fact is that the parliamentary leadership of each party makes the party's policy, though with due regard for the forms and for the sensibilities of the rank and file, and sees that it gets adopted. For example, despite the fact that the Labor rank and file in many of the constituency organizations are enthusiastic followers of Aneurin Bevan, the party itself is unquestionably controlled by Bevan's right-wing opponents—so that in a considerable number of instances Bevanite constituency organizations have to accept and campaign for *anti*-Bevanite Labor candidates. Butler concludes: "Much may be wrong with American parties, but those who have looked to the British system for remedies have surely erred in their analysis of its excellencies."

The "excellency" of the British system most admired by American advocates of more "responsible" American parties, however, is the high cohesion and strong discipline of the British parliamentary parties; and

Butler does not deny that these phenomena exist. But British parties are cohesive and disciplined, according to our second group of writers, because of the special nature of the British community and its belief system, which, in certain crucial respects, differs sharply from the American community and *its* belief system. Concretely, the leaders of both British parties are for the most part drawn from the public-school-Oxford-Cambridge "ruling class"; and the parties operate within a highly centralized culture, in which most Britons read London newspapers, listen to the B.B.C., and have no commitment to anything resembling the American traditions of "federalism" and "states' rights." Until we develop American equivalents for the British traditions of the "gentleman in politics" and unitarism, argue these writers, we are not likely either to want or to be able to get British-type parties.

Great Britain, moreover, pays a price for having the kind of parties it has. In Ernest Griffith's words, when the investigator goes behind the scenes in England, he finds such things as these:

A bureaucracy maturing almost all legislation and increasing by leaps and bounds; the two parties outbidding each other with promises of governmental largesse, so as to attract marginal groups; a division of the nation along class lines; the sacrifice of independence of thought and action on the part of the individual member; the pressing home of such a drastic measure as the nationalization of steel, though a majority of the voters supported candidates opposed to it at the last election.

The British party system, furthermore, breaks down in a crisis every bit as much as does the American system. As Professor Arthur N. Holcombe points out, of the fourteen ministries that have held office since the Parliament Act of 1911, only six, holding office only about a third of the time, have been composed solely of representatives of a single party approved by a majority of all the voters. Of the others, which together have held office about two-thirds of the time, five have been coalition or "national" ministries composed of representatives from several parties, and three have been formed by a single party having less than a majority in the House of Commons and in the nation, and have held office only by the temporary sufferance of the other parties. In the British party system, therefore, the "national" or "all-party" ministry is the equivalent of "presidential dictatorship" in the American system—that is, what the governing system turns to when, in time of crisis, the party system ceases to function "normally." And the incidence of such deviations from the party-system "norm" are certainly at least as frequent in Great Britain as in the United States.

THE PROBABLE PRICE OF CENTRALIZED AND DISCIPLINED PARTIES. In order to determine whether we want centralized and disciplined parties, say our second group of writers, Americans must understand the probable price of such parties and decide whether the probable benefits are worth it. The major items in the bill such parties would present the nation are as follows:

The Breakdown of Federalism. The primary purpose of centralizing and disciplining our parties is to enable them to formulate and execute *national* programs without regard to the demands of state and local interests and organizations. The technique for accomplishing it is to vest control of the state and local parties—and, through them, the state and local governments—in the hands of the national party leaders, so that state and local interference with national programs will be reduced to an absolute minimum. It may well be, therefore, that if such a party system were developed in the United States, it would mean the end of the reality if not of the form of federalism, and the states would become little more than administrative subdivisions of the national government. Perhaps the American people desire—or ought to desire—the demise of federalism and the installation of unitarism; but at least they should recognize that such a development would likely be a part of the price for centralized and disciplined national parties.

A Multiple-Party System. The advocates of more "responsible" national parties seem to assume that the new party alignments would pit a party made up of all the nation's "liberals" against another made up of all its "conservatives," thus retaining at least the two-party feature of our present national party system. But political conflict in the United States is enormously more multifarious and complicated than a simple division between pro-New Dealers and anti-New Dealers; and a great many groups could find their home in neither party. Suppose, for example, that the "conservative" party firmly and unmistakably pledged itself to oppose any federal civil-rights legislation, to end or greatly reduce farm price-supports, to end or greatly reduce our economic and military commitments abroad, and to prevent any further federal development of electric power and water resources. Could such a party hope to carry the South, the rural and urban areas of the East and Middle West, and the Northwest? By the same token, could a "liberal" party taking the opposite stand on each of these issues hope to carry all those sections? If the "liberals," for instance, pledged themselves to a national civil-rights program and meant business about it, the conservatives could hardly do less unless they were resigned to being a permanent minority. In such a situation, what would the South do? Form a third party? Or, as now, simply defy the national platform of whatever party it operated within? In the former case, we would get a multiple-party system; in the latter, there would be no essential change from our present system.

It has often been remarked that the congeries of bipartisan and intraparty "blocs" in Congress is, in effect, a multiple-party system masquerading under the labels and formalities of a two-party system. To the extent that this is an accurate description of our present national party system, it results, not from any mere organizational deficiency in our national party machinery, but rather from the diversity and multiplicity of our interest groups and the heterogeneity and complexity of the political conflict they express. So long as the basic nature of the American community remains the same, therefore, centralizing and disciplining our national parties would very likely result in a multiple-party rather than a two-party system.

But perhaps the new parties could change the nature of the community itself. What would be the likely result of that?

The Breakdown of Consensus. If each of our national parties were centralized and disciplined, it would have to mobilize electoral support in a considerably different manner from that employed by our present parties. It would have to make specific promises to certain groups, and accordingly, reject with equal specificity the demands of certain other groups. Moreover, the winning party would have to fulfill its promises pretty much to the limit, since the groups supporting it might well regard the party's failure to keep its promises as even worse than not making them at all or making them in vague and loose terms. The most likely result of such a situation would be the near-complete identification of particular groups with particular parties—labor and the lower-income groups with the "liberals," business and the higher-income groups with the "conservatives." And this, in turn, would clearly and unmistakably pit one class against another class in such a way that conflicts between them would become cumulative rather than, as at present, blurred and dispersed.

Take, for example, the present bitter controversy over racial segregation in the southern public schools. On the one hand we have a group, spoken for by the NAACP, which regards the ending of all such segregation immediately as a matter of the most sacred rights of man and the most urgent necessity. On the other hand we have opposed to them another group, spoken for by the "Dixiecrat" element of the Democratic party, which regards the continuation of such segregation as absolutely essential to the whole southern way of life and its most cherished values. Clearly there is a high "civil-war potential" in this explosive situation. Our present politico-governmental system, as we noted [elsewhere], is handling it as it handles all such matters: both major parties make vague platform declarations in favor of "equal rights for all races," but neither pledges itself to the federal enforcement of desegregation of southern schools come what may. The Supreme Court greatly pleases the anti-segregation group by declaring segregation unconstitutional—but federal troops are not ordered into South Carolina and Mississippi to make sure the Court's decision is carried out; and if the anti-segregationists were to make any such proposal, the southern senators would certainly filibuster it to death. The situation, however, is not entirely static: in Washington, D.C., and in the border states, segregation is being ended completely in some schools and modified in others. Thus the anti-segregationists and the pro-segregationists each get part—but not all—of what they want; no interracial or intersectional civil war breaks out; and a situation is preserved in which the gradual erosion of southern-white attitudes toward the Negroes that has been taking place during the past quarter-century or more—and in which, in the present writers' opinion, lies the best hope for the ultimate solution of this difficult problem—can continue its work. Certainly this is not the "swift, purposive, and vigorous" national governmental action demanded by the advocates of more "responsible" parties; but it *is* a kind of action which, whatever else can be said about it, preserves our consensus and yet does not permanently fix the status of Negro schoolchildren at its present level.

Suppose, however, we had centralized and disciplined parties. Both the Negroes and the southern whites are large and significant blocs of voters, and it seems unlikely that either would be content with parties which took clear positions on all other issues and acted upon them when in power but remained silent or vague on this particular issue. Either each group would form a third party, or one of the major parties would take up its cause. Suppose, again, that the "liberal" party pledged itself to end segregation and the "conservative" party to defend it. If, as now seems likely, the "liberals" won an election on this issue, they would either have to redeem their pledge, probably by sending federal troops into the South to enforce desegregation, or welsh on it in an "irresponsible" manner. Neither line of action would satisfy *both* groups to the extent that they are being satisfied under our present party system; and the consequences of the former for the American community are too obvious to be described, and should be taken into account in any attempt to calculate the social costs of centralized, disciplined, and programmatically precise national political parties in the United States.

Conclusion

As the reader should be well aware, the present writers, like the second group of commentators whose views we have just summarized, feel that the American party system as it now exists performs a role of great usefulness in our national politics of government; that, judged by the criterion of our conception of democracy, that role is of great value and deserving of high praise; and that the price America would probably have to pay for more centralized and disciplined national parties is, from the standpoint of democracy and in the light of the present nature of the American community, too high. We are, however, aware that other students of these matters have come to quite different conclusions.

A POLITICAL STRATEGY FOR AMERICANS*

James MacGregor Burns

I have tried to describe the four parties today with some objectivity— even more, to put myself in the positions of their leaders, to share their aims and outlook, to see the political world through their eyes. But I shall not pretend neutrality or detachment. The chief results of the ideas and institutions embraced by the Madisonian model are, I believe, as follows:

1. We have been captured by that model, which requires us to await a wide consensus before acting, while we have neglected, except furtively and sporadically, the Jeffersonian strategy of strong leadership, majority rule, party responsibility, and competitive elections. Hence, government action has been unduly delayed, whether measured by the progress of other comparable nations, such as Britain; or by the ascertainable needs of people, such as the jobless of the 1930's or the civil rights of minorities today; or by what the voters wanted or would accept, as reflected in the national platforms of both major parties and in the campaign promises of their presidential candidates.

2. Our four-party system requires coalition government, which is notoriously unable to generate strong and steady political power. To act, American leaders have had to gain the concurrence not simply of a majority of the voters, but of majorities of different sets of voters organized around leaders in mutually checking and foot-dragging sectors of government. The price of this radical version of checks and balances has been enfeebled policy, as major concessions have been made to gain the necessary support.

3. Hence as a nation we have lost control of our politics. We cannot collectively settle the elementary question of who may vote in national

* From the book, *The Deadlock of Democracy*, by James MacGregor Burns. © 1963 by James MacGregor Burns. Chapter 13. Englewood Cliffs, N. J.: Prentice-Hall, Inc., 1963. Reprinted by permission. Mr. Burns is Professor of Political Science at Williams College and biographer of Franklin Delano Roosevelt and of John F. Kennedy.

elections and hence we cannot extend the vote to millions of our fellow Americans, especially Negroes. We cannot exercise the primitive right of controlling congressional and presidential election arrangements, especially gerrymandering, rural over-representation, and one-party districts. We have lost control of political money and its misuse.

4. We lack popular control of the policy-making process. Our splintered parties set up barriers between the people and their national government rather than simplifying the alternatives, clarifying competing party doctrines, and allowing the victorious majority to govern.

5. Our government lacks unity and teamwork or, when it exists, it is often the integration of drift. Ideally, the winning party under a two-party system pulls together the executive and legislative branches in order to deliver on the party's (and candidates') promises to the people. But a fragmented party system cannot do this because the winning party is split into factions warring with each other.

6. We oscillate fecklessly between deadlock and a rush of action. Congress fails to act on crucial long-term problems; inevitably crisis comes, and the President uses his emergency powers. The Senate kills a bill to control harmful drugs; then a drug causes babies to be born without limbs; the Senate passes the same bill unanimously. Congress slashes vital foreign aid appropriations, then passes mammoth arms bills with little debate and without a single dissent.

7. We can choose bold and creative national leaders without giving them the means to make their leadership effective. Hence we diminish a democracy's most essential and priceless commodity—the leadership of men who are willing to move ahead to meet emerging problems, but who are also sensitive to the rights of the opposition and subject to the results of a free and competitive election.

8. We cannot define our national purpose and mobilize our strength to move vigorously against the problems that beset us at home and abroad, or to exploit the enormous possibilities of urban man and world man in the last third of the 20th Century.

"If you ask me—as a historian, let us say—whether a country in the state this country is in today," George F. Kennan has said, "with no highly developed sense of national purpose, with overwhelming accent of life on personal comfort and amusement, with a dearth of public services and a surfeit of privately sold gadgetry, with a chaotic transportation system, with its great urban areas being gradually disintegrated by the headlong switch to motor transportation, with an educational system where quality has been extensively sacrificed to quantity, and with insufficient social discipline even to keep its major industries functioning without grievous interruptions—if you ask me whether such a country has, over the long run, a good chance of competing with a purposeful, serious, and disciplined society such as that of the Soviet Union, I must say that the answer is 'NO'!"

We need a new kind of bipartisanship. The two presidential parties should join forces in Congress and elsewhere just long enough to work out the rules of the game for a fair, orderly, and competitive battle between the two national parties for the decades to come. The presidential parties must singly and jointly overcome the arrangements that thwart political competition, that prevent them from broadening their electoral support, and keep them from dealing with the way-of-life issues that increasingly dominate the nation's future. This means that each presidential party must convert its congressional party into a party wing exerting a proper, but not controlling or crippling hold on party policy.

The overcoming of the congressional parties requires the curbing of the institutional buttresses of their power: the seniority system in Congress, the other minority devices such as Rules Committee veto and the filibuster, mal-apportionment and one-party districts in the states, and, if feasible, midterm elections for the House. It means the shaping of new party structures and procedures. Above all, it means that the parties must protect themselves as organizational entities. Today, as we have seen, they are holding companies for numberless state and local and "candidate" organizations over which they have little control. But some of these organizations—especially those built around officeholders—have a divisive and stultifying impact on the national parties. Other party organizations—especially those oriented around governors who share the national party's style and outlook—could serve as foundation blocks for the national party.

This uneasy relation between the national and local parties poses a severe intellectual and organizational problem. Most of those who favor stronger parties want the national parties to combine more closely with state and local parties for the sake of more party coherence, discipline, and responsibility. Certainly this is desirable when the presidential and state parties are enough akin in doctrine and policy to strengthen each other. But other state and local parties are so different in outlook and doctrine that the presidential party must disentangle itself from them and set up its own separate independent party, at least in the states and congressional districts, with its own officers, finances, and communications channels. This means, for example, that the presidential Republicans would work through the present state parties in New York or California or Michigan, but would work around the parties of Barry Goldwater and Karl Mundt in Arizona and South Dakota.

Members of the presidential parties can resolve this problem only if they keep in mind what end must be sought. The aim is to draw the congressional and presidential party leaderships to each other by drawing the two party electorates more closely together—more specifically, by combining the smaller congressional party electorates with the bigger, more inclusive presidential party electorates in the states. As far as possible the President and his party majorities in Congress should be elected by substantially the same electoral groupings, for the sake of clarity of policy, unity in government, and responsibility to the majority. To do this the parties must pay a price: they cannot be allowed to be all things to all men. In some states a nationally oriented Republican party might not be able to win; but it could still field candidates who would stage vigorous campaigns, put over the message of national Republicanism, and build toward the day when the Republicans would have a fighting opportunity in that area. Such candidates could "bend" the national platforms a bit toward local political needs but what they must not do—what the national party leaders should be in a position to prevent them from doing—is so to distort Republicanism that its national meaning and appeal is perverted and impaired.

Once the Democratic and Republican parties agreed on such assumptions, the specific elements of party consolidation would fall into place:

1. *The national government should control national elections.* There may have once been good reasons for states to control elections of national officials; there are none today. State control of national elections, indeed, is a violation of the Madisonian principle under which each level of government should regulate its own political affairs. It is ridiculous that a man who moves to Alabama or Mississippi must wait two years before he can vote for presidential candidates he has observed for years. It is tragic that state control of senatorial and congressional elections helps congressional leaders to keep their constituencies small, noncompetitive, and exclusive. Both presidential parties must open up the closed politics of these one-party enclaves and ultimately make them into fighting ground.

Republicans may object that enlarging the electorate would help the Democrats more than themselves. So it might, for a time. But in the long run the Republicans would have as much to gain, for the party balance would re-assert itself. The main problem for the Republicans is not a strong Democratic party; without a lively rival party it would not mean much to be a Republican; the main problem is a congressional party that frustrates the Republican party in becoming a formidable national organization.

2. *The national parties must build grass-roots memberships.* Colonels, lieutenants, and sergeants are not enough; the parties need the same foundation that every other big, politically active organization—the AFL-CIO, the Legion, the A.M.A.—already has: an extensive card-carrying, dues-paying membership. There must be a clear channel of direction and

responsibility from party leaders to rank and file. This membership would be united chiefly by their common faith in their party's tradition, doctrine and policy. Hence they could operate effectively at any level, because they would be pursuing the same general objectives whether they were working at the local, state, or national levels.

Membership parties would call for more emphasis on party clubs and less on party committees, for clubs are the haven for party members and committees cater more to the parties' Kentucky Colonels. As the New York and California experiences have shown, the clubs encourage an open, vigorous, and policy-oriented politics. As that experience also shows, the clubs encourage a political independence and purism that will call for ingenious leadership if they are to sustain the old party organizations as well as rejuvenate them.

3. *The presidential and congressional parties must be merged organizationally.* There is no point in drawing a blueprint, especially since conditions will vary from state to state. One electoral change might have a helpful, though limited, effect. This is to alter the organization of the ballot so that candidates for President, Senator, and Representative would be placed in a separate box from candidates for state and local offices, and in such a way that the voters could choose a straight national party ticket simply by marking one party circle or by pulling one party lever. The form of the ballot, studies show, does have some influence on voting; moreover, every proper step should be taken to underline the key relationship of President to Senators and Representatives.

4. *New party leadership must be developed in Congress.* Clearly the institutional bases of minority and obstructionist politics . . . must go. A common defense of the seniority system is that it may be a poor way to run Congress but there is nothing better to take its place. This is nonsense, of course; hundreds of legislatures the world over choose their committees and leaders, on other grounds than the accumulation of uninterrupted years of seniority. What the defenders of the seniority rule are really saying is that given our present congressional party system, a seniority rule is inevitable. And in this they are correct. By the same token, an end of the rule depends on the end of the system.

What would take its place? Representative, responsible, and vigorous party policy committees under the leadership of elected party officials and their whips. The arrangement would not look very different on the surface from the present majority and minority leadership and party and policy committees. But there would be a big difference; the elected party leaders of Congress, working with the President (or the "out" presidential party leadership) would be in charge of the content and handling of party measures.

The seniority rule and related arrangements have been in effect so long that they seem to have divine support. But they are wholly man made, and they can be removed by man just as they were instituted by men. What it takes is majority support for changes in Congress, determination, parliamentary resourcefulness, and persistence. This is where the bipartisanship of the two presidential parties is sorely, though only temporarily, needed. Supported by a Kennedy or a Nelson Rockefeller in the White House, the presidential party in Congress should pool its strength with the other presidential party to strengthen both Senate and House.

5. *The parties and their candidates should be financed on a mass, popular, systematic basis.* It is better that a lot of people give a little money than that a few give a lot. A large dues-paying membership should help on this score, and there should be legal restrictions on the total amount of money that one man (or one family) can contribute. Other specific steps could be taken. Political money in the national party should be put under the national chairman, who should be held accountable for its use. The national committee should allot money to congressional candidates much more generously than it does now. As a beginning, Congress should adopt the President's proposals based on the recommendations of his committee on campaign finance—especially those for government subsidy of certain campaign expenses.

6. *The national opposition party should be better organized and given a clearer voice.* Today the Republicans cannot oppose effectively and responsibly because they speak with two voices, through their two parties. The presidential party should strengthen its All-Republican Conference by giving it money, staff, and organizational effectiveness. It should stage an annual conference, much smaller than the national convention, where national policy could be debated and the party platform publicized and renovated. The national committee should become a vigorous, representative body for which the national chairman could speak authoritatively in advancing and defending his party's position on quickly changing events. He should be the acknowledged spokesman for the "out" party.

The "in" party might also do well to establish an annual conference and perhaps an advisory council. While the need is not so acute for the party in power, since it possesses the unrivaled rostrum of the White House, the President should take care to nurture embryonic party organizations toward the day when his party again becomes the loyal opposition.

These six proposals require only party and minor governmental reforms. With one possible exception, they do not call for constitutional change. (The exception is the nationalization of elections for national officials; but this aim could probably be realized by stringent congressional regulation of national elections administered by the states.) Constitutional reform on the whole is not recommended, partly because it is so difficult. Still, as a capstone to these reforms, certain constitutional amendments would be extremely helpful and might achieve enough support to pass.

One of these is a four-year term for Representatives, to coincide with presidential terms. Today a two-year term for important office is an anachronism, as many states have recognized in shifting to four-year terms for governors and other state-wide offices. A two-year officeholder hardly has time to master his job; he is perpetually mending fences; he is unduly vulnerable to sudden gusts of public opinion. More important, the off-year elections usually raise havoc with the President's support in Congress, and of course form one of the bases of the congressional party system. Parliamentary democracies elsewhere find a four- or five-year term satisfactory for national legislators.

Extending the Representatives' terms to four years raises the thorny problem of the Senate. Politically, and perhaps constitutionally, it would be virtually impossible to shorten the Senate's tenure to four years, at least for the foreseeable future. We may have to accept the staggered six-year term, with a bow to the Framers.

A second needed constitutional change is repeal of the 22nd Amendment, but this would doubtless be more controversial than the proposal for a four-year term for Representative. Most political scientists (and most Presidents) believe that the anti-third term rule threatens a President's power during his second term, no matter how clear he makes his determination to choose his successor, for party and legislative leaders inevitably start moving into the orbits of other presidential candidates. But the impact of the amendment may not be crucial; Paul T. David believes that the amendment actually strengthens the "presidential wing" in both parties by partially balancing the weak position of the out-of-power presidential party, forcing the "in" party to deal seriously with problems of succession, and hence in making presidential party politics more competitive. I believe that the pulverizing impact of the amendment on presidential party unity more than offsets these advantages. In any event, the 22nd Amendment is less likely to be repealed as a result of general reform efforts than as part of a strategy to draft a highly popular President for a third term.

A final desirable constitutional amendment concerns the Electoral College. Today the system helps sustain the gap between the presidential and congressional parties, as we have noted; any change must be calculated in terms of its effect on the four-party system and on the coming of two-party politics. Perhaps the two presidential and the two congressional parties could hold a Four Power summit conference on this matter and adopt a compromise: if the congressional parties give up their gerrymandered and one-party districts (as far as possible) in congressional elections, the presidential parties would yield their own gerrymandering in the Electoral College. The presidential parties might offer, as a compromise, a proposal drafted by Professor Ralph Goldman and introduced into Congress by Senator Humphrey. This plan would eliminate the electors as such but retain the total number of electoral votes. The presidential candidate with a plurality in a state would receive two electoral votes (equivalent to its two Senators). The remaining 435 electoral votes would then be divided between the presidential candidates on a nationwide basis, in proportion to the national vote for each. This proposal recognizes both state equality under the federal system and the Jeffersonian idea of the direct popular election of the President. Barring over-all change in the Electoral College, perhaps party leaders could at least agree on a simple reform to prevent individual electors from voting in defiance of the election mandate, and to correct some of the dangerous mechanical weaknesses of the present system.

All three of these amendments are desirable. But we must not stake our hopes on, or become too much diverted by, the possibility of constitutional reform. The more central need of party and governmental reform is challenging enough.

KENNEDY AND THE CONGRESS

Francis M. Carney

As candidate in 1960, as President-elect, and in his early days in the White House, John F. Kennedy promised an active Presidency. He was, after all, a student of history, and he knew and agreed with Hamilton's prescription of "energy" as the most desirable quality in the executive. Plainly, also, Kennedy was drawn to those Presidents of his own party—Jackson, Wilson, F. D. Roosevelt—who stood in the heroic mold, who were great leaders of legislation and opinion.

As a candidate, Kennedy had given out a long agenda for his Presidency. His campaign theme was the need to get the nation on the move again. He promised a more active diplomacy and a greater flexibility in foreign affairs; a stronger—and more costly—military and space capability; an expanded and liberalized foreign trade; a more vital economy at home through monetary and budget policies to encourage expansion, growth, and full utilization of manpower and industrial plant capacity; farm stability through managed production; liberalized social security benefits; better unemployment insurance coverage and higher minimum wages; revitalization of internal transportation; special governmental assistance to chronically depressed areas; vigorous leadership to secure meaningful civil-rights legislation, hospital insurance for the aged through social security, and improvement of the quantity and quality of the nation's schools through federal aid; tax reform and reduction; and special attention to the problems of urban areas. And this list is not at all exhaustive. In his program, Kennedy stood clearly in the positive government tradition, committed to the view that government has massive and immediate responsibilities for the social and economic health of the nation. In his concept of the Presidency, he was committed to activism. He would be Chief Legislator as well as Chief Executive.

Looking at and listening to the lean, vigorous, and highly articulate young President on Inauguration Day 1961, one could scarcely doubt that it would all come true. Kennedy had demonstrated vigor, toughness, determination, resourcefulness, and intellectual capacity as he wrested the nomination from his party's reluctant leaders and went on to defeat the skillful and favored Richard M. Nixon in November. The inauguration speech was eloquent and confident. Kennedy seemed to be standing in wait, like one of Henry V's "greyhounds in the slips," to hurl himself at the problems standing in wait for him. Captivated newsmen began to talk of a burst of legislative creativity on the order of Roosevelt's "first hundred days" or of the first term of Wilson's New Freedom.

As though to clear the decks for Kennedy's "first hundred days," his party in the House of Representatives handed him an initial crucial victory by voting to expand the size of the Committee on Rules in order to break up that vital committee's dominating coalition of conservative Democrats and Republicans. The Rules Committee vote was intended to ensure that the Kennedy programs could come before the House for a vote, that they would not be silently throttled in committee. In the press, the Rules Committee vote was frequently taken as evidence of the new President's shrewd, tough ability to lead Congress—although Kennedy, of course, shared credit for the victory with the late Speaker Sam Rayburn.

But a Rooseveltian "first hundred days" did not follow on the heels of the Rules Committee fight. There was no burst of legislative creativity at all, despite the fact that in the first session of the 87th Congress the President did score some notable legislative victories. It soon became apparent from the pattern of Presidential messages to the Congress that Kennedy was not going to try to achieve all of the objectives of the campaign.

In early January 1961, Kennedy had given the press a list of "priority" bills he hoped to see pass in the session of Congress. These proposals included an omnibus public housing bill, federal aid to depressed areas, a rise in and an extension of the minimum wage, federal aid to education, and medical care for the aged through Social Security. None of these was a new proposal, none embodied radical new doctrine. All of the Kennedy "must" legislation of the first year had been before Congress in one form or another in the Eisenhower years. It may not even be too strong to say that all five of the new President's proposals could have been enacted under Eisenhower had the former President chosen to support them strongly.

Perhaps the most conspicuous absences from the President's 1961 proposals were civil-rights legislation and a major reform and reduction in federal taxation. Undoubtedly, the decision not to press for civil-rights legislation in 1961 was made to ensure passage of the rest of the President's program. Not only would the southern opponents of civil rights filibuster in the Senate to block a vote on a civil-rights bill, they might even retaliate by withholding support from other Kennedy bills, or use their entrenched power in the committees of Congress to keep the bills bottled up in committee. Kennedy's strategy was to sacrifice controversial new legislation, especially a civil-rights bill, in order to get a modest program of holdover Democratic Party bills through in quick order. The clue to this strategy was given early in January 1961 when Kennedy (then President-elect) refused to give his support as a senator to an effort by a bipartisan group of Senate liberals to change the standing Senate rules to permit a majority vote to halt a filibuster.

Did this strategy of wooing the southern conservatives in his own party work? The President won fairly quick approval of housing, minimum wage, and depressed-area legislation, giving up a little bit of something in each, but getting most of what he had asked for. In national-security policy, too, the President was rather successful in the first session of Congress, as foreign aid and military and space appropriations requests were passed largely in the form and amounts that he requested. On the other hand, no action was taken on medical care for the aged, and no such bill was ever even reported out of the House Ways and Means Committee. The Kennedy proposal for federal aid to education broke on the big rock of the church-state question. The bill was killed in the House Rules Committee— and by the vote of a New York City Democrat normally counted as a Kennedy supporter. Furthermore, the acrimony stirred up by the debate on the bill, the forming of hard lines from which it would be difficult to recede, probably ensured that there would be no general federal-aid-to-public-schools legislation for the balance of Kennedy's term. By the end of 1963 there was still little prospect that such a bill would pass in either session of the 88th Congress. Thus, the Kennedy strategy of 1961 was only partially successful. Steering clear of civil-rights legislation to save the other parts of his program, he wound up with three of his "big five" domestic-policy programs—none of which really broke new ground—and a good record on foreign- and defense-policy proposals.

While stressing the measures discussed above, Kennedy was nevertheless an active, energetic proposer of legislation to Congress. According to *Congressional Quarterly Weekly Report*, 355 specific legislative requests to Congress came forward from the President in 1961—nearly twice the 183 requests that President Eisenhower sent to Congress the previous year. Of the 355 requests Kennedy sent to the Capitol, Congress passed 172, or 48.4 percent. That compares favorably with the 30.6 percent of Eisenhower's final year's requests. If, however, Kennedy's first-year record is compared with the Eisenhower first-year record, the story is far different. For in 1953, according to *Congressional Quarterly*, Congress granted 72.7 percent of Eisenhower's requests, and in 1954 gave him 64.7 percent—as compared with the 44.3 percent approval score won by Kennedy in 1962. The years 1953–54 seem to be fairer comparison years for the legislative "batting averages" of the two Presidents—because of the "honeymoon" effect, and because in 1953–54, Eisenhower was working with a Republican Congress, just as Kennedy has had Democratic Congresses since 1961.

By July 1, 1963, President Kennedy had submitted a record 403 specific legislative requests to Congress. As of the same date, Congress had approved 19 of these, or 4.7 percent, whereas in 1961, Congress had approved 10 percent by July, and in 1962, 7 percent had been approved by July. Thus, the President's success with Congress seems to be declining from what was a modest beginning.

Over-all "box-score" figures do not give a wholly accurate picture, however. For Mr. Kennedy is undeniably a more active President than Mr. Eisenhower was, and his proposed measures are more novel and controversial than those of the former President, who stuck so relentlessly to the middle of the road. Undoubtedly, Mr. Kennedy could have a higher approval score if he adopted a minimal program and sent fewer, less controversial requests to Congress. In the second place, the box-score figures can be misleading because they tell us nothing of the quality or importance of the legislation that does pass. If most of Mr. Kennedy's legislative victories of 1961–63 did but extend and consolidate traditional New Deal–Fair Deal programs, he is nevertheless not without some historic achievements. The passage—in virtually the form requested by Kennedy—of the Trade Expansion Act of 1962 was just such a victory, for it capped this nation's transition from a piecemeal and protectionist foreign-trade policy to a rational free-trade policy. The ratification by the Senate in 1963 of the nuclear test-ban treaty with the U.S.S.R. was another landmark victory for the President. If to these two legislative achievements the President could add in a civil-rights bill of the far-reaching dimensions he has requested and an unemasculated tax-cut measure that would, in effect, ratify his budgetary and fiscal policies, it would have to be said that in qualitative terms he had enjoyed a not unimpressive term as a legislative leader.

But Mr. Kennedy must be judged by his failures as well as by his successes. The failure of federal aid to education, medical care for the aged, major reform of the tax structure, the attempt to create a federal Department of Urban Affairs, and the request for a standby presidential power to cut income taxes; the progressive slashes in his foreign-aid requests, and the resistance in Congress to the Kennedy notion that the federal budget is a positive weapon of national economic policy—all must be set in the debit column of Mr. Kennedy's legislative balance sheet. Finally, when we examine the President's record in the light of candidate Kennedy's predispositions and aspirations, one must conclude that as a legislative leader he has not been a conspicuous success. Certainly, he has been no Roosevelt of the "first hundred days," no "Prime Minister" Wilson of 1913–16.

What has gone wrong with Mr. Kennedy's plans? What palpable factors are there in his relations with Congress that make his lot there so hard? Here we cannot go into all of the elements of Mr. Kennedy's own style that might affect his relations with Congress. But we can look at the built-in or institutional factors that especially affect Kennedy as legislative leader and as leader of his own party.

Extra-Congressional Factors

A DUBIOUS MANDATE. Mr. Kennedy's extremely narrow margin of victory in 1960 must be counted among any list of factors reducing his effectiveness in leading Congress. Walter Lippmann has said that Kennedy was haunted by the fact that he did not even receive a majority of the popular votes cast for President in 1960, and that Kennedy was struck by the conviction that he had, therefore, no mandate to depart radically from the programs and approach of his popular predecessor in office. Such a conviction could account for the generally modest nature of Kennedy's first legislative programs suggested to Congress. It might account also for a reluctance to apply heavy pressure on Congress in behalf of his program, on the grounds that the congressional mandate was at least as valid as his own. On the other hand, the impressive success of the Democratic Party in the elections of 1962 was at least partly attributable to Mr. Kennedy's personal popularity, and notably to the public approval of his handling of the crisis over Soviet missiles in Cuba in October of 1962.

If the narrowness of the victory in 1960 hampered Mr. Kennedy, it could at least be argued that the events of 1962 went a long way toward canceling the dubiousness of the mandate of 1960.

FOREIGN POLICY COMES FIRST. One of the popular myths of American political life is that "politics stops at the water's edge." Sometimes it does, but not always—as several Presidents have found to their sorrow. Both the allies and the adversaries of a democracy must understand that its people are reasonably united behind a foreign policy if that policy is to be successful. Conscious of the need for unity or consensus behind his foreign policy, a President must be loath to risk that unity with domestic policies that are highly controversial and therefore divisive. This need carries over into Congress. A President may have legislation for his foreign-policy designs, and he cannot afford to lose the confidence of Congress. Consequently, he must think twice about introducing domestic legislation that provokes or alienates blocs of potential support for foreign-policy measures. President Kennedy repeatedly stressed the need for support of his Trade Expansion Act, and for the full appropriations requested for foreign aid and the expansions in defense and space spending he sought. It is therefore not unlikely that he muted or toned down his pressure on Congress to give him his whole domestic package.

A COMPLACENT PEOPLE. When F. D. Roosevelt became President in 1933, there was a pent-up demand in the people for action. For three years the nation had floundered in a deepening economic crisis. F.D.R. entered office in the middle of a great emergency, and it was under the cover of that emergency that much of the New Deal program was put through. Roosevelt's public image was in part that of a man embattled.

For Kennedy there was no emergency. There are dissatisfactions among the people, a restlessness and uneasiness about our national character and style of life, a mood of soul-searching; but these things are not directly amenable to government action. Kennedy's long agenda of social and economic problems to be overcome by government action either affect too few people (such as the unemployed), or they do not have enough salience to overcome the general self-satisfaction. There is no surge of public opinion evident behind the President's program, no evidence of any wish to punish those Congressmen who do not support the President.

Congressional Factors

But most of the causes of President Kennedy's difficulties as a legislative leader lie in the Congress itself, and in the differing structures and natures of the modern Presidency and Congress.

THE FRAGMENTATION OF THE PARTIES. Both the 87th and 88th Congresses were organized by heavy Democratic Party majorities. In the 87th Congress, the House divided 263–174 in favor of the Democrats; the Senate, 64–36 in favor of the Democrats. In the 88th Congress, the House had 257 Democrats and 177 Republicans; the Senate, 67 Democrats to 33 Republicans. To say that the Democrats organized the Congress is to say that the officers of each house were Democrats, that the Democrats essentially controlled the order of business for each house, that the chairmen of all the committees in each were Democrats, that the committees were heavily weighted in favor of the Democrats, and finally that most of the professional staff workers of the committees and of each house were Democratic appointees. But, that the *machinery* of the 87th and 88th Congresses was entirely in the hands of Democrats does not mean that a single, unified, directing majority presided over the legislative process.

V. O. Key and James M. Burns have said that in reality ours is a four-party system, consisting of Presidential Democrats and Republicans, and Congressional Democrats and Republicans. The regional strongholds of the Presidential parties are the seaboard and industrial states and cities of the North and the West. The Congressional Democrats have their impregnable redoubt in the South, though border- and mountain-state representatives are at least fellow travelers of the Congressional Party. The Congressional Republicans come mainly from the Middle Western Republican heartland. Of course the accidents of personality and of electoral fate often break up perfect regional symmetry. There are some Middle Western Presidential Republicans and big-city Congressional Democrats, but the regional demarcations as described ordinarily hold. The enduring sources of these party differentiations lie principally in the electoral system and in the traditions and organization of Congress.

INFLUENCE OF THE ELECTORAL COLLEGE. The surest route to victory in a presidential election is to win the votes of the populous, urban, largely industrial northern states, states with big blocs of electoral college votes: New York, California, Pennsylvania, Illinois, Michigan, Ohio, Massachusetts, New Jersey, Connecticut, etc. It is on the populations of these states that the great problems of modernity fall most heavily, the problems of employment, poverty, housing, slums, inflation, crime, schools, and transportation. In the great cities of these states live the ethnic minorities, especially Negroes, for whom the burdens of prejudice and discrimination complicate the other problems of urban modernity. From the time of F. D. Roosevelt, this population has, rightly or wrongly, looked to the national government for solutions to the more pressing of the problems. Presidents are leaders of the whole nation, but they know that their electoral majorities come from the big states with the big cities. The presidential wing of each party makes its appeals to this population and is especially sensitive to its needs; hence, it stands for governmental action to meet these needs.

RURAL DOMINANCE IN CONGRESS. The Congressmen from the populous industrial states also are oriented toward the problems of their constituents, and therefore also stand for governmental action to meet the problems, and in the main belong to the presidential wing of their party. But, if the Presidential Party represents a majority of the nation's population, why isn't that majority reflected more accurately in Congress? Since the Congressional Parties do not have a clear majority in Congress (though there is some overrepresentation of rural areas), it is difficult to state in precise or quantitative terms the extent to which urban and suburban areas are underrepresented in Congress. *Congressional Quarterly* has identified the twenty least populous congressional districts in the nation and the twenty most populous. Of the distinction between these districts, it notes that the most populous twenty are overwhelmingly urban-suburban in character, and that a predominantly rural complexion is the most striking characteristic of the twenty smallest. In fact, according to *CQ*, 96.7 per cent of these least populated districts are rural in character, whereas 80.1 per cent of the most populous are urban or suburban. It is not difficult to see then that there is disproportionate rural and small-town influence in Congress simply in the terms of numbers.

Leaving aside the special case of the agricultural surplus and the cost-price squeeze on the farmer, we find the people of rural and small-town America do not share the pressing problems of the people of metropolitan America, and do not have the same sense of urgency about governmental solutions. Rural and small-town America are the bastions of the American traditions of individual, family, and local self-reliance. Thrift, prudence, doing for one's self and for one's own, not living beyond one's means are still salient values in the American hinterland. What is a "social problem" in the city is a family or community problem in the small town or on the farm. The world of welfare, governmental planning, deficit spending, and deliberately unbalanced national budgets is strange and unpopular in traditional, rural America. The Congressional Parties, while not made up entirely of rural representatives, are nevertheless more oriented toward the values and interests of the small towns than toward the needs of the metropolitan centers. The result is a discordance between the Presidential and Congressional wings of each party, which in many ways is more striking than the differences between Democrats and Republicans normally.

THE SOUTHERN DEMOCRATS. If we think of the South as the eleven states of the Confederacy, plus Oklahoma and Kentucky, there are 105 Southern Democrats in the House, and 23 in the Senate of the 88th Congress. They form the principal part—but by no means the total mass of the Democratic Congressional Party. Why are they so different from their fellow Democrats in the North? On the question of civil rights for Negroes, the answer is obvious and needs no elaboration here. But why do they diverge so on other issues? Not all members from the South do diverge from the Presidential Democrats on all issues, and there are even a few members from the South who on all issues but civil rights are aligned with the Presidential Party. But the southerners as a bloc are more conservative. Let us briefly list some reasons for this.

In the first place the South is still largely a rural section. The large cities of the South, moreover, are discriminated against by unequal apportionment of districts or by gerrymandering. On *CQ's* list of the twenty most populous congressional districts, seven are from southern cities; of the twenty least populous districts, eleven are southern rural areas. Again, the extreme sets the pattern. The typical southern Congressman is from a small town or rural area.

In the second place, the growing sensitivity of the northern Democrats to the Negro protest, and their growing commitment to civil-rights legislation, has progressively alienated the southerners from their nominal fellow partisans. Bitterness begets bitterness. Hostility begets hostility. If northern liberal Democrats are willing to strike the southern Democrat in what the latter considers his vital interests, then the northern liberals must expect retaliation against their vital interests.

In the third place, southern Democrats must look where they can for support against civil-rights legislation in their efforts to use the rules and procedures of each house to stifle majority-backed threats to the "southern way of life." To the extent that they get this support from conservative Republicans, and they do get it, they must give something to their allies— namely their votes against liberal or positive government legislation proposed by the Presidential Democrats.

Finally, though the pattern breaks down in some states in presidential elections, the South has been a one-party area. Most southern Congressmen have not ever faced a stiff challenge from a Republican opponent. The two-party dialogue is barely heard in the South. The tides of debate, conflict, and discussion that wash over the rest of the nation in election years leave most of the South untouched. Southern Democrats usually win their posts in the primary elections, which are rather personality contests and local factional fights than spirited contests over national issues. If a southern Congressman can demonstrate his steadfastness on the civil-rights question and keep his personal life free from scandal he seldom needs to bother much about other issues. This remoteness from the concerns of the rest of the nation contributes, then, to the conservative complexion of the South as a region.

THE STRENGTH OF THE SOUTH. The influence of southerners on legislation is greater than their numbers in both houses of Congress would appear to warrant, at first glance. In Congress, rank and office—and therefore, influence or power—goes with seniority. There is a place for talent, skill, and learning; but in the main, rank depends on seniority. We have noted that the one-party-system areas are removed from the tides of national politics, and that incumbent Congressmen from such areas have a better chance of staying in office than those from a district or state in which there is vigorous two-party competition. The South is our most notable, though not the only, example of a one-party area. A few facts serve to illustrate the consequences in terms of offices and power in Congress.

In the Senate, thirteen of the fifteen most senior Democrats are from the South. In the House, twenty-eight of the fifty most senior Democrats are southerners. Of the fifteen least senior Senate Democrats, only one is from the South. Of the sixteen standing legislative committees in the Senate, nine are chaired by southern members. The House has twenty such committees, eleven of which are headed by southern members. The very powerful Appropriations Committee of the House, which must pass on all bills appropriating federal money for any purpose, has thirteen subcommittees. Eight of these subcommittees, each of which is armed with the power of the full committee, are chaired by southern Democrats. Similarly, eight of the thirteen subcommittees of the Senate Appropriations Committee are chaired by southerners.

In the House, Democratic members are given their committee assignments by the Democratic members of the Ways and Means Committee, who sit as a committee on committees. In the 88th Congress, there are fifteen Democrats on Ways and Means, of whom seven, including the Chairman, are from the South. In the Senate, Democratic committee assignments are made by the Democratic Steering Committee, which is composed of fifteen members, of whom seven are southern Democrats. If to these seven southerners on the Senate Democratic Steering Committee one adds Senator Hayden of Arizona and Senator Bible of Nevada, both of whom are solid members of the Congressional Democratic Party, we can see that in the vital matter of assignment to committee posts, the Presidential Democrats are outmanned by the Congressional Democrats.

Senator Joseph S. Clark of Pennsylvania, a leading Presidential Democrat, has alleged that the Congressional Democrats in general (and the southerners in particular) have used their power over committee assignments to intimidate other Democrats from voting to amend the Senate rules to make it easier to end filibusters, one of the key weapons of any southern fight against civil-rights legislation. Senator Clark asserted that the Senate is run by an "Establishment," which in turn is dominated by southerners and conservative Republicans. The Establishment, according to Clark, opposes a change in the filibuster rule. Clark then showed that eight nonfreshman Democratic Senators voted with the southern faction on the rules change, and also submitted requests for a change in their committee assignments. Seven were granted of the eight requests, and six of the eight Congressmen received the assignment of their choice. Clark then noted that fourteen Democrats who voted against the South for a change in the rules also submitted requests for a change in assignment. But only five received new assignments, and only one the assignment of his choice. It would seem that the Democratic Steering Committee in this instance, at least, rewarded the members who voted with the South and punished those civil-rights liberals who wanted to strip the South of one of its most potent weapons.

The Delicate Balance of the Parties

At the present time neither the Presidential nor the Congressional Parties are in firm control of Congress. If there is no Kennedy majority, neither is there an anti-Kennedy majority. In the 88th Congress, legislation will continue to arise from an elusive process of compromise, leadership, obstruction, and bargaining. Perhaps the delicacy of the equilibrium of Congress can best be appreciated by a brief glance at the struggle in January 1961 over the composition of the House Rules Committee. Kennedy and his Party leadership in the House knew that if the Presidential program was to have a chance at all, they would have to get it out of the Rules Committee and onto the floor of the House. That meant that the make-up of the Committee would have to be changed. The old Rules Committee consisted of six moderate-to-liberal Democrats, two conservative Democrats (including the chairman), and four conservative Republicans. There was a six-to-six stalemate, enough to keep liberal legislation bottled up. Kennedy's congressional supporters agreed that the best way to change the stalemate was to enlarge the committee to fifteen members and appoint two moderate or liberal Democrats, thus ensuring a probable eight-to-seven pro-Kennedy division. After fierce debate the plan carried by the narrow margin of five votes, 217–212. The distribution of the votes offers some clue to the strength of the blocs. To the hard core of about 100 Presidential Democrats from the North and West, the remainder of the Democratic Party outside the South attached itself. In addition, forty-seven southern Democrats were led over by moderate southern leadership and the skill of the late Mr. Rayburn. Finally, twenty-two Presidential

Republicans joined the winning side to give it the margin of victory. All of the rest of the Republicans and sixty-three southern Democrats—the hard core of the Congressional Party—voted against the change. The resulting precarious eight-to-seven split in the Rules Committee reflects the tenuousness of President Kennedy's support in Congress.

The basic liberal-conservative split can be overcome by the interjection of some other issue. In 1961 two otherwise liberal or moderate Roman Catholic Democrats defected to the conservatives on the committee to kill the President's school aid bill because the bill provided no benefits for parochial schools. In 1962, two moderate southerners voted with the conservatives to kill the proposal to establish a Federal Department of Urban Affairs, because it was understood that the President was going to name a Negro as Secretary of the new Department. And so it goes in Congress as a whole.

There is basically a small pro-Kennedy majority in each house, but the President must husband carefully. The civil-rights issue, a religious issue, a matter of local or regional economic concern—a matter of the pork-barrel —or even the ambitions or injured pride of an individual here or there can upset the slender Kennedy majority and frustrate his legislative objectives. Legislation must be put together with an eye to all of the snags and lurking dangers. Then, too, there is the fact that the Congressional Democrats are in the majority of the command posts in the two houses— the committee chairmanships. In the committees, bills can be gutted beyond recognition or silently murdered before ever coming before the full houses, or stalemated when the houses cannot agree.

The majority does not always win in the United States. There are gifted and cogent thinkers who argue that this is as it should be. James Burnham and William S. White, for instance, argue that in small town and rural America, and in the South, too, there are certain great traditions of our society that ought not always to be swept aside by the majority. These minority-borne values, they argue, deserve representation—and that means meaningful protection against unrelenting majority pressure. Both Burnham and White feel that if the representatives of the minorities must resort occasionally to manipulation of the rules and procedures of Congress, if they must from time to time use a certain stealth in blocking the majorities from bringing legislation to a vote that the majority is bound to win, then so be it. Hard-pressed minorities must use the means available. The system of electing the members of Congress, and the organization of Congress itself afford a number of such means.

The President and his "party" in Congress are not disarmed. They have won their victories and they will win more before the 88th Congress adjourns. According to *Congressional Quarterly*, the effectiveness of the coalition of Republicans and Southern Democrats has already been reduced. The coalition appeared on 28 percent of the roll calls in 1961 but on only 14 percent in 1962; whereas in 1962, party lines held firm on 31 percent of the roll calls. Furthermore, when the President employs the weapon of publicity, he can usually coax a great deal more out of Congress. Although Congress passed less than 50 percent of the total Presidential requests in 1961 and 1962 (and ran behind that pace in 1963), when measures are brought to a roll-call vote, the President does much better. On clear-cut roll-call tests in both House and Senate the President was victorious about 85 percent of the time in 1962, indicating that the President's proposals are more popular when Congressmen must take a public stand on them. The task for the President would seem to be to take his case to the public more often and more effectively than he has so far, and through the public to bring pressure on Congress to enact his program. It remains to be seen whether or not the President has the will and the skill to do that, for that process, too, has its risks.

THE THEORY OF BALANCE*

C. Wright Mills

In the old liberal society, a set of balances and compromises prevailed among Congressional leaders, the executive branch of the government, and various pressure groups. The image of power and of decision is the image of a balancing society in which no unit of power is powerful enough to do more than edge forward a bit at a time, in compromised countervailance with other such forces, and in which, accordingly, there is no unity, much less coordination, among the higher circles. Some such image, combined with the doctrine of public opinion, is still the official view of the formal democratic system of power, the standard theory of most academic social scientists, and the underlying assumption of most literate citizens who are neither political spokesmen nor political analysts.

But as historical conditions change, so do the meanings and political consequences of the mechanics of power. There is nothing magical or eternal about checks and balances. In time of revolution, checks and balances may be significant as a restraint upon unorganized and organized

* C. Wright Mills. *The Power Elite*. New York: Oxford University Press, 1956. Pp. 265–268. Reprinted by permission. The late Mr. Mills was Professor of Sociology at Columbia University and author of numerous works on American society and politics.

masses. In time of rigid dictatorship, they may be significant as a technique of divide and rule. Only under a state which is already quite well balanced, and which has under it a balanced social structure, do checks and balances mean a restraint upon the rulers.

The eighteenth-century political theorists had in mind as the unit of power the individual citizen, and the classic economists had in mind the small firm operated by an individual. Since their time, the units of power, the relations between the units, and hence the meaning of the checks and balances, have changed. In so far as there is now a great scatter of relatively equal balancing units, it is on the middle levels of power, seated in the sovereign localities and intermittent pressure groups, and coming to its high point within the Congress. We must thus revise and relocate the received conception of an enormous scatter of varied interests, for, when we look closer and for longer periods of time, we find that most of these middle-level interests are concerned merely with their particular cut, with their particular area of vested interest, and often these are of no decisive political importance, although many are of enormous detrimental value to welfare. Above this plurality of interests, the units of power—economic, political, and military—that count in any balance are few in number and weighty beyond comparison with the dispersed groups on the middle and lower levels of the power structure.

Those who still hold that the power system reflects the balancing society often confuse the present era with earlier times of American history, and confuse the top and the bottom levels of the present system with its middle levels. When it is generalized into a master model of the power system, the theory of balance becomes historically unspecific; whereas in fact, as a model, it should be specified as applicable only to certain phases of United States development—notably the Jacksonian period and, under quite differing circumstances, the early and middle New Deal.

The idea that the power system is a balancing society also assumes that the units in balance are independent of one another, for if business and labor or business and government, for example, are not independent of one other, they cannot be seen as elements of a free and open balance. But as we have seen, the major vested interests often compete less with one another in their effort to promote their several interests than they coincide on many points of interest and, indeed, come together under the umbrella of government. The units of economic and political power not only become larger and more centralized; they come to coincide in interest and to make explicit as well as tacit alliances.

The American government today is not merely a framework within which contending pressures jockey for position and make politics. Although there is of course some of that, this government now has such interests vested within its own hierarchical structure, and some of these are higher and more ascendant than others. There is no effective counter-vailing power against the coalition of the big businessmen—who, as political outsiders, now occupy the command posts—and the ascendant military men—who with such grave voices now speak so frequently in the higher councils. Those having real power in the American state today are not merely brokers of power, resolvers of conflict, or compromisers of varied and clashing interest—they represent and indeed embody quite specific national interests and policies.

While the professional party politicians may still, at times, be brokers of power, compromisers of interests, negotiators of issues, they are no longer at the top of the state, or at the top of the power system as a whole.

The idea that the power system is a balancing society leads us to assume that the state is a visible mask for autonomous powers, but in fact, the powers of decision are now firmly vested within the state. The old lobby, visible or invisible, is now the visible government. This 'governmentaliza-tion of the lobby' has proceeded in both the legislative and the executive domains, as well as between them. The executive bureaucracy becomes not only the center of power but also the arena within which and in terms of which all conflicts of power are resolved or denied resolution. Adminis-tration replaces electoral politics; the maneuvering of cliques replaces the clash of parties.

The agrarian revolt of the 'nineties, the small-business revolt that has been more or less intermittent since the 'eighties, the labor revolt of the 'thirties—all of these have failed and all of these have succeeded. They have failed as autonomous movements of small property or of organized workmen which could countervail against the power of the corporate rich, and they have failed as politically autonomous third parties. But they have succeeded, in varying degrees, as vested interests inside the expanded state, and they have succeeded as parochial interests variously seated in particular districts and states where they do not conflict with larger inter-ests. They are well-established features of the *middle* levels of balancing power.

Among the plurality of these middle powers, in fact, are all those strata and interests which in the course of American history have been defeated in their bids for top power or which have never made such bids. They include: rural small property, urban small property, the wage-worker unions, all consumers, and all major white-collar groups. These are indeed still in an unromantic scatter; being structurally unable to unite among themselves, they do indeed balance one another—in a system of semi-organized stalemate. They 'get in the way' of the unified top, but no one of them has a chance to come into the top circles, where the political out-siders from corporate institution and military order are firmly in com-mand.

When the multifarious middle classes are a political balance wheel, the professional politician is the ascendant decision-maker. When the middles classes decline as a set of autonomous political forces, the balancing society as a system of power declines, and the party politicians of the sovereign localities are relegated to the middle levels of national power.

These structural trends came to political shape during the period of the New Deal, which was of course a time of slump. That our own immediate period has been a time of material prosperity has obscured these facts, but it has not altered them; and, as facts, they are important to the understanding of the power elite today.

CHAPTER FOUR

The Presidency: Nature of the Office

After Lord Bryce returned to England from his visit to the United States in 1883, he observed in *The American Commonwealth* that Americans only infrequently select great men as Presidents. He pondered about the reasons for this and concluded that "after all, a President need not be a man of brilliant intellectual gifts." He noted that while profundity of thought, a wide range of knowledge, and imagination might be assets to the President, these qualities really were not necessary. This, he maintained, was true because "four-fifths of his work is the same in kind as that which devolves on the chairman of a commercial company or the manager of a railway, the work of choosing good subordinates, seeing that they attend to their business, and taking a sound practical view of such administrative questions as require his decision."

Lord Bryce can be excused for this observation. When he viewed the Presidency in 1883, Chester Arthur was sitting in the White House and President Arthur could not be called an energetic President. In the busiest time of the year, when Congress was in session, President Arthur did not arise until nine. He would then eat a "continental breakfast" while dressing, and his official day would be under way. But the day would usually end at four in the afternoon, at which time he went out for a drive or a horseback ride.

In the 1880s, the President exercised certain narrowly defined constitutional, ceremonial, and political duties. He was chief of state, commander in chief of the small military and naval forces, chief of America's diplomatic corps—a diplomatic corps that did not even contain one diplomat with the rank of ambassador—and he was also chief clerk of the federal administration and titular head of his political party.

By the end of the first decade of this century, it was still appropriate to discuss the relative merits of William Howard Taft's "constitutional" or literal view of presidential powers versus Theodore Roosevelt's "stewardship" theory of the Presidency. Today, such theories are of historical interest only. In the 1960s, a President has no choice between being a weak or strong chief executive. All of his traditional duties have mushroomed, and many new responsibilities have been added. Wars, cold wars, depressions, and the welfare state have thrust upon the Presidency continuing responsibilities of such magnitude that no President can safely ignore them. Today, the President must execute his traditional duties, and also be the leader of the Congress, the overseer of the national economy, the tribune of the people, and the leader of the free-world alliance.

In order to discharge effectively the constantly increasing burdens of the Presidency, it has been necessary to equip the office with such staff agencies as the National Security Council, the Council of Economic Advisers, and the Bureau of the Budget. Within the past thirty years, it has become obvious that there is no longer a President, but a President and a Presidency—a man and an institution. This change has meant that the President's personal responsibility to take a policy lead for the nation— to seize the initiative—has become institutionalized in such agencies as the Bureau of the Budget and the Council of Economic Advisers.

Few would seriously contend that Presidents have not needed these policy-planning agencies. The President must be free from petty details before he can assume the responsibility for making decisions. Woodrow Wilson stated: "Men of ordinary physique and discretion cannot be Presidents and live, if the strain be not somehow relieved. We shall be obliged to be picking our chief magistrates from among wise and prudent athletes —a small class."

Keeping the President abreast of every daily crisis and at the same time ensuring the discharge of the continuing duties of the office calls for constant re-examination of executive organization. In the opinion of Governor Nelson Rockefeller, the nature of the office now requires further institutionalization, further attention to "rational" administrative procedures. He has called for the creation of the post of "First Secretary" to relieve the President. However, a Senate group headed by Senator Jackson has cautioned that such a new post could rob the President of his powers in the process of relieving him of burdens. The implication is that presidential burdens are in fact presidential powers.

Granted that presidential burdens are in reality the powers and duties of the office rather than burdens, the problem of the Presidency is not merely one of modernizing its organization. Indeed, Franklin D. Roosevelt violated many canons of modern public administration in developing his competitive theory of administration. FDR realized that the opportunity to make decisions was the opportunity to exercise power, and Professor Arthur M. Schlesinger, Jr. notes that FDR guarded this right to make or not to make decisions. FDR loved power, and he had a politician's expert knowledge of the essence of political power. Nonetheless, FDR was frequently accused of evading decisions. Professor Schlesinger feels that FDR's extraordinary political acumen cautioned him to use dilatory tactics until he sensed the proper political timing. Such close attention to the nuances of public opinion can, however, have serious pitfalls. Sidney Hyman suggests that an overemphasis on maintaining popularity can lead to a "hoarding" of power rather than to its use.

Some students of the Presidency would contend, however, that "hoarding" power really means that a President is preserving power in order to use it at crucial junctures. It is their contention that—particularly on the domestic scene—a President is a molder of national consensus. If a President attempts to be a protagonist in domestic issues that have not developed a wide national consensus, the result is likely to be a loss of interest-group support. To cast the President in the role of protagonist will mean a loss in public prestige. In turn, this loss sacrifices the latitude of support a contemporary President needs in the vital areas of defense and foreign affairs.

If it is true that the modern Presidency must of necessity be strong, and if it is true that the office calls for a man who wants power and who comprehends the nature of power, how then can we reconcile the "aggrandizing" Presidency with democracy? Does the Presidency today constitute a menace to American democracy? Professor Edward S. Corwin suggests that the answer to the question is in the negative, and points out that the developments that have so vastly increased the powers of the Presidency frequently have been the direct result of an ever widening democracy in the United States—for example, the increased powers of the Presidency resulting from welfare legislation. In addition, we must remember that there are limits to the Presidency: it must operate in a constitutional system of checks and balances and in a society of powerful, private, countervailing forces. The American Presidency, then, is a challenge to those who have held that democracies must fail because representative governments can neither decide quickly nor act forcefully.

ON MODERNIZING THE PRESIDENCY*

Governor Nelson Rockefeller

Few realize the tremendous load the President carries in his multiple responsibilities as Chief of State, Chief Executive, Commander-in-Chief of the Armed Forces, the man constitutionally responsible for the conduct of our foreign policy and leader of his political party. More than 50 departments and agencies of the Government report directly to the President. Their number imposes upon him an almost impossible burden—in the need to resolve conflicting approaches and divergent advice, and, from such sources, select and set a determined course of action. . . .

In fact, international affairs involve, one way or another, the activity and responsibility of every department of our Government. There are also some 18 independent agencies, as well as sundry boards and commissions, involved in aspects of international affairs. The field of foreign economic aid alone involves as many as four Government agencies—and six international financial organizations.

This overelaborate pattern of interdepartmental committees has been designed over the years in an earnest effort to meet the legion of complex problems in both foreign and domestic affairs. The simple fact is this: the committees of a democratic government cannot hope to meet or to master these problems by simply trying to outnumber them. The critical need is for a revamped structure of government.

The fact, today, is that the structure of our Government too often moves slowly, even sluggishly to meet this world of swift-moving change. It tends to be stiff and static—when it should be quick, alert, and creative. There is, therefore, a growing public awareness and concern about the structure of Government and the efficiency of its decisionmaking process. And one great proof of this public concern and interest is the existence and the work of your committee.

The Problem

The problem is too complex to be soluble by simply adding more authority or more power or more functions to the Department of State. Foreign operations involve the Department of Defense and other major

---

* 86th Congress, 2d Session, Senate Committee on Government Operations. *Hearings Before the Subcommittee on National Security Policy Machinery*, Part VII (June 28, July 1, 1960).

departments and agencies—each with its own special concern, and attitude toward, international problems.

The crux of the problem is to help develop a coordinated Presidential
policy and program which can then be administered, on a day-to-day
basis, by the existing agencies of Government. The proliferation of agencies and committees in this whole field has tended to increase and complicate—rather than ease and clarify—the burden upon the President in
defining and directing policy.

The reason is obvious. The more numerous and varied the sources of
divergent advice and advocacy—from departments, agencies, committees
and individuals—the less chance or time has been left to the President for
reflective, overall, long-range defining of purpose and planning of policy. . . .

The Objectives

The essential objectives are three.

First. In support and furtherance of our national purpose, we must
integrate fully, at the Presidential level, the international political, diplomatic, economic and social, military, informational, cultural and psychological aspects of foreign affairs.

Second. We also must relate and integrate these matters—from the
perspective of the responsibility of the Presidency—with all of our compelling domestic concerns—economic or social, financial or regulatory—
as all these affect our national conduct in the world.

Third. We must provide the governmental structure that can effectively
assist the President in developing objectives and policies, in all the area
of foreign policy and national security, so clear and so thoughtful that
they will give unified and purposeful direction to America's unique role
in serving—and enhancing—the future of freedom.

The Recommendations

To achieve these objectives—vital equally to our national security and
our world role—I recommend two broad courses of action.

1. I recommend creation of the post of First Secretary of the Government to assist the President in exercise of his constitutional responsibility
and authority in all the area of national security and international affairs.
This means in more explicit detail the following:

(a) The First Secretary should be appointed by the President, subject
to the confirmation of the Senate.

(b) He should have statutory designation as Executive Chairman of
the National Security Council.

(c) He should exercise authority as delegated to him by the President, and subject to withdrawal of such authority by, and at the will of, the President.

(d) He should be empowered at the discretion of the President to act for the President in international matters at the prime ministerial level, with the Secretary of State operating on the level of the ministers of foreign affairs.

(e) He should have a staff of his own and be empowered to use and reorganize all of the interdepartmental planning machinery of the Government in the area of national security and foreign affairs.

While the First Secretary, deriving his authority from the President and acting on his behalf, would have a status above that of the Cabinet, the operating responsibilities of Cabinet officers would not be changed. Thus, the Secretary of State would continue to be in charge of the day-to-day conduct of diplomacy. So, too, the Secretary of Defense would continue to be in the direct line of Presidential command of the Armed Forces.

As Executive Chairman of the National Security Council, the First Secretary could be delegated the authority, by Executive order or by legislation, to appoint the Chairman of such supporting groups as the Operations Coordinating Board, the Council on Foreign Economic Policy, and the National Advisory Council on International Monetary and Financial Problems.

The urgencies are as clear and great in the area of domestic affairs as in the areas of foreign affairs and national security. Here, too, the President needs the service and support of a structure of Government more effectively assisting him to define national purpose and execute national policy, in meeting the swiftness and the complexity of the problems and challenges of our time.

The Problems

Such is the nature of this period of history that the problems confronting the Government have seemed to multiply even faster than the agencies created to cope with them. To be specific:

There is the sheer number of departments and agencies reporting to the President—in essentially domestic affairs, no less than 8 departments and some 40 agencies. . . .

There is the constant and ever more difficult task of resolving conflicts between program objectives and budgetary limitations.

There is the ever-increasing volume of legislation pending in the Congress each year, including legislation proposed by the President—all reflecting new problems, freshly and forcefully challenging all departments of government.

And there is the need for thoughtful long-range planning and development of policy—made ever more difficult, and ever more necessary, by problems ever more complex.

The Objective

The President alone simply cannot undertake to meet the volume of problems and functions today demanding his attention, study, and action. To ignore this fact would be to strain the structure of our Government at its very apex—to allow it to be weak where it must be strong.

The essential objective, then, is to give to the President a strong supporting structure within his own Office for policy formulation and concrete decision.

A second objective, is to assure that, at the level of the departments and agencies themselves, there is an organizational structure adapted to meeting the key domestic problems of today.

The Recommendations

1. I recommend the creation of the post of Executive Assistant to the President and Director of the Office of Executive Management, to assist in planning and management in the sphere of domestic affairs. . . .

The Office of Executive Management . . . would serve the President more effectively than the present structures of government in the general management of administrative matters, including budgetary, personnel, planning, and organizational activities. The Office would assume the functions of various units within the Executive Office of the President and would, over a period of time, remove the need for numerous temporary staff arrangements established to meet special problems.

Thank you very much, Mr. Chairman.

ON MODERNIZING THE PRESIDENCY: A REPLY*

Senate Committee on Government Operations

The Besetting Problem

By law and practice the President is responsible for the conduct of foreign relations. He is Commander in Chief of the Armed Forces. He directs the departments and agencies. He makes the key decisions on the executive budget. He cannot delegate these great tasks to any council or committee. The responsibility is his, and his alone.

New dimensions of national security make the proper exercise of the President's responsibility more difficult than ever before in our history.

The line between foreign and domestic policy, never clear to begin with, has now almost been erased. Foreign policy and military policy have become more inseparable than ever. The tools of foreign policy have multiplied to include economic aid, information, technical assistance, scientific help, educational and cultural exchange, and foreign military assistance.

Historically, a President has looked to the Department of State for his principal help in developing and executing foreign policy. But today the sphere of the Department of State is far narrower than the full range of contemporary foreign relations. As an organization, the Department of State can now claim no greater concern in certain aspects of foreign policy than the Department of Defense. The interest of Treasury and Agriculture in some areas of international affairs is almost equal to that of State.

Indeed, today, almost every department of our Government, and some 18 independent agencies also, are involved with national security policy. Four Government agencies and six international financial organizations work in the field of foreign economic aid alone.

The net result is this: The planning and execution of national security policy cut across the jurisdiction of many departments and agencies. This situation imposes upon the President a heavy burden. A host of responsible protagonists urge divergent advice upon him. He must resolve these conflicting approaches, select his own course of action, and see to its

---

* 86th Congress, 2d Session, Senate Committee on Government Operations. *Organizing For National Security: Super-Cabinet Officers and Superstaffs* (Committee Print, 1960).

faithful and efficient execution by the very officials whose advice he may have rejected.

Presidents have in the past employed the budgetary process as an instrument for policy and program review and coordination. The budgetary process in other words has been traditionally much more than an exercise in accountancy, in the sense of merely keeping ledgers on the cost of on-going and contemplated programs. . . .

Throughout the past decade, increasingly elaborate and complicated interdepartmental mechanisms have been created to assist the President in policy development coordination, and execution. The best known of these bodies is the National Security Council. . . .

This interdepartmental machinery has certain inherent limitations in assisting the President.

Committees, including the National Security Council are primarily coordinating mechanisms. But they can coordinate and integrate only what their members bring to them; they cannot originate national security policy. The role of a committee in policy formulation is essentially critical and cautionary, not creative. The prime source of policy innovations is the contribution of a responsible individual who wrestles day in and day out with the problems of national security. Given imaginative proposals from such individuals, a committee may be helpful in criticizing, countering, or embroidering them. . . .

When policy stakes are high and differences in outlook sharp, department heads traditionally have sought to bypass coordinating committees while keeping them busy with secondary matters. Where this has not been possible, department heads have traditionally tried to keep the product of coordination from binding them tightly or specifically to undesired courses of action. The net result has tended to be "coordination" on the lowest common denominator of agreement, which is often tantamount to no coordination at all.

The President has been left in an unenviable position. He has found it necessary to undertake an endless round of negotiations with his own department heads or else he has been confronted at a very late date by crisis situations resulting from the lack of adequate coordination at an earlier stage. The burdens of the President have been increased correspondingly, and after-the-fact improvisation has too often substituted for forward planning.

A First Secretary of the Government?

Contemplating the problems now faced by a President, some have concluded that he requires the assistance of a new "super-Cabinet" official who would deal across the board with national security problems. The idea is not new. In 1955 former President Hoover suggested creating two appointive Vice Presidents, one responsible for foreign and the other for domestic affairs. More recently, President Eisenhower's Advisory Committee on Government Organization has studied variants of the concept of a "super-Cabinet" official.

In July of this year, Gov. Nelson Rockefeller, former Chairman of the Advisory Committee, appeared before the Subcommittee on National Policy Machinery and made a specific proposal for statutory creation of a "First Secretary" of the Government. . . .

At first glance, the proposal may appear an answer to current difficulties in the operation of policy machinery. The First Secretary's perspective would be expected to encompass the whole range of national security problems. He would be charged with giving committee coordinating mechanisms the stiffening of authoritative direction. Theoretically, he would be no mere White House staff assistant but a super-Cabinet member, thus able to direct fellow Cabinet members in a way that ordinary Presidential aides cannot. Theoretically again, he could relieve a President of many burdens both within the Government and in negotiations with other chiefs of Government. Finally, he could act as a first adviser to the President on foreign policy in its full modern context.

Careful analysis of the First Secretary proposal, however, reveals serious shortcomings and limitations. The proposal would fail to solve the problems it is meant to meet, and would also introduce grave new difficulties into the working of our national policy machinery.

This proposal raises two problems. One concerns a First Secretary's relationship with department heads.

Giving a man the Title of "First Secretary" does not thereby give him power. Under this proposal, the Secretaries of State and Defense and other Cabinet officers would retain their present statutory functions and authority. These officials would continue to be accountable to the Congress for the proper performance of their statutory duties. They would equally continue to be responsible to the President.

Being responsible to the President, the Secretaries of State and Defense and other Cabinet officers would report directly to him. They would be bound to question the decisions of a First Secretary; his placement between them and the President would inevitably generate friction and resentment. The First Secretary could gain the power he needed only if the President consistently accepted the First Secretary's judgment over that of his department heads.

But if the President were consistently so deferential to his First Secretary, who then would be President?

And who would then be willing to be Cabinet officers? The primacy of the First Secretary could conceivably be established by filling Cabinet offices with relatively submissive men who lack strong convictions or much will of their own. But this is a period of history when our Government needs more—not less—vigor and drive in high positions. This end would not be served by choosing for Cabinet positions men who could acquiesce to the downgrading of the historic posts that they are asked to occupy.

A second problem raised by this proposal involves the relations of the First Secretary to the President.

The historical record shows that Presidential assistants draw effective power from their demonstrated intimacy with the President. On numerous occasions in the past, a President has deputized an intimate adviser to take charge of certain plans or operations and to act for him in dealing with department heads. In varying degree, such men as House, Hopkins, Byrnes, and Adams have served effectively as Presidential deputies. But the positions of such men were always very different from that proposed for the First Secretary. Past deputyships have been ad hoc assignments given temporarily at the President's own pleasure to persons in his confidence whose intimacy with him was matched by their complete dependence on him. At the height of their effectiveness in Government, a Hopkins or an Adams drew power, not from statutes, titles, staffs, or paper prerogatives of any sort, but solely from the President's evident confidence in them and reliance on them.

Yet the proposed First Secretary would be in a very poor position to sustain that intimate relationship even if he had it at the outset. His statutory position, his formal status in the Government, his supervision of assorted staffs, his chairmanship of manifold committees, his attraction for the press, and his accountability to the Senate which confirmed him— all would mitigate against the maintenance of his close, confidential, personal relationship with the President.

It is most unlikely that a President would in fact give a First Secretary the consistent backing and support he would require to maintain his primacy over other Cabinet members. To do so would run the risk that the First Secretary would become an independent force, politically capable of rivaling the President himself. It would run the further risk of rousing combined opposition from departmental and congressional sources and from affected interest groups. . . .

Only the President's responsibility is as wide as the Nation's affairs. Only he can balance domestic, economic, and defense needs—and if anyone else were to be given the job the President would become a kind of constitutional figurehead.

In summary: Our governmental system has no place for a First Secretary. He is thought of as a mediator and a judge of the conflicting national security policies advocated by the major departments, the Congress and its committees, and private groups. But in the American system only one official has the constitutional and political power required to assume that role and to maintain it. That official is the President of the United States. He cannot be relieved of his burdens by supplying him with a "deputy" to do what only he can do.

THE DYNAMICS OF DECISION*

Arthur M. Schlesinger, Jr.

. . . The members of the Roosevelt cabinet, as usual, suffered frustration and, as usual, thought their experience unique. In private, they echoed the familiar laments of Gideon Welles and Franklin Lane. "Only the barest routine matters were discussed," burst out Ickes in his diary after a meeting in 1935. "All of which leads me to set down what has been running in my mind for a long time, and that is just what use the Cabinet is under this administration. The cold fact is that on important matters we are seldom called upon for advice. We never discuss exhaustively any policy of government or question of political strategy. The President makes all of his own decisions. . . . As a matter of fact, I never think of bringing up even a serious departmental issue at Cabinet meetings." "It seemed to me," wrote William Phillips, sitting in occasionally for Hull, "that a great deal of time was wasted at Cabinet meetings and much of the talk was without any particular import." "The important things were never discussed at Cabinet," said Morgenthau. "The President treats them like children," Tugwell wrote in his diary, "and almost nothing of any importance was discussed.". . .

Beyond the cabinet there stretched the Executive Branch of the government—an endless thicket of vested usage and vested interest, apportioned among a number of traditional jurisdictions, dominated by a number of traditional methods and objectives. This was, in the popular understanding, the government of the United States—the people and departments and agencies whose office it was to carry out the national laws and fulfill the national policies. The President had few more basic responsibilities than his supervision and operation of the machinery of gov-

* From *The Coming of the New Deal: The Age of Roosevelt*, Vol. 2, by Arthur M. Schlesinger, Jr. Boston: Houghton Mifflin Company, 1959. Pp. 520–532. Reprinted by permission. Mr. Schlesinger is adviser to President Kennedy.

ernment. Little fascinated Franklin Roosevelt more than the tasks of presidential administration. And in few things was he more generally reckoned a failure.

This verdict against Roosevelt derived ultimately from a philosophy of public administration—a philosophy held for many years after by Civil Service professionals, expounded in departments of political science, and commending itself plausibly to common sense. This school's faith was in logical organization of government, founded on rigid definitions of job and function and maintained by the sanctity of channels. Its weapons were the job description and the organization chart. Its unspoken assumption was that the problems of administration never change; and its consuming fear was improvisation, freewheeling or unpredictability—which is nearly to say creativity—in the administrative process. From this point of view, it need hardly be said, the Roosevelt government was a textbook case of poor administration. At one time or another, Roosevelt must surely have violated every rule in the sacred texts of the Bureau of the Budget. . . .

The question remains whether the true test of an administrator may be, not his ability to design and respect organization charts, not his ability to keep within channels, but his ability to concert and release the energies of men for the attainment of public objectives. It might be argued that the essence of successful administration is: first, to acquire the ideas and information necessary for wise decisions; second, to maintain control over the actual making of the decisions; and, third, to mobilize men and women who can make the first two things possible—that is, who can provide effective ideas and information, and who can reliably put decisions into effect. It is conceivable that these things may be more important than preserving the chastity of administrative organization—that, indeed, an excessive insistence on the sacredness of channels and charts is likely to end in the stifling of imagination, the choking of vitality, and the deadening of creativity.

Franklin Roosevelt, at any rate, had some such philosophy of administration. The first task of an executive, as he evidently saw it, was to guarantee himself an effective flow of information and ideas. And Roosevelt's first insight—or, at least, his profound conviction—was that, for this purpose, the ordained channels, no matter how simply or how intricately designed, could never be enough. An executive relying on a single information system became inevitably the prisoner of that system. Roosevelt's persistent effort therefore was to check and balance information acquired through official channels by information acquired through a myriad of private, informal, and unorthodox channels and espionage networks. At times, he seemed almost to pit his personal sources against his public sources. From the viewpoint of subordinates, this method was distracting when not positively demoralizing. But Roosevelt, with his voracity for facts and for ideas, required this approach to cross-check the official system and keep it alert as well as to assure himself the balanced and various product without which he could not comfortably reach decisions. . . .

In seeking information, Roosevelt took care not to confuse the capital with the nation. "Pay no attention to what people are saying in Washington," he once told Molly Dewson. "They are the last persons in the country to listen to." He loved going out to the country himself and got infinite stimulus from faces in crowds, from towns quietly glimpsed out of the windows of slow-moving trains, from chance conversations with ordinary people along the way. But polio and the Presidency limited his mobility. Instead, he had to urge others to get out of Washington. "Go and see what's happening," he told Tugwell. "See the end product of what we are doing. Talk to people; get the wind in your nose." . . .

If information was the first responsibility of the executive, the second was decision. American Presidents fall into two types: those who like to make decisions, and those who don't. One type designs an administrative system which brings decisions to him; the other, a system which keeps decisions away from him. The second technique, under its more mellifluous designation of "delegation of authority," is regarded with favor in the conventional theory of public administration. Yet, pressed very far, "delegation of authority" obviously strikes at the roots of the Presidency. One can delegate routine, but one cannot delegate any part of the serious presidential responsibility. The whole theory of the Constitution makes the Chief Executive, in the words of Andrew Jackson, "accountable at the bar of public opinion for every act of his Administration," and thus presumably accountable in his own conscience for its every large decision.

Roosevelt, in any case, was pre-eminently of the first type. He evidently felt that both the dignity of his office and the coherence of his administration required that the key decisions be made by him, and not by others before him. He took great pride, for example, in a calculation of Rudolph Forster's that he made at least thirty-five decisions to each one made by Calvin Coolidge. Given this conception of the Presidency, he deliberately organized—or disorganized—his system of command to insure that important decisions were passed on to the top. His favorite technique was to keep grants of authority incomplete, jurisdictions uncertain, charters overlapping. The result of this competitive theory of administration was often confusion and exasperation on the operating level; but no other method could so reliably insure that in a large bureaucracy filled with ambitious men eager for power the decisions, and the power to make them, would remain with the President. . . .

Once the opportunity for decision came safely into his orbit, the actual process of deciding was involved and inscrutable. As Tugwell once put it, "Franklin allowed no one to discover the governing principle." He evidently felt that clear-cut administrative decisions would work only if they expressed equally clear-cut realities of administrative competence and vigor. If they did not, if the balance of administrative power would not sustain the decision, then decision would only compound confusion and discredit government. And the actualities of administrative power were to be discovered, not by writing—or by reading—Executive orders, but by apprehending through intuition a vast constellation of political forces. His complex administrative sensibility, infinitely subtle and sensitive, was forever weighing questions of personal force, of political timing, of congressional concern, of partisan benefit, of public interest. Situations had to be permitted to develop, to crystallize, to clarify; the competing forces had to vindicate themselves in the actual pull and tug of conflict; public opinion had to face the question, consider it, pronounce upon it—only then, at the long, frazzled end, would the President's intuitions consolidate and precipitate a result.

Though he enjoyed giving the impression of snap decisions, Roosevelt actually made few. The more serious complaint against him was his weakness for postponement. This protraction of decision often appeared a technique of evasion. And sometimes it was. But sometimes dilemmas did not seem so urgent from above as they seemed below—a proposition evidently proved when they evaporated after the passage of time. And Roosevelt, in any case, justified, or rationalized, delay in terms of his own sense of timing. He knew from hard experience that a person could not regain health in a day or year; and he had no reason to suppose that a nation would mend any more quickly. "He could watch with enormous patience as a situation developed," wrote his wife, "and would wait for exactly the right moment to act." When people pressed proposals on him, he often answered (as he did to Frank Walker in 1936), "You are absolutely right. . . . It is simply a question of time." The tragedy of the Presidency in his view was the impotence of the President. Abraham Lincoln, Roosevelt said, "was a sad man because he couldn't get it all at once. And nobody can." He was responding informally to an important young questioner. "Maybe you would make a much better President than I have. Maybe you will, some day. If you ever sit here, you will learn that you cannot, just by shouting from the housetops, get what you want all the time.". . .

This technique of protraction was often wildly irritating to his subordinates, enlisted passionately on one side or another of an argument and perceiving with invincible clarity the logic of one or another course. It was equally irritating to his opponents, who enjoyed the advantages of oversimplification which come from observation without responsibility. But the President's dilatory tactics were, in a sense, the means by which he absorbed countrywide conflict of pressures, of fears, of hopes. His intelligence was not analytical. He did not systematically assess pros and cons in his own mind. What for others might be an interior dialogue had to be externalized for Roosevelt; and it was externalized most conveniently by hearing strong exponents of divergent viewpoints. . . .

With the conclusion, however reached, a new phase began. When Garner once tried to argue after Roosevelt had made up his mind, the President said, "You tend to your office and I'll tend to mine." ("I didn't take offense at that," said Garner, "because he was right.") "You could fight with Roosevelt and argue with him up to a certain point," said Morgenthau, "—but at no time during his waking hours was he anything else but a ruler." Wayne Coy, who was a Roosevelt assistant for some years, observed that one could say exactly what one thought to Roosevelt, so long as he was saying only "in my judgment" or "I think." When he said "The President thinks," the time for discussion was over. To another assistant, James Rowe, who insisted that he should do something in a particular way, Roosevelt said, "I do not have to do it your way and I will tell you the reason why. The reason is that, although they may have made a mistake, the people of the United States elected me President, not you."

Often he announced his decisions with bravado. He liked to tell advisers, "I'm going to spring a bombshell," and then startle them with novel proposals—or rather with proposals novel to them, not perhaps to another set of advisers. "He delights in surprises—clever, cunning and quick," said Hugh Johnson. "He likes to shock friends as well as enemies with something they never expected." But he seems rarely to have supposed that any particular decision was in a final sense correct, or even terribly important. "I have no expectation of making a hit every time I come to bat. What I seek is the highest possible batting average." He remembered Theodore Roosevelt's saying to him, "If I can be right 75 per cent of the time I shall come up to the fullest measure of my hopes." "You'll have to learn that public life takes a lot of sweat," he told Tugwell, "but it doesn't need to worry you. You won't always be right, but you mustn't suffer from being wrong. That's what kills people like us." After all, Roosevelt said, suppose a truck driver were doing your job; 50 per cent of his decisions would be right on average. "You aren't a truck driver. You've had some preparation. Your percentage is bound to be higher." And he knew that the refusal to decide was itself a form of decision. "This is very bad," he said to Frances Perkins, "but one thing is sure. We have to do something. We have to do the best we know how to do at the moment." Then, after a pause: "If it doesn't turn out right, we can modify it as we go along."

This dislike of firm commitments, this belief in alternatives, further reduced the significance of any single decision. As Miss Perkins observed, "He rarely got himself sewed tight to a program from which there was no turning back." The very ambiguity of his scheme of organization—the overlapping jurisdictions and duplicated responsibilities—made flexibility easy. If things started to go bad, he could reshuffle people and functions with speed which would have been impossible in a government of clear-cut assignments and rigid chains of command. Under the competitive theory, he always retained room for administrative maneuver.

Only a man of limitless energy and resource could hold such a system together. Even Roosevelt at times was hard put to keep it from flying apart. But he did succeed, as no modern President has done, in concentrating the power of executive decision where the Constitution intended it should be. "I've never known any President," said W. M. Kiplinger, "who was as omnipresent as this Roosevelt." "Most people acting for Roosevelt were messenger boys," said Ed Flynn. "He really made his own decisions."

PRESIDENTIAL POPULARITY IS NOT ENOUGH*

Sidney Hyman

When John F. Kennedy bid for the White House . . . he made his concept of the Presidency a prime issue of the 1960 contest. Today, . . . he has served notice of a shift of emphasis. The prime issue in the contest ahead—in so far as he can make it so—will be the way the . . . Congress has dealt with his legislative program.

Taken jointly, these two events—the 1960 debate about the Presidency itself, and the impending . . . debate about the state of Presidential-Congressional relations—squarely raise three questions. Why has the . . . Congress vetoed key items in Mr. Kennedy's domestic program, while supporting his initiatives in foreign policy? In view of Mr. Kennedy's great popularity as a President, why couldn't he convert that popularity into Congressional support for his domestic measures? Beyond what the President has already done, is there anything more he can do to help insure the enactment of those domestic measures?

---

* Condensed from the *New York Times Magazine* (August 12, 1962). Copyright by The New York Times. Reprinted by permission. Mr. Hyman is a staff writer for the *Washington Post*.

It may help clear the air by saying straight off that any activist President is bound to clash with the Congress. The first of the reasons why can be found in the Constitution. It not only arms the President and the Congress with overlapping powers and duties in the same sphere of action and with mutual veto powers. It also arms the House and the Senate for war against each other, so that what often seems a clash between a united Congress and the President can really be a House-Senate clash with the President caught in the cross fire.

Second, the President and the Congress can be set on a collision course by the different pressures stemming from the profoundly different constituencies they represent.

The Presidential constituency extends from the individual to the nation to the world of nations. Nowadays, to be sure, Presidential elections are decided in the great urban centers of the North. Yet the President is not politically responsible to them alone. The entire American electorate expects him to serve the historic interests of the nation as a whole. At the same time, his vast nonvoting constituency—represented by the people of the Western alliance—looks to him as the commander in chief of the alliance, and expects him to serve it as a whole.

The Congressional constituency is something else again. Structurally, it is a collection of individual districts and states and their component special interests. Yet these do not necessarily add up to the national interest, any more than the sum of all the members of Congress adds up to the national voice. A Congressman is under no direct pressure to take into account the views of people who do not vote within the fixed geographical area he respresents. Nor is he under any direct pressure to take into account any historical play of far-off forces. It is the immediate needs and views of his voting constituents that form the prime pressure points on his thoughts. And in the decisions he makes with them in mind, he is ruled by an estimate of what local opinion is like at the moment of decision, and what it may be like when he must stand for re-election.

. . . When all is said and done, why can't President Kennedy's popularity be turned into a residual source of power he can draw on to win Congressional support for his domestic program? In the fairly new-style attitudes Americans show toward any popular President, there is something of the attitude the people of Siena showed toward a general they hired to wage war against a neighboring town. When the general triumphed and the word was received, it occurred to some townspeople that he was now in a position to conquer them as well. So a public meeting was held to determine how to reward him in ways that would combine gratitude with prudence. At last a solution was hit upon. The general was killed, then worshiped as Siena's patron saint.

So, too, with a popular President. He is universally loved provided he reigns like the British Crown—provided he is content to be the patron saint of national unity, the apotheosis of all the Sunday school virtues, the embodiment of connubial bliss. He is universally loved so long as he is the royal and remote figure through whom the people can vicariously enjoy a sense of personal involvement in the affairs of the high and the mighty, and the beautiful.

These millions of Americans glory in the power of the President. And they know that the national interest cannot be served without their own power. Yet they cannot shake off a nagging fear, especially after they have witnessed Presidential power in action, that the President will make their love for him an instrument of injury to them, in any matter where he ceases to be merely the Crown and proceeds to rule as a President.

A paradox seems to follow from this.

The more popular a President is—as in the case of President Eisenhower—the more there is a tendency to make him the prisoner of his popularity, and the more the state of his own popularity seems to be the essence of his Administration. Conversely, and ignoring Election Day opinions, a President like Harry S. Truman who was constantly accused of "lowering the dignity of the Presidency," is left at liberty to revolutionize the whole focus of American life because he was unpopular, reviled and hence not feared.

President Kennedy, like President Eisenhower before him—but for different reasons—is supremely suited to represent in the American imagination an American counterpart to the British Crown.

Yet the sense of commitment this evokes is not, basically, a commitment to his politics but to his person. Insofar as it is a commitment to his politics, it seems limited to his conduct of foreign affairs and stops short of being a commitment to his domestic politics.

If the foregoing analysis is plausible, and if, as I believe, President Kennedy has his heart in most of the domestic measures he has advocated, then it seems to me that there is at least one great way he can help along the cause of his legislative program.

This is to forget about his popularity entirely. By doing this, he will at least be liberated from all illusions that (except on Election Day) it represents some sort of magic power in reserve, and that it therefore becomes of great moment to the success or failure of his program whether he is "hoarding" it or being a "spendthrift" with it. He will be set at liberty to speak his mind on what he thinks is in the best interests of the nation. He will not have to weigh his words first in the balance of how they are likely to move the decimal points on Dr. George Gallup's scale.

The fact remains that Mr. Kennedy was not elected just to be loved. He was elected to run the government to the best of his ability. If he runs it well, and everyone comes to hate him, future generations will still raise monuments of gratitude to his memory. If he runs it poorly or not at all, and everyone loves him, the panegyrics heard during his incumbency will become a dirge in the ears of later generations.

In any case, his popularity will not save his domestic program. A number of its measures went down to defeat at a time when eight out of ten Americans loved him. Since his popularity can never again stand so high, why look for salvation from this source? But supposing it is said that, since war or peace is the great issue of the day, the President's personal popularity counts for a great deal as a source of national unity and massed effectiveness?

The answer is, that President Truman brilliantly managed the conduct of American foreign policy though his personal stock was low. As long as he was the President, his foreign policy moves were supported by the Congress and the nation—however grudgingly—for there was no alternative.

Meanwhile, we have seen with our own eyes that Mr. Kennedy's great personal popularity in the United States has not been a factor in the way Mr. Khrushchev, General de Gaulle, and Chancellor Adenauer have responded to his moves. All three opposed him when his personal popularity at home was at its zenith. They will continue to oppose him or not, depending on their estimate of how his proposals will affect their national interest, and whether the power of the United States, exercised through his hands, arms him with the material means to make his will prevail over theirs in any case at issue.

If the President can help along his domestic program by forgetting his popularity, he can then follow through by appealing over the heads of the Congress to the people.

For an appeal of this sort to be effective, the audience must see where a particular proposition fits in with a larger design. Such a spirit was conveyed by President Kennedy, for instance, when he belatedly took what threatened to be a bread-and-butter fight over the trade bill, and showed where it fitted in the design for an Atlantic partnership.

Yet, with an Administration full of highly articulate men, it is to be wondered that the trade bill should stand virtually alone in this regard. There stands, in sharp contrast to this, the fact that the Administration, in economic matters, has allowed the mentality of the nation to be ruled by the dogmas of "Poor Richard's Almanac," as promulgated posthumously by the Eisenhower Administration. Except as the matter might have appeared in the shorthand language of a forgotten economic message, the Administration has yet to make clear, for general understanding, how its particular domestic measures are related in the grand design to "get America moving again."

A single Presidential speech will not do the trick. But a systematically conceived effort led by the President and pressed by every means at hand and on every occasion—award ceremonies, dedications, press conferences, conventions of national organizations, television "fireside chats," all addressed to aspects of the same central theme—cannot help but materially change the climate of national opinion. None of this may reach and sway a backwoods area where public opinion is inert, and which returns to the Congress a committee member or chairman who has been bottling up a Presidential measure. Yet such an appeal to the people is worth making for at least three reasons.

First, it can help breathe new life into the expiring idea that the people are the source of all power over the Government and are the ultimate judges of what the President and the Congress say or do. Second, it will inspire the President's own troops, and make the waverers more disposed to risk themselves in support of purposes they will understand. And third, it can generate national pressures that will be felt by Congressional hierarchs who have the personal and professional prestige "rightly" to sway other Congressional hierarchs—something the President, as an "outsider" could not do by direct appeal.

There is one last thing to be done that can help along the cause of the President's domestic program, without waiting for the changes that will eventually overtake the Congress once the states, in line with the Supreme Court decision, establish voting districts along fairer lines.

It is to have the Congress re-create a counterpart to the La Follette-Monroney committee that inquired into the institutional procedures of the Congress, and whose recommendations, when adopted, made the Congress for a while an instrument of responsible power. As Mr. Kennedy made the nature of the Presidency a central issue in the 1960 election contest, he would do well by himself and the country if he made the re-examination of Congressional procedures a central issue of the . . . elections.

A HISTORY OF AGGRANDIZEMENT*

Edward S. Corwin

It is an axiom of American history that the Constitution came from the Framers "a bundle of compromises." Not so generally recognized is the confirmation lent this observation by those clauses of the Constitution most nearly affecting the office and powers of the President. The vagueness of the constitutional grants of power to the President has always furnished matter for comment, sometimes favorable, sometimes otherwise, depending on the commentator's bias. "The executive power shall be vested in a President of the United States of America"; "the President shall be Commander-in-Chief of the Army and Navy"; with the advice and consent of the Senate he shall make treaties and appoint to office; he shall have power to "grant pardons for offenses against the United States"; he shall "recommend . . . such measures to Congress as he shall judge necessary and expedient"; and so on and so forth. Yet in order to exercise any of these powers—in order, indeed, to subsist—he must have money, and can get it only when and if Congress appropriates it. Likewise, he is dependent on Congress for the very agencies through which he must ordinarily exercise his powers, and Congress is the judge as to the necessity and propriety of such agencies. Again, he is bound to "take care that the laws" that Congress enacts are "faithfully executed"; for this purpose all his powers are in servitude; and Congress has the power to investigate his every official act, and can, by a special procedure, if it finds him guilty of "high crimes and misdemeanors," impeach him and throw him out of office. Moreover, by the standard set by the prerogative of the British monarch in 1787, his "executive power" and his power to protect were both seriously curtailed. The power to "declare war" was vested in Congress; the Senate was made a participant in his diplomatic powers; he was given a veto on all legislative acts, but one that the houses can override by a two-thirds vote.

In short, the Constitution reflects the struggle between two conceptions of executive power: that it ought always to be subordinate to the supreme legislative power, and that it ought to be, within generous limits, autonomous and self-directing; or, in other terms, the idea that the people are

* Edward S. Corwin, *The President: Office and Powers, 1787–1957*, Fourth Revised Edition. New York: New York University Press, Inc., 1957. Pp. 306–313. © 1957 by New York University. Reprinted by permission. Mr. Corwin was McCormick Professor of Jurisprudence, Princeton University.

re-presented in the Legislature *versus* the idea that they are *embodied* in the Executive. Nor has this struggle ever entirely ceased, although on the whole it is the latter theory that has prospered. . . . Taken by and large, the history of the presidency has been a history of aggrandizement.

The office got off to a good start under a very great man. The principle of the Separation of Powers was not yet regarded as forbidding the executive to initiate legislation. In the act establishing the State Department Congress itself laid down a "practical construction" of the Constitution that, save for the interregnum of the Reconstruction Period, has left the President absolute master of his official family. A dangerous foreign situation in 1793 brought that family into existence, while it also enabled the President to translate his position as the organ of communication with other governments into a substantive, creative power. Finally, the Whisky Rebellion provided the occasion for the first step in that course of legislation and of presidential action that has long since invested the President, in situations of widespread disorder or threat of it, with powers of dictatorship.

Under Jefferson and the "Virginia School of Presidents" a certain retrogression took place from the notion of Presidential autonomy toward that of legislative supremacy. Under Jefferson himself the retreat was theoretical rather than actual. As the founder and leader of the first national party he was able to dominate Congress by personal influence, and it was shown for the first time what accession of strength political skill can bring the presidency. But Jefferson's successors, caught between the upper and nether millstones of their self-abasing conception of the presidency and their lack of personal force, were reduced to official insignificance. The War of 1812 marked the near elimination for the time being of presidential prerogative in the field of foreign relations; the Monroe Doctrine announced to the world at large that opportunities for aggrandizing the presidency from foreign adventuring were to be confined strictly to the Western Hemisphere. Jefferson pronounced the dictum that no President could with safety to our democratic institutions be eligible for a third term, albeit he might nominate his successor; and the successors whom Jefferson himself nominated ratified the ban.

Jackson's presidency was more than a revulsion to earlier ideas: it was a revolution. A new electorate was organized into a new party whose wide ramifications, focusing in the National Convention, rendered its continuance independent of accidents of personality. Guaranteed this powerful and persistent support among the people at large, Jackson extended the doctrine of the President's autonomy to embrace his obligation to the law; constitutional obligation was reduced—or exalted—to the level of moral obligation. At the same time the President's duty to "take care that the laws be faithfully executed" was asserted to comprise the right to read the law for any and every member of the Executive Department; and through a vigorous and expanded use of his veto and removal powers Jackson for the time being made this claim good. Through the latter power, moreover, the Spoils System was for the first time engrafted on the national government, thereby adding one more weapon to the presidential armory.

Except nevertheless for a few unfortunates like John C. Calhoun and Nicholas Biddle, the Jacksonian "dictatorship" was more bark than bite, more proclamation than performance. The Monroe Doctrine, the taboo on a third term, and, what was even more important, the States Rights conception of national legislative power, all set conspicuous landmarks that Jackson himself had not the slightest inclination to disturb. His most outstanding assertions of power, and especially in the field of legislation, were negative and exercised by veto. Moreover, despite the permanency of the party organization reared by his henchmen in every quarter of the Union the prominence of the office during his incumbency was predominantly a reflection of his own energetic personality. When he left office he left behind him a political vacuum that a resuscitated Congress presently filled, and, thanks to the manipulations of the slavery interest, continued to fill— if exception be made of slavery's tool, the sly, pious Polk—till the outbreak of the Civil War.

For all that, the Jacksonian conception of the presidency was not forgotten. Indeed, its champions and its critics contributed about equally to render it more articulate than ever—a fact of the first magnitude when Lincoln became President and found himself confronted with a nation in dissolution. Lincoln's claim to "the war power" was derived from three sources: Jackson's doctrine that *all* the President's powers are autonomous; the Supreme Court's doctrine in *Luther v. Borden* (1849) that insurrection is "war"; and the measures that Pierce and Buchanan had taken in their efforts to put down civil war in Kansas, together with the budget of doctrine that a legal genius of Caleb Cushing had furnished them in justification of their policy.

At first, as we pointed out on an earlier page, Lincoln laid claim only to an *ad interim* war power, one operative only until Congress could ratify and reinforce its measures; but the Supreme Court's sweeping language in the Prize cases (1863) encouraged him to take a more forthright stand, and this, combined with his indisposition to co-operate with Congress, led him to break over constitutional bounds and become a dictator even exceeding the Roman model. Nor was the constitutional corrective applied until after the war was comfortably over, by the Court's decision in *ex parte Milligan* and by Congress's uprising against Johnson. The implication of Lincoln's course that the President has power to meet an emergency without awaiting action by Congress is accordant with the

most ancient traditions of Anglo-American law; but when on this implication Lincoln sought to erect a plan of Reconstruction in which the role
of the national legislative power was negligible, he brought the presidency
in the person of his too zealous apostle Johnson to the verge of disaster.
Even so, it fell to Johnson, by escaping impeachment, to demonstrate
the impracticability of this medieval method of controlling presidential
power. Moreover, it was during his term that the Supreme Court virtually
underwrote, in Mississippi v. Johnson (1867), Jackson's contention that
the President's duty to the Constitution is solely the duty of conscience
that his oath imposes.

But again the cyclical character of presidential power demonstrated
itself. As from 1809 to 1829, so again from 1865 to 1885 the legislative
power became the dominant element of the national government. Indeed,
except for the success of Presidents Hayes and Cleveland in using the
Army to put down "domestic violence" within the states the period of
congressional preponderance reached to the death of McKinley. But
meantime Congress by its own headiness had paved the way for the re-
crudescence of its constitutional rival, by forcing on McKinley the war
with Spain. By that act and the consequences that ensued from it the
restrictive effect of the Monroe Doctrine on presidential prerogative was
seriously undermined. The United States was now a "world power," and
presently it found itself involved in a World War.

The great accession to presidential power in recent decades has, however, taken place in the *internal* equally with the *external* field of government, and has been signalized by the breakdown of the two great
structural principles of the American Constitutional System, the doctrine
of dual federalism and the doctrine of the Separation of Powers; while
along with this breakdown has gone an even more fundamental change
in popular outlook regarding the purpose and scope of governmental
power. I mean, of course, the replacement of the *laissez-faire* theory of
government with the idea that government should make itself an *active,
reforming* force in the field of economic enterprise, which means necessarily that the *national government* should be active in this way, inasmuch
as the field in question has long since come to transcend state lines.

The result for the presidency has been twofold. On the one hand,
Presidents have made themselves spokesmen of the altered outlook, have
converted their parties to it—a conversion not infrequently accompanied
by backsliding—and, with the popular support thus obtained, have asserted a powerful legislative initiative. On the other hand, Congress, in
responding to the President's leadership in its own peculiar field, has
found it convenient to aggrandize his executive role enormously, by
delegating to him the power to supplement its measures by a type of sub-
legislation called "administrative regulations." Not all this delegated

power, it is true, has gone to the President, but a vast proportion of it has; and it constitutes a realm of presidential power of which the Framers had little prevision, although it began to appear in the field of foreign relations even as early as Washington's second administration.

The first exponent of the new presidency was Theodore Roosevelt, but his achievement was to some extent negated by faults of method. Woodrow Wilson was enabled by the advantage of having critically observed his predecessor, by his knowledge of political methods abroad, by a taste for institution-building, which was later to divert him into an abortive effort at world organization, and finally by the opportunity afforded by our entrance into the First World War, to illustrate on an unprecedented scale both the new roles of the President—that of legislative leader and that of recipient of delegated legislative power. The First World War was prosecuted for the most part under laws drafted under the appraising eye of the President and conferring on him far greater powers than those Lincoln had exercised as Commander-in-Chief.

But it is the second Roosevelt who beyond all twentieth-century Presidents put the stamp both of *personality* and *crisis* on the presidency. In the solution of the problems of an economic crisis—"a crisis greater than war"—he claimed for the national government in general and for the President in particular powers hitherto exercised only on the justification of war. Then when the greatest crisis in the history of our international relations arose he imparted to the President's diplomatic powers new extension, now without consulting Congress, now with Congress's approval; and when at last we entered the Second World War he endowed the precedents of both the Civil War and the First World War with unprecedented scope.

The presidency of this present year of grace, so far as it is explicable in terms of American constitutional law and theory, is the product of the following factors: (1) social acceptance of the idea that government should be active and reformist, rather than simply protective of the established order of things; (2) the breakdown of the principle of dual federalism in the field of Congress's legislative powers; (3) the breakdown of the principle of the Separation of Powers as defining the relation of President and Congress in lawmaking; (4) the breakdown of the corollary principle that the legislature may not delegate its powers; and (5) the impact of the President's power as Commander-in-Chief and the organ of foreign relationship of two world wars and the vastly enlarged role of the United States in the international field.

Does the presidency, then, in the light of these facts, constitute a standing menace to popular government and to those conceptions of personal liberty to which popular government is, in part, traceable? So far as concerns popular government in the sense of majority rule, the exact contrary is the case: all the developments named are the direct consequence of democracy's emergence from the constitutional chrysalis. That, on the other hand, these developments leave private and personal rights in the same strong position as they once enjoyed would be quite impossible to maintain. Nor is it feasible in this connection to distinguish too acutely between the property and other rights. Not only in the past, but today as well, the property right is the right best capable of holding its own against political power. This is the principal lesson to be drawn from the history of Liberalism.

As matters have stood till the other day, presidential power has been at times dangerously *personalized,* and this in two senses: first, that the leadership that it affords was dependent altogether on the accident of personality, against which our haphazard method of selecting Presidents offers no guarantee; and, secondly, that there is no governmental body that could be relied on to give the President independent advice and that he was nevertheless bound to consult. As a remedy calculated to meet both phases of the problem I have suggested a new type of Cabinet. At least, if a solution is to be sought in *institutional* terms, it must consist in *stabilizing* in some way or other the relationship between President and Congress.

Recent developments, however, may have relegated my proposal, even if it ever had any real prospect of acceptance, to the limbo of happy untried ideas—happy, perhaps, because untried. In the "Institutionalized Presidency" the President becomes merged with—albeit not submerged in—a cluster of institutions designed to base government in the national area on conference and consensus. The "Institutionalized Presidency" is the contribution of Congress and of recent Presidents, but particularly of President Eisenhower, whose temperament, training, and needs it obviously meets. But is it a permanent structure? In our "world in transition" no confident prediction can be safely vouchsafed. The incalculables are too many and too formidable.

CHAPTER FIVE

The Presidency: Emergence of the Candidates

The American Presidency makes incredibly imposing demands on the man in the White House. The office calls for a man who has the dignity of a monarch, the sagacity of an elder statesman, the adroitness of a professional politician, and the physical stamina of a track star. The question which arises in this chapter is: How do we find the man to meet the demands of the office? The answer is that "we" do not find the man, but rather that a political party "finds" a man at its national convention who will claim to be able to meet the challenges of the office. The central problem, then, is to examine against the nature of the presidential office this method of selecting presidential candidates.

The national conventions date back to the early 1830s, and were a product of Jacksonian democracy. Prior to this time, a small group of party and congressional leaders, "King Caucus," had determined who would be the presidential candidate. With the increase in suffrage that accompanied Jacksonian democracy, demands were made for a nominating method that would allow a far greater number of people to participate directly in the selection of the nominees. Thus the convention system was born.

However, the convention system has long been under attack. Many have wondered just who the delegates represent. Others have questioned the appropriateness of its circus atmosphere. As one critic observed, it is a "colossal travesty of popular institutions." Dissatisfaction with the system grew to such proportions that toward the end of the last century many states adopted the presidential-preference primary. By this method, the voters of a state select the delegates to the national convention. These delegates are pledged to support a specified candidate—at least on the first ballot. Today, twenty states have some form of preference primary; but the majority of the delegates continue to be selected by state or district conventions or by the state party committees. Even in the states that use the primary, some people question whether primaries amount to anything more than popularity polls.

Despite this doubt, and with the coming of television, the presidential primary has taken on added dimensions. As Theodore H. White suggests, the Wisconsin and particularly the West Virginia primaries in 1960 played a vital if not a decisive part in John F. Kennedy's campaign for the nomination. These primaries gave Kennedy a national audience, and afforded him the chance to impress upon key Democratic leaders across the nation that a Kennedy ticket could win.

In any given presidential-election year there are only a limited number of potential candidates. In a broad sense, there is a natural political aristocracy: membership in this group of white males is equivalent to "availability" for the nomination. These political aristocrats have certain features in common: a middle- to upper-class social and economic status; a residency in a large urban state; an unblemished family life; and some political experience, preferably as a state governor. Formerly, the unwritten rules of availability excluded non-Protestants. Kennedy's election broke that tradition, as well as the tradition favoring candidates of English, Scotch, or German background. How soon a Jew or an Italian-American will break the rule against his candidacy is unknown.

The most "available" candidate for any party's nomination is a first-term White House incumbent. The 1964 Democratic nominee is thus a foregone conclusion. The 1964 Republican nominee will be selected from a dozen available candidates. All are politicians (some more seasoned than others), all are members of the upper socio-economic group, and all are Protestants. However, they vary in family life, in political philosophy, and in their urban identification. William A. Rusher sees the 1964 GOP convention as a crucial crossroad. The obvious choice for a nominee—in his eyes— is based on an increasingly attractive Southern strategy for the GOP— ignoring the large Eastern urban states while concentrating on the traditional Republican areas of upper New England and the Middle West, and on the South. Still, such a strategy is a November plan: one aimed at election day, not directly at winning convention delegates.

Convention delegates, however, must weigh the Southern strategy against the large electoral votes that can be amassed in such states as New York and California. The exchange of remarks between Senators Daniel, Kennedy, and Lehman on proposals to amend the presidential-electoral system sheds some light on the problem. The Presidency has an urban bias, for the reason that, under the "winner-take-all" electoral system, the large urban centers in a given state have the major voice on election day. (Thus, in the past, conventions have not selected a nominee who would have no appeal to the great mass of urban voters.) To select a nominee with a strong Southern appeal might alienate substantial numbers of urban voters in a "swing" state like New York: for example, the important Negro vote in New York City. The seven "swing" states of New York, Michigan, Illinois, Texas, California, Pennsylvania, and Ohio have a combined vote of 210 votes, and 268 votes are all that are necessary for victory.

In 1960, it was obvious that the primary campaigns largely predetermined the nomination of Kennedy. Whether the GOP nomination will be so predetermined in 1964 is largely dependent on whether the major contestants engage in a series of tough primary battles. In the absence of primary battles, the nominating convention will again loom large. It might be possible for the "smoke-filled room" of Mark Sullivan's era again to take over the nominating process, and to dictate to the Republican convention who will be the party's standard-bearer in 1964. In any event, Professor James MacGregor Burns holds that the "smoke-filled room" is not necessarily as sinister a force as some have pictured it to be. He sees it as part and parcel of a political process that has produced outstanding men as nominees. He also points out that the convention is the best means available for achieving party unity and compromise, by on-the-spot bargaining and maneuvering. Perhaps the advent of TV, and the resultant showcase atmosphere of the convention, will make it increasingly difficult to achieve this goal of bargaining and maneuvering. The result might be to make the smoke-filled room even more an inner sanctum than it is today.

Preconvention primary battles can mean that the national conventions serve only as a rubber stamp—to ratify the previously fought popularity contests. On the other hand, a convention where smoke-filled rooms dominate the scene could imply that conventions are controlled by the party elite, the bigwigs. The question is whether either alternative is consistent with the nature of the Presidency or responsible government.

THE ART OF THE PRIMARY*

Theodore H. White

A primary fight, at any level, is America's most original contribution to the art of democracy—and, at any level, it is that form of the art most

---

* From *The Making of the President, 1960*, by Theodore H. White. Copyright © 1961 by Atheneum House, Inc. Reprinted by permission of the publishers. Mr. White is a Pulitzer Prize winning journalist.

profanely reviled and intensely hated by every professional who practices politics as a trade.

In theory a primary fight removes the nomination of candidates from the hands of cynical party leadership and puts it directly in the hands of the people who make the party. When, indeed, theory matches fact (for, in some states, primaries are absurdly meaningless), primary contests result in disastrous and unforgettable explosions. A genuine primary is a fight within the family of the party—and, like any family fight, is apt to be more bitter and leave more enduring wounds than battle with the November enemy. In primaries, ambitions spurt from nowhere; unknown men carve their mark; old men are sent relentlessly to their political graves; bosses and leaders may be humiliated or unseated. At ward, county or state level, all primaries are fought with spurious family folksiness—and sharp knives.

Bosses and established leaders hate primaries for good reason; they are always, in any form, an appeal from the leaders' wishes to the people directly. Primaries suck up and waste large sums of money from contributors who might better be tapped for the November finals; the charges and countercharges of primary civil war provide the enemy party with ammunition it can later use with blast effect against whichever primary contender emerges victorious; primary campaigns exhaust the candidate, use up his speech material, drain his vital energy, leave him limp before he clashes with the major enemy.

And whatever ill can be said of local primaries can be multiplied tenfold for the Presidential primaries. For the amount of money used in a series of Presidential primaries across the breadth of this land is prodigious; the stakes of the Presidency are so high and dramatic that a horde of self-winding citizens and amateurs suddenly insists on participation; and the wreckage that a primary usually leaves of a well-organized local machine is as nothing compared to the wreckage that two political giants from alien states can make of an instate organization, whose private ambitions they abuse and whose delicate local balances and compromises they completely ignore as they strive for power to command the whole country.

Yet, when all is said, there remains this gross fact: were there no Presidential primaries, the delegates sent to the National Conventions would be chosen by local party bosses, and the decision of the Convention, made blind by inability to measure candidates' voting strength, would rest in the back room, with the bosses. When, for a period of thirty-five years, from 1865 to 1900, the choice of Presidential candidates was left to the bosses in convention assembled, their selections resulted in such mediocre leadership of this country that it could be truly written that "No period so thoroughly ordinary had been known in American politics since Christopher Columbus first disturbed the balance of American society." It was only with the turn of the twentieth century that the Presidential primary was introduced, soon to spread over the union. Many states in the next half-century experimented with the Presidential primary—some making it a permanent feature of their politics, some finally abolishing it, most of them altering its rules from decade to decade. By 1960, only sixteen states still retained a legal, open primary, in which all seekers for the Presidency of the United States, of either party, might offer themselves to the people directly. These sixteen states were as diverse in their politics and sociologies as the diversity of American civilization itself; they had been chosen by no superior reason or plan. Altogether to the foreign eye they must have seemed the most preposterous field of battle on which men who aspire to the leadership of American freedom and control of its powers should choose to joust. Yet these states were, and remain, vital to the play of American Presidential politics.

For John F. Kennedy and Hubert Humphrey there was no other than the primary way to the Convention. If they could not at the primaries prove their strength in the hearts of Americans, the Party bosses would cut their hearts out in the back rooms of Los Angeles. Thus, as they approached their combat, they had a sense of multiple audience—first, the folksy audience of the primary state to be won directly, along with the local delegates that could be harvested in the primary victory (this, of course, was the least of their considerations); next, the national audience, as the nation first paid its attention to the combat and assessed the men; and, at last, there were the bosses of the big Eastern states and the smaller organized states who would coldly watch the race to observe the performance of political horseflesh.

Of the sixteen primary states, Hubert Humphrey had by late winter chosen five as his field of battle; of the same sixteen, John F. Kennedy had similarly chosen seven. And they were first to clash head-on in Wisconsin on April 5th. . . .

By Tuesday, April 5th, as Wisconsin prepared to vote, it was (or so the prognosticators felt) a walkaway.

The fact that it was not a walkaway, as shown by the actual result of the voting, was to shape all the rest of Kennedy's strike for the Presidency, from then until November.

. . . Within two hours after the polls had closed the profile of voting had become apparent. He was to lose the Western tier conclusively—the Third, Ninth, Tenth—whether because they were farm districts or Protestant districts he could not judge. He was to lose the Second equally heavily—whether because it was Protestant or loved Humphrey or was Stevensonian again he could not judge. He was to carry the Seventh narrowly; the Sixth and Eighth (heavily Catholic, old Joe McCarthy country) substantially; the First District and Milwaukee's Fourth and

Fifth (again heavily Catholic) decisively. No one could tell whether Humphrey's districts had voted against Kennedy because they were Protestant or because they were farmland closest to Minnesota; nor whether Kennedy had won his own six districts because they were heavily Catholic or because they were heavily industrial. The returns had shown their character by eight o'clock; by then, the entire message was clear to him.

"What does it mean?" asked one of his sisters.

"It means," he said quietly yet bitterly, "that we have to do it all over again. We have to go through every one and win every one of them—West Virginia and Maryland and Indiana and Oregon, all the way to the Convention." . . .

If Kennedy received his six-district-to-four margin as a setback, Humphrey received the short end of 4 to 6 almost as a victory.

Humphrey had expected defeat, had accepted the prognosis of the experts as certain tidings of devastation. Yet here he now was, having run a tight race, finding in the figures hope, cheer and comfort. . . .

He emerged from this inner scene of homespun gaiety to greet the TV cameras and the press briefly. Exuberant, he told them, "You can quote me as being encouraged and exhilarated and sorry it's all over." He quipped for a few minutes, then said he was going directly back to Washington the next day and on to West Virginia.

It is quite clear now, in retrospect, that John F. Kennedy owes his nomination as much to Hubert Humphrey's decision that night in Milwaukee as to any other man's decision except his own. . . .

If, realizing this, Humphrey had withdrawn at that moment, Kennedy would have faced zero opposition in the West Virginia primary; thus, any Kennedy victory there would have proved nothing and been meaningless in terms of bargaining power vis-à-vis the big Eastern bosses. . . .

In American life political patterns are rarely determined by geography, and the states of the union group themselves in distinct political families more by past history than by simple neighborliness.

Only 640 miles separate Madison, the capital of Wisconsin, from Charleston, the capital of West Virginia. Yet centuries of time and tradition, immeasurable gulfs of culture, separate these two states. If one were to choose as a proud grouping those American states whose politics are probably the most decent and worthy of respect, one would group Wisconsin, certainly, with Minnesota, California and Connecticut. And if one were to choose those states whose politics (excluding the baroque courthouse states of the South) are the most squalid, corrupt and despicable, then one would add West Virginia to that Jukes family of American politics that includes Indiana, Massachusetts and Texas. . . .

Over the past thirty years coal has molded West Virginia politics. Starting with the era of Franklin D. Roosevelt (who let John L. Lewis organize the miners against an industrial savagery unique in American industry), West Virginia became a Democratic state; the Mine Workers Union became a force in politics equal to the United Automobile Workers in Michigan or the clothing workers in New York.

When coal began to die some fifteen years ago, West Virginia began to die with it. Technology helped kill coal. . . . High union wages also helped kill coal employment—as the union shoved wages up and up, it became not only cheaper but also imperative for the operators to automate their mines with the superb new machines of the postwar era. Gradually, as these pressures made themselves felt, the miners were dismissed, then they hungered. . . .

West Virginia had long attracted the interest of John F. Kennedy—perhaps longer than any of the other states in the union outside his own. Two years before, while running for re-election as Senator from Massachusetts, he had retained Louis Harris to make the very first probe of public opinion outside his home state—in West Virginia, in June of 1958. (The result of the poll then was 52 for Kennedy, 38 for Nixon, balance undecided.) . . .

By April of 1960, however, after the Wisconsin primary, it was uncertain whether it was Humphrey who was caught in the trap or Kennedy himself. For between February and April the political atmosphere of the country had begun to heat. The Wisconsin primary had attracted the attention of the national press and the national television networks; and the nation had become aware that a religious issue was beginning to develop in its national politics for the first time since 1928; men and women from West Virginia to Alaska were slowly learning the identity and religion of the major candidates; and the tide in West Virginia had turned against the Boston candidate. Sampling in Charleston now, three weeks before the primary voting day of May 10th, Harris discovered that the citizens of Kanawha county—which includes Charleston, the capital—had shifted vehemently in sentiment. They were now, he reported, 60 for Humphrey, 40 for Kennedy. When Kennedy headquarters inquired of their West Virginia advisers what had happened between his 70-to-30 margin of December and the short end of the present 40-to-60 split, they were told, curtly, "But no one in West Virginia knew you were a Catholic in December. Now they know." . . .

As usual with the Kennedy operation, solutions proceeded at two levels —one strategic and one organizational. . . . The organizational solution was, of course, O'Brien's. After ten years in the service of John F. Kennedy, Lawrence F. O'Brien is certainly one of the master political operators of the new school.

What distinguishes the new school from the old school is the political approach of exclusion versus inclusion. In a tight old-fashioned machine, the root idea is to operate with as few people as possible, keeping decision and action in the hands of as few inside men as possible. In the new style, practiced by citizens' groups and new machines (Republican and Democratic alike) the central idea is to give as many people as possible a sense of participation: participation galvanizes emotions, gives the participant a live stake in the victory of the leader. . . .

A first meeting in the morning for the northern chairmen took place at the Stonewall Jackson Hotel in Clarksburg. A second meeting for the southern chairmen took place that afternoon at the Kanawha Hotel, 100 miles away, in Charleston.

Jobs to be done:

Organization of volunteers for door-to-door distribution of the Kennedy literature.

Rural mailings.

Telephone campaign. (The West Virginians explained the problem of telephoning in a state where the party line still reigns, but O'Brien insisted nonetheless.)

Receptions to be organized. (And since tea and coffee receptions were too effete for West Virginia, it was all right to call receptions an "ox roast" in the northern part of the state, a "weenie roast" in the southern part.)

Finally, all county chairmen were told which members of the Kennedy family (plus Franklin D. Roosevelt, Jr.) would be available to tour in what areas on which day.

Above all: work.

. . . But beyond organization was the raw stuff of American politics: those things blurted out by simple people that show their emotion, their misgiving, their trust. And there could be no doubt about the issue that bothered these people . . .

The issue, it was clear, over and beyond anything O'Brien's organizational genius could do, was religion: the differing ways men worshiped Christ in this enclave of Western civilization.

All other issues were secondary. The Kennedy tacticians had already refined several minor lines of attack on Humphrey. They had begun and continued to stress the war record of John F. Kennedy, for in West Virginia, a state of heroes and volunteers, the stark courage of the Boston candidate in the Straits of the Solomons in the Fall of 1942 found a martial echo in every hill. ("To listen to their stuff," said an irate Humphrey man, "you'd think Jack won the war all by himself.") The Kennedy men continued to hammer at Humphrey as being "front man" for a gang-up crowd of Stevenson-Symington-Johnson supporters who refused to come into the open. They stressed their candidate's sympathy and concern for the hungry and unemployed. Humphrey, who had known hunger in boyhood, was the natural workingman's candidate—but Kennedy's shock at the suffering he saw in West Virginia was so fresh that it communicated itself with the emotion of original discovery. Kennedy, from boyhood to manhood, had never known hunger. Now, arriving in West Virginia from a brief rest in the sun in the luxury of Montego Bay, he could scarcely bring himself to believe that human beings were forced to eat and live on these cans of dry relief rations, which he fingered like artifacts of another civilization. "Imagine," he said to one of his assistants one night, "just imagine kids who never drink milk." Of all the emotional experiences of his pre-Convention campaign, Kennedy's exposure to the misery of the mining fields probably changed him most as a man; and as he gave tongue to his indignation, one could sense him winning friends.

Yet the religious issue remained, and as the days grew closer to the voting the Kennedy staff divided on how it must be handled. . . . It was up to the candidate alone to decide. And, starting on April 25th, his decision became clear. He would attack—he would meet the religious issue head on.

Whether out of conviction or out of tactics, no sounder Kennedy decision could have been made. Two Democratic candidates were appealing to the commonalty of the Democratic Party; once the issue could be made one of tolerance or intolerance, Hubert Humphrey was hung. No one could prove to his own conscience that by voting for Humphrey he was displaying tolerance. Yet any man, indecisive in mind on the Presidency, could prove that he was at least tolerant by voting for Jack Kennedy.

Up and down the roads roved Kennedy names, brothers and sisters all available for speeches and appearances; to the family names was added the lustrous name of Franklin D. Roosevelt, Jr. Above all, over and over again there was the handsome, open-faced candidate on the TV screen, showing himself, proving that a Catholic wears no horns. The documentary film on TV opened with a cut of a PT boat spraying a white wake through the black night, and Kennedy was a war hero; the film next showed the quiet young man holding a book in his hand in his own library receiving the Pulitzer Prize, and he was a scholar; then the young man held his golden-curled daughter of two, reading to her as she sat on his lap, and he was the young father; and always, gravely, open-eyed, with a sincerity that could not be feigned, he would explain his own devotion to the freedom of America's faiths and the separation of church and state. . . .

The orchestration of this campaign infuriated Humphrey. Once the issue had been pitched as tolerance versus intolerance, there was only one way for a West Virginian to demonstrate tolerance—and that was by voting for Kennedy. Backed against the wall by the development of an issue for which there was no conceivable response either in his heart or practical politics, Humphrey fell back on the issue of money. ("There are three kinds of politics," he would say. "The politics of big business, the politics of the big bosses, and the politics of big money, and I'm against all of them. I stand for politics of the people.") . . .

Strangled for lack of money (Humphrey's expenditures in West Virginia were to total only $25,000—nothing, in the scale of American politics), knowing himself in debt, aware of the nature, depth and resources of this final Kennedy drive, as the final week end approached Humphrey became a figure of pathos. He needed advertising, he needed workers, above all he needed TV to show himself across the state.

West Virginia voted on May 10th, a wet, drizzly day. By eight o'clock the polls were closed. With 100 names on some of the local ballots, all of them more important as jobs to West Virginians than the Presidency, the count was very slow. Shortly before nine o'clock, however, came the first flash: Old Field Precinct, Hardy County, Eastern Panhandle, a precinct acknowledging only twenty-five Catholic registered voters, had counted: For Kennedy, 96; for Humphrey, 36.

The count dragged on. By 9:20, with ten precincts out of 2,750 in the state having reported, the first faint trend became visible: Kennedy, 638; Humphrey, 473—a 60-to-40 break. Yet these were from northern West Virginia, the sensitized civilized north. How would the candidate do in the fundamentalist, coal-mining south? By 9:40 the count read Kennedy, 1,566 and Humphrey, 834; and someone in the Humphrey headquarters muttered, "We're dead." . . .

The Senator's eyes gleamed with tears in the bright lights that television had installed to catch the surrender. It took him a moment to get his voice under control.

"I have a brief statement to make," he said. He read the words, "I am no longer a candidate for the Democratic Presidential nomination."

. . . The first of the seven had been scratched from the list of candidates for the Presidency of the United States by the people of the hills. In the morning, when Hubert Humphrey woke, the Presidential image had evaporated. Outside the Ruffner Hotel his parked bus had overnight been given a ticket for illegal parking.

CROSSROADS FOR THE GOP*

William A. Rusher

America's most accomplished tea-leaf readers have now concluded their study of the November election results, and they are turning up with an interpretation so unexpected and so unsettling that many of them profoundly wish they had never investigated the matter at all.

Just about all of them have long agreed that the *only* relevant question, in choosing a Republican presidential nominee, is "Who has the best chance of winning?" And it seemed perfectly safe to let this problem merge imperceptibly into the technically subordinate question, "Who can carry New York and California?"—on the hitherto sound principle that these two large states are indispensable if a Republican nominee is to win nationally. The 1964 answer to this not terribly complicated conundrum is, of course, supposed to be Nelson Rockefeller.

Imagine, therefore, the shock to the neural ganglia of these practiced pragmatists when a hard look at the 1962 election returns revealed 1) that neither Nelson Rockefeller nor any other Republican, real or nominal, has much more prospect of wresting New York and California from John F. Kennedy in 1964 than Mao Tsetung; 2) that the GOP has, nevertheless, an astonishingly good chance of up-ending Kennedy nationally, by taking most of the 165 electoral votes of the southern and border states away from him; and 3)—fasten your seat-belts, please—that the man with the best chance of carrying these states, and therefore of winning, is not Nelson Rockefeller, nor even George Romney or William Scranton, but Arizona's soft-spoken and conservative junior senator, Barry Goldwater. . . .

The Rockefeller Showing

. . . Rockefeller defeated incumbent Democratic Governor Averell Harriman four years ago by 573,034 votes. Kennedy, however, managed to carry the state against Nixon in 1960 by 383,666. In 1962 the Democrats nominated for Governor a cigar-store Indian named Robert Morgenthau, and frugally held their campaign expenditures to just $420,000—the smallest such figure in the modern political history of the Empire State. Rockefeller and the GOP, determined to "win big" in order to make the

---

* Reprinted from *National Review*, 150 East 35th Street, New York 16, New York, by permission. Mr. Rusher is the publisher of the *National Review*.

indispensable demonstration of puissance in supposedly crucial New York, publicly admit to having spent $2,184,000, or more than *five times* as much as the Democrats. (And that, of course, doesn't include the salaries of the windrows of ghostwriters, analysts and advisers palmed away in various Rockefeller family foundations and businesses.) Rockefeller himself campaigned tirelessly for almost a full year before November—kissing babies, patting cows and munching blintzes as if there were no tomorrow. His opponent, on the other hand, in his all but motionless two-month campaign, richly earned the mocking sobriquet, "the Democratic Calvin Coolidge." Small wonder that Rockefeller's official campaign manager openly predicted, the day before the election, that his tiger would win by 800,000—perhaps even by a million—votes.

And yet on Election Day 1962 Rockefeller's margin over Morgenthau was actually 43,865 votes *less* than his 1958 margin over Governor Harriman. And when we take into account the 141,877 votes rolled up by the gubernatorial candidate of New York's brash new Conservative Party (which is now a legal party in the state, and which has sternly warned that it will run a full slate of independent presidential electors against any Liberal nominated by the GOP in 1964), Rockefeller's overall margin sinks to a phthisic 387,292. Seldom has so much been so mauled by so little. . . .

Well, say there is no kingdom then for Nelson. Can the Republican Party do better? Surprisingly enough, the signs are multiplying that it can: that, in fact, 1964 can prove as dramatic a turning-point in the fortunes of the GOP as 1932 did for the Democrats. It will take courage; it will take imagination; it will compel the GOP to break the familiar mould that has furnished it with every presidential nominee for a quarter of a century—but it can be done. One can almost prophesy that it *will* be done —if not in 1964, then inevitably in 1968. The Republican Party, like it or not, has a rendezvous with a brand new idea.

Prospects in the South

And that brings us to the second great lesson of the 1962 elections. Ever since Reconstruction, the southern states have been as relentlessly Democratic as Rose Kennedy herself. This mulish but understandable prejudice has forced them into unnatural association with northern entities and ideas that every true Southerner instinctively loathes (Mencken once described the Democratic Party as "two gangs of natural enemies in a precarious state of symbiosis"), but it worked: it provided almost every Democratic Presidential candidate for 80 years with a guarantee of well over 100 electoral votes before he opened his mouth.

But, as the Bible reassuringly predicts, "This too shall pass away." Erosion has steadily undermined the one-party South—most notably during and since World War II, which ruthlessly homogenized American youth and (perhaps even more important) laid the foundations of a modern mixed economy in this once almost wholly agricultural region. Swifter means of communication and transportation—national newsmagazines, television networks and jet aircraft—have further diluted the ancestral tendencies. In scores of southern cities today, white-collar and professional workers drive home to split-level suburban ranch houses every evening, looking and acting for all the world like their northern and western counterparts.

And they are voting Republican. In the eleven states of the old Confederacy, according to *Time,* Republican candidates for the House of Representatives received 31 per cent of all votes cast in 1962—as against only 16.3 per cent in 1958. (And this, mark you, despite the fact that a substantial number of seats were not even contested by the GOP.) In Alabama, hitherto presumed to be as safe for Democracy as Tammany Hall, a smooth-talking 43-year-old Republican named James Martin, who had never sought public office before, ran against veteran Democratic Senator Lister Hill, lost by just seven-tenths of one per cent—and carried every major *city* in Alabama. And other strikingly strong showings were made by Republican gubernatorial or senatorial candidates in such unfamiliar territory as Arkansas (30.8 per cent), South Carolina (42.6 per cent) and Texas (45.9 per cent).

It takes no seer, therefore, to recognize that the Republican Party is at last within measurable distance of becoming what it has never been since Reconstruction: a truly national party, with a powerful state-by-state organization and successful local candidates in the South as well as elsewhere.

And what are the Republicans of this new South saying? What will they be arguing, as they foregather with their fellow Republicans of the North and West in the convention of 1964? "Nominate Rockefeller"? Far from it. With a unanimity that cannot fail to impress, *they are calling for a conservative GOP and a conservative presidential candidate.*

"I am against Rockefeller," says 34-year-old Tad Smith, recently-retired Republican State Chairman of Texas, "because his nomination would, quite simply, destroy the Republican Party of Texas. At one Resignation Rally after another, life-long Democrats now turning Republican have warned me that they will vote for a conservative Republican in 1964—but not for Rockefeller or any other Liberal." And the same story is told by leading Republicans in state after state across the South.

But the showing of Southern Republicans in 1962, encouraging as it may be, is still almost uniformly short of the 51 per cent in each state that would be needed to carry the South's electoral votes in 1964. Is there any evidence that a Republican *presidential* nominee could improve on this showing by the GOP's local candidates? Once again, the answer is an emphatic Yes—*provided he is a conservative.*

In the first place, it should be remembered that voting Republican for the presidency is far commoner in the South than voting Republican for congressional candidates (a practice which threatens the prized seniority of conservative Southern Democrats in the Congress). The following southern and border states have all gone Republican, primarily as a means of conservative protest, in at least two of the three presidential elections during the past eleven years: Florida, Kentucky, Maryland, Oklahoma, Tennessee, Texas and Virginia. (Louisiana and West Virginia went Republican once apiece.) There is no reason to suppose that any of these states is beyond the grasp of a Republican candidate chosen precisely because of his proven appeal to the South.

In addition, consider the cold estimate of the vigorous young men who are the Republican state chairmen in two of the Democratic Party's strongest remaining southern redoubts: John Grenier of Alabama and Wirt Yerger, Jr., of Mississippi. *Both insist that their own states will vote for a conservative Republican,* if one is nominated in 1964. Says Grenier: "It'd be the easiest campaign I ever ran."

Moreover, their prediction is echoed by some surprising sources. Within the past two months, a senior Democratic Senator from the Deep South confided to a friend that, in his opinion, Goldwater could carry all 165 southern and border state electoral votes against Kennedy in 1964—and underlined his view by quoting Attorney General Robert Kennedy as having told him privately that the First Family fears Goldwater far more than Rockefeller. . . .

Nature of the Counterattack

Which brings us to the nature and validity of the inevitable counter-attack. . . . Even disregarding the slightly mildewed laurels and still-smoldering ambitions of Nelson Rockefeller, the New York GOP has naturally enjoyed, and will not readily give up, its familiar role as Most Popular Girl at the Ball. More broadly, the Liberal Republicans, who have won every convention since (and including) 1940 by urging the necessity of wooing Liberal votes in the big cities of the North, are certainly not going to accept demotion without a fight. So the cry is up: *any Republican concession to Southern sentiment is a venture in sheer racism, and will lose the GOP crucial votes in the North and West.*

It is tempting to dismiss this argument by observing that the GOP will have to drink deep indeed at the racist trough before it equals the record of John Kennedy's own Southern allies on this score. The Democratic nedy conquests in the big industrial states of the North and still stand a serious chance of winning the election.

Whether Senator Goldwater is willing to shoulder the burden of a campaign of this sort—first against Nelson Rockefeller's millions, and then against John Kennedy and the massed batteries of the American Left—is not presently known. Certainly a man could be forgiven for praying that he might be spared that cup.

But the arithmetical imperatives speak with a logical force of their own, and it is not in the final analysis Barry Goldwater's personal wishes that are paramount: it is the overarching necessities of the Republican Party, and, in a larger sense, of the nation itself.

And this remains true, whatever we believe will be the final outcome of the 1964 election. For what if, despite everything, 1964 is fated to be a Democratic year? How can the Republican convention, then, best build for a successful future? By turning its back on the new, conservative and increasingly Republican South and gumming blintzes with Nelson Rockefeller? Or by nominating a candidate who—win or lose—will galvanize the party in a vast new area, carry fresh scores and perhaps hundreds of Southern Republicans to unprecedented local victories, and lay the foundations for a truly national Republican Party, ready to fight and win in 1968 and all the years beyond?

ELECTORAL COLLEGE REFORM*

Mr. DANIEL. I have heard discussion on the floor today by several Members of the Senate to the effect that they would like to change the system so as to provide a direct vote of the people for President and Vice President. As has been explained by the senior Senator from Tennessee [Mr. Kefauver], that would be almost impossible to accomplish, because about 31 States would lose some of their representation in the electoral vote—and that is particularly true of the smaller States—because at the present time, instead of the vote being based simply on population or on qualified voters, the States are entitled to 2 votes for their Senators and 1 vote for each Representative in the total electoral vote.

For that reason, and for other reasons, such as differences in voting

---

* 84th Congress, 2d Session. *Congressional Record*, pp. 5148–5149, 5236, 5263. Mr. Daniel was a Senator from Texas, Mr. Kennedy a Senator from Massachusetts, and Mr. Lehman a Senator from New York.

Party for 80 years has run with the hares down South on
while riding with the hounds up North—nominating loudl
presidential candidates, while calmly raking in, on locally
platforms, 95 per cent of all Senate and House seats (n⌐
governorships and legislatures) south of the Mason-Dixon L

On this issue of integration, truth is difficult to separate f⌐
The Southern Republicans understand and accept the fact th
not dictate a national Republican platform—or candidate—c⌐
segregation. They make, on the other hand, no apology for o⌐
Warren Court's breezy ventures in social pioneering—and it m
that here they have something to teach conservatives of the No⌐
objected that, nonetheless, a gap remains between Northern and
Republican sentiment on this issue, the only honest answer is
American society is deeply riven on the subject, and no party that
to national scope can, by definition, do other than reflect—as the
cratic Party has for 80 years reflected—this division in itself.

Certainly there is not a shred of evidence that any large bloc o
now sustaining Republican dominance in any northern or western
will bolt to the party of Kennedy (and Eastland, and Ellender) be
the GOP chooses to bid vigorously for the support of the new m
class of a changing South. Republican National Chairman William M
was much nearer the mark when he exhorted the December meetin⌐
the Republican National Committee: "Don't let them give you a sens⌐
guilt [about seeking votes in the South]." The American people, No⌐
and South, are entitled to be heard on the question of which party
treating the complex issue of race relations most honestly and with th
most real statesmanship. (As a matter of fact, one of the tantalizing by
products of a 1964 decision by the GOP to nominate a conservative would
be precisely this: that it would compel the Democrats, for the first time in
almost a century, to pay a reasonable amount of attention to their own
hitherto captive Southern conservatives.)

But what the Republican delegates in 1964 will want to do is *win*, and
it is here that the case for a conservative (meaning, in practice, Barry
Goldwater) must be rested and can be won. No Republican—not Rockefeller, not Goldwater, and neither Romney nor Scranton—has a serious
prospect of carrying either New York or California against Kennedy in
1964. Probably any one of them can hold the GOP's Midwestern heartland, and such peripheral fiefs as northern New England and certain of
the Mountain states, amounting in all to perhaps 140 electoral votes (with
270 needed to win). But Goldwater, *and Goldwater alone* (for in this respect Scranton and Romney are in no better position than Rockefeller),
can carry enough southern and border states to offset the inevitable Ken-

qualifications in the various States, it would be impossible for us to have a direct vote for President and Vice President. . . .

Therefore, it seems to me . . . that the closest we can get to the people themselves having a direct vote for President and Vice President is to divide the electoral vote within each State in accordance with the popular vote. That is the amendment I have sponsored: . . . to let each State keep its present electoral votes but elect named electors in the same manner that named Senators and Representatives are elected.

. . . In other words, the substitute which I shall call up in a moment would put into effect the so-called Lodge-Gossett proposal, with only this change:

We would provide that instead of requiring 40 per cent of the vote for election, as it was provided in the original amendment, the electoral vote will be distributed among the highest 3 candidates for President and Vice President. This is to get rid of the argument of splinter parties, to try to get rid of any possibility that dividing the vote in that way would increase splinter parties.

Mr. KENNEDY. Let me make one point as to what the effect of the Daniel proposal would be on the large States. I think the point is made most clear by the 1944 election.

Twelve Southern States, polling a vote of 5,609,000, showed a plurality of 2,263,270 for Roosevelt, which brought him 186 electoral votes, and none for his opponent.

A proportional division would have cut his lead by 65.697 electoral votes, giving him, under the proportional system, 99.576 with 33.879 for Dewey, and 4.445 for minor candidates.

The five States with the largest voting population, all with active party competition, cast a total vote of 20,621,569, returning to Roosevelt a plurality of 1,026,256, which gave him 135 electoral votes, to 25 for Dewey, an advantage of 110. A proportional division would have cut the lead to less than 8. The point is made that that would have given the 5 most populated States a margin of only about 8 electoral votes. The southern margin, with a voting turnout of a quarter of the 5 top States, would be 66.

The point I make is that in the case of the States with the largest population, their influence would be almost nil, and that it would make the influence of the Democratic Party in the South far greater than it is.

Mr. LEHMAN. Mr. President, what is going on here is an attack against the political influence of the big States in the nomination and election of a President of the United States.

Statements have been made about reducing the influence of so-called minority groups and splinter blocs. What minority groups are thus referred to? Let us speak openly and frankly with each other in debating so critical a proposition as a drastic change in the Constitution of the United States.

Is it organized labor? Farmers? Small-business men? Is it the veterans? Naturalized citizens? Negroes? Catholics? Jews? Masons? Which are these minority groups that we must guard against by constitutional amendment?

What events and what tendencies of the past do we mean to forestall in the future?

What influence have New York, Pennsylvania, Illinois, and California had which must be neutralized now by this constitutional amendment?

Mr. President, it is my responsiblity to my State of New York to defend its influence in national affairs. But first, I want to know, specifically, in what way it is claimed that that influence has been bad and has worked to the disadvantage of the United States and of the cause of democracy?

Let us have the facts on the table, in full view, so that we may know why we are asked to follow the incredible and chaotic formula recommended by the Judiciary Committee.

Mr. President, I am in favor of reforming our present system of electing the President of the United States, but not this way. I am aware of the so-called dangers, which have been pointed out by political scientists, of electing a so-called minority President.

I am aware that the electoral college system was originally designed as a means of selecting, and not of electing, a President.

I am in favor of the direct election of a President of the United States by the people, by the direct vote of the people, just as we elect Senators and Members of the House of Representatives.

If 16 million people in New York State can be trusted to elect a United States Senator by direct vote, 160 million people can be trusted to elect a President of the United States by direct vote.

Radio, television, and the press have made the United States one community with instantaneous and comprehensive communication. The direct election of a President is the only democratic way. We will come to it, in good time, I am sure. Even if a constitutional amendment to this effect is not adopted this year, it will be adopted eventually. It is the only logical way of electing a President.

The present system of electing an electoral college which elects a President is obviously archaic. It should be changed.

But, Mr. President, so wise were the drafters of our Constitution—even beyond their own realization—and so flexible is that system, combined with the political genius of the American people, that out of this archaic system has evolved a more or less democratic manner of electing a President. And the people do, in fact, elect the President. And it is a fact of our history, that with but the rarest exceptions, the President elected in this manner has been the actual choice of the majority of the voters of our country.

Now comes this proposal—this political potpourri, this political hash, if I may characterize it as such—which is seriously advocated as means of electing a President of the United States.

The sponsors of the resolution would have us elect a President in a way which would permit State legislatures to gerrymander an election in a positively nightmarish manner. They would permit 36,000 votes cast in Mississippi to be worth as much as 200,000 votes in New York State.

They would permit low-vote one-party States to have more influence in the election of a President than the huge States where elections are fought out under conditions of the keenest competition, where the candidates must prove themselves or lose.

The President is the only officer in the United States who represents all the people of the country. He should and must be elected in the most democratic manner possible, by the closest approach we can make to pure democracy.

In form, the present electoral college system is not so organized. But in actual operation it does, by some miracle, succeed in reflecting a democratic choice.

I want to eliminate the chance that on some future occasion it may not repeat this miracle. I want to see the President elected by the direct vote of the people. But failing that, I must oppose, with all the strength I have, this dangerous and ill-conceived formulation for the amendment of our Constitution, which would make the election of a President subject to a hundred, a thousand whims, vagaries and unpredictable decisions and actions on the part of State legislatures.

Mr. President, New York State is already far underrepresented in proportion to its population, both in the Senate and in the House. The people who live in the congested cities and counties in New York are far underrepresented in the Congress, just as they are underrepresented in the New York State legislature.

Shall we, then, compound and intensify this situation by reflecting this multiple underrepresentation in the choice of a President? Not only would we intensify the underrepresentation, but we would splinter our influence in the nominating conventions and the electoral college.

The sponsors of this proposal would do New York no favor by giving the party which loses the election a proportional representation in the electoral vote, while at the same time they would make every individual vote in New York count for only a fifth as much as a vote in Mississippi, South Carolina, or Arkansas.

I hope we will not tamper with the Constitution, if this is the way we are to do it. . . .

Presidential Electoral Vote

STATE	1952	1956	1960	1964
Alabama	D	D	D (1)	10
Alaska			R	3
Arizona	R	R	R	5
Arkansas	D	D	D	6
California	R	R	R	40
Colorado	R	R	R	6
Connecticut	R	R	R	8
Delaware	R	R	D	3
Florida	R	R	R	14
Georgia	D	D	D	12
Hawaii			(2)	4
Idaho	R	R	R	4
Illinois	R	R	D	26
Indiana	R	R	R	13
Iowa	R	R	R	9
Kansas	R	R	R	7
Kentucky	D	R	R	9
Louisiana	D	R	D	10
Maine	R	R	R	4
Maryland	R	R	D	10
Massachusetts	R	R	D	14
Michigan	R	R	D	21
Minnesota	R	R	D	10
Mississippi	D	D	U (3)	7
Missouri	R	D	D	12
Montana	R	R	R	4
Nebraska	R	R	R	5
Nevada	R	R	D	3
New Hampshire	R	R	R	4
New Jersey	R	R	D	17
New Mexico	R	R	R	4
New York	R	R	D	43
North Carolina	D	D	D	13
North Dakota	R	R	R	4
Ohio	R	R	R	26
Oklahoma	R	R	R (4)	8
Oregon	R	R	R	6
Pennsylvania	R	R	D	29
Rhode Island	R	R	D	4
South Carolina	D	D	D	8
South Dakota	R	R	R	4
Tennessee	R	R	R	11
Texas	R	R	D	25
Utah	R	R	R	4
Vermont	R	R	R	3
Virginia	R	R	R	12
Washington	R	R	R	9
West Virginia	D	R	D	7
Wisconsin	R	R	R	12
Wyoming	R	R	R	3

KEY
D—Democrat
R—Republican
U—Unpledged

(1) Six out of 11 electors voted for Senator Harry Byrd.

(2) Hawaii's three votes not cast because of a recount.

(3) Eight independent electors voted for Byrd.

(4) One Oklahoma vote cast for Byrd.

TOTALS	1952	1956	1960
Percent Popular Two-Party Vote	R:55 D:45	R:58 D:42	D:50.08 R:49.92
Percent Electoral Vote	R:83 D:16	R:86 D:14	D:56 R:41

We have been operating for 180 years under the present system. It has not been perfect, by any means. One could make a good argument, on logical grounds, against it. But in the main it has worked well, and in only a few cases was the man who became President of the United States not elected by an actual majority of the people of the country.

I very much desire direct election of the President; but to substitute this amendment for what we have been using for 180 years, with 98 or 99 per cent satisfaction, certainly does not make sense to me. I think it would be a great mistake to adopt this amendment. I hope with all my heart that it will not be approved. I shall work with all my strength to cause the defeat of the amendment. I think it would be a serious step backward in the democratic processes of this country.

THE NOMINATION OF
WARREN GAMALIEL HARDING*

Mark Sullivan

. . . In two rooms of a dingy old hotel in Washington, Daugherty set up Harding headquarters. (The Wood and Lowden candidacies had whole floors and immense staffs in the leading hotels of Chicago and New York.) To a newspaper man who called at the Harding headquarters, Daugherty explained his strategy. With a candor that was part of his intellectual armory, to be used where his instinct told him candor would serve him best, and with a pictorial vividness of speech that was part of his rich endowment of imagination, he said: "I won't try to fool you; you can see what we've got here, it's only a shoestring. I'll tell you, in confidence, what's in my mind. All I'm doing is getting in touch with the leaders and delegates who are for Wood and Lowden, being friendly with them. . . ."

Toward the newspapers generally, and the public, Daugherty practised a finesse that was the ultimate refinement in subtlety. For the sake of Ohio looking on, he had to seem to be pushing the Harding candidacy seriously. But if he actually pushed it seriously, he would destroy the only chance he had, by antagonizing the major candidates and their delegates.

* Reprinted with the permission of Charles Scribner's Sons from OUR TIMES, *The Twenties*, Vol. VI by Mark Sullivan. Copyright 1935 Charles Scribner's Sons; renewal copyright © 1963 Mark Sullivan, Jr., Sydney B. Parker, and Narcissa Siegchrist. The late Mr. Sullivan was a journalist and historian.

However, to be between the devil and the deep sea was a familiar experience with Daugherty. He enjoyed it and spent most of his life in that exhilarating strand, or in pulling clients out of it. His present dilemma was no great tax on his resourcefulness.

. . . He told them [newspaper men] exactly what he was relying on— but told it in such a way as to let them think he didn't believe it himself.

"Well," he said, in answer to skeptical questions, "there will be no nomination on the early ballots. After the other candidates have failed, after they have gone their limit, the leaders, worn out and wishing to do the very best thing, will get together in some hotel room about 2:11 in the morning. Some fifteen men, bleary-eyed with lack of sleep, and perspiring profusely with the excessive heat, will sit down around a big table. I will be with them and present the name of Senator Harding. When the time comes, Harding will be selected, because he fits in perfectly with every need of the party and nation. He is the logical choice, and the leaders will determine to throw their support to him." . . .

As the 1920 Republican National Convention approached, the leading candidate was General Wood [not closely associated with any state]. He was, by any fair estimate, one of the half-dozen most distinguished Americans of the time, perhaps better equipped than any other individual to provide America with leadership in the difficult postwar and reconstruction years ahead. As a young man he had entered the Army as a medical officer during the eighties, when Indian troubles, while they had ceased to be common and had diminished in formidableness, were still occasional; he had become an officer of the line, had served as superior in command to Theodore Roosevelt in the Rough Riders during the Spanish War, had become Governor-General of Cuba and had been Chief of Staff of the Army. Though without professional training at West Point, he became the best type of Army-man. Just before the Great War, and during the early part of it, he had been leader of the movement, later well justified, for preparedness. That service, as well as his other distinctions, had commended him for a corresponding part in America's participation; refusal by President Wilson to let him serve in France had increased Wood's standing among Republicans, made him appropriate as the man to lead the Republicans in the election which would choose a successor to Wilson. Wood, because of his association with Theodore Roosevelt in the Rough Riders and in the fight for preparedness, had the support of most of the conservatives among Roosevelt's followers. At the same time, the fact that he was a soldier was a handicap to him. The country had just gone through the Great War, had not liked the experience, and to some degree disliked military men. As the shrewd Harry Daugherty put it, "There's not enough money in the world to buy the nomination for a man with epaulettes on his shoulders in 1920." This handicap to Wood was increased by his advocacy, during his campaign, of universal military service for America. . . .

Next to Wood, the principal candidate was Frank O. Lowden. He had been a poor boy in Minnesota and Iowa, had become a successful lawyer in Chicago; had married a daughter of one of the powerful rich of the day, George Pullman; had been a long-time member of the Republican National Committee, and had recently made a striking record as Governor of Illinois. He had served five years in Congress, and had been distinguished in that body at a time, 1906 to 1911, when the quality of Congress was exceptionally high. In mind, he was able; in temperament hearty and forceful; in personality agreeable. He was of the best of the type from which the United States had been accustomed to choose its Presidents.

Third, in numerical strength, was Hiram Johnson. He had first come to the country's attention by his conduct of a famous criminal prosecution in San Francisco, had been Governor of California, had been the candidate for Vice-president on the ticket with Theodore Roosevelt when the latter started the Progressive party in 1912, and had been, since 1917, United States Senator from California. His support included the more progressive part of the old Theodore Roosevelt following. Another large area of support accrued to him from strong opponents of America's joining the League of Nations; Johnson, with some ten others in the Senate, had composed the group whose unceasing opposition to the League had brought them various designations of implacability, the "bitter-enders," the "battalion of death," the "last-ditchers."

Others among the candidates included a Governor of Massachusetts, named Calvin Coolidge, who had arrested nation-wide attention by his attitude toward a strike of Boston policemen; Coolidge had sent to the head of the American Federation of Labor, Samuel Gompers, a telegram as notable for its laconic force of style as for the principle it declared: "There is no right to strike against the public safety by anybody, anywhere, any time.". . .

And there was Harding—his rank, as subsequently measured by strength on the first ballot, was sixth, below Wood, Lowden, Johnson, Butler, and Governor Sproul of Pennsylvania. He was identified with no conspicuous group or cause; the country knew no more of him than it knows of any inconspicuous Senator. . . .

The tensity of opposition between the two foremost contenders which Daugherty had been hoping for, upon which he had built all his own plans, had developed as Daugherty had foreseen. Beginning with the earliest primaries for the election of delegates, there had been strong rivalry between the camps of Wood and Lowden—rivalry which had soon turned to bad feeling and to over-eagerness, expressing itself in competitively lavish organizations. This grew into large expenditures of money, to which the country's attention was called by one of the other candidates, Johnson of California, and his Senate colleague, Borah of Idaho. Promptly the outcry was taken up by other Republican leaders and by press and public. Borah in the Senate charged that a "plot" was afoot to "buy the Presidency," that the use of money by Wood and Lowden constituted a "saturnalia of corruption.". . .

On the board as it lay when the balloting was about to begin, Wood had about a third of the delegates and Lowden about a third. For Harding, Daugherty had somewhat less than a tenth. The rest were scattered among some fifteen minor candidates and favorite sons. As between Wood and Lowden, Wood had a few more, hence Wood would be in the lead in the early ballots.

With the board standing thus, Daugherty arranged his little army of Harding delegates with a skill composed of alertness and patience. Most of them, of course, must vote for Harding on the first ballot, and continuously. But others he would save, concealing them, spreading them about among other candidates, so as to be able to add them to Harding's tally little by little on later ballots, and thus make that impression of steady growth which operates powerfully on convention psychology.

Yet others of his Harding delegates Daugherty reserved for another purpose. He knew his first task must be to "kill off" Wood. For killing off Wood, he knew the best instrumentality, indeed the only one, was Lowden. So Daugherty went to Lowden's manager and made an alliance, a carefully qualified alliance. Daugherty would, he told the Lowden manager, help Lowden beat down Wood, would devote to that purpose as many of his Harding delegates as he could spare. "We can't allow," Daugherty said, "Harding's vote to be too small, but we'll loan you every vote we can until you pass Wood." Daugherty was explicit about the strictly limited duration of the alliance. He carefully told the Lowden manager that "the minute you pass Wood, the minute Wood is out of the race, all friendship between us on the floor of this convention ceases— you understand that." The Lowden manager said, "Certainly, you couldn't make a fairer proposition." The two shook hands and Daugherty went off to deploy his delegates.

The balloting, when it began, took the course that Daugherty had sensed it would. The two principal candidates, Wood and Lowden, had each about the same number of delegates. On the first ballot, there was material difference; Wood having 287½, Lowden only 211½. But from the beginning, Lowden grew more rapidly than Wood. (Partly with the aid of the delegates temporarily "loaned" to him by Daugherty.)

By the fourth ballot, Wood was still in the lead, with 314½, but Lowden had come up close behind, with 289. And it was apparent to persons who were experienced in such battles and knew the present conditions, that on the next ballot, Lowden would pass Wood. Yet it was equally apparent, to the elder statesmen paternally watching the scene, if not to the candidates or delegates, that Lowden could not win. The law of human nature that Daugherty had counted on would now work. Each of the two major candidates would prevent the nomination of the other. . . .

The time when this became apparent was about five o'clock of the first day's balloting, Friday afternoon, with the convention only one day to go. The condition constituted a considerable concern to the party elders. Two of them acted.

Senators Reed Smoot of Utah and Henry Cabot Lodge of Massachusetts—the latter was the presiding officer—whispered together on the platform. Smoot stepped forward to the edge of the platform. "I move," he said, "that the convention do now stand adjourned until ten o'clock tomorrow morning." In the silence of a surprised convention, Lodge put the motion, put it with characteristic Harvard precision—always Lodge preserved the manner of the scholar in politics. "Those in favor of the motion to adjourn will signify it by saying 'Aye.'" There were a few scattered "Ayes." Again Lodge intoned, "Those opposed 'No.'" There was a roar of "Nos." The delegates, especially those of Wood and Lowden who composed the majority of the convention, were still in fighting heat, still expected their respective candidates to win, were still eager to be at each other and were in no mood for adjournment. But Lodge, with complete insouciance, ceasing to be the scholar in politics and becoming the practised political manipulator—Lodge announced, turning boredly from his desk before he completed the sentence, "The 'Ayes' have it and the convention is adjourned until tomorrow morning at ten o'clock." Every delegate knew the "Nos" had far outnumbered the "Ayes," but accepted the chairman's decision calmly, rather smilingly. Assuming that the party gods must have some good reason, the delegates accepted the palpably false decision in the spirit of "father knows best." Both the Wood delegates and the Lowden delegates, and their leaders, continued to think their respective candidates would win the next day. . . .

That night four of them [party elders] dined together, Senator Charles W. Curtis of Kansas (later Vice-President), Senator Frank Brandegee of Connecticut, Senator Henry Cabot Lodge of Massachusetts, and George Harvey. . . .

The four agreed that Wood and Lowden would deadlock each other next morning, and that thereafter the nomination would be likely to go to whoever among the other candidates should have the first "pick-up," that is, whoever should show strength in the first ballot after the deadlock and the ensuing "break.". . .

Of the four, Curtis was the most confident they had best take Harding.

Energetic and competent, Curtis started out to call on stated leaders and arrange to have delegates vote for Harding in the morning, so that Harding should be the one to have the first "pick-up." The others remained in Harvey's suite. From time to time during the night, Curtis came back to the room; he brought other leaders with him; yet other leaders dropped in. On each, as he came, the Harding suggestion was tried out. Some opposed the notion; none had any enthusiasm or conviction for it. From time to time they renewed their discussion of the other possibilities. Harvey suggested Will Hays, but the suggestion did not take hold. Discussion of one suggestion after another was succeeded by intervals of moody silence. . . .

The room became, so far as there was any such thing, the "smoke-filled room" that Daugherty had anticipated. Daugherty, however, was not in it—but his logic was, and his logic was as effective as his presence. From time to time, procrastination was discussed to adjourn the convention over Sunday. But Daugherty had taken that, too, into account. From long experience and insight into human nature, especially delegate nature, Daugherty knew that the next day, Saturday, the delegates would be tired, that they would be coming to the end of the funds they had brought to Chicago with them, that two-thirds of them would become disgusted by realization that their candidates could not win, and that in their emotional exhaustion they would make some nomination before Saturday night. Daugherty was in a position to sit tight, and he did. In the end, the "fifteen men" came to a kind of indifferent, tired unanimity—more a negation of other candidates than an affirmative agreement on Harding.

About two o'clock in the morning— . . . Harvey sent for Harding. Harding came, heavy-eyed, heaving from time to time the sighs of strain and anxiety. Harvey received him alone, in another room.

. . . "We think," Harvey said to Harding, "you may be nominated tomorrow; before acting finally, we think you should tell us, on your conscience and before God, whether there is anything that might be brought up against you that would embarrass the party, any impediment that might disqualify you or make you inexpedient, either as candidate or as President.". . .

The ten minutes that Harding spent alone in that room were fateful. It would be interesting to know what went on in Harding's mind. Some years later, a story about Harding emerged sensationally, a story which if based on facts would have constituted an impediment to Harding as candidate and as President. It was what politicians call a "woman story," precisely the kind covered by the question Harvey had asked. Did Harding think about this? Conjecture is made difficult and Harding's personal situation at the time was made complex by the fact that in his heart he had not wanted the nomination; had tried, in his too easy-going way, to escape it. Was this story one of his reasons for not having wanted the nomination? Did he now give consideration to finally renouncing the nomination by telling Harvey there was an impediment?

Harding, after some ten minutes alone, opened the door into the room where Harvey was waiting. He told Harvey there was no impediment. Harvey went back to the smoke-filled room where the others were still in conference.

At ten o'clock the next morning, when the convention came together, the elders took hold of the situation. . . .

The elders, partly to let Lowden and his delegates save face, conducted one ballot, the fifth of the convention, in which Lowden took the lead, registering 303 to Wood's 299. That gave pleasure to Lowden and his delegates; it was to be a kind of consolation prize.

Then there were three ballots in which Wood and Lowden were exactly even or practically so: 311½ to 311½ in the sixth ballot; 312 for Wood to 311½ for Lowden in the seventh; and 299 for Wood to 307 for Lowden in the eighth. Those three ballots, with the two major candidates seesawing within a margin of eight delegates, was notice to both that neither could win. It left each, and the friends of each, with no grievance, nor any reason to sulk in the coming campaign against the Democrats.

By the ninth ballot all the amenities and anticipatory prudences had been taken care of. It was late Saturday afternoon, 46 minutes past 4; it was time to conclude. On this ballot Harding was given 374½ votes— his highest preceding had been 133½. That ballot was notice to all that Harding was the man; notice to all who desired to ride on the bandwagon that the wheels were about to roll. The delegates rushed for it. On the tenth ballot, Harding's total was 692⅕ and he was nominated.

It was late on a Saturday afternoon, 6:23 P.M. Harding, sought by every reporter at the convention, focus-point now of all the country's instrumentalities of light, the whole country awaiting what he should say— Harding, flustered, not at his best, not even at *his* modest best, but very accurate, put his comment in words that reflected his background and habit of mind: "We drew to a pair of deuces, and filled." He said it with more ruefulness than elation. . . .

THE CASE FOR THE SMOKE-FILLED ROOM*

James MacGregor Burns

The American suspicion of backroom politicking goes back a long way. Almost two centuries ago a young Bostonian named John Adams confided to his diary that he had just learned that some local politicians were holding secret meetings in Tom Dawes' garret.

"There they smoke tobacco till you cannot see from one end of the garret to the other," wrote the future President. "There they drink flip, I suppose, and there they choose a moderator, who puts questions to the vote regularly; and selectmen, assessors, collectors, wardens, fire wards, and representatives are regularly chosen before they are chosen by the town."

This was one of the first, but by no means the last, attack on the smoke-filled room and all it stands for. Years later, when Senator Warren G. Harding's manager made his famous prediction before the 1920 Republican convention that at the critical moment "some fifteen men, bleary-eyed with loss of sleep, and perspiring profusely with the excessive heat, will sit down in seclusion around a big table," the popular suspicion of conventions and smoke-filled rooms was once again vindicated. The decision reached at 2 A.M. in a suite in the Blackstone Hotel in Chicago to "put Harding over" has come to stand as the acme of boss control and popular betrayal.

Today, with the two great party conclaves only a few weeks off, the national party convention and its smoke-filled room are again under attack. The bosses will be in control, we are told. The people will be left out in the cold. While the rank-and-file delegates cheer themselves hoarse, wave banners, ride donkeys or elephants into hotel lobbies, and indulge in childish horse-play, a small group of wire-pullers will put their man across in a series of unprincipled deals. The party platforms will be a meaningless hodgepodge.

A dissenting opinion is in order. The national party conventions are, I believe, a vital part of the American political system. Smoke-filled rooms are indispensable to their successful operation. The convention must be improved, not weakened. We must make more use of it, not less.

The main argument for the convention is simple. It works. During the

---

* From *The New York Times Magazine* (June 15, 1952), 9+. Reprinted by permission.

last century it has brought before the country men of the caliber of Lincoln, Cleveland, McKinley, Bryan, Wilson, Hughes, Smith, Willkie, both Roosevelts and others. The critics of the convention argue that such men were nominated despite the system rather than because of it. Is this really so?

Take the case of Lincoln's election in 1860. That year, when the Republican convention opened in the Wigwam in Chicago, Senator William H. Seward, a distinguished New Yorker, looked like the most promising candidate. He was strong in much of the East and North; he had vigorously opposed the extension of slavery. But his long record had vulnerable points and he had little appeal for states like Illinois and Indiana that might be crucial for Republican victory in the fall.

Lincoln's men worked feverishly. They had the active support of the candidate himself, who had been soliciting votes from the state delegations and who had paid the railroad fare of at least one delegate out of his own pocket. One of Lincoln's supporters worked on Indiana. "By the Lord," he said, "we promised them everything they asked." Pennsylvania delegates were won over with the promise of a Cabinet post for their favorite son, Simon Cameron. (Lincoln later honored this promise.)

The candidate wired, "I authorize no bargains and will be bound by none." But the convention manager said, "Lincoln ain't here, and don't know what we have to meet, so we will go ahead as if we hadn't heard from him, and he must ratify it." They organized a filibuster to prevent Seward's men from speaking. Using tickets with forged signatures, they jammed the Wigwam with thousands of Honest Abe's supporters, who set up a clamor on Lincoln's nomination that sounded like, "all the hogs ever slaughtered in Cincinnati giving their death squalls together." At the crucial moment, the managers swung over Ohio delegates with a promise to their leader of "anything he wants." Far behind on the first ballot, Lincoln won on the fourth.

Sordid politics? Perhaps. Yet out of this political rough-and-tumble emerged one of the two or three greatest American leaders. Out of it came a candidate who vindicated his party's choice in the fall election by making a clean sweep of the free states. Such strong political backing was indispensable to the new Administration facing bitter civil strife.

Time and time again conventions have helped produce a man to meet the needs of the hour. Another case in point was the Democratic convention in 1932 in Chicago. The fight for the nomination was intense, for the Democrats scented victory in the fall. In the first roll-call Franklin D. Roosevelt had a commanding lead of 666¼ votes—more than a majority but not enough to win (in 1932 the Democrats still had the two-thirds rule). In the next balloting he won only eleven more votes, and in the third only five more. The Roosevelt machine seemed to be grinding to a halt. But if it did, who would be nominated? The convention might become hopelessly deadlocked in a fight among Alfred E. Smith, Newton D. Baker, John N. Garner and a host of other candidates.

At this point James A. Farley, Roosevelt's campaign manager, hastily arranged a meeting with Representative Sam Rayburn of Texas in a hotel room. The parley was brief and to the point. Farley needed the bloc of delegates controlled by Speaker Garner of Texas. In exchange he offered the Vice Presidency to Garner. Rayburn telephoned the Speaker, who authorized the release of his delegates. On the next ballot Roosevelt went over, and the next day Garner was nominated as Vice President. If Illinois had been willing to shift to Roosevelt on an earlier ballot, Farley said later, the Vice Presidency would have gone to that state. . . .

Conventions usually come up with the men the people want. Those who use the nomination of Harding as an argument against the conventions and smoke-filled rooms should remember that he won almost twice as many votes as his Democratic opponent in the fall election.

The cases of Lincoln and Roosevelt not only tell us something about convention mechanics. They also illustrate the genius of the convention for sifting through the candidates, casting aside extremists and narrowing down the choice to a man acceptable to the major elements of the party. Such a man can expect united support in the main battle against the opposing party. More important, no one has a better chance than he of enjoying firm party backing on entering the White House. Given our divided form of government, this is no mean virtue of the convention system.

Those who look aghast at convention horse-trades and hijinks often forget that compromise is the very essence of democratic politics. Some of the deals may not be pretty ones, but in any case bargaining and even manipulation are inevitable. The convention is simply the arena where the final negotiations take place, subject to a number of ground rules. The proceedings are not exclusive. Any delegate can take part in the bargaining in one way or another—and many of them do. At the same times that the Lincoln and Roosevelt managers were winning delegates from enemy camps, their own delegations were in a state of siege as a result of maneuvers by their rivals.

The smoke-filled room is essential to the convention, for it serves as the mechanism that allows party leaders to shift their choices toward a compromise candidate. Without such a mechanism there would be eternal deadlock. The Democratic convention of 1924, which went through 103 harrowing roll-calls before settling on a candidate, might have done its job better with more smoke-filled rooms, not fewer.

Is there any way to achieve party compromise and unity without all this bargaining and maneuvering? The only real alternative to the convention system is a nation-wide direct presidential primary system. President Woodrow Wilson in 1913 advocated legislation providing for primary elections throughout the country "at which the voters of the several parties may choose their nominees for the Presidency without the intervention of nomination conventions." Similar proposals have been made more recently.

The difficulties with such a plan are twofold. It would not guarantee an end to "boss control"; experience with primaries has proved that party organizations often can dominate primary elections as easily as they dominate conventions. More important, primary elections on a national scale could disrupt party solidarity and effectiveness. They might allow organized groups to move in and take over control of party selections. Candidates of such groups are often poorly equipped to lead a united party in the general election or to command firm party backing in office.

The point is that we need consensus *within* the party so that all major elements—geographical, economic, ideological—can take part in choosing party leaders and shaping party goals. We need division *between* the major parties so that the people will have a meaningful choice at the polls. The primary system often gives us the reverse. It disrupts party consensus by foisting on the party candidates who may be alien to party traditions and principles. It may produce candidates in the fall elections who are either so close to each other in viewpoint that the voters see little choice between them, or so far apart that the voters look in desperation for some middle ground.

Primaries, moreover, cannot perform an important job that the convention can—the adoption of a party platform. It is fashionable to deride the platform as a useless collection of platitudes, resembling a train platform in that it is "something to get in on, and not to stand on." If this were the case, hard-headed politicians would not sweat over the planks as hard as they do. Actually the platforms are important because they tell, in Herbert Agar's words, "not what a party will do, but who is pushing and pulling for what, and with how much success."

Does all this mean that we should give the convention a clean bill of health? Not at all. Political scientists and practical politicians alike have urged the following improvements:

(1) Make the conventions more representative. Too many delegates are allowed from states where the parties have little strength. Both parties give a "bonus" to areas where they are strong but apportionment of delegates still is far from perfect.

(2) Make the conventions smaller. Around 3,000 delegates and alternate delegates will crowd into each of the major conventions next month. One-third of this number would allow for more orderly and coherent deliberation. Party conventions should never become small, however, because one of their chief functions is to whip up enthusiasm that will send the party workers home eager for the battle to come.

(3) Make more use of the convention. The greatest weakness of the convention is that it meets only once every four years. This seems a bit ridiculous when one considers that small business, labor and professional organizations assemble at least annually. The convention should meet every year in order to invigorate the party organization and to bring the platform up to date. The minority party should use the occasion to nominate a leader to organize opposition to the party in power. Nothing would improve our convention system more than fuller use of it.

So much for needed reforms in the convention itself. At least as desirable are changes in the methods of selecting delegates to conventions. This phase of the convention system has aroused the most criticism. The indictment is two-fold: first, that methods of choosing delegates are baffling to the voters and discourage them from taking part; second, that the bosses actually choose and control delegates and the people are left out.

The first charge is true. The average voter in a presidential primary finds a ballot covered with names of people he does not know and whose positions on either candidates or principles are not clear. Delegates to be elected are in all stages of commitment to some candidate, of semi-commitment, or of no commitment at all. . . . The whole system of electing delegates needs to be enormously simplified. Moreover, eligibility requirements for voters should be clarified to prevent fracases and misunderstandings such as the recent ones between Taft and Eisenhower supporters in the South.

The second charge bears close examination. Certainly one can find a good deal of "boss control" in the selection of delegates, but as in most of our political processes, there is a good deal of both democracy and oligarchy in the system and it is hard to tell where one ends and the other begins. . . .

The national party convention in its present form is well over a century old. A peculiarly American institution, it has had many triumphs and a few failures. Like most of the devices of democracy, the system works about as well as the people make it work.

CHAPTER SIX

The Process of Persuasion

Is a presidential campaign really a national soap opera, or is it a national effort to educate and inform the public about the political issues confronting the nation? Has Madison Avenue invaded political parties to the degree that the process of persuasion is simply the systematic manipulation of the mass mind? Has television basically altered the nature of campaigns, or are they today essentially the same as in 1860?

If we could turn the clock back to Lincoln's first presidential campaign, the four-party race of 1860, we would watch a number of campaign tactics that are still in use today. The nation was bitterly divided over the slavery issue, the aftermath of which is still an issue in 1964. The recently born Republican Party smelled victory in the winds. Out of caution, their nominee assumed a lofty, noncommittal pose. An "old campaigner," William Cullen Bryant, advised Lincoln to make no speeches, write no letters as a candidate, and enter into no pledges. Why alienate large groups of voters already committed to Lincoln, for the sake of a few uncommitted voters? Lincoln stayed in Springfield during the entire campaign and never made a single campaign speech.

Thus, Lincoln's strategy in 1860 was what V. O. Key's article describes as the "front-porch" campaign: he waited in Springfield for the press and the party workers to visit him—and they did. The campaign had wide press coverage, and Lincoln's party had most of the Northern press "sewed up"—a press which at least on the editorial page is still largely committed to the same party one hundred years later.

But Lincoln's principal opponent, Senator Stephen A. Douglas, could not afford to conduct a "front-porch" campaign. The "Little Giant" had to carry his cause to the people. Undaunted by imminent defeat, Douglas conducted a "whistle-stop" campaign. Harry Truman, laboring under similar odds, achieved different results when in 1948 he decided to "give 'em hell" via a whistle-stop campaign.

Although the 1860 campaign was sobered somewhat by the threat of secession, still it had its ballyhoo and color. Republican speakers made an estimated 50,000 speeches, and the people flocked to political rallies all over the nation. There are few torchlight parades today, yet there is still a lot of martial music, political rallies, and stomping of feet. Another Senator from Illinois, Paul Douglas, one hundred years later, has said that there is nothing to replace this old strategy of meeting the voters face to face.

What has changed since 1860? Adlai E. Stevenson, an experienced campaigner, observes that modern political campaigns are placing incredibly heavy demands on a candidate; that showmanship is replacing ideas. In other words, Mr. Stevenson senses that a premium is being placed on huckstering rather than on political statesmanship. In early 1960, he called for a national debate by the two major candidates, an event which came in the Kennedy-Nixon television debates during the fall campaign. Evaluating these debates, Stanley Kelley, Jr. feels that a step in the right direction has been made. It is his position that campaigns have shifted from the politics of personal favors, which characterized the machine-boss age, to the politics of personalities and issues. Nonetheless, the discussion of campaign issues has been filled with ambiguities and distortions—largely because TV has not been exploited as an instructive political media.

Although there is little question that TV presents new opportunities in political education, TV also illustrates one of the major problems which the national parties face—the high cost of a nation-wide presidential campaign. As the President's Commission on Campaign Costs reported in 1962, the parties are faced with rising costs, the small number of financial donors, and the consequent fear that a major democratic process is critically dependent on a few influential contributors.

The huckstering Madison Avenue influence in presidential campaigns has disturbed students of democratic politics for the past ten years. There was even a fear at one time that professional public-relations men were not only invading the inner councils of the major parties, but more importantly, that the PR men were about to dominate the campaigns and the candidates. Nonetheless, Anthony Howard, looking back at the 1960 election, infers that the PR men failed to prove their value, and he ventures to predict that the "proud persuaders" of Madison Avenue will never again occupy decisive power positions in the inner councils of the major parties.

Even if the Madison-Avenue PR men have been relegated to technical advisory positions, there is still an unanswered question. Just how phony is a campaign? Is it all sound and fury, or does it have some educational effects on the electorate? In order to answer this, we would have to know more than we presently do about what goes on in the mind of the voter during the campaign. An even more crucial issue is how we can at least maintain the present campaign standards, if not improve them, in the face of the growing complexity of political issues in an age of cold wars, nuclear defense, the Negro revolt, and the perennial problems of budgets, welfare legislation, and economic growth.

CAMPAIGN TECHNIQUES*

V. O. Key, Jr.

Art and Artifice in Campaigning

. . . One may speak of grand campaign strategy, rationally formulated and executed with precision, but a great deal of campaign management rests on the hunches that guide day to day decisions. The lore of politics includes rules of thumb that are supposed to embody the wisdom of political experience as guides to action. Whether the maxims of the practicing politician have any validity, they do have an interest as an element of the art of politics, an interest frequently capitalized upon by the writers for the Sunday supplements.

Front porch, swing around the circle, or whistle stop. An old problem of campaign tactics is the question of the extent of the speaking and traveling schedule of the head of the ticket. Should the candidate make an extensive swing around the country and speak at as many places as practicable or should he make a "front-porch" campaign? The decision on this question may depend on the qualities of the candidate. In 1920 the Republican strategy was to keep Harding at home in Marion, Ohio. "Keep Warren at home," the Republican leader Penrose is reported to have said. "Don't let him make any speeches. If he goes out on a tour, somebody's sure to ask him questions, and Warren's just the sort of damn fool that'll try to answer them." "The Front Porch campaign," according to Samuel Hopkins Adams, "was determined upon. The role assigned to the candidate was that of the modest, simple, sagacious, home-loving, home-staying statesman. He was to be 'just folks.' To the Mecca of Marion would come the devout, and the Prophet would edify them with the sound doctrine of orthodox Republicanism.". . .

---

* From *Politics, Parties, and Pressure Groups,* Fourth Edition, by V. O. Key, Jr. New York: Thomas Y. Crowell Company, 1958. Pp. 512–530. Reprinted by permission. Mr. Key is Professor of Government at Harvard University.

Television has made the vine-clad front porch obsolete. The choice becomes one of whether the candidate is to travel about the country and mingle with the multitude or stay at home near a television camera. In 1956 Mr. Eisenhower's managers intimated in the early stages of the campaign that their candidate would limit himself to a few television speeches from Washington. An appearance or so by the General in a television studio quickly persuaded those concerned that the General's talents could be better employed on the stump.

Picturing the candidate to the public. Given the bearing of the personal qualities of the candidate on electoral decision, the outcome of an election may be determined by the image of the candidate implanted in the minds of the voters. The nature of the image to be propagated depends on the strategy and circumstances of the campaign. Within limits, skillful propagandists can convert a candidate into a mythical character possessing in distilled form the qualities thought to be advantageous for the campaign. Television, instead of obstructing this process by making the candidate's qualities perceptible to all, may aid in the transformation —so long as the candidate can find his way through the speeches that have been ghosted for him. . . .

The fictional picture of the candidate expedient and profitable to propagate varies with circumstances and, to some extent, with the talents of the candidates. In 1932, for example, Franklin Roosevelt thought it desirable to "dramatize himself as a breaker of custom, a daring, resolute champion of action, establishing a bold contrast with the country's picture of Hoover as timid, hesitant, irresolute.". . . In 1952 Eisenhower's managers sought to merchandise him as a man who embodied the homely virtues, a simple and sincere man of unmatched integrity, yet possessed of an experience and wisdom beyond compare that would enable him "to go to Korea" and bring peace, order, and security to a troubled world. . . .

The lofty, nonpartisan pose. If a presidential candidate has attained great popularity, it may be possible for him to assume a position above the battle. His lofty eminence makes attack difficult; it may create an impression of assurance of victory, of a great figure who rises above his petty associates, of a man above politics, of a giant beyond reach of quixotic sallies by the pygmies of the opposition. Perhaps the popular expectation that Presidents should be something more than partisans contributes to the beatification of presidential candidates, but some of them succeed in becoming more saintly than do others. Franklin D. Roosevelt demonstrated some skill in this respect, as various candidates who challenged him learned to their dismay, but Eisenhower undoubtedly demonstrated greater genius in disentangling himself from the ruck and the muck of the political battle. He managed to disengage himself so completely from politics, even from his own Administration, that he provided a target beyond range. From this point he could in the campaign of 1956 look down on the "locust-swarm of partisan orators" in the Democratic ranks, he could belittle the moans of a "few politicians," he could dismiss criticisms of his farm policy as "drivel" concocted by "partisan orators" and "anguished politicans." This disengagement from politics also permitted him to disassociate himself from the dubious tactics of his allies. . . .

The silent treatment. Some campaigners are so circumstanced that they may be correct in regarding it as sound policy never to mention the name of the opposing candidate. He may be referred to as our opponent, as the gentleman from New York, or he may be completely ignored. Roosevelt explained this policy on the theory that many people could not remember names. They voted for names they knew. To name the opponent was to advertise his name and to impress it on the public mind. Roosevelt knew that there would be no lack of mention of his own name by his enemies. . . .

Defensive strategy: Reply or ignore? As a presidential campaign moves along the question recurs of what to do about the opposition's attacks. Should a candidate answer them or should he ignore them? "There's an old bromide in politics that goes something like this: 'If your opponent calls you a liar, do not deny it—just call him a thief.' ". . .

The basic difficulty in answering attacks is that the enemy chooses the terrain of battle, which is favorable to his cause. For that reason it may be preferable to ignore an attack altogether. Or an unwise attack by an irresponsible member of the opposition may be chosen for reply, a tactic that shifts the initiative to the defense. . . .

Campaigners, as they avoid or parry charges, naturally place emphasis on what they regard as their strong points; likewise they say little about the weaker elements in their record or program. The opposition follows a like policy of speaking endlessly of the popular features of what it has to offer and of minimizing mention of the less attractive aspects. In consequence the issues seem never to be joined in the campaign oratory. . . .

Driving a wedge between the opposing candidate and his followers. An old campaigning maxim is that "a candidate should always separate his opponent from the rank and file of the party." Willkie in 1940 strove to draw a line between Roosevelt and the Democrats. The "New Dealers" (not the Democratic Administration) had, he argued, departed from the precepts of Democratic heroes and saints. "So if there is any Democratic disciple of Thomas Jefferson in Dubuque he ought to vote for me. Surely any Andrew Jackson Democrat should vote for me and not for my opponent. . . . No Cleveland Democrat should vote against me." He talked to the Democrats as if they had been betrayed by Roosevelt and the "New Dealers.". . .

The art of the smear. Although presidential campaigns may be cleaner than they were a century ago, fine specimens of the smear turn up now and then. A smear is a charge regarded as not quite cricket. Most smears are lies, nothing more, nothing less, but they also include lines of attack that attribute unpatriotic or selfish motives to the opposition or that raise questions no honorable man would raise. A simple falsehood must, of course, be presented in a manner to appear to be the truth. Thus, in 1932 a photograph of a sign before a "Hoover Ranch" reading "No White Men Wanted" was widely circulated; the enterprising photographers had hung a placard prepared for the occasion alongside a sign in front of a California ranch named for Mr. Hoover by one of his admirers. . . .

Obviously the head of a ticket cannot be associated with the dissemination of the more obvious sorts of smears. At times lesser leaders may make a public smear but the more personal smears travel by word of mouth; sometimes the movement of stories is deliberately expedited; sometimes they originate spontaneously and travel under their own power. The ancestry of a candidate, his extramarital exploits, his meanness, his disposition to rob his fellow man, his association with doubtful characters, his wife's alcoholism, the peccadillos of his children, and a variety of other matters are dealt with in yarns that find their way across the country during a campaign. . . .

Communications Media

The appeals determined upon by the campaign strategists must be gotten to the voters. The candidate in a small rural county may have a word with and shake the hand of every voter in the jurisdiction before election day. The conditions of national politics differ radically from the suppositions of democratic theorists who see the entire citizenry assembled under a spreading chestnut tree to settle the affairs of state. A presidential candidate, save through the shadows of television, can show himself to only a few voters. Nor can he, given the looseness of national party organization, depend exclusively upon party workers over the nation to carry his message to the people. He must utilize the media of communication—press, radio, television—to project his image and to transmit his appeals to the people. . . .

The press: Reporter and partisan. American political parties have fewer and fewer newspapers openly allied with them as partisan journals. The decline of the partisan press, often supported by public advertising or other patronage, has affected the Democratic party far more than it has the Republican party. The independent or nonparty press tends by and large to be Republican in sympathy. Yet the managers of both parties must deal with a press that professes to function as a more or less neutral conduit through which news of events flows. Campaigners must contrive ways and means to inject their propaganda into the channels of the press.

The candidate cannot afford to be ignored by the press; his entourage, as well as the national headquarters, includes men whose job it is to facilitate the work of the newspapermen and to feed materials to the press. The politician believes that unfavorable treatment by the press is better than no coverage. Frank R. Kent put the maxim: "It is better to be roasted than ignored." The late Claude A. Swanson phrased it: "When they stop writing about you in politics, you are dead." Candidates strive to keep in the headlines; every day there must be a story for the press. When the presidential candidate goes on tour, provision is made for correspondents to accompany him; they are furnished advance copies of speeches and facilities to aid them in covering the campaign. . . .

What of the influence of newspapers? Do people vote as their favorite editors recommend? Do slanted news columns win votes? Do the great publishers swing elections? The evidence on such matters is extremely limited, although it is evident that newspaper influence differs enormously from situation to situation. Roosevelt won four presidential elections over the opposition of most of the press; Truman enjoyed no widespread newspaper support. Eisenhower, on the other hand, had the support of the bulk of the daily press. With newspaper support Roosevelt might have won by wider margins; without newspaper support Eisenhower might have won by narrower margins. The chances are that newspapers exert greater influence in state and local matters than in presidential campaigns. Voters in jurisdictions that elect obscure candidates to fill inconspicuous positions may rely to a greater extent on the press for guidance. In party primaries the press may, other things being equal, exert more influence than in general elections, but in some jurisdictions newspaper opposition is said to be a positive advantage. In turn, newspapers themselves may to some degree be under the same sorts of influences as is the electorate; some newspapers do cross party lines from time to time.

The effect of the press is not to be measured solely by its impact on the fortunes of the candidates during the course of a campaign. By steadily hammering their policy predilections, campaign or no campaign, newspapers over the long pull affect the attitudes of their readers, an influence that may be reflected in the voting when an election rolls around. The cumulative educational effect of the press in individual communities may become both pervasive and durable. . . .

Party literature. . . . Of the millions of pieces of literature printed in each campaign—some estimates run into the hundreds of millions— a great deal probably never reaches the voters. Its distribution is both a wearisome and costly task. If it is mailed, a large outlay for postage and clerical labor is required. If it is entrusted to party workers for distribution, it may not be distributed, for the party organization is seldom as efficient as it is reputed to be. Shipments of literature in bulk to state committees often stop at state headquarters. Louis Howe, secretary to Franklin Roosevelt, found that only about 3 to 5 per cent of the literature distributed to state committees by national headquarters ever reached the voters. . . .

Radio and television. Television and radio have reduced the press to a secondary role in the calculations of the managers of presidential campaigns. These new communications media give the candidate direct access to the people of the nation. He can speak to the voters with no fear that his remarks will be misrepresented by the headline writers or buried on the back pages. If he is a skilled TV performer and the party war chest allows, he can use TV and radio to counterbalance newspaper opposition. Moreover, radio and TV are, in their capacity as reporters of the news, under more of a compulsion than the press to give an even-handed account of events. . . .

Obviously the new media require at campaign headquarters technical specialists in addition to speech writers. They pose new problems of tactics as well as new opportunities to reach the people. In 1952, for example, the Democrats made extensive use of television beginning early in the campaign in order to overcome the handicap from the fact that Stevenson was comparatively unknown. Eisenhower, on the other hand, had not yet developed a TV technique and the calculation was that barnstorming would be advantageous to enable as many voters as possible to see the General's folksy manner at first hand. Beyond such questions that grow out of the circumstances of specific campaigns are numerous problems of technique in the use of TV and radio, such as the timing of presentations, the relative emphasis on spot announcements and set speeches, and the minimization of interference with popular programs of entertainment.

Although television even by 1956 had had a powerful impact on campaigning for the Presidency, its full effects have probably not been felt. They certainly have not been systematically identified. One consequence that seems indisputable is that individuals can by dramatic television performances attain a national recognition and attract a national following much more rapidly than by reliance on older communciations media. . . . Whether television facilitates the manipulation of the electorate by campaigners remains open to doubt, although its existence compels campaigners to adapt their styles to it. Nor has television supplanted other media as a source of information. The evidence indicates that reliance on television as a source of information about campaigns declines with increase in educational level.

Political rallies: The personal touch. The radio and TV are no substitute for the old-fashioned political rally where the candidate can be seen and heard; the tactical problem in campaigning has been to contrive ways and means of combining the personal touch of the rally with the marvels of electronic communication. The psychological evidence indicates that individuals in crowds are rendered suggestible. The applause picks up the doubters in the audience and carries them along. Listeners to a radio speech lack the emotional stimulus of the crowd; one or a handful of persons may be listening. Television adds the bearing, the gestures, the smiles of the speaker to the voice of radio, but the "personality" of the candidate may not make its way to the image on the television screen. . . .

CHOICE BY HULLABALOO*

Adlai E. Stevenson

It seems to me that we ought to revise the hit-or-miss system by which every four years we select a man to lead us. With the primary season . . . beginning, and the New Hampshire election almost at hand, maybe this is a good time to review the process. . . .

I yield to no man in my affection for the lovely state of New Hampshire; but does it make sense that, solely because New Hampshire votes early, the opinion of a few thousand of its inhabitants should wield great influence in deciding who shall preside over 180 million of us? And in a state primary seldom more than 25 per cent of the eligible voters participate anyway.

A primary campaign is a state campaign, in many respects not unlike a campaign for state office—Governor, Attorney General, Auditor. A candidate makes his speeches to meetings of party workers or to groups of citizens gathered in halls, hotels and picnic grounds. Such groups often don't want to hear much about complex national issues; they are more concerned with local party affairs and with meeting "the candidate." . . .

Actually primaries are more likely to destroy good candidates than to make them. The plain truth is that a primary campaign is not a suitable testing ground for Presidential candidates.

Now as to the general election campaign, it presents one overwhelming problem: how to communicate ideas on complex issues to an audience of

---

* Reprinted from THIS WEEK *Magazine*. Copyright © 1960 by the United Newspapers Magazine Corp. Reprinted by permission of Harold Ober Associates, Incorporated. Mr. Stevenson is the United States Ambassador to the United Nations.

180 million. In a simpler society, a political candidate could stand in the forum in Athens and carry his message to the voters by merely speaking in a loud voice. But not in America.

Traditionally we have attempted to reach American voters through a hodgepodge of rallies of party workers, huge public meetings, radio talks and whistle stops, all reported nationally in the press.

The whistle stop is a venerable political institution and I daresay that in the days when the railroad tracks ran right down Main Street it was an eminently useful one. But at that time we were only a few million, not 180. Today it is utterly impossible for a candidate to reach more than a handful of the populace in this manner.

Moreover, whistle stopping has an inherent weakness. Woodrow Wilson put his finger on it when, at Michigan City in the 1912 campaign, he told a crowd of six hundred what he did not like about speaking from a rear platform: "I have tried discussing the big questions of this campaign from the rear end of a train. It can't be done. They are too big, that is the long and short of the matter. By the time you get started and begin to explain yourself the train moves off. I would a great deal rather make your acquaintance than leave a compound fracture of an idea behind me."

In recent years candidates have attempted a variation on the whistle stop, the prop stop—a brief airborne stopover during which the candidate speaks from a platform beside his airplane while an uneasy audience stands blinking in the sun or shivering in the wind.

My own experience at prop-stopping has been almost wholly unhappy. The sounds the candidate makes compete with the sounds of aircraft (which may be merciful to all!). And an airport is remote from the city's center: to go out to it to hear, or try to hear, a political speech is almost unthinkable to anybody but a loyal party worker, who is already convinced.

A City May be Insulted

Finally, a city may be insulted by a candidate who deigns only to descend briefly on its airport. Airports and planes for some reason have not managed to arouse people's affection as did the iron horse. I have a feeling that the whistle stop is dead and the prop stop will never get off the ground.

Rallies of party workers are useful. The candidate may inspire his workers. He gives them arguments they can use in discussing issues with voters. He binds them tighter to their party. But I sometimes think candidates spend too much time addressing their workers and not enough trying to reach the public at large.

And I have never been convinced that such party rallies should be televised. A successful rally must be a noisy emotional experience of the convinced, and an independent voter sitting in his living room, not converted to the candidate's faith but willing to listen to his arguments, must be repelled or at best only amused by the spectacle of eager partisans laughing uproariously at the candidate's every feeble witticism and roaring with glee at each intemperate assault on the opposition—and the more extravagant his language the better. A good political rally is no place for a sober, sensible discussion of intricate problems and policies.

As for large public meetings, they, too, are useful and a candidate, by incessant effort, can reach a good many thousand this way—provided the people come!

Whether they come depends on the strength of his local political organization and to a far greater extent on whether the local press and radio arouse interest in advance to get out a crowd.

Those, then, are the traditional methods of reaching the voters face to face. And by using them, even if campaigns lasted much longer than two months, a candidate could reach but a tiny fraction of the 180 million Americans.

Now, of course, all these meetings are reported nationally in the press. But that way the candidate's views reach the voters second hand, and I am talking about reaching them directly.

Moreover, to depend upon the press to report the speeches of the rival candidates with equal fullness and fairness, one must assume that newspapers are generally neutral and have plenty of space for politics. The press in the United States has always had the right to free expression of opinion.

How to Reach the Public?

But a newspaper's editorial slant often affects the way it displays and balances the news. It is my experience that the press as a whole reflects a greater warmth for a Republican candidate than for a Democratic one—with, of course, notable exceptions.

It has been proposed that to reach more voters directly the candidate, instead of trying to leap rapidly from one city to another, visit regional centers around the country for a series of speeches and meetings with people who come in from the surrounding territory.

We attempted something on this order—a quick trip around the country —as a preliminary to the 1956 campaign. As a preliminary it was fine—it enabled us to address most of the party leaders in a series of strategic areas and to meet a good many of them. But I doubt if it would work well during the campaign itself.

A hundred years ago people would travel long distances to hear a candidate for President, but nowadays who would journey to any distant city to hear a candidate except a party worker? Regional meetings would ease the strain of travel on the candidate but I doubt if they would solve the problem of how he is to communicate directly with the people.

Stevenson Tried a New Approach

I tried another device in 1956: That of issuing a series of printed program papers setting forth in detail my views on various issues and proposals for dealing with them. They were detailed documents and they set forth programs for legislative and executive action in specific terms, not in the platitudes and generalities that make up most campaign oratory; and had I been elected I would have put them into effect.

I thought these documents useful and I wish all candidates would issue similar ones—no one would ever again need vote for a man without knowing exactly what to expect of him. But I am realist enough to know that the number of Americans who would read these documents was small. As a method of reaching the vast American public, they were a predestined failure. And as a stimulant for meaningful, thoughtful discussion they were a failure too, for the Republican candidates ignored them and so did most of the press.

What then do we do? If candidates can't communicate by party rallies, large public meetings, whistle stops, regional meetings and program papers, where shall they turn?

They have already turned—to television.

National political television came of age during the nominating conventions of 1952. It played an important role that year during the campaign and an even more important one in 1956. Soon it may be decisive. For by no other means can a candidate hope to communicate with so many voters *directly*.

So I suggest we give some thought to the way political television has been used in the past and to whether in the future it is likely to do what it ought to do in a democratic system: enlighten the electorate on the issues and on the candidates' views of those issues.

And about this I have many misgivings.

Television is fantastically expensive. In a dark hour of the 1956 campaign, my manager Jim Finnegan muttered with fine irony: "If somebody doesn't come up with $70,000 in the next hour and a half, 'that eloquent voice of the western world' ain't gonna be on TV tonight."

Each half hour my voice burdened the networks cost my party $70,000— which may explain why my speeches so often ran overtime. I was trying to crowd as many ideas as possible into the half hour.

Should Money Decide a Campaign?

In 1956 the Republicans spent $4,036,935 on radio and TV and the Democrats $2,971,143, a total of $7,008,078. No doubt they will spend more this coming year.

But this raises a serious problem, for it gives the best financed party a tremendous advantage. Should money decide who can carry his case to the people?

Again fifty years ago audiences listened for hours while Bryan or La Follette held forth on such abstruse questions as monopoly and the tariff; but radio shortened the time of a political speech to half an hour. And in 1956 I was told that no television speech should be longer than 15 minutes, that five minutes was better and that a one-minute "ID"—a spot commercial—was best of all.

So here is another serious question: How can a candidate possibly deal honestly in one, or five, or 15 minutes with any complex question—with inflation or disarmament, for example? Plainly, he cannot. He is reduced to sloganeering, to huckstering, to oversimplifying.

If he has ideas on a complex subject, he is not permitted to set them forth. Instead he must reduce them to a slogan. Slogans may be all very well to sell soap. But in politics they are dangerous. To reduce a foreign policy decision to a phrase is to give no hint of the perils, alternatives, and secondary issues that lie behind it. The slogan "Liberation" for the satellites may have been a good vote catcher for the Republican candidates, but the tragic fate of the Hungarian rebellion demonstrated its fraudulence as a policy.

Dancing Girls or Ideas?

Again, from the earliest times politicians have sought to please, to entertain; but television encourages this weakness. We are already familiar with rigged campaign performances on TV, with candidates that don't simply appear on TV but are "produced." Television watchers expect to be entertained. Dare politicians disappoint them? Will showmanship be substituted more and more for discussion, dancing girls for ideas?

And may not all this lead to even greater apathy on the part of the voters? Everyone decries apathy and agrees it can, if extended indefinitely, lead only to the death of democracy. I should think that the television of the future, if it follows the pattern of the past, can only increase voter apathy. People will "consume" political broadcasts as they "consume" TV comedies, Westerns and spectaculars. They will sit back in their chairs and enjoy themselves—or they will switch to something else. Their attitude will be, let the performers perform.

This is apathy. TV requires no effort on the part of the viewer. Fifty years ago, men were not apathetic toward politics, for citizenship was highly prized and made demands on them. They had to travel long distances by wagon and stand in the hot sun for hours to hear or see Bryan, La Follette, McKinley, or Theodore Roosevelt.

Politics Should be Serious

Not today; a man need not even leave his living room to be entertained by Mr. X—candidate for President of the United States, the most powerful office on earth. Politics may have been "entertainment" in the old days, too, for there weren't very many other distractions. But in those days people took their politics seriously and were willing to work for their entertainment.

Today we have to find some means of making politics "serious" again— of making the business of presenting issues to the voters so interesting and so compelling that the voters will want to listen.

That's our problem.

ELECTIONS AND THE MASS MEDIA*

Stanley Kelley, Jr.

What influence have the media on voters? . . . Early researchers expected to find the mass media a direct and potent force in shaping and changing voting behavior. Their expectations were not borne out. How a person votes and whether he votes seems most closely related to his party affiliation, his perceptions of the interests of the groups with which he identifies himself, his opinions about several long-standing issues of public policy, his perceptions of the personal qualities of candidates, and his view of party performance in the management of governmental affairs. These affiliations, opinions, perceptions, and views are relatively stable. They are not easily altered by current communications of any kind and so perforce not by communications conveyed to the voter by the mass

* Reprinted from a symposium, The Electoral Process, Part I, Vol. 27, No. 2 (Spring 1962) by permission from Law and Contemporary Problems, published by the Duke University School of Law, Durham, North Carolina. Copyright, ©, 1962, by Duke University. Mr. Kelley is Associate Professor of Politics at Princeton University.

media. Campaign communication is, in fact, more likely to reinforce than to alter them. . . .

At this juncture, however, one point ought to be made clear. To say that campaign discussion in the media does not change voter behavior radically is not to say that it has no significant effect on voting. That it reinforces partisan allegiances is in itself a significant effect. That it induces marginal changes in opinions about parties, issues, and group interests is another. Finally, it is probable that the media exert a very considerable influence on the voter's perceptions of the personal qualities of candidates. . . .

The personal attributes of candidates as perceived by voters influence the voting decision independently of the other factors that help to determine it; a significant number of people, in fact, seem to bring no other criterion to bear in voting than their evaluation of "the man." The personal qualities of new candidates are, furthermore, new issues for a great many people. What newspapers and magazines say about a new candidate and the candidate's appearances on radio and television are likely, therefore, to be major factors in creating his public image—either to his damage or benefit.

In contests for nomination, the treatment the media give candidates may have even more important consequences than it does in general election campaigns. It may serve as an indication to the public of the candidacies that are to be taken seriously and those that are not. . . . What the media are contributing to is a definition of the alternatives in contests for the nomination; and, in "making decisions, recognition of the alteratives for choice is always a first and vital step."

Arousing interest in the electoral decision, and in discussion about it, is also a vital step in electoral decision-making. The mass media probably do as much as any institution to overcome voter apathy about campaign talk. To the extent that they succeed in doing so, they succeed because they dramatize elections, because they make them entertaining. This is conjecture, but highly plausible conjecture.

What difference does it make whether or not the voter's interest in elections is aroused? First, an interested voter, quite obviously, is likely to act differently from an uninterested one. He is more likely to expose himself to campaign discussion on his own initiative and more likely to participate politically in other ways as well. Second, both the outcome of particular elections and the functioning of the electoral system in the long run are in large part determined by the extent to which election contests arouse the interests of voters. Voter interest is an important factor in determining the scope of electoral conflict; and, as E. E. Schattschneider has observed, "the outcome of all conflict is determined by the scope of its contagion. The number of people involved in any conflict determines what happens; every change in the number of participants, every increase or reduction in the number of participants affects the result."

Arousing the voter's interest in elections in modern times has proved an exceedingly difficult task. If there is one thing known about the audience for campaign discussion in the mass media, it is that most of it is inconstant, inattentive, easily distracted. In campaign periods most voters expose themselves to the political output of the media to some extent. Few follow it closely. As newspaper readers, probably a majority of voters read little beyond the headlines. Most campaign speeches that are broadcast find a relatively small proportion of the potential electorate in their audiences. Many voters read about campaigns in magazines, but very few rate them as their most valuable source of information on campaigns. . . .

The media seek to capture the voter's attention for campaign discussion by appealing to his sense of civic duty. They also inculcate in him an essentially unrealistic notion of the efficacy of his vote and so, probably, succeed in getting more of his attention than they would otherwise. More important, however, they present election stories in a manner calculated to dramatize elections, emphasizing their elements of conflict, their uncertainties, the personal fortunes that ride on their outcomes. The language of campaign reporting—"infighting," "counter-attack," "the next move," "homestretch"—is the language of sports, games, and military action. Stories about the early lives of candidates, about how their wives feel about the coming decision at the polls, about the tensions and frustrations of campaigning—these are for the most part irrelevant to anything but the presentation of elections as drama. Reporters and broadcasters present campaigns in this way, undoubtedly, simply because they do not want to carry dull stories or broadcast dull programs. If one were to try deliberately to conceive of a strategy that would arouse the voter's interest in campaign discussion, however, it would be difficult to conceive of a strategy more effective than that which the media have unconsciously adopted. To dramatize politics is to make paying attention to campaign discussion its own reward.

The public reaction to the television debates in the 1960 presidential race suggests that the power of campaign discussion may not only depend in large measure on its value as entertainment, but may vary very radically when that value varies. Unlike most political shows, the debates were exceedingly well designed to exploit the drama inherent in a presidential election. They brought the two candidates face to face in an atmosphere of uncertainty, tension, and deadly seriousness. Whatever the outcome might mean for the voter, he could see and feel what it must mean for John F. Kennedy and Richard M. Nixon.

By any applicable standard each of the debates drew an enormous audience: bigger than that for the Sunday World Series game, bigger than that for the most popular regularly scheduled commercial show, bigger than that reached by either of the two national conventions in any given time period, far bigger than that attracted by any paid political telecast. They held their audiences more effectively than hour-long commercial entertainment shows and far more effectively than programs like *CBS Reports*. The average paid political broadcast in 1960 attracted seventy per cent of the audience normally attracted by the show it replaced. The debates, on the average, attracted 120 per cent of the audiences of the programs they replaced. . . .

The role of the mass media in the electoral process is not defined solely by the impact of media activities on the attitudes of voters. The media also do things both for and to politicians, and to modes of political action, organization, and discourse.

The modern candidate is acutely interested in gaining access to the media and in using that access effectively. He spends a large proportion of his campaign funds for the purchase of broadcast time. He adjusts the output of his statements to the rhythms of newspaper production. Even his whistle-stopping, and now his jet-stopping, is intended as much to capture the front pages of local newspapers as it is to expose the candidate to local crowds.

In view of what has been said about the relatively modest capabilities of campaign communication to change votes, all this concern with the media might seem misguided. Of course it is not. To win office in a competitive two-party system the campaigner normally must make marginal changes, but need not make more than marginal changes, in the political situation in which he finds himself. And that is what the realistic campaigner will try to do. He will try to increase the enthusiasm of his supporters in an effort to increase somewhat the numbers of them that go to the polls. He will try to give a somewhat wider currency to his name and project a more attractive image among independents, the undecided, and the uninterested. He will take stands on issues designed both to increase his appeal to the main body of his supporters and to "swing" groups in the population.

In realizing these objectives the sheer size of the audience he can reach is important to him, for the larger the audience he reaches, the more likely it is to include the most malleable elements of the population. Television and newspapers—the mass media *par excellence*—enable him to reach maximum audiences more cheaply than he could by any alternative means. In 1960 Vice President Nixon was seen in person by an estimated ten million people. In 1952 party workers solicited the votes of perhaps fifteen million people. Both these figures are less than the normal audience for one paid political telecast in a presidential campaign. Presumably candidates could reach as many voters by direct mail as they can *via* newspapers and television, but the cost per voter reached would be far higher. The communications that the campaigner aims at the general public through the mass media are important not only for their direct effects, but also because they reinforce and support other campaign activities. The candidate may reach an understanding with farm leaders or business leaders; what farm magazines or business magazines say about the candidate help to translate such understandings into votes. He may reach an agreement with the leader of an opposing faction within his party—as President Eisenhower did in his Morningside Heights meeting with the late Senator Robert A. Taft—and the media will carry news of the agreement to the party rank and file. He may use the mass media to facilitate the efforts of party workers to get voters registered and to the polls, just as the commercial advertiser facilitates over-the-counter sales of his product by advertising in the media. The very fact of his ability to mount a campaign of impressive proportions in the media may contribute greatly to maintaining the morale of his campaign workers.

These are some of the things the mass media can do *for* politicians. As has already been noted, however, they also do things *to* politicians and to politics. The nature of these influences can be made clearer if we contrast the properties of the media with the properties of the political communications systems that ante-dated their rise. Probably the most important of these was the political machine, and the contrast can be made the clearer because the rise of the mass media has been accompanied by the machine's gradual decay.

Both the machine and the mass media can enable the politician to establish a relationship with voters and to give a partisan direction to their opinions and actions. They perform these functions, however, in quite different ways. The machine's precinct workers sought direct, personal ties with the voter. They performed services and expected loyalty in return: Elections are won, Chicago's Jacob Arvey has observed, "by what you do all year round, by the day-to-day good will you generate in each precinct." However true this may once have been (and may still be in some localities), the media do not lend themselves to this kind of political action—one cannot fix parking tickets, keep a boy out of jail, or deliver food to the needy *via* newspapers and television. The mass media are useful to the politician as instruments of propaganda. The decline of the machine and the increasing dependence of politicians on the media, therefore, has meant a gradual shift in American political life from the politics of personal favors toward a politics of issues and images. . . .

New weapons systems bring new kinds of military specialists to the fore. The battleship admiral gives way to the carrier admiral, the airplane general to the missileman. New political communications systems act in a similar fashion. The rise of the mass media has altered the personnel of political organizations to include, and to give greater weight to the opinions of, those skilled in their use and in the politics of issues and images that their use entails. Among those with the required skills are the public relations man, the advertising man, the academic braintruster, the editor, and the publisher.

Editors and publishers are not newcomers to the inner councils of political organizations, although their presence there undoubtedly has a different significance now than it did when the political machine was at the height of its power. Nor do all editors and publishers become actively involved in their parties' affairs. Those who wish to become involved, however, have three strong claims to the practical politician's attention: Their knowledge of the media and their use, the power of their editorial columns, and their power to give a partisan bias to the news. Probably a relatively small proportion of the nation's publishers exercise this last power in any flagrant manner—at least so one would conclude from one of the best recent studies of press campaign coverage. But all bias need not be flagrant: Newspapers and news magazines can devote comparable space to what campaigners are saying while emphasizing or de-emphasizing themes in their propaganda. They can, by carefully chosen words, subtly suggest the heroes and villains of the events they are reporting. The best judgment would seem to be that if most of the press uses its power to bias with moderation, it nevertheless uses it; that if it is a limited power, it is nonetheless real.

In arguing that the modern campaigner plays a politics of issues and of personality appeals, we have not, of course, meant to imply that issues and personality appeals assumed importance in politics only with the rise of the mass media. The argument is rather that they are of greater importance now than they were previously. Does the modern politician also treat issues differently than his pre-mass media counterpart? The answer would seem to be: In some respects, yes; in some important respects, no.

The mass media form a network of communication that transmits messages almost instanteously to national audiences. The fact has at least two important consequences. First of all, it forces the politician to maintain consistency in his appeals; he cannot profitably pander to local prejudices by saying one thing in one place, another in another. Indeed, it has become a fashion for presidential candidates to make their first statements on civil rights questions in the South, to repeat them later (with suitable notice of their original source) to Negro audiences in the North. Second, the modern politician is compelled to give his campaign a pace, an appearance of movement. Before the rise of the mass media the campaign speaker could develop—just as the Chautauqua speaker developed—an act in which he could use repeatedly all his most successful rhetorical embellishments. The modern campaigner still uses a basic speech which he repeats with variations, but he must search day after day for new pegs to hang it on, if he is to furnish newsmen with new headlines and voters with new topics of conversation. . . .

As has already been noted, the formats that the media provide for political expression not only serve as its vehicles, but also discipline it. A campaigner must make a series of decisions as to the way he will handle issues. He must decide what issues to stress, which (if possible) to avoid; with what degree of specificity to state his positions; how much attention to give to his opponent; how to portray his opponent's record and positions on policy problems. The form in which he expects his communications to reach the public will be an important factor in determining the nature of these decisions.

Propaganda designed to capture the headlines or to reach the public through spot announcements, for instance, is normally characterized by gross distortions and a failure to define party differences. It is so characterized because the propagandist works on the assumption that communications distributed in this manner will reach many voters whose attention is so sporadically attracted to campaign discussion that they are unlikely to hear the answers of one side to the assertions of the other. It is good strategy, therefore, for propagandists on both sides to present their opponent's position in as poor a light as possible and to ignore attacks on their own weaknesses. With a debate, however, good propaganda strategy becomes quite a different thing. Both sides have equal and simultaneous access to the same audience, an audience that includes the partisans of both and of neither. In this situation to distort the position of one's opponent is to invite a quick and authoritative reply. To fail to answer challenges is to invite a conclusion by the audience that a good answer is not possible. To fail to define differences with one's opponent is to invite him to define them in the way most advantageous to himself. Debates thus tend to increase the accuracy, specificity, and relevance to the voting decision of statements in campaign discussion. . . .

Once these sorts of media influence on political discourse have been acknowledged, however, it remains true that the revolution in communication has not been accompanied by any comparable revolution in the way campaigners treat issues. James Bryce's description of campaign discussion applies in its essentials equally well to such discusion both before and after the rise of the mass media:

"The object of each party naturally is to put forward as many good political issues as it can, claiming for itself the merit of having always been on the popular side. Anyone who should read the campaign literature of the Republicans would fancy that they were opposed to the Democrats on many important points. When he took up the Democratic speeches and pamphlets he would be again struck by the serious divergences between the parties, which however would seem to arise, not on the points raised by the Republicans, but on other points which the Republicans had not referred to. In other words, the aim of each party is to force on its antagonist certain issues which the antagonist rarely accepts, so that although there is a vast deal of discussion and declamation on political topics, there are few on which either party directly traverses the doctrines of the other. Each pummels, not his true enemy, but a stuffed figure set up to represent the enemy."

Today, as in Bryce's day, the campaign discussion that the media convey to their audiences is, in very large measure, a discussion where the candidates talk past each other, one that is filled with distortions, ambiguities, and meaningless generalities.

Why? Among other reasons, because the potentialities of the media for altering the quality of campaign discussion have just begun to be explored.

Before the 1960 election, spokesmen for the broadcasting networks, particularly those for the Columbia Broadcasting System, argued that television's capacities for presenting campaign discussion in its most instructive forms remained largely unexploited. They were arguing to a point. They wanted revision or repeal of section 315 of the Federal Communications Act. . . .

In 1959 and in the 1960 post-convention session of Congress, the television industry got about what it had been after. Congress revised section 315 to enable broadcasting license holders to feature appearances by a candidate—without incurring any legal obligation to provide equal time to his opponent—in bona fide newscasts, news documentary shows, and news interview programs. Moreover, the application of section 315 to presidential and vice presidential candidates was suspended altogether for the duration of the campaign.

How did television use its new freedom? The industry's most spectacular contribution to the campaign was, of course, its presentation of the four Nixon-Kennedy joint appearances. But it also led the two candidates down other paths previously untrodden by presidential contenders on campaign. Both appeared on NBC's "Meet the Press" and Kennedy appeared on CBS's "Face the Nation." Both were interviewed at great length—on "Person to Person," "Tonight," "Presidential Countdown," and "The Campaign and the Candidates." Both had a number of their more important appearances featured *via* tapes in documentary treatments of the campaign. Vice Presidential candidates Lyndon Johnson and Henry Cabot Lodge, Jr., appeared on many of these same programs.

These innovations in television's campaign coverage did not escape criticism. One editor termed the debates "electronically contrived bad dreams" and a leading historian ventured the opinion that George Washington "it is safe to say, would not have come out very well" in a television debate. The superficiality of the questions posed by members of the debate panels drew complaints, as did the necessity for the candidates to give snap answers to their questioners. The severest critics contrasted the Nixon and Kennedy performances unfavorably with what they felt was really needed—a long, deep, serious, "thorough and concentrated consideration of the great issues that face our generation," a consideration in which the candidates could have engaged in "the slow questioning of alternatives before decision" or have lapsed into "thoughtful silence." While the other industry-sponsored programs aroused less comment than the debates, there were those who found distasteful the mixture of politics and gags that attended the candidates' appearances on comedian Jack Paar's show.

The majority reaction to television's innovations in campaign discussion, however, was clear. They had been good additions to campaigning, particularly the debates. I concur in the majority opinion.

A good deal of the criticism of the debates seems to have been based on a thoroughgoing misunderstanding of what campaigning is all about. Candidates are not university lecturers. They are not disinterested analysts of public affairs. They are seekers after public office, pleaders in their own cause. Before seeking public office they *ought* to have given previous thought to issues like aid to education, foreign aid, medical care for the aged, inflation, and farm surpluses. They ought to be able to say what they think should be done about such issues. They must at least seem to have thought about them.

Many of the critics, moreover, seem not to have compared what Nixon and Kennedy said in the debates and what they said (or was said on their behalf) in speeches, spot announcements, five-minute trailers, leaflets, pamphlets, and billboards. In their joint appearances Kennedy and Nixon frequently acknowledged agreement, rarely attributed false positions to each other, exposed quite clearly their differences on a number of significant issues, challenged each other and responded to each other's challenges. This kind of behavior is not typical of campaigners and it was not typical of Nixon and Kennedy when they made their appeals for public support in other ways.

Finally, the critics ignored one of the most striking achievements of the debates. They gave both candidates an equal opportunity to present reasonably comprehensive statements of their respective cases to what was substantially the total potential electorate. They were an answer to one of the principal problems associated with our present system of financing campaigns—inequalities in the abilities of parties and candidates to raise money. Such inequalities have never been a danger because they enabled the well-financed candidate to reach too many people with his views. They have been a danger because his poorly-financed opponent was able to reach too few. The debates equalized the opportunities of the two presidential candidates to communicate far more effectively than we have ever been able to by putting restrictions on contributions and expenditures.

THE HUCKSTER'S LAMENT*

Anthony Howard

'And so', said the agency vice-president earnestly leaning over his desk, 'I suppose what we really are is Jeffersonian Democrats. I mean at least we believe in trusting the people—which is apparently more than all those ivory-tower professors do. You know, the battle that's going on between us and our critics—Vance Packard, David Riesman and all that crowd—is, when you put it in its historical context, exactly that which was fought out between Thomas Jefferson and Alexander Hamilton. And I don't have to tell you that Jefferson, and the people, won.'

For Madison Avenue it deserved to be rated a brave try if only because ever since 8 November, in the 3,000-odd advertising agencies of New York, coats have been worn tightly buttoned at the neck against the suspected draught to come. The ad-men cannot forget, and anyway the Democrats are unlikely to let them do so, that in 1952, 1956, and 1960 the Democratic party account virtually had to go begging. In 1952 no large Madison Avenue agency would touch it; in 1956 an appeal for fair play brought an eventual (and, as it turned out, unhappy) acceptance by the small but lively agency of Norman, Craig & Kummel; and in 1960, perhaps as a result of that mutually painful experience, the account was again exiled all the way to San Francisco. By then, however, the Democrats had learnt how to hit back: from the moment their campaign was launched (by the key-note speaker at their convention) phrases like 'pitch-man prosperity' and 'government by hucksters' began to recur with a relentless regularity. By the end of the 1960 presidential election Madison Avenue was looking almost as badly knocked about as Wall Street had in 1932. For the first time in 30 years the bankers and the stockbrokers could afford to sit back and enjoy the spectacle of others being portrayed as enemies of the people. The conspiracy theory of politics had claimed a fresh victim; and the biter had been well and truly bitten.

---

* Reprinted from *New Statesman* (27 January 1961) by permission. Mr. Howard is a British writer.

Yet the ad-men seem to have sensed what was coming to them. In 1960, for the first time since Governor Dewey entered into his love-match with America's third largest agency in the late 1940s, the mammoth advertising firm of Batten, Barton, Durstine and Osborn baulked at handling the Republican national committee's account. Instead it took the lead in setting up a special *ad hoc* political agency called 'Campaign Associates' to which other Madison Avenue firms allowed their more eager partisan members to be drafted (quaintly, an expedient that had first been suggested—and rejected—in the case of the Democrats in 1956). The ruse, though, appears to have deceived no one. As the Republican ship finally went down some of the last heads to be seen above the waves were those of BBD&O executives who had defiantly arranged Mr. Nixon's $200,000, four-hour telethon on election eve. To irreverent observers at least, Mr. Carrol P. Newton (a vice-president of BBD&O who had been placed in charge of Campaign Associates) seemed, when all was over, to have very much the same kind of puzzled look on his face that Sir Alec Guinness wore in *Kind Hearts and Coronets* as he stood firmly saluting on the bridge while the dreadnought which he commanded plunged into oblivion.

For Madison Avenue had not only tried to steer the Republican vessel through the electoral waters: it had also largely built it, riveting complacency on to confidence, and satisfaction on to optimism, in its copywriters' wordyards. Not the least of the obstacles that Mr. Kennedy had to overcome in order to attain his presidency was the whole tone of commercial advertising. No one taking his impression of the nation's mood from it could possibly have gathered that anything was wrong with the state of America (which a new product could not put right), or that things could conceivably in any way be improved (except in so far as advertising would loyally continue to chase the twin hares of mass production and consumption).

Whether it was the girl dreaming that she 'stopped the traffic in my Maidenform bra', or the diplomat sending his son to Groton on the money he saved by buying an Austin, everything (including wish-fulfillment and vicarious ambition) seemed to be provided by a beneficently organized industry. The final tribute to the ad-man's art was perhaps paid by the *New York Times* reporter who, towards the end of the 1956 campaign, wrote: "The symbol of this election has been the smile on the face of the crowd in the President's wake. It is a peaceful, dreamy, faraway smile of pure contentment . . ."

In 1960, however, that smile was wiped off the face of the electorate, and as it vanished Madison Avenue lost its traditional buoyant bonhomie and began instead to look extremely bothered. It is not, of course, that the men from the agencies are today huddled into little shivering groups;

they have, after all, their consolations—including the reflection that a Democratic administration, unlike a Republican one (which occasionally gets inconveniently carried away by notions of thrift), normally believes in 'priming the pump'. With perhaps this in mind, the accounts departments of the various agencies are already estimating that in 1961 'for the first time in history the total advertising volume will probably break through the $12 billion mark'. The ad-man's current anxiety is rather a more personal one, stemming from a sudden realisation that the price of the industry's eight years of supposed omnipotence has been a steadily increasing resentment on the part of the public. A few months ago beatitude itself seemed to be within grasp; now even empire has been discovered to be far away. . . .

Yet far more than any threat to the future, it is probably what has already occurred that most worries Madison Avenue. For eight glorious years the men who worked there were able to persuade themselves (and their clients) that they alone were the people to whom all hearts were open and all desires known—merely to discover at the end that not only was this carefully constructed vision widely resented, but that it also simply was not true.

If it did nothing else, Mr. Kennedy's close victory, and the manner in which it was won, showed that some secrets remained hidden even from 'motivational research'. Somewhere some subliminal dissatisfactions had gone undetected; and as Mr. Kennedy came into office, American advertising was left sadly to mourn its mistakes with the plaintive but basically unrepentant cry: 'We have changed the connotation of so many products and companies. Surely we are smart enough to do it for ourselves.' On that basis—in Mr. Kennedy's America—it does not promise to be an easy task.

PART TWO

THE ISSUES

CHAPTER SEVEN

Poverty, Abundance, and Government

If President John F. Kennedy were to say "I see one-third of a nation—ill-housed, ill-clad, ill-nourished," there would be more than a few looks of astonishment. But Franklin D. Roosevelt said it in 1936, and the phrase stuck. It stuck, not because FDR had discovered something new, but because he expressed warm concern for the obvious—the poor, the forgotten man. America knew about poverty in the 1930s by firsthand experience. And then came the New Deal, welfare legislation, and the economic prosperity of the postwar years.

By the 1960s, the poor were assumed to be an aberration. In 1958, John K. Galbraith wrote in his famous *The Affluent Society* that poverty was "no longer a massive affliction [but] more nearly an afterthought." How can poverty be a problem in America, when the average family income is over $7,000? There would seem to be no problem. Nonetheless, there is a growing opinion among scholars that the poor, at least relatively speaking, are still with us—still ill-housed and ill-nourished, but not so ill-clad that we can so readily recognize them. Michael Harrington develops the thesis that the poor are invisible—that poverty lies off the beaten track of middle-class America. These millions of Americans were bypassed by the economic and social gains of the 1930s, and many of them have joined the ranks of the hard-core poor—those who because of age, race, or physical or mental defects cannot be lifted out of their poverty by general economic prosperity. Good times have not trickled down to them.

As such conditions have been perceived, a frequent reaction has been to call for some type of massive federal intervention to help the poor. If part of today's poverty can be ascribed to inadequate education—as with the functional illiterates—then the federal government needs to do more to assist the states. President John F. Kennedy's address to the Congress in February 1961 outlines a program of federal assistance in secondary and elementary education. His proposals have been defeated in the Congress. In part, they were defeated because of the controversy over aid to church-related schools, but they were also defeated for the reasons which Senator Barry Goldwater discusses. First, Senator Goldwater is not convinced that the primary problem in education is financial. Second, the Senator shares with many the fear that federal aid to education will result in centralization of authority, and a consequent loss of the local freedom to shape education to local needs.

A similar juxtaposition of views can be seen when proposals for federal medical aid are examined. Dr. Edward R. Annis, president of the American Medical Association, discusses the reasons the AMA has opposed the King-Anderson medicare program for the aged. Dr. Annis sees medicare as an attack on individual freedom and self-respect, and he lists specific charges against the program. Gilbert A. Harrison attempts to answer Dr. Annis's charges by citing statistics—medical and financial—on the condition of the aged in America. He also attempts to refute the charge that medicare is a drastic and revolutionary program.

To the perplexed voter, all of the charges and countercharges in debates about solutions to poverty have a ring of truth. When social workers reveal that we now have third-generation full-time welfare recipients, one can be legitimately concerned about the effect of government aid programs on self-respect. On the other hand, a call for "free-enterprise medicine" seems to fall somewhat short of the traditional humanitarian goals of American medicine. What the voter must look for, then, are politicians who will discuss the problems of poverty, education, and health without resorting to shibboleths and slogans.

OUR INVISIBLE POOR*

Michael Harrington

There is a familiar America. It is celebrated in speeches and advertised on television and in the magazines. It has the highest mass standard of living the world has ever known.

In the 1950s this America worried about itself, yet even its anxieties were products of abundance. The title of a brilliant book was widely misinterpreted, and the familiar America began to call itself "the affluent

---

* Reprinted with permission of The Macmillan Company from *The Other America* by Michael Harrington. Chapter 1, "The Invisible Land." Copyright 1962 by Michael Harrington. Mr. Harrington is a contributing editor of *Dissent.*

society." There was introspection about Madison Avenue and tail fins; there was discussion of the emotional suffering taking place in the suburbs. In all this, there was an implicit assumption that the basic grinding economic problems had been solved in the United States. In this theory the nation's problems were no longer a matter of basic human needs, of food, shelter, and clothing. Now they were seen as qualitative, a question of learning to live decently amid luxury.

While this discussion was carried on, there existed another America. In it dwelt somewhere between 40,000,000 and 50,000,000 citizens of this land. They were poor. They still are.

To be sure, the other America is not impoverished in the same sense as those poor nations where millions cling to hunger as a defense against starvation. This country has escaped such extremes. That does not change the fact that tens of millions of Americans are, at this very moment, maimed in body and spirit, existing at levels beneath those necessary for human decency. If these people are not starving, they are hungry, and sometimes fat with hunger, for that is what cheap foods do. They are without adequate housing and education and medical care.

The Government has documented what this means to the bodies of the poor, and the figures will be cited throughout this book. But even more basic, this poverty twists and deforms the spirit. The American poor are pessimistic and defeated, and they are victimized by mental suffering to a degree unknown in Suburbia. . . .

The millions who are poor in the United States tend to become increasingly invisible. Here is a great mass of people, yet it takes an effort of the intellect and will even to see them. . . .

There are perennial reasons that make the other America an invisible land. Poverty is often off the beaten track. It always has been. The ordinary tourist never left the main highway, and today he rides interstate turnpikes. He does not go into the valleys of Pennsylvania where the towns look like movie sets of Wales in the thirties. He does not see the company houses in rows, the rutted roads (the poor always have bad roads whether they live in the city, in towns, or on farms), and everything is black and dirty. And even if he were to pass through such a place by accident, the tourist would not meet the unemployed men in the bar or the women coming home from a runaway sweatshop.

Then, too, beauty and myths are perennial masks of poverty. The traveler comes to the Appalachians in the lovely season. He sees the hills, the streams, the foliage—but not the poor. Or perhaps he looks at a run-down mountain house and, remembering Rousseau rather than seeing with his eyes, decides that "those people" are truly fortunate to be living the way they are and that they are lucky to be exempt from the strains and tensions of the middle class. The only problem is that "those people," the quaint inhabitants of those hills, are undereducated, underprivileged, lack medical care, and are in the process of being forced from the land into a life in the cities, where they are misfits.

These are normal and obvious causes of the invisibility of the poor. They operated a generation ago; they will be functioning a generation hence. It is more important to understand that the very development of American society is creating a new kind of blindness about poverty. The poor are increasingly slipping out of the very experience and consciousness of the nation.

If the middle class never did like ugliness and poverty, it was at least aware of them. "Across the tracks" was not a very long way to go. There were forays into the slums at Christmas time; there were charitable organizations that brought contact with the poor. Occasionally, almost everyone passed through the Negro ghetto or the blocks of tenements, if only to get downtown to work or to entertainment.

Now the American city has been transformed. The poor still inhabit the miserable housing in the central area, but they are increasingly isolated from contact with, or sight of, anybody else. Middle-class women coming in from Suburbia on a rare trip may catch the merest glimpse of the other America on the way to an evening at the theater, but their children are segregated in suburban schools. The business or professional man may drive along the fringes of slums in a car or bus, but it is not an important experience to him. The failures, the unskilled, the disabled, the aged, and the minorities are right there, across the tracks, where they have always been. But hardly anyone else is.

In short, the very development of the American city has removed poverty from the living, emotional experience of millions upon millions of middle-class Americans. Living out in the suburbs, it is easy to assume that ours is, indeed, an affluent society.

This new segregation of poverty is compounded by a well-meaning ignorance. A good many concerned and sympathetic Americans are aware that there is much discussion of urban renewal. Suddenly, driving through the city, they notice that a familiar slum has been torn down and that there are towering, modern buildings where once there had been tenements or hovels. There is a warm feeling of satisfaction, of pride in the way things are working out: the poor, it is obvious, are being taken care of.

The irony in this . . . is that the truth is nearly the exact opposite to the impression. The total impact of the various housing programs in postwar America has been to squeeze more and more people into existing slums. More often than not, the modern apartment in a towering building rents at $40 a room or more. For, during the past decade and a half, there has been more subsidization of middle- and upper-income housing than there has been of housing for the poor.

Clothes make the poor invisible too: America has the best-dressed poverty the world has ever known. For a variety of reasons, the benefits of mass production have been spread much more evenly in this area than in many others. It is much easier in the United States to be decently dressed than it is to be decently housed, fed, or doctored. Even people with terribly depressed incomes can look prosperous. . . .

Then, many of the poor are the wrong age to be seen. A good number of them (over 8,000,000) are sixty-five years of age or better; an even larger number are under eighteen. The aged members of the other America are often sick, and they cannot move. Another group of them live out their lives in loneliness and frustration: they sit in rented rooms, or else they stay close to a house in a neighborhood that has completely changed from the old days. Indeed, one of the worst aspects of poverty among the aged is that these people are out of sight and out of mind, and alone. . . .

Forty to 50,000,000 people are becoming increasingly invisible. That is a shocking fact. But there is a second basic irony of poverty that is equally important: if one is to make the mistake of being born poor, he should choose a time when the majority of the people are miserable too.

J. K. Galbraith develops this idea in The Affluent Society, and in doing so defines the "newness" of the kind of poverty in contemporary America. The old poverty, Galbraith notes, was general. It was the condition of life of an entire society, or at least of that huge majority who were without special skills or the luck of birth. When the entire economy advanced, a good many of these people gained higher standards of living. Unlike the poor today, the majority poor of a generation ago were an immediate (if cynical) concern of political leaders. The old slums of the immigrants had the votes; they provided the basis for labor organizations; their very numbers could be a powerful force in political conflict. At the same time the new technology required higher skills, more education, and stimulated an upward movement for millions.

Out of the thirties came the welfare state. Its creation had been stimulated by mass impoverishment and misery, yet it helped the poor least of all. Laws like unemployment compensation, the Wagner Act, the various farm programs, all these were designed for the middle third in the cities, for the organized workers, and for the upper third in the country, for the big market farmers. If a man works in an extremely low-paying job, he may not even be covered by social security or other welfare programs. If he receives unemployment compensation, the payment is scaled down according to his low earnings.

One of the major laws that was designed to cover everyone, rich and poor, was social security. But even here the other Americans suffered discrimination. Over the years social security payments have not even provided a subsistence level of life. The middle third have been able to supplement the Federal pension through private plans negotiated by unions, through joining medical insurance schemes like Blue Cross, and so on. The poor have not been able to do so. They lead a bitter life, and then have to pay for that fact in old age. . . .

Today's poor, in short, missed the political and social gains of the thirties. They are, as Galbraith rightly points out, the first minority poor in history, the first poor not to be seen, the first poor whom the politicians could leave alone.

The first step toward the new poverty was taken when millions of people proved immune to progress. When that happened, the failure was not individual and personal, but a social product. But once the historic accident takes place, it begins to become a personal fate.

The new poor of the other America saw the rest of society move ahead. They went on living in depressed areas, and often they tended to become depressed human beings. In some of the West Virginia towns, for instance, an entire community will become shabby and defeated. The young and the adventurous go to the city, leaving behind those who cannot move and those who lack the will to do so. The entire area becomes permeated with failure, and that is one more reason the big corporations shy away. . . .

In the past, when poverty was general in the unskilled and semi-skilled work force, the poor were all mixed together. The bright and the dull, those who were going to escape into the great society and those who were to stay behind, all of them lived on the same street. When the middle third rose, this community was destroyed. And the entire invisible land of the other Americans became a ghetto, a modern poor farm for the rejects of society and of the economy. . . .

Physical and mental disabilities are, to be sure, an important part of poverty in America. The poor are sick in body and in spirit. But this is not an isolated fact about them, an individual "case," a stroke of bad luck. Disease, alcoholism, low IQ's, these express a whole way of life. They are, in the main, the effects of an environment, not the biographies of unlucky individuals. Because of this, the new poverty is something that cannot be dealt with by first aid. If there is to be a lasting assault on the shame of the other America, it must seek to root out of this society an entire environment, and not just the relief of individuals. . . .

Finally, one might summarize the newness of contemporary poverty by saying: These are the people who are immune to progress. But then the facts are even more cruel. The other Americans are the victims of the very inventions and machines that have provided a higher living standard for the rest of the society. They are upside-down in the economy, and for them greater productivity often means worse jobs; agricultural advance becomes hunger.

In the optimistic theory, technology is an undisguised blessing. A general increase in productivity, the argument goes, generates a higher standard of living for the whole people. And indeed, this has been true for the middle and upper thirds of American society, the people who made such striking gains in the last two decades. It tends to overstate the automatic character of the process, to omit the role of human struggle . . . Yet it states a certain truth—for those who are lucky enough to participate in it.

But the poor, if they were given to theory, might argue the exact opposite. They might say: Progress is misery.

As the society became more technological, more skilled, those who learn to work the machines, who get the expanding education, move up. Those who miss out at the very start find themselves at a new disadvantage. A generation ago in American life, the majority of the working people did not have high-school educations. But at that time industry was organized on a lower level of skill and competence. And there was a sort of continuum in the shop: the youth who left school at sixteen could begin as a laborer, and gradually pick up skill as he went along.

Today the situation is quite different. The good jobs require much more academic preparation, much more skill from the very outset. Those who lack a high-school education tend to be condemned to the economic underworld—to low-paying service industries, to backward factories, to sweeping and janitorial duties. If the fathers and mothers of the contemporary poor were penalized a generation ago for their lack of schooling, their children will suffer all the more. The very rise in productivity that created more money and better working conditions for the rest of the society can be a menace to the poor. . . .

It is too early to say whether or not this phenomenon is temporary, or whether it represents a massive retrogression that will swell the numbers of the poor. To a large extent, the answer to this question will be determined by the political response of the United States in the sixties. If serious and massive action is not undertaken, it may be necessary for statisticians to add some old-fashioned, pre-welfare-state poverty to the misery of the other America.

MEDICARE: BAD MEDICINE FOR EVERYONE*

Edward R. Annis, M.D.

Mr. Chairman, some of us are Democrats, some of us are Republicans, and some of us are political independents. We therefore are not here to promote the fortunes of either political party or the hopes of any particular political candidates. Rather, we are here to help spread the faith in freedom which is shared by millions of Americans in both parties.

Unfortunately, our faith is not shared by some people in this country—and we find them, too, under a variety of political labels. There is a hard core of Fabian socialists, government bureaucrats, social and economic planners, and political opportunists who believe that there is just one basic answer to any and all national problems. That answer is more and more government programs, bigger and bigger federal budgets to carry out the programs, and higher and higher taxes to finance the budgets to carry out the programs.

Unfortunately, also, this behind-the-scenes group of social architects has been able to influence large numbers of sincere, well-meaning people. Over the years—through artful propaganda, clever distortion of facts, easy generalities, and falsely emotional appeals cloaked in humanitarianism—they have managed to mislead many Americans who did not perceive the ultimate design of the completed fabric, the eventual cost in both money and freedom.

Fortunately, however, the pendulum seems to be swinging the other way. More and more of our fellow citizens are becoming concerned over the increasing costs of government, the mounting threat of governmental controls and regulations, the shrinking purchasing power of their paychecks, the growing loss of freedoms. They are becoming less vulnerable to the blandishments of fantasy, as compared with the facts. They are becoming less gullible about promises of pie-in-the-sky, as compared with the facts. They are becoming more realistic in their viewpoint toward grandiose federal panaceas, as compared with the facts.

I think I can say, honestly and with pride, that my profession—the entire medical profession—has played a major role in bringing about this trend. More than any other single group, and for many years, we physi-

---

* Condensed from a speech delivered before the Fifth Political Action Conference, Washington, D.C., January 11, 1963. Reprinted by permission of the author. Dr. Annis is President of the American Medical Association.

cians have been threatened—persistently, doggedly and closely—by the various legislative proposals of the social planners. So far, we have resisted them with courage and success, and in so doing I believe we have caused a lot of people to think twice about a lot of things.

The courage we can claim as our own. But the success was achieved only by going to the American people with the facts, and thereby gaining millions of allies through the avenues of communications and public opinion. In these efforts—first against the Murray-Wagner-Dingell Bill in 1949–1952, then against the Forand Bill which first came up in 1957, and more recently against the King-Anderson Bill of the past two years—we have had great help from organizations and individuals like yourselves who share our opposition to creeping socialism. . . .

And we shall continue to go to the American people with the facts— not only the facts about why we oppose the King-Anderson type of legislation, but also the even more important facts about the progress and potential of existing, voluntary mechanisms. . . .

Unfortunately, this whole subject has been turned into a political football during the past three years. Actually, it is a non-partisan issue which should be resolved on a basis of facts instead of emotion, reason rather than rallies. It involves principles and approaches which go beyond the fortunes of any political party or the political ambitions of any individual.

Fortunately for American democratic processes, the facts gradually overtook and passed the emotion during the first eight months of 1962. As a result of public opinion based upon the facts, the U.S. Senate last July defeated an attempt to enact a compromise version of the King-Anderson Bill. This proposal would have established a limited, government-regulated system of health care for the aged, financed by higher Social Security taxes on all working people.

In early 1962 the proponents of the King-Anderson Bill boasted that public opinion polls and mail to Washington showed a majority of the people in favor of Social Security health care for the aged. By last summer they no longer wanted to hear about public opinion and letters to the members of Congress.

The Gallup Poll, in 1961, had reported that 67 per cent of the public favored the King-Anderson type of legislation. By April, 1962, that percentage had dropped to 55. In July, just before the Senate vote, support for the plan had declined to 48 per cent. And in August the Gallup Poll showed only 44 per cent of the people favoring Social Security health care for the aged.

What accounted for this change in public attitude during 1962?

The answer lies mainly in one word—facts. The American people began to see through the emotional appeals, false generalizations and inaccurate statistics employed by the King-Anderson advocates. They learned the following basic facts about the issue:

1. The great majority of Americans over 65 are *not* poor, ill and without proper health care.

2. Both the *health* and *finances* of our senior citizens are far better than they have been pictured, and they will be improving constantly in the years ahead.

3. The medical cost problems that do exist among the aged are problems of individuals, not of an entire age group.

4. Those problems can be met most efficiently and economically by methods which fit individual needs and the great variety of state and local situations.

5. Our nation already has voluntary, flexible programs to accomplish that purpose. Our job now is to expand and improve them.

6. One of those programs is the Kerr-Mills Law, which Congress passed in 1960. This law enables the states to provide medical assistance for all low-income people over 65, regardless of whether or not they are covered by Social Security.

7. As of today, under the Kerr-Mills Law, 38 states and territories had improved or expanded their Old Age Assistance medical programs, and 31 had established *new* medical assistance programs for old people who are *not* on public assistance. The medical profession is working actively to promote full, efficient use of the Kerr-Mills Law in all states which need it.

8. The other existing method is voluntary health insurance and prepayment plans which already protect 55 per cent of our senior citizens. New plans and ideas are developing at a fast pace, and within the next three years voluntary plans will be protecting 70–75 per cent of the people over 65.

9. By promoting full use and development of these tools already at hand, we can solve the problem and avoid the faults and dangers of the King-Anderson type of program.

10. The King-Anderson type program, for example, would meet neither the medical nor the financial needs of the old people who really need help.

11. It would scatter certain limited benefits, at public expense, to millions of people over 65 who neither need nor want such help.

12. It would raise Social Security taxes on all workers—including young people just starting out in their careers—to provide these limited benefits for only one age group.

13. It would radically alter the whole purpose and nature of our American system of Social Security.

14. It would be the first major step toward national compulsory health insurance for our entire population.

15. Its enactment would have a far reaching influence on the social, economic and political future of our nation.

The medical profession asks only two things in 1963:

That the American people continue to study carefully all the facts and realities involved in this issue, and

That the U.S. Congress in 1963 base its judgment on common sense rather than common politics.

This year, in Washington, the words may be slightly different. The tune will be the same. Hardly waiting for the nation's voting machines to be stacked away in warehouses across the country, the Kennedy administration hastened to proclaim it will resume its drive for foot-in-the-door socialized medicine when the new Congress convenes.

And there is no other way to read the Administration's medicare bill. It provides for a *compulsory* hospitalization program for the aged, regardless of need. It would be financed by increased Social Security *taxes* levied on younger workers and their employers.

If it is passed, only two steps would be necessary to push the U.S. into full-scale nationalized medicine—providing full medical care (including all physicians' services) for the aged, and then lowering the age restrictions until all Americans are legislated into a government "health" program from the cradle to the grave.

The measure was defeated in the Senate by two votes in the last session. It never did get out of the House Ways and Means Committee, the only congressional group to hold hearings on it in two years. Nevertheless, in the wake of an *inconclusive* election, the zeal of Administration planners to secure a greater and greater concentration of power in Washington over the lives of citizens burns with undiminished fervor. . . .

Whatever the wrappings of the package delivered to the new Congress, there will be no compromise on this point. For the Washington bureaucrats, spurred by the pressure of organized labor, are relentless in their determination to expand government welfare programs to cover an increasing proportion of the population in the name of humanitarianism.

It is against this overall objective that the struggle to come must be waged.

Federalized hospitalization for the aged was exposed before the last Congress and the people as a hoax and a fraud. It was demonstrated again and again that the program would do what the proponents piously denied it would do: namely, permit government intervention in the practice of medicine in this country for the first time and begin destruction of the twin traditions of freedom of the patient's choice and freedom of the doctor's practice which have made American medicine one of the wonders of the modern world.

At the same time, it was shown that the cost of the program would be staggering and the end result would have little real meaning for the needy aged. The measure provided only 25 per cent of complete medical care; physicians' fees were not covered; no drugs were included; about 4 million elderly citizens were arbitrarily excluded because they are not on Social Security.

But bureaucrats with a mission are a tireless breed. They can lose time and again, and keep coming back and coming back, confident that they will at last wear down their opposition and win their way. Those against them can lose only once. For them there is no second chance.

Americans must recognize this peril as the stage is set for another struggle over medicare.

If they surrender a fragment of freedom under the guise of compromise or because they weary of the fight, that fragment of freedom is gone—never to be retrieved. Or, stated another way, a federal government take-over is like poured cement. If you do not struggle as it is being poured, but wait until it is an accomplished fact, it hardens and you never escape.

Medicare is not an isolated issue. Far from it. Medicare is part of a greater struggle which has as its goal the surrender of individual freedom and self-respect on promise of unearned government handouts. The people's votes and control of their personal lives and destinies would be purchased with their own money, collected in higher taxes and doled back to them by an all-knowing bureaucracy which claims to have a monopoly on sympathy and good will. A more vicious or cynical combination of forces striking at the keystone of liberty would be impossible to imagine.

Whatever form these welfare schemes assume, the aim is the same—complete centralization of authority in Washington, corruption of a truly independent franchise, and the end of democratic government in this country.

Whatever alternative proposals or purported medicare compromises are put forward in the months to come, Americans should see them all as merely different routes to the same destination—government control of the practice of medicine.

Only a resolute and clear-thinking electorate, proud of its heritage and determined to hold to its principles of self-reliance and personal integrity, stands between the Administration and its objective in this fight.

Medicine, in order to continue to progress in the future as it has in the past, must continue to operate under a free enterprise system which fosters competition, the striving for excellence, the never-ending attempt to "build a better mousetrap."

For the benefit of the American public, we shall welcome and appreciate the vigorous support of all those who believe in initiative, self-reliance, progressive action within the framework of the American way of life—and, above all, personal freedom.

WARD-HEALERS OF THE AMA*

Gilbert A. Harrison

The American Medical Association may succeed in frightening the Congress away from financing medical care for the aged through the Social Security system, but no amount of AMA propaganda can frighten away some elementary facts to which the President's program is addressed. For example, of 15.3 million individuals 65 and over who were not in institutions in 1959, 55 percent had an annual income of less than $1,000. Twenty-three percent $1,000 to $2,000, and nine percent $2,000 to $3,000. Only 13 percent had incomes of $3,000 or more. And these figures include those still working. And in the case of married couples, some of the income which is attributed to the husband goes for support of his wife, who may be under 65. Of 6.2 million *families* where the head of the family was 65 years of age or more, *half* had an income of less than $2,830; one-fourth less than $1,620 a year. More startling: of 3.6 million aged persons who live alone or with persons other than relatives, half had incomes of less than $1,010; four-fifths less than $2,000.

How do they get by, even if they get through the year without a day's illness? The answer is that many barely do. The Bureau of Labor Statistics in a study of 20 large cities in the autumn of 1959 concluded that a retired couple in reasonably good health for their age, *requiring no unusual medical or other services*, and keeping house by themselves in a small rented unit could get along modestly but adequately on a budget ranging from the minimum of $2,390 in Houston, Texas, to $3,110 in Chicago. This, remember, is premised on no unusual demand for medical care. Even so, this absolute minimum in a great many cases is higher than the actual income of aged couples. The BLS also estimated that a person of 65 or over who lives alone could get by, modestly but adequately, with from $1,410 to $1,835 in the 20 cities studied. But the actual median income for single persons in this age bracket living in these cities was only $1,140 in 1959.

Couldn't they fall back on their savings? Some could. But a Federal Reserve Board survey of consumer finances in 1959 found that of some 8 million "spending units" (in families the head of which was 65 years or more) 29 percent had *no* liquid assets (i.e., bank accounts or savings

---

* Reprinted from *The New Republic* (April 17, 1961) by permission. Mr. Harrison is the editor and publisher of *The New Republic*.

bonds), 17 percent had $1 to $500 in reserve, 21 percent had $500 to $2,000. And of the aged whose income was under $3,000 a year (70 percent of the total), 47 percent had less than $200 in liquid assets; 44 percent had assets of $500 or more.

From such statistics it is apparent that the affluent society is not the society of a very great many old folks. And when we read the medical statistics, moreover, we are reading about the aged who do enter hospitals, who see their physicians. We don't know how much suffering, how much neglect is endured privately, with little or no treatment.

We are sure, however, that the number of days spent in a general hospital annually is two to three times as large on an average for persons 65 and over as for younger persons. A National Health Survey study in 1957–58 found that of those discharged from general hospitals after a short stay, those of 65 or over spent 1,778 days in the hospital (per 1,000 persons) as compared with 764 days (per 1,000 persons) for those under 65. The average length of hospitalization for the aged was 14.7 days; for those under 65, 7.8 days.

But in addition to using general hospitals more frequently and for longer periods than younger persons, the aged make special demands on nursing homes and other institutions which keep patients for more than a week or a month. They likewise need more of the doctors' time. An aged person on an average has 6.8 doctor visits a year. The number for the rest of the population is 4.8. In those families with less than $2,000 a year income (as surveyed from July, 1957, to June, 1959), 48 percent of the aged members of the family had some chronic condition which limited their activity; the average number of days spent in bed was 16.5 a year. And in families whose income was $7,000 or more, 37 percent of the aged had some chronic illness; the average number of bed disability days was 10.8 per year.

Nor is the picture complete yet. Usually a doctor's fee is higher for a house call than for an office visit, which helps explain a statement by the Health Information Foundation that "private outlays for physicians in behalf of persons 65 or over averaged almost twice as much per person per year (in 1957–58) as for persons under 65—$55 and $29 respectively."

We also know, from information compiled by the Health Information Foundation, that the aged spend over twice as much per person for *total* medical care in a year as others. (This is what is spent by individuals—not what should be spent. And it does not include the heavy costs of terminal illnesses among those who live alone, or the cost of care for the aged in nursing homes or mental or tubercular hospitals.) For the years 1957–58, the average private expenditure for medical care of those 65 and over was $177; for those under 65, $86.

But even these averages are misleading: they give no true picture of the heavy financial burden of an illness that requires hospitalization. For example, of elderly people who were not married but who were entitled to Old Age, Survivors and Disability Insurance benefits in 1957, more than one in seven spent some time in a hospital, nursing home or other institution, and the median medical costs amounted to $600 for all such beneficiaries. This figure is higher today, for since 1957 the rates for all medical care items have gone up by 14 percent, and rates for hospital rooms have risen by 22 percent. Among the beneficiaries who spent some time in a general hospital during 1957, only 57 percent of those who were married and 38 percent of those non-married were able to meet all their medical bills by themselves (over and above any cost met by insurance). Of the rest, some went into debt, a sizable number received help from relatives or other outsiders.

Many of the aged have, of course, some medical insurance. About half of the OASDI beneficiaries who entered a general hospital sometime during 1957 had a part of their medical bill paid by insurance. But in many instances the insurance was inadequate; and for some who were insured against hospitalization, either the specific illness was excluded from coverage or the general hospital stay was too short (or the deductible too large) for the insurance to go into effect. Thus, of the aged OASDI beneficiaries who were insured and who went to a hospital during 1957, 16 percent of the couples had *no* portion of their year's total medical costs met by insurance; and 57 percent found that their insurance covered less than one-half of their total medical bills. Less than half (46 percent) of the aged have insurance against hospitalization costs (compared with 69 percent of the population under 65).

Furthermore, those most likely to suffer the most hardship—the retired, those with low incomes or with major chronic health problems—are least likely to have the advantage of *any* health insurance coverage. Many private insurance organizations will not even enroll persons 65 or over. To illustrate, as of early 1960, only about two-fifths of the Blue Cross plans accepted initial non-group enrollment from persons over 65. A study by the National Opinion Research Information Foundation shows that, as of four years ago, of those older persons who wanted coverage, 34 percent couldn't afford it and 16 percent had been refused insurance or had it cancelled.

The Kennedy Program

How has the Administration responded to these facts? It has recommended that some, but not all, of the cost of medical care for older people be financed by contributions to the Social Security system. The proposal is described this way by the Assistant Secretary of Health, Education and Welfare, Wilbur J. Cohen (confirmed by the Senate last week by *one* vote): "[It] would make it possible for the people of this country during their working years to provide for their health needs in their old age. Like the present social security benefits, health insurance protection would be provided as a *right* that is earned through work." Care would not be "free" or be a "hand-out." The plan "is based upon a recognition that expensive illness only too often forces the aged after a lifetime of independence to become dependent upon their children or to submit to the humiliation of inquiry into their personal affairs. . . . The health insurance proposal, like the Old Age, Survivors and Disability Insurance program now in effect, would not provide more than basic protection. It would provide payment for the cost of in-patient hospital care (after a deductible), skilled nursing home convalescence after hospitalization, hospital out-patient diagnostic services (after a deductible), and visiting nurse and related health services. . . . The prerogatives of doctors and patients would remain unchanged. The patient would choose his own doctor, who in turn would be absolutely unhindered in practicing his profession."

Specifically, patients would be entitled to 90 days of in-patient hospital care for a single spell of illness at a minimum charge of $20 and a maximum charge of $90. But at no extra cost, the patient would be entitled to another 180 days of skilled nursing home care, and hospital out-patient clinic diagnostic services would be available for all costs exceeding the first $20 for each diagnostic study. Finally, the aged who benefit from this program could have as many as 240 *home* health care visits in a calendar year. Some 14¼ million persons (out of a total of 17¾ million 65 or over) would be eligible for benefits as of January, 1963.

Who pays the bill? The program would be financed entirely by an increase in social security tax contributions of one-fourth of one percent each for employers and employees, and three-eighths of one percent for self-employed persons. . . .

Despite AMA propaganda this can be fairly termed a modest program; it leaves out, for example, any payment from the insurance fund to patients for their physicians' fees, except in very special instances. The patient would have full responsibility for picking his own doctor and his hospital.

But the trade association of the doctors does not see it this way; it sees revolution. The AMA is fighting back with every resource at its command. Last year, the AMA acknowledged spending $72,634.76 on lobbying activities in Washington, but one can be sure that that represents only a fraction of what was spent or will be spent. . . . Already, members of the House Ways and Means Committee are receiving considerable mail— "most of it running against the bill and coming from doctors and their organizations"—but Congress ain't seen nothin' yet. . . .

The AMA strategy was carefully outlined at a confidential get-together of the Association's high command . . . in Chicago. At this meeting, from which reporters were barred, those present were given a complete rundown on the members of the Senate and the House in terms of their likely positions on the President's medical care program. The meeting was told that if the "undecided" vote breaks evenly, the AMA will have the President licked.

Psychological Warfare

This private session was devoted primarily to a discussion of propaganda tactics. . . . When someone raised the question of whether it was really accurate to call the President's program "socialized medicine," he was advised that the AMA's public relations experts had studied this very carefully and found that this is the label best guaranteed to raise the voters' blood pressure.

Quite a variety of propaganda items was previewed in Chicago to be seen later by millions of Americans. There is a "digest of information"— eight pages, single-spaced—giving the AMA's arguments against the President's plan. There is a six-page, single-spaced "selected statistics concerning medical economics," designed to prove that Americans receive "the finest care of any nation." A special report was given at Chicago by the women's auxiliary to the AMA, outlining what ladies can do: "inform each member as to the danger of a compulsory medical care program based on a social security tax. This is socialized medicine."

Texts of a canned talk for delivery at community meetings arranged by auxiliary members have been distributed. Specific lobbying instructions are being supplied: "Since each auxiliary member is a voter in her own right it is suggested that the individual letters which the auxiliary members write to Congressmen should be written on the member's own stationery in longhand or type and signed in her own name rather than that of her husband."

Chicago strategists were also told that headquarters will supply, in quantity, a special edition of the AMA News entirely devoted to this issue. In a red-bordered box on the front page of the News, the AMA speaks directly to doctors: "The medical profession bears the threat of this attack, and physicians can't afford to close their eyes and hope that when they open them again the whole unhappy business will have disappeared. They may awaken to the fact of government medicine. If they are socialized, their patients will be socialized as well. Physicians, individually and collectively, must wrest the initiative from the labor leaders and others who are determined to destroy free medicine. . . ."

The AMA has prepared an instruction sheet for district and county medical societies which recommends that: "Physician members must write and initiate a great number of individual letters to the Congress from their own membership and from friends in other organizations." Detailed suggestions are given on how the local medical society can unite "the allied health, professional and business groups in your community. . . ."

Alongside Life and Holiday

Not only do most physicians have a Representative and two Senators, however; they have patients. And for them, there is a leaflet entitled (in red) "Socialized Medicine and You," to be placed in the doctors' waiting rooms, alongside *Life* and *Holiday*. It is "an open letter to my patients," and begins: "The time has come for all of us to stand and be counted on the question of socialized medicine." In large type we read "Your freedom is at stake." The patient is told that if he agrees "that preserving the freedoms of medical service is vital, then write to your Senators and Congressmen. Join me in telling them that socialized medicine is not for us. . . ."

And that's not all. The AMA has special hand-outs for "editorial writers," reprints from *Nation's Business*, the *Wall Street Journal*, the *Saturday Evening Post*, the *Chicago Sun Times*, the *Chicago Tribune*, the *Richmond Times Dispatch*. There is also a sample letter to editorial writers for the doctors to copy and mail. There is a "communications" kit with ad mats for local newspapers. Space is left at the bottom of each ad for the signature of the particular medical society. One is entitled "Socialized Medicine and You" and can be ordered by number from the AMA, P.O. Box 5037, Chicago 80, Illinois. Five sample one-minute radio or television scripts are likewise available. Simplicity is stressed: "This is [doctor's name]. As a practicing physician, I believe that any American (young or old) who needs medical care should get it. . . . That's why I favor the program of medical aid for the aged enacted in the Kerr-Mills law. (Pause) But some people don't want this law to succeed. They propose a *compulsory* program of medical services to the aged covered by social security—*regardless of need*. To me this represents *Socialized Medicine* for the elderly—with federal control abridging the patient's freedom to choose his doctor . . . compromising the privacy of the doctor-patient relationship. (Pause) For more facts, ask your family doctor for the pamphlet titled "*Medical Aid for the Aged*."

None of this is true; none of it is relevant to providing adequate medical care for older people, who are not for the most part getting it and cannot get it through charity or private insurance plans; the reference to "compulsion" is fraudulent. For what ails so many of the aged is being compelled to endure illness without proper treatment, or to be dependent on charity or on younger members of a family which is struggling itself to keep ahead of the bill collector.

EDUCATION: A PROGRAM FOR THE 1960s*

President John F. Kennedy

To the Congress of the United States:

Our progress as a nation can be no swifter than our progress in education. Our requirements for world leadership, our hopes for economic growth, and the demands of citizenship itself in an era such as this all require the maximum development of every young American's capacity.

The human mind is our fundamental resource. A balanced Federal program must go well beyond incentives for investment in plant and equipment. It must include equally determined measures to invest in human beings—both in their basic education and training and in their more advanced preparation for professional work. Without such measures, the Federal Government will not be carrying out its responsibilities for expanding the base of our economic and military strength.

Our progress in education over the last generation has been substantial. We are educating a greater proportion of our youth to a higher degree of competency than any other country on earth. One-fourth of our total population is enrolled in our schools and colleges. This year 26 billion dollars will be spent on education alone.

But the needs of the next generation—the needs of the next decade and the next school year—will not be met at this level of effort. More effort will be required—on the part of students, teachers, schools, colleges and all 50 states—and on the part of the Federal Government.

Education must remain a matter of state and local control, and higher education a matter of individual choice. But education is increasingly expensive. Too many state and local governments lack the resources to assure an adequate education for every child. Too many classrooms are overcrowded. Too many teachers are underpaid. Too many talented individuals cannot afford the benefits of higher education. Too many academic institutions cannot afford the cost of, or find room for, the growing numbers of students seeking admission in the 60's.

Our twin goals must be: A new standard of excellence in education— and the availability of such excellence to all who are willing and able to pursue it.

A successful educational system requires the proper balance, in terms

---

* 87th Congress, 1st Session, Special Message of the President to the Congress on Education (February 20, 1961).

of both quality and quantity, of three elements: students, teachers and facilities. The quality of the students depends in large measure on both the quality and the relative quantity of teachers and facilities.

Throughout the 1960's there will be no lack in the quantity of students. An average net gain of nearly one million pupils a year during the next ten years will overburden a school system already strained by well over a half-million pupils in curtailed or half-day sessions, a school system financed largely by a property tax incapable of bearing such an increased load in most communities.

But providing the quality and quantity of teachers and facilities to meet this demand will be major problems. Even today, there are some 90,000 teachers who fall short of full certification standards. Tens of thousands of others must attempt to cope with classes of unwieldy size because there are insufficient teachers available.

We cannot obtain more and better teachers—and our children should have the best—unless steps are taken to increase teachers' salaries. At present salary levels, the classroom cannot compete in financial rewards with other professional work that requires similar academic background.

It is equally clear that we do not have enough classrooms. In order to meet current needs and accommodate increasing enrollments, if every child is to have the opportunity of a full-day education in an adequate classroom, a total of 600,000 classrooms must be constructed during the next ten years.

These problems are common to all states. They are particularly severe in those states which lack the financial resources to provide a better education, regardless of their own efforts. Additional difficulties, too often overlooked, are encountered in areas of special educational need, where economic or social circumstances impose special burdens and opportunities on the public school. These areas of special educational need include our depressed areas of chronic unemployment and the slum neighborhoods of our larger cities, where underprivileged children are overcrowded into substandard housing. A recent survey of a very large elementary school in one of our major cities, for example, found 91% of the children coming to class with poor diets, 87% in need of dental care, 21% in need of visual correction and 19% with speech disorders. In some depressed areas roughly one-third of the children must rely on surplus foods for their basic sustenance. Older pupils in these schools lack proper recreational and job guidance. The proportion of drop-outs, delinquency and classroom disorders in such areas is alarmingly high.

I recommend to the Congress a three-year program of general Federal assistance for public elementary and secondary classroom construction and teachers' salaries.

. . . this program would assure every state of no less than $15 for every public school student in average daily attendance, with the total amount appropriated (666 million dollars being authorized in the first year, rising to $866 million over a three-year period) distributed according to the equalization formula contained in the last year's Senate bill, and already familiar to the Congress by virtue of its similarity to the formulas contained in the Hill-Burton Hospital Construction and other acts. Ten percent of the funds allocated to each state in the first year, and an equal amount thereafter, is to be used to help meet the unique problems of each state's "areas of special educational need"—depressed areas, slum neighborhoods and others.

This is a modest program with ambitious goals. The sums involved are relatively small when we think in terms of more than 36 million public school children, and the billions of dollars necessary to educate them properly. Nevertheless, a limited beginning now—consistent with our obligations in other areas of responsibility—will encourage all states to expand their facilities to meet the increasing demand and enrich the quality of education offered, and gradually assist our relatively low-income states in the elevation of their educational standards to a national level.

The bill which will follow this message has been carefully drawn to eliminate disproportionately large or small inequities, and to make the maximum use of a limited number of dollars. In accordance with the clear prohibition of the Constitution, no elementary or secondary school funds are allocated for constructing church schools or paying church school teachers' salaries; and thus non-public school children are rightfully not counted in determining the funds each state will receive for its public schools. Each state will be expected to maintain its own effort or contribution; and every state whose effort is below the national average will be expected to increase that proportion of its income which is devoted to public elementary and secondary education.

This investment will pay rich dividends in the years ahead—in increased economic growth, in enlightened citizens, in national excellence. For some 40 years, the Congress has wrestled with this problem and searched for a workable solution. I believe that we now have such a solution; and that this Congress in this year will make a land-mark contribution to American education.

EDUCATION: IMAGINARY AND REAL PROBLEMS*

Senator Barry Goldwater

I am . . . opposed to the enactment of the committee bill for the reason that if there is a need for Federal aid to education, that need, if it really exists, cannot be met by the committee bill.

However, I introduced early in this session of Congress, a three-part program dealing with education which I believe if enacted, would provide the solution to all problems real and imaginary, confronting our educational system today. . . .

My proposal sets forth a program dealing with the proper role of the Federal Government with respect to education at all levels—elementary school, high school, and college, university, and other institutions of higher learning.

This is a role which must be directed toward helping our people to help themselves without the direct intervention of the Federal Government. It must recognize first and foremost the danger of centralized control over the vitally important areas of life encompassed by the education of our children. Then, it must take account of the actual need which exists for expanding and augmenting the facilities which we now have for meeting the Nation's educational needs. Finally, it should use the power of the Federal Government to place at the disposal of the people and the States and local governments the means to handle the needs that may exist or arise.

The problem is one of letting the people decide, in their own communities where that decision can best be made, just what are their educational needs. After that, it is one of equipping them to handle their needs locally, through their own school boards and without the direction of Washington bureaucracy.

The major domestic problem now facing our Nation is the threat of inflation with its disastrous impact on private savings, insurance, pension funds and social security. This threat has enormous ramifications when applied to our educational problems. . . .

It is my belief that what is primarily wrong with American precollege education is not lack of money but lack of quality. The deterioration in the standards of the American elementary and secondary school has been

---

* 87th Congress, 1st Session. Senate Report No. 255, "School Assistance Act of 1961," pp. 30–35 (1961).

recognized not only by leading scholars in and out of the academic community but finally, by the vast majority of the long-suffering American people as well. It seems obvious that huge sums of additional money should not be spent in perpetuating and aggravating our educational shortcomings. Any program which makes additional funds available for use by our elementary and secondary school systems should be accompanied simultaneously by a program designed to induce improvements in the quality of education. . . .

In spite of the tremendous job which the States and local communities have done during the past 15 years to overcome the backlog of school facilities needed in some areas, a backlog brought on by the depression, World War II, and Korea, the proponents of direct Federal aid to education are nevertheless absolutely insistent that the only way to reduce the backlog is by way of a massive infusion of Federal grants into the States. In recent years, these same proponents have added to their propaganda the claim that teachers are not paid enough by the local school districts and therefore, that it is the responsibility of the Federal Government to correct that situation as well.

It is interesting and significant that the demands for Federal aid to education have grown louder and more insistent as the need for expanding our school facilities diminishes. It is fully apparent that many of those promoting the idea of Federal aid to education are interested only in the element of centralized control and, consequently, refuse to recognize that the States and local communities have been rapidly solving the backlog problem. They have seen their "crisis" selling point melt away in the face of determined local responsibility and are attempting to cover it up by adding new items to their list of needs and more power to their propaganda efforts. The present offensive for Federal aid to and control of the Nation's education is the heaviest ever mounted and it must be met with a courageously sound proposal incorporating the principles of individual freedom and personal responsibility.

I am fully aware that a growing student enrollment has made it difficult for some localities completely to overcome classroom shortages despite the expenditure of considerable amounts of money and effort. I am also conscious of the fact that teachers' salaries have lagged behind those of other professions and vocations, causing some qualified instructors to resign from teaching and enter more highly paid occupations and making it difficult to attract qualified replacements.

However, recently published school statistics dealing with pupil population, enrollment, teachers, and public school expenditures are most revealing. Between 1950 and 1960, public school enrollment increased by 44.4 percent; during this same period, the number of teachers in elementary and secondary schools increased by 51.9 percent, thus reducing the pupil-teacher ratio to 26.4 to 1 as compared to 27.8 to 1 in 1950. But while pupil enrollment and number of teachers are increasing in these ratios, total expenditures for public elementary and secondary schools rose by more than 150 percent.

It is quite obvious from these figures that the States and local communities have been making enormous, and effective efforts to meet their school needs. Wherever the problem of the need for additional classrooms has not been solved, it has not been due to any reluctance on the part of the local community or the State to find and expend the necessary funds.

In view of the willingness of the State and local communities to keep pace with growing educational needs, I reject the wasteful and undemocratic measures to appropriate for school aid, billions of Federal dollars extracted from the States only to be partially funneled back to them again with strict limitations on the use to which these funds may be put.

I believe that the alleged evil plight of our schools has been grossly exaggerated and that the magnificent efforts of our State and local governments to find the money to meet school needs has been largely and purposely ignored.

These efforts represented the quiet response of millions of "forgotten Americans" to the educational problems arising in their communities. The job was done without fanfare by the people who meet their responsibilities on a day-to-day basis without the benefit of prodding by nationwide pressure group organizations. It represents a monument to the efforts of a free people, working with initiative and enterprise in their own communities to meet the problems of those communities as they arose. This is where the big job of meeting the Nation's educational problems has been accomplished up until now and this is where the job, rightfully, should be finished.

My proposal will provide the means for solving additional school problems, if they really exist, but it will leave the determination of this highly debatable question where it properly belongs—with the State and local communities and not with the Federal Government. The basic problem, if there is one, is financial. If State and local governments in some parts of the country are unable to keep pace with their school needs, it is because the Federal taxing power has preempted State and local sources of revenue. Hence, the proper approach is to compel the Federal Government to restore to the States and localities at least a portion of the tax resources which it has taken away. This is precisely what my measure will do.

The proposal is a simple one. Every homeowner, every owner of real estate in the United States pays a real property tax to his local community government. In most cases, a substantial part of this tax is used to meet the primary and secondary public school needs of the community whether for new construction or for maintenance, teachers' salaries or other past or current school costs. S. 991 would merely provide that every taxpayer who pays a school tax on his real property or as a part of his real estate tax, shall after having calculated the amount of Federal income tax which he must pay Uncle Sam, be permitted to subtract from the Federal income tax which he owes, the full amount of such school property tax, or such proportion of it as will result in a total additional tax benefit to these taxpayers of between 3 and 4 billion dollars.

Under existing Federal income tax law, State and local school taxes are deductible from gross income but the amount actually saved by the taxpayer depends on his Federal income tax bracket. Thus, for example, a taxpayer who has paid $200 in school taxes as part of the local real property tax on his home, and is in the 20-percent Federal income tax bracket, realizes a saving of $40. My proposal would retain this present practice, but in addition would permit him to take a $100 credit against what he owed Uncle Sam, i.e., against his net Federal income tax. Hence, instead of a saving of $40, the homeowner under S. 991 would save $140 of the $200 he paid in school taxes on his home. Of course, if the taxpayer's school tax were less than $100, he would be permitted to save in toto no more than the actual amount of his school tax.

This credit would be available to real property-school taxpayers whether they itemize their Federal income tax returns or take the standard deduction.

The concrete advantages of this approach are overwhelming, as will be shown in the following:

1. The tax benefits provided would go directly to approximately 40 million taxpayers, including about 34 million homeowners, who with their families constitute almost 90 percent of our population.

2. With the Federal Government completely excluded from the program, there would be no danger of Federal control over education. Depending on State law, each community itself, or the State, would be the final judge of how much more it would like to spend on its educational needs than it is currently spending.

3. The funds made available to the taxpayers are greater than the sums contemplated under any of the other Federal aid-to-education measures which are seriously being considered; greater even than the sums contained in the committee bill and S. 1241, the administration's higher education bill.

4. Because of the complete exclusion of the Federal Government, there would be no expanded bureaucracy, no Federal administrative costs, and every dollar of tax money thus made available would purchase a full dollar's worth of school aid if the community decided to expand its expenditures for education.

5. Inasmuch as the tax resources of every State and locality would be substantially increased under this proposal, each would have ample funds to provide for its own school needs as it chooses, for none know better what these needs are than the citizens of the States and localities themselves.

6. The so-called richer States would not be required to help finance the school needs of the allegedly poorer States, for under my proposal every State would have sufficient funds to meet its school needs out of its own resources. Rich State A would not be required to pay to the Federal Government in taxes twice or three times as much as it gets back in Federal school aid while poor State B was receiving back in Federal aid two or three times the amount of tax money it paid to the Federal Government as its share of financing the Federal school-aid program.

7. Under any of the other proposed Federal school-aid measures, those States which have fully met their schools needs and would not, if given a free choice, expand their school facilities during the next few years, would nevertheless be compelled to pay their share in Federal taxes to finance the program. The only way these States could recover any of the money thus extracted from them under these various proposals would be to accept the Federal grants and use them to expand their school facilities. The result would be the highly uneconomic and wasteful extension of school facilities in many areas where such extension is unnecessary and where other more urgent needs exist and must perforce remain unsatisfied. Under my proposal, the use made of their money is not dictated to the taxpayers by the bureaucrats in Washington—it is determined by the taxpayers themselves, i.e., by the parent, the citizen, the local school board, and the community.

8. Any objection to my proposal based on the assertion that it would bite into the Federal Treasury is equally applicable to the committee bill. We believe that yours would lead to a good look at the Federal budget and the discovery of many items of less importance, or even of no importance, which could be readily eliminated with no ill effects for the public welfare.

9. If unemployment does not decrease and business continues to falter, my proposal will provide the necessary tax relief which some of the proponents of expanded Federal-aid programs assert to be necessary to stimulate the economy.

10. The preemption of State and local tax resources by the Federal Government would be diminished, and thus an important step would be taken in contracting big central government and strengthening State and local government.

CHAPTER EIGHT

The Federal Government and the Economy

Whether myth or reality, it is still widely accepted in the United States that democracy and the free-enterprise system are inexorably linked. Our first Secretary of the Treasury, Alexander Hamilton, blended mercantilism with *laissez faire* when he made his famous reports and recommendations in the 1780s to the Congress, notably, in his Report on Manufactures. Following Hamilton, government subsidies and taxes were used to aid the development of American capitalism in the nineteenth century. Nonetheless, American capitalism and economic democracy at least until 1913 were generally free of governmental controls.

Both nineteenth-century *laissez faire* capitalism and democratic theory held that the individual was to be allowed the widest scope of freedom consistent with the general welfare. There was no consensus to support a contention that the government had any responsibility for the material welfare of the individual. President Grover Cleveland, a foe of paternalism in government, vetoed a congressional bill appropriating $10,000 for seed to aid the drought-stricken farmers of Texas. Cleveland responded to the bill with "I can find no warrant for such an appropriation in the Constitution, and I do not believe that the power and duty of General Government ought to be expended to the relief of individual suffering which is in no manner properly related to the public service or benefit." Government was pure, just, and economical, but not benevolent! Today, aid to drought- or flood-stricken counties is perhaps the least thing the American farmer expects and gets from his government. Wars and cold wars, depressions, and recessions have altered our views about just what constitutes a "public benefit." Today, government control as well as government assistance is widely accepted. There is a consensus to support the belief that the public welfare is tied to the welfare of farmers, businessmen, and laborers. The area of disagreement concerns just how extensive that relationship should be.

Regardless of how antiquated nineteenth-century rugged individualism might appear in the economy of the 1960s, there is, nonetheless, a strong antipathy to the phrase "state planning." State planning brings to mind collectivism, and from collectivism the mind jumps to socialism and communism. The reality of *ad hoc* federal government fiscal and welfare programs is accepted; but to go from such adaptive policies to a rationally coordinated fiscal plan is something else again. Gunnar Myrdal notes that in both Western Europe and the United States governmental responsibility for the fiscal health of the nation is no longer debatable. Governments plan against mass unemployment, for better housing, against a breakdown in transportation facilities, etc. He feels, however, that it is past time for the governments to coordinate these plans by means of their tax and budget policies into a national means of influencing the whole national economy.

If Mr. Myrdal believes that "spending one's way out of a depression" is becoming orthodox, or if he believes coordinated national economic planning is in the immediate future of the United States, many would disagree. Congressman Thomas B. Curtis denies that the government can spend its way to national prosperity. Ludwig Von Mises' essay has a basic message for planners of the welfare state: there is no Santa Claus! Like former President Eisenhower, Von Mises believes that there is no inexhaustible fund to pay for welfare programs. But going beyond the views of Eisenhower, Von Mises attacks the whole theory of governmental intervention in the economy as a vicious theory that spreads economic havoc.

On the other hand, President Kennedy, in his Yale speech, defends deficit spending and, inferentially, government intervention in the economy. He denies that deficits necessarily create inflation or that budget surpluses necessarily prevent inflation. Both Mr. Eisenhower and Congressman Curtis see deficits as fiscal irresponsibility, and in examining President Kennedy's 1964 budget proposals, they called for cuts in expenditures to wipe out the proposed deficits.

The complexity of the budget issue is evident when one examines the 1964 Kennedy budget proposals. In his Yale speech, President Kennedy called the old administrative or conventional budget a misleading myth. In the 1964 proposals, if the conventional approach is used, the planned deficit would be $11.9 billion; using the consolidated cash budget, the deficit would be $10.3 billion; and using the national-income-accounting approach, the deficit would be $7.6 billion—and all of these are based on the same expenditures and appropriations!

The 1964 Kennedy budget of approximately $100 billion was coupled with a tax-cut proposal designed to promote new capital investment and additional consumer buying. Leon Keyserling, former economic adviser to President Truman, attacks the budget deficit and the proposed tax cut with a view from the left—that neither the deficit nor the tax cut are big enough to prime the pump of the national economy. Keyserling follows the Keynesian view of the response of the economy to governmental stimulation by budget and tax policies. He is seconded by Kermit Gordon, director of the Bureau of the Budget. Gordon sees the deficit as one result of a budget policy; but the purpose of this deficit is to stimulate economic growth. An accelerated economic growth in turn will wipe out deficits, and help attack the unemployment problem.

The political lines on the issues of federal spending and tax policy are never clearly drawn. Generally, the Republicans share a more orthodox fiscal position, whereas the Democrats frequently believe that the orthodox policy of balanced budgets is unrealistic. In the past, the Republicans have called for tax cuts to stimulate business and the Democrats have shared Myrdal's redistributional theories. These positions on tax policy have shifted somewhat. In 1964, the electorate will face Democrats advocating new tax-cutting policies coupled with increased spending, and Republicans advocating a cautious position on taxation and spending.

PLANNING IN THE WELFARE STATE*

Gunnar Myrdal

The Historical and Causal Order

In the last half century, the state, in all the rich countries in the Western world, has become a democratic "Welfare State," with fairly explicit commitments to the broad goals of economic development, full employment, equality of opportunity for the young, social security, and protected minimum standards as regards not only income, but nutrition, housing, health, and education for people of all regions and social groups. The Welfare State is nowhere, as yet, an accomplishment; it is continually in the process of coming into being. In no country was it originally planned in advance—certainly not as a structure of its present imposing ramifications and importance for the individual citizens. In all countries, even in those where the building of the Welfare State is most advanced, the architects are continually laboring with the tasks of simplification, coordi-

---

* Reprinted by permission from *Beyond the Welfare State*, by Gunnar Myrdal. Copyright 1960 by Yale University Press. Pp. 62–72. Mr. Myrdal is a well-known Swedish economist and author of *An American Dilemma*.

nation, rationalization and achievement of efficiency. Indeed, this planning becomes pressing as the edifice of the Welfare State rises.

That this must be so, should be clear from the analysis I have given of the forces behind the trend towards planning in the Western countries. The historical and causal order has been that acts of intervention in the play of market forces came first, and that planning then became a necessity. In a process of cumulative causation, the secular increase in the volume of intervention has been spurred on by the sequence of violent international crises since World War I, the increasing rationality of people's attitudes, the democratization of political power, and the growth of provincial and municipal self-government and of large-scale enterprises and interest organizations in all markets. Thus, as public and private intervention became more frequent and more far-reaching and closely related to the other constituents of this mighty process of social change, so there arose situations of growing complexity, contradiction, and confusion. With ever greater impact, the need for a rationalizing coordination of them all was pressed upon the state as the central organ for the public will.

Coordination leads to planning or, rather, it *is* planning, as this term has come to be understood in the Western world. Coordination of measures of intervention implies a reconsideration of them all from the point of view of how they combine to serve the development goals of the entire national community, as these goals become determined by the political process that provides the basis for power. The need for this coordination arose because the individual acts of intervention, the total volume of which was growing, had not been considered in this way when they were initiated originally.

As the state is increasingly involved in coordinating and regulating the national economy, it becomes compelled to make short-term and long-term forecasts, and to try to modify its policies for commerce, finance, development, and social reform in the light of what these forecasts show. A very much improved basis of statistical and other information is also becoming available to the governments. This coordination of policies, and their continued modification in order to remain appropriate in the setting of factual trends revealed by the forecasts, does not take the shape of a rigid, all-embracing plan. Nevertheless, it constitutes a steadily developing approach to planning, which tends to become firmer and more embracing as present tendencies work themselves out.

From Intervention to Planning

As regards the activities of the big enterprises and the organizations in the infrastructure beneath the formal constitutional structure, it is, of course, clear at the outset that they were not from the beginning part of a rationally coordinated national plan. They regularly represented special interests, not the general and common interests of the nation. But, as a matter of fact, the lack of coordination is equally apparent in public policies as they were initially motivated and decided upon. The history of economic policies in every country, as regards, for instance, tariffs and taxes, gives abundant proof of this thesis.

There is further proof in the records of how the huge structures for primary and higher education and for public health were built up, and also in the big redistributional reforms, such as the social security schemes and other measures for the care of the sick, the disabled, the unemployed, the aged, and the children. All these complexes of economic and social intervention, as they now exist, have been the end product of a long process of piecemeal, gradually induced changes, which in the different fields have been pressed forward, at first as independent and unrelated policy measures, motivated on their own merits or undertaken in response to group pressures.

It is, for instance, remarkable that the social security schemes, which are becoming increasingly expensive, were initially supported only by arguments of social justice and welfare for specific groups of people in need; and such arguments remained predominant for a long time. When the opponents of these schemes, who argued all the time that they would ruin the economy of the country, were again and again proved wrong, this was largely the result of the effect of these reforms in raising the productivity of the mass of the people—an effect which had never played an important part in their motivation. As considerations of these wider effects and interrelations gradually come to the fore in public discussion, the explanation is mainly that these policy measures have by now become so numerous and important, and that they re-direct the distribution of such a very large portion of the national product, that they simply must be coordinated with one another, and with the development of the entire national economy. Thus we arrive at planning in the modern sense.

Public intervention in the field of housing and construction of new houses, affords another example. Since the scanty and diffuse beginnings of a few decades ago, it has been increasing tremendously in all Western countries. The state now finds itself responsible for influencing decisively—directly through its legislation and administration and that of the provincial and municipal authorities, or indirectly through the organizations in the infrastructure that operate under the state's indulgence and sanction—the conditions under which people can find houses to live in, and under which some people can make it a business to provide homes. This involved complex of intervention concerns the level of rents, the availability and price of building and mortgage credits, the conditions on the several labor markets and the markets for building materials, and, indeed, every aspect of the entire economic process by which houses are built, owned or rented, and inhabited. The future number and the age composition of families and other factors determining both human need and effective demand for housing, must be predicted and allowed for, as must the effects of building activity upon trends of general business activity, in the short and long run. The latter effects are so important that the level of building activity has to be watched carefully, even from the point of view of general economic policy. As the cities grow, and as more public investment becomes involved in preparing for such growth, town planning becomes ever more necessary, as does the general public preoccupation with planning and directing the location of industry.

In the same way, the rapid development of higher and professional education now absorbs so much money, and concerns so many young people in all these countries, that it is gradually becoming realized that this activity cannot continue as an independent process of dispersed public policies. Instead, it has to be planned carefully on the basis of calculations of future demand for, and supply of, labor trained in different ways. This necessarily involves a forecast and a plan for the whole national economy. Again, the converse also applies; no long-range forecast or plan for the national economy can any longer be made without including policies for education and training.

Sweden is now inaugurating, as a final effort to complete the edifice of social security, a compulsory provident and pension scheme, aimed at eradicating what are almost the last remnants of class distinction between manual workers and other employees of public and private enterprises. It is probably taking the lead in a reform movement which other Western countries will soon join. All old people will, by legislation, be guaranteed an income corresponding to two-thirds of their earnings during the best fifteen years of their working life. It is clear that a redistributional reform of this huge magnitude must be founded on the most careful forecast of the development of the entire national economy for a long period ahead, and must be integrated into the whole system of public policies influencing this development. Otherwise it would represent the most reckless gambling with the future economy of the country, risking the frustration of national efforts in all fields. This is more evidently the case as the social security payments to the old are being guaranteed in real terms. It is characteristic of the situation Western countries have now reached in regard to planning that a main criticism raised in Sweden against this reform is that the calculations of its effects on the total economic development of the country are not complete and tight enough. This preoccupation with planning is not least prominent in the minds of the conservatives, who oppose the reform.

"Full Employment"

In a sense, the biggest commitment to economic planning in the Welfare State of the Western countries is that they are all now pledged to preserving "full employment," though the definition, as well as the form, of the commitment varies. The political process by which governments have gradually reached this situation illuminates this trend towards planning.

Not many decades ago the periodic appearance of mass unemployment was accepted as a more or less natural consequence of necessary market adjustments to changing business conditions, about which not much could be done. As, however, the political power of the workers increased in the process of democratization, to which I have referred, and as the social conscience became more alert to the sufferings of the unemployed and their families—two changes which, of course, are closely related—measures of financial aid to the unemployed were instituted in one country after another.

At first, these policy measures were all of a compensatory nature, aimed merely at providing the unemployed workers with some of the incomes they had lost by becoming unemployed. It was the symptom, not the cause, of unemployment that was being dealt with. Unemployment insurance, which now forms an integral part of the social security system in all Western countries, represents the consummation of this line of social policy. But soon the demand was raised that the state should take positive measures in order to create additional work opportunities for the unemployed. In the twenties, and still more during the Great Depression, public works policies spread in all Western countries. At the same time, the workers began to press for full wages even in these public works.

These developments represented only steps towards demanding that the state should so direct all its financial and economic policies as to create demand for labor sufficient to liquidate mass unemployment and to keep the national economy uninterruptedly in high gear. Economic theory now responded to the ideological needs of the time by placing the responsibility for economic depressions and unemployment on an imbalance between aggregate demand and supply, opening up a rational way for the state to raise investment and production and to create employment simply by raising its expenditure while keeping down taxation. In Sweden, which amongst the Western countries was the first, both theoretically and practically, to adopt this policy, "pump priming" worked fairly well even in the early years of the Great Depression, as it happened to be supplemented by other simultaneous changes in general business conditions which were favorable to a recovery but not part of intentional policy. Similar policies in the United States and many other countries were less successful, the main explanation being that the over-spending was too small to have much effect.

After World War II we have all become accustomed to much bigger budgets and also to taking huge budget deficits less seriously. The expansionist theory of spending one's way out of a depression is now on the way to becoming orthodox, even in the more conservative sections of the business world. It has, as yet, not been put to much of a test, however, as first the urgent reconstruction needs and the pent-up demands immediately after the war, and later the immense armament expenditures and other financial consequences of the cold war, have contributed in mighty fashion to sustain total demand. Inflation and not deflation has been the continuous worry. But, whatever the explanation, it is in any case a fact that on the whole all the Western countries have enjoyed full employment, not only during but also after the war. Now only a dwindling minority of workers in these countries have any personal experience of mass unemployment or any recollection of the situation some few decades ago, when even in boom years the fear of unemployment was a sinister cloud on the horizon for every working-class family. It is safe to predict that in none of the Western countries will a period of severe unemployment ever again be tolerated by the people.

In a sense, this determination to preserve full employment is the crowning accomplishment of the democratic Welfare State. It is generally understood and accepted that this implies a preparedness to use even radical policy measures, when needed, in order to keep the entire labor force employed, and also that this assumes a most careful watch on the entire economic development and a planned coordination of all economic policies.

The Fiscal Budgets

All these developments towards planning in the Western world have, of course, had their consequences for the fiscal budgets, which integrate a certain type of public intervention and, in one way or another, reflect others. A steady rise in the size of these budgets and an increased level of taxation were secular trends in Western countries even before World War I. These trends would have continued their course upwards, even without the push of the crises and the world wars, although they would have risen much less steeply. A convenient way of illustrating what has happened to fiscal policy may be to focus our attention on the science of public finance.

Public finance remained for centuries primarily a study of the rational conduct of the households of the states, the provinces, and the municipalities. Modern science took over directly from the Cameralists. Taxes were studied from the point of view of their ultimate incidence and their just distribution among the citizens. The relation between the public finances and the total economy of a country was dealt with in the same way as is natural and appropriate for an individual person or a business concern: exclusively as a one-way relation, from economy to taxation and public spending. The problem was how the development of the total economy reflected itself in changes in the need for public expenditure and in the yield of taxes and other public incomes at given rates.

For, before World War I, the public finances were not a large enough part of the total economy of a country to have any very significant influence in the other direction, i.e., on the business situation. And during this era, people, including the economists, were not interested enough anyhow in directing the national economy in a planned way to give much importance to this other problem. It lacked political actuality. This is the science of public finance we still find in our old textbooks.

This characterization of the science of public finance before 1914 is broadly correct. However, it must be borne in mind that even before the eighteenth century there had been plenty of speculation and discussion as to the role of fiscal policy, and especially of the effects of state borrowing on the general business situation. That interest, though, was usually centered upon one particular practical issue; it never determined the structure of fiscal theory as a whole. National budgeting was never approached with a view to its general effect upon the trade cycle or economic growth.

World War I had vast fiscal consequences, in many ways, and these were widely discussed. But such discussion never mentioned the possible use of the budget as a tool in social or economic engineering.

When the Great Depression set in during the thirties, public finances had already, because of the growth of public intervention in economic life, come to absorb so large a proportion of the national product that a variation of public incomes and expenditures could have a substantial influence on the development of the economy as a whole. And the interventionist spirit was rising. The science of public finance during the thirties became, therefore, focused on the problem of how to manipulate the fiscal budgets in such a way as to counteract business variations downwards.

This second stage turned out to be very short. Now, after World War II we are in the third stage. Often something around a third of the national income passes through treasury accounts and the trend is still rising. It thus becomes impossible to distinguish a separate public finance problem any longer. Both the old textbooks and our discussion during the thirties of a planned, counter-cyclical budgetary policy appear outmoded.

The problems of public finance are now inseparably merged with problems of international trade and payments, wages and incomes, money and credit. The theoretical organizing device is the national budget, conceived as the central bookkeeping control in the service of an overall state economic forecasting and planning network. The national budget accounts for the composition of the entire national income and its disposal for investment and consumption by private as well as public agents. In this national budget, the fiscal budget appears only as a set of items to be analyzed as part of the whole.

The problems of the two earlier stages of the development of the science of public finance still exist and are important: the incidence and the equitable distribution of taxes and the influence of public finances on the general business situation. But they are now integrated inextricably with all other problems of economic policy and are subordinated to the one dominating question of the direction of the whole national economy. In the short span of a lifetime, the science of public finance has had its scope and content radically changed, not once but twice. This illustrates the impact of the growth of public policies and points to the final result of this trend towards overall state economic planning, even if this planning is as yet of a compromise character and anything but comprehensive, programmatic or politically ostentatious.

THE CRISIS OF INTERVENTIONISM*

Ludwig Von Mises

The Harvest of Interventionism

The interventionist policies as practiced for many decades by all governments of the capitalistic West have brought about all those effects which the economists predicted. There are wars and civil wars, ruthless oppression of the masses by clusters of self-appointed dictators, economic depressions, mass unemployment, capital consumption, famines.

However, it is not these catastrophic events which have led to the crisis of interventionism. The interventionist doctrinaires and their followers explain all these undesired consequences as the unavoidable features of capitalism. As they see it, it is precisely these disasters that clearly demonstrate the necessity of intensifying interventionism. The failures of the

---

* Reprinted by permission from *Human Action: A Treatise on Economics*, by Ludwig Von Mises. Pp. 851–857. Copyright 1949 by Yale University Press. Mr. Von Mises is an economist, author, and lecturer.

interventionist policies do not in the least impair the popularity of the implied doctrine. They are so interpreted as to strengthen, not to lessen, the prestige of these teachings. As a vicious economic theory cannot be simply refuted by historical experience, the interventionist propagandists have been able to go on in spite of all the havoc they have spread.

Yet the age of interventionism is reaching its end. Interventionism has exhausted all its potentialities and must disappear.

The Exhaustion of the Reserve Fund

The idea underlying all interventionist policies is that the higher income and wealth of the more affluent part of the population is a fund which can be freely used for the improvement of the conditions of the less prosperous. The essence of the interventionist policy is to take from one group to give to another. It is confiscation and distribution. Every measure is ultimately justified by declaring that it is fair to curb the rich for the benefit of the poor.

In the field of public finance progressive taxation of incomes and estates is the most characteristic manifestation of this doctrine. Tax the rich and spend the revenue for the improvement of the condition of the poor, is the principle of contemporary budgets. In the field of industrial relations shortening the hours of work, raising wages, and a thousand other measures are recommended under the assumption that they favor the employee and burden the employer. Every issue of government and community affairs is dealt with exclusively from the point of view of this principle.

An illustrative example is provided by the methods applied in the operation of nationalized and municipalized enterprises. These enterprises very often result in financial failure; their accounts regularly show losses burdening the state or the city treasury. It is of no use to investigate whether the deficits are due to the notorious inefficiency of the public conduct of business enterprises or, at least partly, to the inadequacy of the prices at which the commodities or services are sold to the customers. What matters more is the fact that the taxpayers must cover these deficits. The interventionists fully approve of this arrangement. They passionately reject the two other possible solutions: selling the enterprises to private entrepreneurs or raising the prices charged to the customers to such a height that no further deficit remains. The first of these proposals is in their eyes manifestly reactionary because the inevitable trend of history is toward more and more socialization. The second is deemed "antisocial" because it places a heavier load upon the consuming masses. It is fairer to make the taxpayers, i.e., the wealthy citizens, bear the burden. Their ability to pay is greater than that of the average people riding the nationalized railroads and the municipalized subways, trolleys, and busses. To ask that such public utilities should be self-supporting, is, say the interventionists, a relic of the old-fashioned ideas of orthodox finance. One might as well aim at making the roads and the public schools self-supporting.

It is not necessary to argue with the advocates of this deficit policy. It is obvious that recourse to this ability-to-pay principle depends on the existence of such incomes and fortunes as can still be taxed away. It can no longer be resorted to once these extra funds have been exhausted by taxes and other interventionist measures.

This is precisely the present state of affairs in most of the European countries. The United States has not yet gone so far; but if the actual trend of its economic policies is not radically altered very soon, it will be in the same condition in a few years.

For the sake of argument we may disregard all the other consequences which the full triumph of the ability-to-pay principle must bring about and concentrate upon its financial aspects.

The interventionist in advocating additional public expenditure is not aware of the fact that the funds available are limited. He does not realize that increasing expenditure in one department enjoins restricting it in other departments. In his opinion there is plenty of money available. The income and wealth of the rich can be freely tapped. In recommending a greater allowance for the schools he simply stresses the point that it would be a good thing to spend more for education. He does not venture to prove that to raise the budgetary allowance for schools is more expedient than to raise that of another department, e.g., that of health. It never occurs to him that grave arguments could be advanced in favor of restricting public spending and lowering the burden of taxation. The champions of cuts in the budget are in his eyes merely the defenders of the manifestly unfair class interests of the rich.

With the present height of income and inheritance tax rates, this reserve fund out of which the interventionists seek to cover all public expenditure is rapidly shrinking. It has practically disappeared altogether in most European countries. In the United States the recent advances in tax rates produced only negligible revenue results beyond what would be produced by a progression which stopped at much lower rates. High surtax rates for the rich are very popular with interventionist dilettantes and demagogues, but they secure only modest additions to the revenue. From day to day it becomes more obvious that large-scale additions to the amount of public expenditure cannot be financed by "soaking the rich," but that the burden must be carried by the masses. The traditional tax policy of the age of interventionism, its glorified devices of progressive taxation and lavish spending, have been carried to a point at which their absurdity can no longer be concealed. The notorious principle that, whereas private expenditures depend on the size of income available, public revenues must be regulated according to expenditures, refutes itself. Henceforth, governments will have to realize that one dollar cannot be spent twice, and that the various items of government expenditure are in conflict with one another. Every penny of additional government spending will have to be collected from precisely those people who hitherto have been intent upon shifting the main burden to other groups. Those anxious to get subsidies will have to foot the bill themselves for the subsidies. The deficits of publicly owned and operated enterprises will be charged to the bulk of the population.

The situation in the employer-employee nexus will be analogous. The popular doctrine contends that wage earners are reaping "social gains" at the expense of the unearned income of the exploiting classes. The strikers, it is said, do not strike against the consumers but against "management." There is no reason to raise the prices of products when labor costs are increased; the difference must be borne by employers. But when more and more of the share of the entrepreneurs and capitalists is absorbed by taxes, higher wage rates, and other "social gains" of employees, and by price ceilings, nothing remains for such a buffer function. Then it becomes evident that every wage raise, with its whole momentum, must affect the prices of the products and that the social gains of each group fully correspond to the social losses of the other groups. Every strike becomes, even in the short run and not only in the long run, a strike against the rest of the people.

An essential point in the social philosophy of interventionism is the existence of an inexhaustible fund which can be squeezed forever. The whole doctrine of interventionism collapses when this fountain is drained off. The Santa Claus principle liquidates itself.

The End of Interventionism

The interventionist interlude must come to an end because interventionism cannot lead to a permanent system of social organization. The reasons are threefold.

First: Restrictive measures always restrict output and the amount of goods available for consumption. Whatever arguments may be advanced in favor of definite restrictions and prohibitions, such measures in themselves can never constitute a system of social production.

Second: All varieties of interference with the market phenomena not only fail to achieve the ends aimed at by their authors and supporters, but bring about a state of affairs which—from the point of view of their authors' and advocates' valuations—is less desirable than the previous state of affairs which they were designed to alter. If one wants to correct their manifest unsuitableness and preposterousness by supplementing the first acts of intervention with more and more of such acts, one must go farther and farther until the market economy has been entirely destroyed and socialism has been substituted for it.

Third: Interventionism aims at confiscating the "surplus" of one part of the population and at giving it to the other part. Once this surplus is exhausted by total confiscation, a further continuation of this policy is impossible.

Marching ever further on the way of interventionism, first Germany, then Great Britain and many other European countries have adopted central planning, the Hindenburg pattern of socialism. It is noteworthy that in Germany the deciding measures were not resorted to by the Nazis, but some time before Hitler seized power by Bruning, the Catholic Chancellor of the Weimar Republic, and in Great Britain not by the Labor Party but by the Tory Prime Minister Mr. Churchill. The fact has been purposely obscured by the great sensation made in Great Britain about the nationalization of the Bank of England, the coal mines, and other enterprises. However, these seizures were of subordinate importance only. Great Britain is to be called a socialist country not because certain enterprises have been formally expropriated and nationalized, but because all the economic activities of all citizens are subject to full control by the government and its agencies. The authorities direct the allocation of capital and of manpower to the various branches of business; they determine what should be produced and in what quality and quantity, and they assign to each consumer a definite ration. Supremacy in all economic matters is exclusively vested in the government. The people are reduced to the status of wards. To the businessmen, the former entrepreneurs, merely quasi-managerial functions are left. All that they are free to do is to carry into effect the entrepreneurial decisions of the authorities within a neatly delimited narrow field.

It has been shown that the managerial system, i.e., the assignment of ancillary tasks in the conduct of business to responsible helpers to whom a certain amount of discretion can be granted, is possible only within the frame of the profit system. What characterizes the manager as such and imparts to him a condition different from that of the mere technician is that, within the sphere of his assignment, he himself determines the methods by which his actions should conform to the profit principle. In a socialist system in which there is neither economic calculation nor capital accounting nor profit computation, there is no room left for managerial activities either. But as long as a socialist commonwealth is still in a position to calculate on the ground of prices determined on foreign markets, it can also utilize a quasi-managerial hierarchy to some extent.

It is a poor makeshift to call any age an age of transition. In the living world there is always change. Every age is an age of transition. We may distinguish between social systems that can last and such as are inevitably transitory because they are self-destructive. It has already been pointed out in what sense interventionism liquidates itself and must lead to socialism of the German pattern. Most of the European countries have already reached this phase, and nobody knows whether or not the United States will follow suit. But as long as the United States clings to the market economy and does not adopt the system of full government control of business, the socialist economies of Western Europe will still be in a position to calculate. Their conduct of business still lacks the characteristic feature of socialist conduct; it is still based on economic calculation. It is therefore in every respect very different from what it would become if all the world were to turn toward socialism.

It is often said that one half of the world cannot remain committed to the market economy when the other half is socialist, and vice versa. However, there is no reason to assume that such a partition of the earth and the coexistence of the two systems is impossible. If this is really the case, then the present economic system of the countries that have discarded capitalism may go on for an indefinite period of time. Its operation may result in social disintegration, chaos, and misery for the peoples. But neither a low standard of living nor progressive impoverishment automatically liquidates an economic system. It gives way to a more efficient system only if people themselves are intelligent enough to comprehend the advantages such a change might bring them. Or it may be destroyed by foreign invaders provided with better military equipment by the greater efficiency of their own economic system.

Optimists hope that at least those nations which have in the past developed the capitalist market economy and its civilization will cling to this system in the future too. There are certainly as many signs to confirm as to disprove such an expectation. It is vain to speculate about the outcome of the great ideological conflict between the principles of private ownership and public ownership, of individualism and totalitarianism, of freedom and authoritarian regimentation. All that we can know beforehand about the result of this struggle can be condensed in the following three statements:

1. We have no knowledge whatever about the existence and operation of agencies which would bestow final victory in this clash on those ideologies whose application will secure the preservation and further intensification of societal bonds and the improvement of mankind's material well-being. Nothing suggests the belief that progress toward more satisfactory conditions is inevitable or a relapse into very unsatisfactory conditions impossible.

2. Men must choose between the market economy and socialism. They

cannot evade deciding between these alternatives by adopting a "middle-of-the-road" position, whatever name they may give to it.

3. In abolishing economic calculation the general adoption of socialism would result in complete chaos and the disintegration of social cooperation under the division of labor.

SOME MODERN ECONOMIC MYTHS*

President John F. Kennedy

President Griswold, members of the faculty, graduates and their families, ladies and gentlemen: Let me begin by expressing my appreciation for the very deep honor that you have conferred upon me. As General DeGaulle occasionally acknowledges America to be the daughter of Europe, so I am pleased to come to Yale, the daughter of Harvard. It might be said now that I have the best of both worlds, a Harvard education and a Yale degree.

I am particularly glad to become a Yale man because as I think about my troubles, I find that a lot of them have come from other Yale men. Among businessmen I have had a minor disagreement with Roger Blough, of the Law School Class of 1931, and I have had some complaints too from my friend Henry Ford, of the class of 1940. In journalism, I seem to have a difference with John Hay Whitney, of the class of 1926—and sometimes I also displease Henry Luce of the class of 1920, not to mention also William F. Buckley, Jr., of the class of 1950. I even have some trouble with my Yale advisors. I get along with them, but I am not always sure how they get along with each other.

I have the warmest feelings for Chester Bowles of the class of 1924 and for Dean Acheson, of the class of 1915, and my assistant, McGeorge Bundy, of the class of 1940, but I am not 100 per cent sure that these three wise and experienced Yale men wholly agree with each other on every issue.

So this Administration which aims at peaceful cooperation among all Americans has been the victim of a certain natural pugnacity developed in this city among Yale men. Now that I, too, am a Yale man, it is time for peace. Last week at West Point, in the historic tradition of that Academy,

---

* Commencement Address, Yale University, June 1962.

I availed myself of the powers of Commander in Chief to remit all sentences of offending cadets. In that same spirit, and in the historic tradition of Yale, let me now offer to smoke the clay pipe of friendship with all of my brother Elis, and I hope that they may be friends not only with me but even with each other.

In any event, I am very glad to be here and as a new member of the club, I have been checking to see what earlier links existed between the institution of the Presidency and Yale, I found that a member of the class of 1878, William Howard Taft, served one term in the White House as preparation for becoming a member of this faculty. And a graduate of 1804, John C. Calhoun, regarded the Vice Presidency as too lowly a station for a Yale alumnus—and became the only man in history to ever resign that office.

Calhoun in 1804 and Taft in 1878 graduated into a world very different from ours today. They and their contemporaries spent entire careers stretching over 40 years in grappling with a few dramatic issues on which the nation was sharply and emotionally divided, issues that occupied the attention of a generation at a time: the National Bank, the disposal of the public lands, nullification or union, freedom or slavery, gold or silver. Today these old sweeping issues very largely have disappeared. The central domestic issues of our time are more subtle and less simple. They relate not to basic clashes of philosophy or ideology but to ways and means of reaching common goals—to research for sophisticated solutions to complex and obstinate issues. The world of Calhoun, the world of Taft had its own hard problems and notable challenges. But its problems are not our problems. Their age is not our age. As every past generation has had to disenthrall itself from an inheritance of truism and stereotype, so in our own time we must move on from the reassuring repetition of stale phrases to a new, difficult but essential confrontation with reality.

For the great enemy of the truth is very often not the lie—deliberate, contrived and dishonest—but the myth—persistent, persuasive and unrealistic. Too often we hold fast to the cliches of our forebears. We subject all facts to a prefabricated set of interpretations. We enjoy the comfort of opinion without the discomfort of thought.

Mythology distracts us everywhere—in government as in business, in politics as in economics, in foreign affairs as in domestic policy. But today I want to particularly consider the myth and reality in our national economy. In recent months many have come to feel, as I do, that the dialogue between the parties—between business and government—is clogged by illusion and platitude and fails to reflect the true realities of contemporary American society. . . .

There are three great areas of our domestic affairs in which, today, there is a danger that illusion may prevent effective action. They are, first, the question of the size and the shape of government's responsibilities; second, the question of public fiscal policy; and third, the matter of confidence, business confidence or public confidence, or simply confidence in America. I want to talk about all three, and I want to talk about them carefully and dispassionately—and I emphasize that I am concerned here not with political debate but with finding ways to separate false problems from real ones. . . .

Let us take first the question of the size and shape of government. The myth here is that government is big, and bad—and steadily getting bigger and worse. Obviously this myth has some excuse for existence. It is true that in recent history each new Administration has spent much more money than its predecessor. Thus President Roosevelt outspent President Hoover, and with allowances for the special case of the Second World War, President Truman outspent President Roosevelt. Just to prove that this was not a partisan matter, President Eisenhower outspent President Truman by the handsome figure of $182 billion. It is even possible something of this trend may continue.

But does it follow that big government is growing relatively bigger? It does not—for the fact is for the last 15 years, the Federal Government—and also the Federal debt—and also the federal bureaucracy—have grown less rapidly than the economy as a whole. If we leave defense and space expenditures aside, the Federal Government since the Second World War has expended less than any other major sector of our national life— less than industry, less than commerce, less than agriculture, less than higher education, and very much less than the noise about big government.

The truth about big government is the truth about any other great activity—it is complex. Certainly it is true that size brings dangers—but it is also true that size also can bring benefits. Here at Yale, which has contributed so much to our national progress in science and medicine, it may be proper for me to mention one great and little noticed expansion of government which has brought strength to our whole society. The new role of our federal government as the major patron of research in science and in medicine. Few people realize that in 1961, in support of all university research in science and medicine, three dollars out of every four came from the federal government. I need hardly point out that this has taken place without undue enlargement of government control—that American scientists remain second to none in their independence and in their individualism.

I am not suggesting that federal expenditures cannot bring some measure of control. The whole thrust of federal expenditures in agriculture has been related by purpose and design to control . . . as a means of dealing with the problems created by our farmers and our growing productivity. Each sector, my point is, of activity must be approached on its own merits and in terms of specific national needs. Generalities in regard to federal expenditures, therefore, can be misleading—each case, science, urban renewal, education, agriculture, natural resources, each case must be determined on its merits if we are to profit from our unrivaled ability to combine the strength of public and private purpose.

Next, let us turn to the problem of our fiscal policy. Here the myths are legion and the truth hard to find. But let me take as a prime example the problem of the federal budget. We persist in measuring our federal fiscal integrity today by the conventional or administrative budget—with results which would be regarded as absurd in any business firm—in any country of Europe—or in any careful assessment of the reality of our national finances. The administrative budget has sound administrative uses. But for wider purposes it is less helpful. It omits our special trust funds; it neglects changes in assets or inventories. It cannot tell a loan from a straight expenditure—and worst of all it cannot distinguish between operating expenditures and long term investments.

This budget, in relation to the great problems of federal fiscal policy, is not simply irrelevant; it can be actively misleading. And yet there is a mythology that measures all of our national soundness or unsoundness on the single simple basis of this same annual administrative budget. If our federal budget is to serve, not the debate, but the country, we must and will find ways of clarifying this area of discourse.

Still in the area of fiscal policy, let me say a word about deficits. The myth persists that federal deficits create inflation and budget surpluses prevent it. Yet sizeable budget surpluses after the war did not prevent inflation, and persistent deficits for the last several years have not upset our basic price stability. Obviously deficits are sometimes dangerous—and so are surpluses. But honest assessment plainly requires a more sophisticated view than the old and automatic cliche that deficits automatically bring inflation.

There are myths also about our public debt. It is widely supposed that this debt is growing at a dangerously rapid rate. In fact, both the debt per person and the debt as a proportion of our gross national product have declined sharply since the Second World War. In absolute terms the national debt increased only 8 per cent, while private debt was increasing 305 per cent, and the debts of state and local governments increased 378 per cent. Moreover, debts, public and private, are neither good nor bad, in and of themselves. Borrowing can lead to over-extension and collapse—but it can also lead to expansion and strength. There is no single, simple slogan in this field that we can trust.

Finally, I come to the problem of confidence. Confidence is a matter of myth and also a matter of truth—and this time let me take the truth of the matter first.

It is true—and of high importance—that the prosperity of this country depends on assurance that all major elements within it will live up to their responsibilities. If business were to neglect its obligations to the public; if labor were blind to all public responsibility; above all, if government were to abandon its obvious—and statutory—duty of watchful concern for our economic health—if any of these things should happen, then confidence might well be weakened and danger of stagnation would increase. This is the true issue of confidence.

But there is also the false issue—and its simplest form is the assertion that any and all unfavorable turns of the speculative wheel—however temporary and however plainly speculative in character—are the result of, and I quote, "lack of confidence in the national administration." This I must tell you, while comforting, is not wholly true. Worse, it obscures the reality—which is also simple. The solid ground of mutual confidence is the necessary partnership of government with all of the sectors of our society in the steady quest for economic progress.

Corporate plans are not based on a political confidence in party leaders but on an ecomonic confidence in the nation's ability to invest and produce and consume. Business had full confidence in the Administrations in power in 1929, 1954, 1958, and 1960—but this was not enough to prevent recession when business lacked full confidence in the economy. What matters is the capacity of the nation as a whole to deal with its economic problems and its opportunities.

The stereotypes I have been discussing distract our attention and divide our effort. These stereotypes do our nation a disservice, not just because they are exhausted and irrelevant, but above all because they are misleading—because they stand in the way of the solution of hard and complicated facts. It is not new that past debates should obscure present realities. But the damage of such a false dialogue is greater today than ever before simply because today the safety of all the world—the very future of freedom—depends as never before upon the sensible and clear-headed management of the domestic affairs of the United States. . . .

FISCAL RECKLESSNESS*

Dwight D. Eisenhower

. . . If the Government is to accept deliberately a massive deficit, and simultaneously embark upon lavish new spending and a huge tax cut, the Nation is headed for trouble. If we do this we will convict ourselves of fiscal recklessness and a failure to heed the plain lessons of history.

Moreover, I am particularly concerned, in this situation, for our children. If we irresponsibly keep on passing them our bills, they will inherit, not a free country with bright opportunities, but a vast wasteland of debt and financial chaos. Our youngsters have the right to expect more from us than a confession of our unreadiness or inability to pay for the things we demand from our Government.

Of course, there is no compulsion upon us to be so foolish. I believe the new spending programs in the pending budget can be drastically reduced without hurting a single essential function and still leave the level of Federal operations billions higher than I thought necessary only two years ago.

My last budget—for fiscal 1962—called for authority to spend 81 billion dollars. The 1964 budget before you asks for 108 billion dollars. Such a pyramiding of programs will inevitably create higher and higher spending in coming years and more and more difficulty in ever bringing our finances into balance. If this 27 billion dollar increase were cut in half, we would still have the fastest growing budget we have ever had in peacetime. Cuts of that magnitude would seem to be both reasonable and desirable, if only we will keep in mind the adverse consequences of failing to make them.

Take defense—up 10 billion dollars in two years. In my view, it is almost incredible to say this program cannot be safely pared. The defense budget I left behind provided amply for our security. Even allowing for costly developments since then, I have no doubt that the enormous defense sums can well stand a judicious and sizable pruning. The space program, in my opinion, is downright spongy. This is an area where we particularly need to demonstrate some common sense. Specifically, I have never believed that a spectacular dash to the moon, vastly deepening our debt, is worth the added tax burden it will eventually impose upon our citizens.

---

* 88th Congress, 1st Session. Letter to Representative Charles Halleck, 109 *Congressional Record*, 5172 (April 2, 1962).

I am sure there are many other areas in the voluminous budget where substantial economies can be made, to the great benefit of the Nation.

May I stress this point: there is not a trace of partisanship in the views here expressed. Responsible government is not a partisan issue. Leading citizens, in both parties in and out of government, have most emphatically stated that they share similar convictions. Among these are my last two Budget Directors, whom I asked to appraise the pending programs, because I am not now in a position to specify the detailed reductions that can be made. They believe that a cut of 10 or 12 billion dollars in spending authority would be practicable, without injuring any necessary activity. I agree with them that, at the very least, major surgery on the proposed programs, old and new, is a necessary accompaniment to a cut in taxes.

My hope is that our countrymen will grow indignant enough over these dangers to our country's future to make their views vigorously known to you gentlemen in the Congress. If this does come to pass, then we will face the happy prospect of reducing spending, reducing taxes, and looking after our children's tomorrow all at the same time.

AN ARTIFICIAL DICHOTOMY*

Leon H. Keyserling

My Proposals for Action Now

. . . My suggestions for revising the President's program emerge clearly from the foregoing analysis.

1. I suggest that the Federal budget, for fiscal 1964, lift domestic public outlays by about $3 billion above the fiscal 1964 level proposed by the President, as a start towards lifting them by about $16 billion by calendar 1966. The suggested apportionment of these increases, in accord with our great national priorities, are set forth on my charts 29 and 30. Acceptance of my suggestion, by affirming that the servicing of our great priorities of public needs, with appropriate help from the Federal Government, should grow as our population and our per capita productive resources grow in consequence of the advancing technology, would remove the most objec-

---

* 88th Congress, 1st Session, testimony of Leon H. Keyserling before the Joint Economic Committee (January 1963). Mr. Keyserling is a former chairman of the Council of Economic Advisers and currently a consulting economist and attorney in Washington, D.C.

tionable feature of the President's whole program—that these Federal domestic outlays in the aggregate be frozen for several years ahead, which actually means a cutback when measured against population growth and a growing GNP. Moreover, in the years immediately ahead, the increasing Federal outlays, in accord with my suggestion, would provide a substantial stimulus to the economy during the interval when we shall not yet have attained maximum employment and production, and in my view a much more effective stimulant, both as an activating economic force and in terms of the ultimate product results, than the kind of spreadout tax changes contained in the President's program.

2. I suggest that first priority and immediate tax changes be limited to the following: (a) Cutting the 20 percent flat rate, applicable to the first $2,000 of taxable income, to an average rate of less than 15 percent, with much larger reduction in the rate applicable to the first $1,000 than to the second $1,000, and (b) acceptance of the President's proposal which broadens the 10 percent standard deduction in a manner which is most favorable to lower income groups. The effect of my suggestion would be to make the tax reduction very much more progressive than it is in the President's program, by concentrating it very much more heavily in the low and middle-income groups. My proposal would be a one-shot affair, and would have an annual value of about $7 billion to $8 billion. This, combined with my $3 billion suggested increase in public outlays above the President's budget, would be a deliberately contrived net increase in the Federal Deficit of $10 billion to $11 billion, or about the amount which the President would spread out over 3 years through his tax program, but in an entirely different pattern. The concentration of this stimulus to the economy within a 1-year period would be enormously more effective than spreading it out over 3 years, and I submit also that the pattern which I suggest is much better adjusted to the restoration of economic equilibrium and to considerations of social justice and equity than the pattern proposed by the President.

3. I suggest that, after this first priority tax reduction is accomplished as rapidly as feasible, reforms in the personal and corporate tax structure should thereafter be undertaken, with the recoupments due to these reforms roughly equivalent to further reductions in tax rates, applicable to higher income families, and in corporate tax rates. This would have the merit of deferring, until what is needed most is accomplished first, that which is important but secondary and also extremely complex, time-consuming, and fraught with many uncertainties to ultimate enactment. However, I do not mean to infer, by my suggestion, that all of the reforms proposed by the President are desirable at any time. Some of these seem undesirable in that they appear to repeat some of the imbalances and inequities contained in the President's proposals for tax reduction.

4. I suggest that the administration—and the Congress if necessary—exert all needed pressure upon the Federal Reserve System, toward a much more liberal monetary policy and toward much lower interest rates. The balance of payments and gold problem can better be dealt with in entirely different ways from those which have been used to date, and which have so grievously damaged the whole U.S economy.

5. I suggest that the Council of Economic Advisers be directed by the President to formulate a long-range set of quantitative targets for economic growth, with meaningful components, with due regard for the great priorities of our national needs, and with due emphasis upon the central problem of the need to induce changes in the structure of demand which will be responsive to the challenge of the new technology and automation. This alone, in accord with the express intent of the Employment Act of 1946, would provide proper guides to all needed national economic policies.

Why We Are Going Wrong Now

What would seem to be the central reasons why people so capable, so well-informed, and so well-intentioned as those who are helping the President in economic matters are moving so far afield from what they should be doing and saying? I suggest two basic reasons:

1. Economic policies in Government, no less than in business, should be a means rather than an end. In order that the policies be relevant and adequate, the ends must first be stated in terms of meaningful and thorough quantitative targets or end objectives, both long-range and short-range. The relevant targets, in this instance, are the needed levels of employment, production, and purchasing power, broken down into major components, and projected for a reasonable number of years ahead. This the Employment Act of 1946 not only contemplates, but indeed requires. The Council of Economic Advisers, in its current report, has abandoned even some tentative and fragmentary efforts to do this, which it earlier had commenced.

The explanation of this abandonment is not available to me; the consequences should be apparent to all. Policies not carefully adjusted to well-developed targets, related to our potentials and our needs, are policies flying in the dark; lacking integration one with another; excessively responsive to the inertia of outdated thinking; and unduly responsive to the desire to do that which the most people will agree to without being informed, instead of seeking to inform them. Economic education, emanating in proper degree from national leadership, is the hallmark of the evolution of sound national economic policies;

2. The second explanation resides in the artificial dichotomy between

economic and social purposes, resulting in two reports so disappointingly devoid of adequate policies expressly related to these social purposes. It is not enough to say that everybody will be better off, and our social purpose thus served, if our economic performance is improved. For the very nature of our chronic and current economic trouble is that those social programs which add directly to human well-being, which improve the distribution of the fruits of our production, are at the very heart of potentially successful economic efforts.

After all, the real challenge of the unused resources, resulting from not meeting this problem, is in the form of opportunity—the opportunity to eradicate the poverty and deprivation which still afflict two-fifths of our population, and to lift all Americans to decent levels of living compatible with our soaring power to produce; to take millions of families out of slums; to provide them with more educational opportunities and better health services in line with our technical competence to do so; to cleanse their cities and purify their waters; to enlarge their security in their old age; to enable them to be transported more conveniently; to improve the natural resources which will be the heritage of their descendants; and even to enable a larger proportion of them to enjoy the more conventional material comforts of life, and to enjoy more leisure— and not in the form of involuntary unemployment. These are not merely the byproducts of a successful economy program; they are an essential and major portion of the implementation of such a program. An economic program which does not recognize this sufficiently will fall far short of economic restoration, because it does not accurately sense the very nature of the task. And it will not rally the American people fully to the task, because it does not come close enough to their most profound needs and aspirations.

GROWTH IS THE ANSWER TO DEFICITS*

Kermit Gordon

I welcome the opportunity to discuss the budget transmitted by the President for the fiscal year 1964.

Budget estimates must be based in part upon assumptions concerning

* 88th Congress, 1st Session. *Hearings,* Joint Economic Committee (January 29, 1963). Mr. Gordon is Director of the Bureau of the Budget.

the future behavior of the national economy. It is best that these assumptions be made explicit, so that those who appraise the economic outlook differently may judge the budget estimates in the light of their own views.

The economic assumptions underlying the 1964 budget take into account the fact that we have had seven quarters of economic expansion since the recession trough, during which the gross national product has risen by $61 billion, personal income by $43 billion, and corporate profits by more than $11 billion. They also are influenced by the fact that the rate of expansion was substantially slower in 1962 than in 1961, and the widespread expectation that the pace of expansion in 1963 is not likely to better the 1962 performance in the absence of new fiscal stimulus.

However, with early enactment of the President's new tax proposals, we would expect that the economic expansion of the last twelve months will begin to accelerate in the coming year. Specifically, the budget is based on the expectation that the gross national product which reached $554 billion in calendar 1962 will rise to around $578 billion in calendar 1963. Personal incomes in calendar 1963 are expected to advance to $459 billion, nearly $20 billion higher than last year, and corporate profits to $53 billion, up about $2 billion from a year earlier. Since economic projection, however, is an imprecise art, I should add that such expectations encompass a range of possible levels of gross national product for 1963 extending to perhaps $5 billion on either side.

Looking at the trend of the economy more closely, we note that the current recovery has carried the gross national product to a new high of $562.0 billion, annual rate, in the fourth quarter of calendar 1962. This is $10 billion above the rate in the second quarter of the same year. The budget estimates are based on a continuation of economic recovery at about this same rate of advance through the middle of the calendar year 1963. Thereafter, assuming early enactment of the proposed tax program, the rate of growth in economic activity would be expected to pick up as we approach the end of the year.

As this Committee has often observed, there is a mutual relationship between budget policy and the economy. An economy operating substantially below its full potential not only irrevocably loses private production and income and Federal revenues but also generates Federal expenditures which could, under happier circumstances, be avoided. The Federal budget thus depends on the state of the economy and, at the same time, significantly influences the level of economic activity.

Under the President's recommendations, Federal payments to the public in the fiscal year 1964 are estimated to total $122.5 billion, an increase of $5.7 billion over 1963. On an administrative budget basis, total expenditures are estimated at $98.8 billion, $4.5 billion above the present fiscal year.

Increased outlays for national defense, space, and interest are about equal to the increase in total administrative budget expenditures. For all other programs, combined, administrative budget expenditures in 1964 are about the same as—actually slightly below—1963. Although this large segment of expenditures is approximately unchanged in total, it contains a number of increases and offsetting decreases. I shall cover these changes in more detail later.

At this point, however, I want to emphasize the fact that a large part of the civilian expenditures recommended by the President represent an investment in the future progress of the Nation—facilitating the long-run growth of our economy. They include new programs and expansions in existing Federal activities in such areas as education, health, manpower retraining, area redevelopment, youth employment opportunities, conservation and development of natural resources, scientific research, and transportation.

Of the total Federal cash payments to the public estimated for 1964, about $17.6 billion, or almost one-seventh, are for Federal civil public works, for highways, hospitals, and other State-local assets, for small business, rural electrification, and other loans and additions to civilian Federal assets, and for such developmental activities as education, health, and nondefense scientific research and development. Taken as a proportion of nondefense payments, rather than of the total of all payments, the ratio becomes more than one-fourth instead of one-seventh. Of this $17.6 billion, $10.8 billion is for additions to civil assets and $6.8 billion is for education, training, health, and nondefense research and development.

Since the war, as the President pointed out in the budget message, the pressures of a growing population, rising wages and prices, and demands for improved public services have resulted in sharp increases in expenditures at all levels of government. Since 1948, State and local government expenditures have more than trebled. Federal outlays for nondefense purposes have more than doubled, and these outlays include an expanding amount of aid to State and local governments.

The most important aspect of fiscal policy in this year's budget is, of course, the President's program for tax reduction and reform. The details of that program were spelled out in the tax message, and its economic impact has been analyzed both in the Economic Report and in Chairman Heller's testimony. I should like, today, to look briefly at the tax program in relation to the budget as a whole, as it affects both fiscal year 1964 and later years.

Given the prospective level of gross national product, the tax and expenditure policies reflected in the fiscal 1964 budget will yield a large deficit on the basis of each of the three budgetary concepts. The 1964 deficit is a result, but not the means or the purpose, of fiscal policy. The means is the economic stimulus provided by a carefully phased program of tax reduction and reform. The purpose is the achievement of full prosperity and more rapid growth in the American economy—the attainment of an economic climate within which the chronic deficits of recent years will disappear.

As economic activity responds to the successive steps of tax reduction and reform, the advance in output and incomes towards full employment levels will be accompanied by a more than proportional increase in Federal revenues. It is characteristic of our economy that corporate profits are more volatile than other forms of income. As a consequence, the advance toward full employment should see a particularly large rise in profits, and in the Federal revenues derived from the corporate income tax. Within a few years after enactment, total revenues under the new tax system should be larger than those which would have been yielded by the existing tax structure.

The fact that under certain conditions a decrease in tax rates can lead to an increase in tax revenues should not be surprising. It is analogous to the situation which often confronts a business firm. A firm's revenues depend both on the price of its product and the volume of its sales. It has been typical of many of our industries that a reduction in prices can often so stimulate the volume of sales that total revenues are eventually increased. Since the response of volume to price reduction often takes time to work itself out, it may sometimes be necessary to accept a temporary reduction in receipts—to incur a 'deficit' if you will—until the full effects of the price reduction are felt.

Eliminating the slack in our economy, returning to full employment, and speeding up the rate of economic growth are vital objectives in and of themselves—both for what they imply for the well being of our citizens and for their effect on our position of world leadership. Fiscal policy, as reflected in the 1964 budget, lays the foundation not only for a more prosperous economy but also for an improved budgetary position. As the tax reduction becomes fully effective and as the economy moves back towards full employment a substantial part of the accompanying rise in revenues will be available and will be used to reduce the transitional deficit.

Many have wondered why the Administration did not reduce expenditures in order to make room for a tax cut within a balanced budget. The answer to this is twofold:

First, the expenditures contemplated in the 1964 budget are, in the judgment of the Administration, the minimum necessary to safeguard our national security and to fulfill our pressing domestic responsibilities. As I indicated earlier, expenditures for programs other than defense, space, and debt service have been held slightly below last year's level.

To have gone even further in expenditure restraint would have been a disservice to the national security and the national welfare.

Second, a reduction in the proposed level of Federal expenditures, not matched by a larger tax reduction, would be self-defeating under current conditions. Reduced Federal purchases of goods and services in fiscal 1964 would, of course, reduce private production, employment, profits, and wages. This, in turn, would lead to lower Federal revenue collections and a deficit would remain. In the end, the problem of Federal deficits can be solved only in a prosperous and growing economy—it is to this goal that the Administration has directed its tax and expenditure policies.

DEFICIT SPENDING WON'T WORK*

Representative Thomas B. Curtis

. . . the President is not cutting expenditure in nondefense areas but actually is embarking us upon a continued increase in expenditure levels primarily in nondefense areas which began with the last Eisenhower budget of $81 billion expenditure request to an $87 billion mark for fiscal year 1962 to a $94 billion mark for fiscal year 1963 and now to something that is well over $100 billion for fiscal year 1964.

Let it not be forgotten that the 1963 budget, although calling for an expenditure level of $92.5 billion, actually had requests for obligational authority of just under $100 billion. The 1964 budget request for new obligational authority is $107.9 billion. This indeed is fiscal irresponsibility. It is a deceitful presentation to the Congress and to the public.

Let us find out early in this Congress whether or not we are going to follow the fiscal irresponsibility set out in the President's budget or whether we in Congress are going to assume some fiscal responsibility in behalf of the people.

To put it in capsule, it is a theory of deficit financing at the Federal level. That the Federal Government, by spending more money than it takes in, can stimulate the economy to greater economic growth. This theory, incidentally, was implemented to some degree in the thirties during the Roosevelt depression days. It did not work then but those who

---

* 88th Congress, 1st Session. 109 *Congressional Record*, 521+, 1554+ (January 17, February 4, 1963). Mr. Curtis is a Republican Representative from Missouri.

promote this theory say that it is wrong to say that it did not work. Their answer is that it did not work because we did not spend enough, that the deficit financing was not enough.

The proponents of the deficit financing theory say, to prove that we did not spend enough, "Look what did happen when we did spend vast sums of money in World War II." In other words, the argument is that heavy deficit spending in World War II brought us out of the Roosevelt depression of the thirties. I think that that certainly ignores a very basic point, the point of difference between an economy based upon war and one based upon peacetime activities.

We can put it in this context: There were 10 million people unemployed in 1940 when America became the arsenal for democracy. One way we solved unemployment was simply to put uniforms on over 10 million of our young men and women. The way we solved the inflationary impact of these policies was to impose price and wage controls, and I might say controls of materials and of certain goods and services. These restrictions on freedom our people will put up with during a war period, but these must be recognized as giving up freedoms. This business of freedom and liberty has, I think, a direct bearing on our economic theories and what our economy is really all about. What we are seeking to do is not only provide the good life for our people in terms of tangible goods and services but also in terms of this very precious intangible, human liberty and freedom. You can get three meals a day, plenty of clothing and shelter and protection in a jail, but none of us wants that. So we must relate our economic policies to this precious element of freedom.

The expenditure rate that the President has presented in this budget is $98 billion. I suggest that we hold the expenditure rate to $93 billion, the rate of fiscal year 1963. Then just take the actual expenditures of fiscal year 1963 and apply those cuts with some understanding of give and take, using $93 billion as your total figure. I think we probably could go back an entire fiscal year to 1962 where the expenditure rate was $87 billion or go back to fiscal year 1961 when the expenditure rate was $81 billion. You see what we have been doing is just upping Federal expenditures each year. The President has tried to create the impression, and I regret that he has done it in this way, that the expenditure increase is primarily in defense. Actually, the bulk of these increases are in nondefense expenditures exclusive of space exploration which is not defense oriented as yet. I might say in this budget that the President has presented to us, to the Congress, for fiscal year 1964, the increase in nondefense expenditures—and counting space separate if he wants to do so—is an increase of about $3 billion. But how has he done that and yet created the impression of not increasing these items: by taking out nonrecurring items which were in the 1963 expenditures and cashing in capital items. I will give you one item just to illustrate the magnitude of it—$2 billion for the Export-Import Bank Agency. This is a 1963 expenditure. Everyone knows it is a nonrecurring item. That is a minus figure in the 1964 budget. The President has put in recurring items in his expenditure column for 1964. A $1.4 billion increase in Department of Agriculture and $1.7 billion increase for Department of Health, Education and Welfare for example. Now this, frankly, is juggling statistics.

Foreign aid could well be cut and we would improve our relations abroad.

I think we could probably wipe the whole thing out for the next fiscal year, inasmuch as the carryover balances equal twice the amount of the expenditure rate. I imagine we could well not appropriate another cent for fiscal year 1964. Expenditure on previous obligations would still continue, so it would be in there; I think that we could probably cut that expenditure rate to about a billion and a half. But, again, this would depend on careful work being done in the Appropriations Committee. I am not like some of my colleagues on both sides of the aisle who think that the theory of foreign aid is unsound; I think the theory is sound, but the requests for appropriations and the expenditure policies have just been fantastic in their extravagance, in their lack of planning or lack of policy—just about everything I can think of has been in error in the foreign aid programs.

We could save a great deal of money by holding down employment. For instance, the Federal Government put on 160,000 men and women civilian employees during the last year. This and salary increases cost us close to a billion dollars.

The Republican-controlled 83d Congress which came into power in 1953 cut the Truman prepared budget by $14 billion, and they did it in a scalpel method, not with a meat ax.

I want to put that in context, though. It is true that we were then shifting from war to peace, and therefore we could appropriately cut some. Just because of this shift. But, you must recognize that the $14 billion cut in 1 year was accomplished intelligently. And it was not confined to the shift from war to peace.

We should have this national debate. Whether we are Democrats or Republicans, we must decide whether we agree or disagree with this new theory of planned deficit financing.

Unless we eschew the theory of deficit financing, there is not the discipline nor the incentive to cut expenditures.

CHAPTER NINE

The Negro Revolt

The year 1963 witnessed the end of an era in the history of the American Negro. It was an era in which, as Professor H. Frank Way's article suggests, the pace of Negro freedom had been painfully slow. However, 1963 also witnessed a sudden increase in the tempo of Negro militancy. Under the pressures of this new militancy, white America—from Birmingham to Los Angeles, from New Orleans to Englewood, New Jersey—became acutely aware of the Negro revolt. In no small way, the leader of the revolt was the Reverend Martin Luther King, Jr. In the spring of 1963, while in a Birmingham jail, he wrote an open letter justifying the "creative tension" of direct action—the tension necessary to arouse white America to face the changing reality of race relations in the United States.

In his letter, Dr. King advocated disobedience to unjust laws in order to change those laws. Columnist and editor David Lawrence raises the question of what becomes of "law and order" when individuals or groups do not utilize existing governmental machinery to satisfy their grievances. Mr. Lawrence feels that an unjust law must be corrected in the courts or in the legislatures, not in the streets.

If Dr. King is one of the spiritual leaders of the Negro revolt, author James Baldwin is one of its intellectual leaders. James Baldwin has come to symbolize the new pride and confidence of the Negro—and some would say the hate the Negro harbors for the white man. Baldwin does not recognize a "Negro problem." To Baldwin, the race issue in the United States is a "white problem"—a need for a white self-examination, an inner search to discover why he invented the "nigger" and why he cannot recognize the Negro as a man.

For many years, Northern white liberals have been champions of the Negro cause. But, to many of these liberals, the Negro problem always seemed to be a Southern problem, and the solutions seemed as easy as they were remote from the Northern suburbs. But recently, the Northern white liberal has had to face for the first time his own feelings about the

Negro. The issue is no longer sectional, and the Negro is no longer contented just to be living in Englewood or Chicago. He is making demands now, not just in the South, but also in the North.

In the spring of 1963, President Kennedy said that the heart of the race issue was the question whether all Americans are to be afforded equal rights and equal opportunities, ". . . whether we are going to treat our fellow Americans as we want to be treated." But John Fischer suggests that while the Negro may secure full legal rights, he will never be accepted on equal terms in the ordinary operations of society, unless he shows new evidence of willingness to assume responsibilities with these rights. Mr. Fischer examines some common white fears about the Negro, fears that he believes are indeed "Negro problems": Negro civic apathy, Negro moral irresponsibility, the Negro crime rate, and the deterioration of Negro homes. Mr. Fischer suggests that white America will not treat the Negro as an equal unless the Negro demonstrates that he is in fact equal to the tasks of good citizenship. The charges Mr. Fischer makes are not new. But in the past, these charges were suspect because they were so frequently uttered by those who were callous to racial injustice. They may still be suspect—civic virtues are not generally spawned in poverty—but they may not be dismissed merely as the rantings of racists.

THE PACE OF FREEDOM

H. Frank Way, Jr.

Did it start with Birmingham, or was it Oxford or Albany? Perhaps it began when William Lloyd Garrison wrote in the *Liberator* in January 1831, "Yea, till every chain be broken, and every bondsman set free! Let Southern oppressors tremble—let their secret abettors tremble—let their Northern apologists tremble—let all the enemies of the persecuted blacks tremble." But the struggle for Negro freedom must have started even before 1831. It must have started in the heart of the first Virginia slave who came to realize that to his Christian master he was only a faceless black and not the image of God.

But whether the struggle for freedom began three hundred years ago or one hundred years ago, the fact remains that the pace of freedom has been painfully slow. One hundred years after the Emancipation Proclamation, the American Negro has grown impatient and restive in his endeavor to be accorded the dignity of a human being. The Negro wants to be a full man *now*. Today the Negro is militant; indeed, "uppity." He flirts with rioting in New York, and in Jackson, Mississippi. When he is told of the dangers of his new militance he can only reply "Being a Negro has always been dangerous in America." Twenty-two unsolved bombings of Negro homes in Birmingham are testimony of that. "Wait" is a white man's word, and "moderation" the voice of defeat. The Negro knows that white America played a tragic game with him—it set him free, but it did not give him freedom.

The Rise of Jim Crow

In 1863, the Negro was freed from slavery. In 1868, the Fourteenth Amendment was adopted, providing that no state shall deny to any person the equal protection of its laws. Yet, by the late 1880s, it was obvious that the federal government—indeed most of white America—had lost interest in the blacks. By this time, a more subtle form of racial persecution was replacing slavery. It was given the euphemistic title "segregation." Jim Crowism became the order of the day, and the Negro became isolated in religion, in politics, in the economy, in social life, and in education. The "equal protection of the laws" became the separation of the races by unequal laws. And the whole legal fabric of state-supported inequality was upheld by the United States Supreme Court.

In 1896, the Supreme Court announced, with only one dissenting Justice, its decision in *Plessy v. Ferguson*. The Court upheld a Louisiana statute that required the separation of Negro and white passengers in railway carriages. In announcing its "separate but equal" doctrine, the Court was only responding to the growing sentiment in favor of Jim Crow codes. The Court closed its eyes to the likelihood that its doctrine would be used to justify separate but unequal facilities for the Negro.

One of the observations of the Court in the Plessy case merits quoting. It was a position widely held in 1896, and one that is still reflected in the current racial crisis. The Court said: "Legislation is powerless to eradicate racial instincts or to abolish distinctions based upon physical differences, and the attempt to do so can only result in accentuating the difficulties of the present situation. If the civil and political rights of both races be equal, one cannot be inferior to the other civilly or politically. If one race be inferior to the other socially, the Constitution of the United States cannot put them upon the same plane."

The basic fallacy of this position was the assumption by the Court that the civil and political rights of Negroes were in practice equal in Louisiana, or elsewhere. The contrary was true. The 1890s and early 1900s witnessed the final steps in the total isolation of the Negro. In the year of the Plessy decision, there were 130,334 Negroes registered to vote in Louisiana; by 1904 there were only 1,342. In 1902, Louisiana adopted a segregation statute for all streetcars. In 1914, it adopted a segregation statute for circuses and tent shows, and New Orleans adopted a residential segregation law—creating a legalized ghetto. Finally, New Orleans passed an ordinance that segregated white and Negro prostitutes into separate districts.

Mr. Justice Harlan, the lone dissenter in the Plessy case, read the majority opinion and then wrote, "We boast of the freedom enjoyed by our people above all other peoples. But it is difficult to reconcile that boast with a state of the law which, practically, puts the brand of servitude and degradation upon a large class of our fellow citizens, our equals before the law. The thin disguise of 'equal accommodations' . . . will not mislead anyone, or atone for the wrong done this day."

As the years after the Plessy decision slipped by, racial discrimination hardened. Lynchings increased; Theodore Roosevelt's Square Deal and Wilson's New Freedom came and went and the problems of the Negro remained untouched. In fact, it was during the liberal Wilson's administration that a segregation policy was adopted in the federal offices in the District of Columbia.

The First World War had an important effect on the Negro. It started a migration north to better jobs. But the Negro simply exchanged his rural shack for a city ghetto. The North experienced its first serious race riots. The KKK spread into the Northeast and the Midwest. At the close of the 1920s, the Negro's position in America remained relatively unchanged—he was still a second-class citizen.

The advent of the Roosevelt years witnessed tangible improvements in Negro rights. More importantly, in the 1930s, there was a growing public consciousness of racial injustice. The Anti-Defamation League, The Catholic Interracial Council, the CIO, and, of course, the NAACP and the National Urban League all pressed the issue of racial justice. Some hesitant steps were taken by the federal executive to recognize the Negro and his rights. The previous "lily-white" policy in federal employment was modified, and FDR created in 1939 a civil-rights division in the Department of Justice.

But neither the federal executive nor the Congress attempted to outstrip public opinion, which remained largely insensitive to the plight of the Negro. No civil-rights legislation was passed, nor was any advocated by the President. The benefits of the Roosevelt years for the Negro were mainly indirect. These came as a result of New Deal legislation designed to improve the material welfare of the underprivileged.

Of even greater consequence to the Negro was the liberal atmosphere of the 1930s, and this was mirrored in the Supreme Court. The Court, during the Roosevelt and Truman administrations, became more sympathetic to Negro demands for equal treatment by the states. It refused to allow the states to enforce racially restrictive covenants; it declared the white primary unconstitutional; it repeatedly warned the states against Negro discrimination in state criminal cases; and it took an increasingly critical position of the "equal" in the "separate but equal" doctrine of public education.

The Second World War brought about further migration of Negroes to the North. When they faced employment discrimination in defense industry, they were able to pressure the Roosevelt administration into establishing a Fair Employment Practices Committee to investigate race discrimination by government contractors. By the end of the war, the first state antidiscrimination commissions had been established. The period of the war and the immediate postwar years saw improvement in the Negro's material security, in his organizational support, and in his self-confidence. He was still a faceless black, segregated in the North and in the South, but his economic and political power, particularly in the large urban centers of the North, was on the increase.

The Truman administration did more perhaps than any previous administration since the Lincoln years to bring the race issue to the public. In December 1946, President Truman appointed a President's Committee on Civil Rights, and fourteen months later he urged the Congress to enact the Committee's recommendations. Although the Congress failed to act on the recommendations, the Committee's report, *To Secure These Rights,* was widely acclaimed outside the South.

In 1948, President Truman issued an executive order that desegregated the armed services and prohibited race discrimination in federal employment. In 1949, the Federal Housing Administration reversed its previous policy, and announced it would not in the future insure homes that had restrictive covenants.

The Supreme Court and Jim Crow

The greatest single blow to race discrimination was delivered neither by the Congress nor the President. Congress, under the strong influence of rural representatives and Southern Democrats, had long been paralyzed on the race issue. In the early 1950s, President Eisenhower was little inclined to sweep away the support of the conservative coalition in Congress, a coalition which bartered Negro rights for Southern Democratic votes in the Senate and the House of Representatives. But the third branch of the federal government, the judiciary, although the least powerful branch of the government, was under no political obligation to entrenched blocs. Once before, in 1857 in the Dred Scott case, the Supreme Court tackled the Negro issue—and brought down the wrong side. It took the Court almost thirty years to recover the prestige it lost—and prestige is the essence of the Court's power. Nearly one hundred years later, the Court tackled the race issue again.

In 1954, the Supreme Court handed down its now famous decision in *Brown v. Topeka Board of Education*. A unanimous Court reversed the Plessy doctrine, and held that state segregation by race in public schools was inherently unequal. The Court pointed out that to separate Negro children ". . . from others of similar age and qualifications solely because of their race generates a feeling of inferiority as to their status in the community that may affect their hearts and minds in a way unlikely ever to be undone." The Court now saw what only Justice Harlan could see in 1896. At long last, the equal protection clause was to have some relationship to equality.

Judicial Desegregation

The Court was of course not unaware of the monumental nature of its decision. To give the public and the other branches of the government time, the Court waited until 1955 to hand down a final order in the case. And even in 1955, it did not require immediate compliance with integration, but consciously—or unconsciously—invited delay. The Court told the lower federal courts they could consider a wide variety of factors that might affect integration; and, with studied ambiguity, it ordered segregated schools to desegregate "with all deliberate speed."

For the Court to have demanded immediate compliance would have weakened its prestige, and thus the ultimate impact of its decision. If the Court is without obligation to entrenched blocs, by the same token it is politically isolated. Without congressional and presidential support, which was not forthcoming, the Court had to experiment with "good-faith compliance" on the part of the South. In turn, when the South adopted a policy of open defiance—when it became obvious that there would be no speed, but rather years of deliberation—the Brown decision began to gain its impact on the public mind.

The importance of the Brown decision has not been in its immediate impact on desegregation. This is understandable, because the judiciary is not equipped to solve broad social and economic problems. The judicial process is an *ad hoc* process, with decisions legally binding only on the immediate parties to a particular suit. Such a piecemeal approach can have only minimal influence on solutions to controversial social issues. Furthermore, the Supreme Court does not stand at the top of a monolithic judiciary. The Court must depend on the good faith of the lower federal courts to carry out its guidelines. And the lower federal courts have demonstrated, in desegregation cases after 1955, that local school boards and state legislatures have no monopoly on "deliberation" without speed.

The Brown decision is important, however, because it afforded the Negro a respected forum, not to end race discrimination, but to generate public sympathy for his cause.

Desegregation in Public Education

In 1954, eighteen Southern and border states and the District of Columbia had public-education segregation laws. The Brown decision, in effect, declared these laws unconstitutional. Almost ten years later, the vast majority of Negro students in these states continue to attend racially segregated and generally inferior schools. There was some initial voluntary compliance with desegregation in the border states of Missouri, Maryland, and Delaware, and in the District of Columbia. But in most of the segregated states, the school districts have awaited Negro litigation. When faced with a court order, they have made only token compliance with integration or, in some instances, openly defied a court order and forced the President to use armed power to secure compliance, as in Little Rock, Oxford, and Birmingham.

In 1958, in the Little Rock case, the Court warned the South that delay in any guise in order to deny the constitutional rights of Negro children could not be countenanced, and that only a prompt start, diligently and earnestly pursued could constitute good-faith compliance. The Supreme Court also warned the states that governmental support of racially segregated schools "through any arrangement, management, funds or property cannot be squared with the . . . command that no state shall deny to any person within its jurisdiction the equal protection of the laws."

The South again ignored the Court. Instead of compliance, the Southern states established a complex "legal" facade—to prevent integration— of pupil-placement laws, school-closing laws, tuition grants, and elaborate provisions for pupil transfers in districts forced to integrate by a federal court order.

School-closing laws coupled with tuition grants have had little support in the South. Only one school district, Prince Edward County, Virginia, successfully closed its public schools to avoid integration. Even the Deep South cities of Birmingham and Mobile, Alabama, opposed closing the schools. On the other hand, pupil-placement laws have been adopted in all of the states of the Confederate South. On the surface, these laws have no connection with race. They merely direct school boards to assign pupils individually to schools, using such criteria as orderly administration, the pupil's academic ability, and the pupil's personal standards.

Although the Supreme Court has thus far refused to strike down these laws, it is becoming apparent to the lower federal courts that pupil-placement laws are being administered to discriminate against Negro children. In 1962, the United States Fifth Circuit Court of Appeals condemned the New Orleans pupil-placement act because ". . . it is hailed as an instrument for carrying out a desegregation plan and all the time the entire public knows that in fact it is being used to maintain segregation by allowing a little token integration."

Even in the absence of pupil-placement laws, desegregation in Southern schools would be stymied by *de facto* residential segregation—which results, at least on the elementary school level, in *de facto* school segregation. This type of school segregation has also become a major problem in the urban communities of the North and the West. The neighborhood school zone, consciously or unconsciously drawn along racial lines, is one of the greatest roadblocks to integration. When the Negro, or the Mexican-American, or the Puerto Rican is allowed equal opportunities in housing, *de facto* segregation will no longer be a major problem in education.

The beginning of the 1963–1964 school year in the South brought evidence of a hopeful change. One hundred and thirteen school districts dropped racial barriers. This was the highest figure since 1956, and it was over two and a half times the figure for the previous school year. Perhaps even more important than the number of districts involved, 95 of the 113 adopted integration voluntarily. It would be misleading, however, to assume that these 113 districts will operate on a truly integrated basis. The important figure is not the number of desegregated districts but the percentage of Negro students attending integrated public schools. By the spring of 1963, less than 8 percent of the Negro students in the Southern and border states were attending integrated schools. Tokenism will continue to be a major problem in these so-called integrated districts. Furthermore, one state (Mississippi) has no integrated elementary or secondary public schools, and Louisiana, Georgia, South Carolina, and Alabama have less than ten.

Suffrage and Color

> The right of the citizens of the United States to vote shall not be denied or abridged by the United States or by any State on account of race, color, or previous condition of servitude.
>
> —The Fifteenth Amendment, ratified March 30, 1870

The right of citizens to participate in free elections is surely one of the great dividers between a democratic and an authoritarian society. For the great bulk of American citizens, this right is so taken for granted that it frequently falls into dangerous disuse. However, for thousands of Negroes living in the Deep South today, the right to vote is as remote as an integrated school. Although Negro voter registration has increased since the end of World War II, only about one of five voting-age Negroes in the South is registered. In part, this can be attributed to the voter indifference that is characteristic of lower-income groups. But voter indifference cannot explain the political isolation of the Negro in the South today. Even in the urban centers of the South, such as Atlanta, where the Negro is gaining a political voice, political discrimination is not unknown. In the rural areas of the South, particularly in the Black Belt counties, it takes a supreme act of courage for a Negro to walk into the county courthouse to seek registration.

Despite Supreme Court decisions and protective federal legislation, the Negro is denied the right to vote by delaying action on his registration application, by intimidation, and by requiring a higher standard of literacy for Negroes than for whites in the administration of literacy tests. Perhaps the classic example of discrimination in literacy tests occurred when a registrar of voters in a Louisiana parish failed a Negro and gave as the reason an "error in spilling."

In the first test case under the 1957 Civil Rights Act, a federal district court reported that Terrell County, Georgia, officials failed at least two Negro applicants who held master's degrees. In 1960, of a white population of 4,533 there were 2,894 registered voters. But, of a Negro population of 8,209 there were only 51 registered voters. The federal court cases in Terrell County increased the latter figure to just short of one hundred by 1963. Nonetheless, in the Black Belt counties of the South, such as Terrell County, the Negro sharecropper or tenant farmer lives in such a feudalistic relationship to the white property owners that the discussion of his right to vote is perhaps the most academic question he faces.

Public Accommodations

One of the many outrages that the Negro faces is the denial of opportunities in public accommodations. A Negro family living, for example, in New York City who plans a motor vacation through New England will face pockets of discrimination, particularly in motel facilities. But the same Negro family, who plans a motor vacation to visit relatives in the South, must either sleep in the car or seek shelter in inadequate rooms in a Negro ghetto. In the South, the pattern of racial segregation in hotels, department stores, restaurants, public parks, and beaches is almost totally Jim Crow. A few cities in the South are making hesitant steps to break the tradition of Jim Crow, but in general, the Negro eats, plays, shops, and rests in inferior segregated facilities.

Where racial segregation in public facilities, such as city or county parks, libraries, or swimming pools, is maintained by local policy or laws, there is clearly a violation of the equal-protection clause. The Supreme Court and the lower federal courts have repeatedly struck down local laws supporting segregation in public facilities. But here, as in other areas of segregation, the South has evaded integration by a variety of legal subterfuges, or by simply closing the facilities.

Public accommodations that are not owned, operated, or leased by governmental units present a somewhat different legal problem. In the late 1950s, various civil-rights groups, particularly the Congress on Racial Equality and the Student Non-Violent Coordinating Committee, began to focus their attention on "sit-ins" and demonstrations in or around public accommodations such as segregated lunch counters in drug and variety stores. The equal-protection clause prohibits state racial discrimination. It does not apply directly to voluntary private racial discrimination.

However, when voluntary segregation is supported by the use of a state's coercive powers, such as the arrest and prosecution of sit-in demonstrators merely because of their race, then it seems that the equal-protection clause should apply. In such instances, the state—the police and the courts—is acting to protect private property from trespass; but the motivating factor is race, and race is not a permissible criterion in executing the laws, either in education or trespass.

The Supreme Court has thus far avoided ruling directly on this issue, although it has reversed the convictions of sit-in demonstrators on other grounds. In one of the cases, Mr. Justice Douglas did remark, in a concurring opinion, that "When the doors of a business are open to the public, they must be open to all regardless of race if *apartheid* is not to become engrained in our public places. It cannot by reason of the Equal-Protection Clause become so engrained with the aid of state courts, state legislatures, or state police."

✿ ✿ ✿

In 1942, the Swedish scholar Gunnar Myrdal observed that the Negro problem was America's greatest and most conspicuous scandal. He called it "An American Dilemma." Some twenty years later, America faced its scandal, but the dilemma remains. The Negro problem is a great moral crisis for American democracy, but solutions are often as perplexing as the problem. It is easier to recognize injustice than it is to solve injustice, though recognition is certainly a necessary first step. The hope is that knowledge will give America the capacity to understand race relations, and that through understanding lasting solutions will evolve.

LETTER FROM A BIRMINGHAM JAIL*

Martin Luther King, Jr.

My Dear Fellow Clergymen:

While confined here in the Birmingham city jail, I came across your recent statement calling our present activities "unwise and untimely." Seldom, if ever, do I pause to answer criticism of my work and ideas. . . .

I think I should give the reason for my being in Birmingham, since you have been influenced by the argument of "outsiders coming in." I have the honor of serving as president of the Southern Christian Leadership Conference, an organization operating in every Southern State with headquarters in Atlanta, Ga. . . . I am here, along with several members of my staff, because we were invited here. I am here because I have basic organizational ties here. Beyond this, I am in Birmingham because injustice is here. . . .

You deplore the demonstrations that are presently taking place in Birmingham. But I am sorry that your statement did not express a similar concern for the conditions that brought the demonstrations into being. I am sure that each of you would want to go beyond the superficial social analyst who looks merely at effects, and does not grapple with underlying causes. I would not hesitate to say that it is unfortunate that so-called demonstrations are taking place in Birmingham at this time, but I would say in more emphatic terms that it is even more unfortunate that the white power structure of this city left the Negro community with no other alternative.

In any nonviolent campaign there are four basic steps: (1) collection of the facts to determine whether injustices are alive; (2) negotiation; (3) self-purification; and (4) direct action. We have gone through all of these steps in Birmingham. There can be no gainsaying of the fact that racial injustice engulfs this community. Birmingham is probably the most thoroughly segregated city in the United States. Its ugly record of police brutality is known in every section of this country. Its unjust treatment of Negroes in the courts is a notorious reality. There have been more unsolved bombings of Negro homes and churches in Birmingham than any city in this Nation. These are the hard, brutal, and unbelievable facts. On

---

* This letter was written on April 16, 1963, at the time of the Birmingham riots in response to a letter from clergymen urging Negro moderation. The Reverend Mr. King is chairman of the Southern Christian Leadership Conference.

the basis of these conditions Negro leaders sought to negotiate with the city fathers. But the political leaders consistently refused to engage in good-faith negotiation. . . .

You may well ask, "Why direct action? Why sit-ins, marches, etc.? Isn't negotiation a better path?" You are exactly right in your call for negotiation. Indeed, this is the purpose of direct action. Nonviolent direct action seeks to create such a crisis and establish such creative tension that a community that has constantly refused to negotiate is forced to confront the issue. It seeks so to dramatize the issue that it can no longer be ignored. I just referred to the creation of tension as a part of the work of the nonviolent resister. This may sound rather shocking. But I must confess that I am not afraid of the word tension. I have earnestly worked and preached against violent tension, but there is a type of constructive nonviolent tension that is necessary for growth. Just as Socrates felt that it was necessary to create a tension in the mind so that individuals could rise from the bondage of myths and half-truths to the unfettered realm of creative analysis and objective appraisal, we must see the need of having nonviolent gadflies to create the kind of tension in society that will help men rise from the dark depths of prejudice and racism to the majestic heights of understanding and brotherhood. So the purpose of the direct action is to create a situation so crisis-packed that it will inevitably open the door to negotiation. . . .

We know through painful experience that freedom is never voluntarily given by the oppressor; it must be demanded by the oppressed. Frankly I have never yet engaged in a direct action movement that was "well timed," according to the timetable of those who have not suffered unduly from the disease of segregation. For years now I have heard the word "wait." It rings in the ear of every Negro with a piercing familiarity. This "wait" has almost always meant never. It has been a tranquilizing thalidomide, relieving the emotional stress for a moment, only to give birth to an ill-formed infant of frustration. We must come to see with the distinguished jurist of yesterday that "justice too long delayed is justice denied." We have waited for more than 340 years for our constitutional and God-given rights. . . .

I guess it is easy for those who have never felt the stinging darts of segregation to say wait. But when you have seen vicious mobs lynch your mothers and fathers at will and drown your sisters and brothers at whim; when you have seen hate-filled policemen curse, kick, brutalize, and even kill your black brothers and sisters with impunity; when you see the vast majority of your 20 million Negro brothers smothering in an air-tight cage of poverty in the midst of an affluent society; when you suddenly find your tongue twisted and your speech stammering as you seek to explain to your 6-year-old daughter why she can't go to the public amusement park that has just been advertised on television, and see tears welling up in her little eyes when she is told that Funtown is closed to colored children, and see the depressing clouds of inferiority begin to form in her little mental sky, and see her begin to distort her little personality by unconsciously developing a bitterness toward white people; when you have to concoct an answer for a 5-year-old son asking in agonizing pathos: "Daddy, why do white people treat colored people so mean?"; when you take a cross-country drive and find it necessary to sleep night after night in the uncomfortable corners of your automobile because no motel will accept you; when you are humiliated day in and day out by nagging signs reading "white" men and "colored"; when your first name becomes "nigger" and your middle name becomes "boy" (however old you are) . . . and when your wife and mother are never given the respected title "Mrs."; when you are harried by day and haunted by night by the fact that you are a Negro, living constantly at tiptoe stance never quite knowing what to expect next, and plagued with inner fears and outer resentments; when you are forever fighting a degenerating sense of "nobodiness"—then you will understand why we find it difficult to wait. There comes a time when the cup of endurance runs over, and men are no longer willing to be plunged into an abyss of injustice where they experience the bleakness of corroding despair. I hope, sirs, you can understand our legitimate and unavoidable impatience.

You express a great deal of anxiety over our willingness to break laws. This is certainly a legitimate concern. Since we so diligently urge people to obey the Supreme Court's decision of 1954 outlawing segregation in the public schools, it is rather strange and paradoxical to find us consciously breaking laws. One may well ask, "How can you advocate breaking some laws and obeying others?" The answer is found in the fact that there are two types of laws: There are just laws and there are unjust laws. I would be the first to advocate obeying just laws. One has not only a legal but moral responsibility to obey just laws. Conversely, one has a moral responsibility to disobey unjust laws. I would agree with Saint Augustine that "An unjust law is no law at all."

Now what is the difference between the two? How does one determine when a law is just or unjust? A just law is a man-made code that squares with the moral law or the law of God. An unjust law is a code that is out of harmony with the moral law. To put it in the terms of Saint Thomas Aquinas, an unjust law is a human law that is not rooted in eternal and natural law. Any law that uplifts human personality is just. Any law that degrades human personality is unjust. All segregation statutes are unjust because segregation distorts the soul and damages the personality. It gives the segregator a false sense of superiority and the segregated a false sense of inferiority. To use the words of Martin Buber, the great Jewish philosopher, segregation substitutes an "I-it" relationship for the "I-thou" relationship, and ends up relegating persons to the status of things. So segregation is not only politically, economically, and sociologically unsound, but it is morally wrong and sinful. Paul Tillich has said that sin is separation. Isn't segregation an existential expression of man's tragic separation, an expression of his awful estrangement, his terrible sinfulness? So I can urge men to obey the 1954 decision of the Supreme Court because it is morally right, and I can urge them to disobey segregation ordinances because they are morally wrong. . . .

Of course there is nothing new about this kind of civil disobedience. . . . It was practiced superbly by the early Christians who were willing to face hungry lions and the excruciating pain of chopping blocks, before submitting to certain unjust laws of the Roman Empire. To a degree academic freedom is a reality today because Socrates practiced civil disobedience. . . .

I must make two honest confessions to you, my Christian and Jewish brothers. First, I must confess that over the last few years I have been gravely disappointed with the white moderate. I have almost reached the regrettable conclusion that the Negroes' great stumbling block in the stride toward freedom is not the White Citizens' "Counciler" or the Ku Klux Klanner, but the white moderate who is more devoted to "order" than to justice; who prefers a negative peace which is the absence of tension to a positive peace which is the presence of justice; who constantly says, "I agree with you in the goal you seek, but I can not agree with your methods of direct action"; who paternalistically feels that he can set the timetable for another man's freedom; who lives by the myth of time and who constantly advises the Negro to wait until a "more convenient season." Shallow understanding from people of good will is more frustrating than absolute misunderstanding from people of ill will. Lukewarm acceptance is much more bewildering than outright rejection.

I had hoped that the white moderate would understand that law and order exist for the purpose of establishing justice, and that when they fail to do this they become the dangerously structured dams that block the flow of social progress. I had hoped that the white moderate would understand that the present tension in the South is merely a necessary phase of the transition from an obnoxious negative peace, where the Negro passively accepted his unjust plight, to a substance-filled positive peace, where all men will respect the dignity and worth of human personality. Actually, we who engage in nonviolent direct action are not the creators of tension. We merely bring to the surface the hidden tension that is already alive. . . .

Let me rush on to mention my other disappointment. I have been so greatly disappointed with the white church and its leadership. . . . I have heard numerous religious leaders of the South call upon their worshippers to comply with a desegregation decision because it is the law, but I have longed to hear white ministers say follow this decree because integration is morally right and the Negro is your brother. In the midst of blatant injustices inflicted upon the Negro, I have watched white churches stand on the sideline and merely mouth pious irrelevancies and sanctimonious trivialities. In the midst of a mighty struggle to rid our Nation of racial and economic injustice, I have heard so many ministers say, "Those are social issues with which the gospel has no real concern," and I have watched so many churches commit themselves to a completely other-worldly religion which made a strange distinction between body and soul, the sacred and the secular. . . .

I have wept over the laxity of the church. But be assured that my tears have been tears of love. There can be no deep disappointment where there is not deep love. Yes, I love the church; I love her sacred walls. How could I do otherwise? I am in the rather unique position of being the son, the grandson, and the great grandson of preachers. Yes, I see the church as the body of Christ. But, oh how we have blemished and scarred that body through social neglect and fear of being nonconformist. . . .

I must close now. But before closing I am impelled to mention one other point in your statement that troubled me profoundly. You warmly commended the Birmingham police force for keeping "order" and "preventing violence." I don't believe you would have so warmly commended the police force if you had seen its angry violent dogs literally biting six un-armed, nonviolent Negroes. I don't believe you would so quickly commend the policemen if you would observe their ugly and inhuman treatment of Negroes here in the city jail; if you would watch them push and curse old Negro women and young Negro girls; if you would see them slap and kick old Negro men and young Negro boys; if you will observe them, as they did on two occasions, refuse to give us food because we wanted to sing our grace together. I'm sorry that I can't join you in your praise for the police department. . . .

I wish you had commended the Negro sit-inners and demonstrators of Birmingham for their sublime courage, their willingness to suffer, and their amazing discipline in the midst of the most inhuman provocation. One day the South will recognize its real heroes. They will be the James Merediths, courageously and with a majestic sense of purpose, facing jeering and hostile mobs and the agonizing loneliness that characterizes the life of the pioneer. They will be old, oppressed, battered Negro women, symbolized in a 72-year-old woman of Montgomery, Ala., who rose up with a sense of dignity and with her people decided not to ride the segregated buses, and responded to one who inquired about her tiredness with ungrammatical profundity: "My feets is tired, but my soul is rested." They will be young high school and college students, young ministers of the gospel and a host of the elders, courageously and nonviolently sitting in at lunch counters and willingly going to jail for conscience sake. One day the South will know that when these disinherited children of God sat down at lunch counters they were in reality standing up for the best in the American dream and the most sacred values in our Judeo-Christian heritage, and thus carrying our whole Nation back to great wells of democracy which were dug deep by the Founding Fathers in the formulation of the Constitution and the Declaration of Independence.

Yours for the cause of peace and brotherhood.

Martin Luther King, Jr.

WHAT'S BECOME OF "LAW AND ORDER"?*

David Lawrence

We pride ourselves on being a Nation governed by law. We boast of a society based on order—preserved by the volition of the citizenry or, if necessary, by force of law.

Yet we see minority groups today pretending that they cannot express their will effectively except through marches in the streets or lie-down and sit-in demonstrations which interfere forcibly with motor traffic or the carrying on of private business.

What has become of our famed system of communication for the expression of ideas on controversial questions—through the press, through television, through radio, in meeting halls and auditoriums, and even in the pulpits? Have all these facilities been unavailable to minority groups?

Why have so many clergymen, Negro and white, forsaken the pulpit and the spiritual way of inculcating ideas of justice and morality? One minister, a white man of prominence, who was himself arrested as a participant in a demonstration, told a congressional committee the other day that everything was peaceful until the counterdemonstrators arrived on the scene. But isn't it natural that counterdemonstrators should want to express themselves, too?

Church organizations have passed resolutions and individual ministers have preached sermons on civil rights. The Negro has not been without

* Reprinted from *U. S. News & World Report*, August 5, 1963, published at Washington. Mr. Lawrence is the editor of *U. S. News & World Report*.

champions in every walk of life. Why, therefore, have so many Negro ministers become the active leaders and managers of street demonstrations that have resulted in disturbance of the peace, arrests, bloodshed and death?

Do the Negro ministers—those who on Sunday encourage the members of their congregations to participate in the marches—really feel that people of other races cannot be impressed with the merits of their cause except through so-called nonviolent demonstrations which so often lead to violence?

The dangers of the course which certain Negro leaders have adopted must in due time become apparent. If the only way to get attention for any cause is to organize provocative demonstrations, what lesson does this teach to a nation which believes in a government of law and order? Will not other groups of citizens, intent on attaining their objectives, be encouraged to adopt similar tactics? . . .

Why can't the demonstrators gather in big stadiums and listen to an exposition of views by their leaders? Are we approaching the day when in democratic America the slogan "law and order" is to be shunted aside with a dishonest rationalization that to disturb the peace is the only way to secure redress of grievances?

We hear the cry: "But we've waited a hundred years, we can't wait any longer."

Yet what happened in those hundred years? Was there no Congress or Supreme Court in session to proclaim "the law of the land" in the usual manner? Was anyone prevented from challenging the laws or the court decisions in a formal way through the judicial or legislative processes established by our Constitution? Was there in those decades no discussion in the press and no public debate on the principles involved in the racial controversy? Would the ruling in the 1954 desegregation decisions of the Supreme Court have been achieved earlier if Negro demonstrations had been organized and many participants had been arrested for disturbing the peace?

Government is, in fact, a system developed by evolution. We believe in rule by the majority. The minds and hearts of a majority, however, cannot be won by disregarding the fundamental precepts of government itself— that "law and order" must be preserved while the facilities of debate and lawful communication are made available to all citizens, no matter how unpopular their causes may be.

But constitutional guarantees become worthless if the process of "law and order" is forsaken and we substitute the pressures of the mob in the precincts of government itself.

THE WHITE PROBLEM*

James Baldwin

I want you to somehow make a certain leap with me, . . . I want to give you, and this comes from Nietzsche. . . . It has been on my mind all week long. At some point, the man says:

I stand before my highest mountain. And before my longest journey. And therefore, must I descend deeper than I have ever before descended.

Now there are several thousand things that one has got to say in the context out of which we are speaking. I suppose the first thing that I have to suggest is that one consider the fact that in the life of a man, the life of a woman, in anybody's life, there are several elements always at work. But the crucial element I want to consider here is that element of a life which we consider to be an identity. The way in which one puts oneself together, the way one imagines oneself to be, the reality, for example, the invented reality, standing before you now, arbitrarily called Jimmy Baldwin, who maintains a great many other things. We've agreed we've succeeded in striking a certain kind of bargain with the world; this is his name, and this is what he does, and this is who he is. Okay, but that's not it. The neat fact, forever, for everybody, is something else, is a stranger, the stranger with whom one is forced to deal, day in and day out, forced, in fact, to discover, forced, in fact, to create, as distinct from invent. Life demands of everyone a certain kind of humility, the humility to be able to make the descent that Nietzsche was talking about. . . .

One of the things that one cannot imagine, especially when one is young, is how to pay your dues. You don't even know there are dues to be paid. And later on, one begins to discover, and with great pain, and very much against one's will, that if you want something, whatever it is you want, and whatever it is you want at bottom, must be *to become yourself;* there is nothing else to want. Whatever that is, whatever that journey is, one's got to accept the fact that disaster is a condition under which you will make it. The journey, I mean, not make it in the American sense. And you will learn a certain humility because the terms that you have invented, what you think describe and define you, inevitably collide with the facts

* From "James Baldwin Speaks on the White Problem," condensed from *Frontier* (June 1963). Reprinted by permission. Mr. Baldwin is an American novelist and essayist.

of life. And when this collision occurs, and make no mistake, this is an absolutely inevitable collision, when this collision occurs, like two trains in a tunnel, one's got the choice, and it's a very narrow choice, of holding on to your definition of yourself, or saying, as the old folks used to say, and everybody who wants to live has to say,

"Yes Lord."

Which means to say yes to life. Until you can do that, you've not become a man, or a woman. Now in this country, [this is] part of the dilemma, which could become a tragedy, of being what is known somewhat arbitrarily as an American. The collective effort until this moment, and the collective delusion until this moment, has been precisely my delusion when I was a little boy, that you could get what you wanted, and become what you said you were going to be, painlessly. . . .

I think that it might be useful, in order to survive our present crisis, to do what any individual does, is forced to do to survive his crisis, which is to look back on his beginnings. The beginnings of this country (it seems to me a banality to say it, but alas, it has to be said) the beginnings of this country have nothing whatever to do with the myth we have created about it. The country did not come about because a handful of people in Europe, various parts of Europe, said "I want to be free," and promptly built a boat, or a raft, and crossed the Atlantic Ocean. Not at all, not at all. In passing, let me remark that the word liberty, the word freedom, are terribly mis-used words. Liberty is a fact which is also used as a slogan, and freedom may be the very last thing that people want. The very last thing. Anyway, the people who settled the country, the people who came here, came here for one reason, no matter how disguised. They came here because they thought it would be better here than where they were. That's why they came. And that's the only reason that they came. Anybody who was making it in England did not get on the Mayflower. This is important. It is important that one begin to recognize this, because part of the dilemma of this country is that it has managed to believe the myth it has created about its own past, which is another way of saying that it has entirely denied its past. And we all know, when we think about it, what happens to a person who is born, let us say, where I was born, in Harlem, and goes into the world pretending he was born in Sutton Place. And what happens to a person, however odd this may sound, also happens to a nation, a nation being, when it finally comes into existence, the achievement of the people who make it up. And the quality of the nation being absolutely at the mercy, defined, dictated by, the nature and quality of the people who make it up. . . .

In this extraordinary endeavor to create the country called America, a great many crimes were committed. And I want to make it absolutely clear, or as clear as I can make it, that I understand perfectly well the crime is universal and common, and I trust no one will assume that I am indicting or accusing. I'm not any longer interested in the crime. People treat each other very badly and always have, and very probably always will. I'm not talking about that; I'm talking about denying what one does. This is a much more sinister matter. We did several things in order to conquer the country. There was, at the point we reached these shores, a group of people who had never heard of machines, or as far as I know, of money. . . . We promptly eliminated them and killed them. I'm talking about the Indians, in case you don't know what I'm talking about. Well, people have done this for centuries, but I hazard, I'll bet you, as they say in Harlem, a fat man, that not many American children being taught American history have any real sense of what that collision was like, or what we really did, how we really achieved the extermination of the Indians, or what that meant. . . .

. . . the other thing we did in order to conquer the country, physically speaking, was to enslave the Africans. Now slavery, like murder, is one of the oldest human institutions. So we cannot quarrel about the facts of slavery. That is to say, we could, but that's another story. But we enslaved them because in order to conquer the country, we had to have cheap labor. And the man who is now known as The American Negro, who is one of the oldest American citizens, and the *only* one who never wanted to come here, did the dirty work, hoed the cotton. . . . In fact, I think it is not too strong a statement to say—I'm going to put it this way—without his presence, without that strong back, the American economy, the American nation, would have had a vast amount of trouble creating its capital. If then, if one had not had the [Negro] totin' the barge and liftin' the bales, as we put it, it would be a very different country, and it would certainly be much poorer. And that's all right.

But the people I'm speaking of who settled the country had a fatal flaw. They could see, they could recognize a man when they saw one. They knew he wasn't, I mean *you can tell*, they knew he wasn't anything else but a man, but since they were Christian, and since they had already decided that they came here to establish a free country, and some of them really meant it, by the way, the only way to justify the role this chattel was playing in one's life was to say that he *was not* a man. Because if he wasn't a man, no crime had been committed. That is the basis, that lie is the basis of our present trouble. Because that is an extremely complex lie. If on the one hand, one man cannot avoid recognizing another man, it is also true then, obviously, that the black man who is in captivity and treated like an animal, and told that he was one, *knew* that he was a man, and knew that something was wrong. . . .

Anyway, it was the black man's necessity, once he got here, to accept the cross, because he had to survive, to somehow manage to outwit his

Christian master, because what he faced when he got here was really the Bible and the gun. And that's all right too. What is terrible in it, is that American white men are not prepared, first of all, to believe, for example, my version of this story, to believe that it happened. In order to avoid believing that, they have set up in themselves a fantastic system of evasions, denials, and justifications, which destroyed, or is about to destroy, their grasp of reality, which is another way of saying, their moral sense.

What I am trying to say is that the crime is not the most important thing here. What makes our situation serious is that we have spent so many generations pretending that it did not happen. If you doubt me, ask yourself on what assumptions rest those extraordinary questions that white men ask, no matter how politely. On what assumption rests the question, would you let your sister marry? It's based on some preoccupation in somebody's mind. God knows, you know, I have never given any evidence of having that particular problem. I'm not interested in marrying your sister, my God. I mean that. On what assumption, again, rests the extraordinary question, "What does the Negro want?" This again, comes out of some extraordinary preoccupation in the mind, something entirely, if I may say so, divorced from reality. It's like saying, What do seals eat?, or, I don't know, it's as unreal as unreal can be. . . .

Let's go back, for a minute, to where I started, let's go back to Nietzsche. "I stand before my highest mountain, and before my longest journey. And therefore, must I descend deeper than I ever before descended." And we spoke a little earlier about the necessity, when the collision between your terms and life occurs, of saying yes to life. That's the descent. The difference between a boy and a man is that a boy imagines there is some way to get through life safely, and a man knows he's got to pay his dues. In this country, the entire nation has always assumed that I would pay their dues for them. What it means to be a Negro in this country is that you represent, you are the receptacle of, you are the vehicle of, all the pain, disaster, sorrow, which white Americans think they can escape. This is what is meant, really what is meant, by keeping a Negro in his place. It is why white people, until today, are still astounded and offended, if by some miscalculation, they are forced to suspect that you are not happy in your home. This is absolutely true, and I'm not talking about the deep South. People finally say to you, "But you're so bitter!"

In this country, for a dangerously long time, there have been two levels of experience. One, to put it cruelly, but I think quite truthfully, can be summed up in the image of Doris Day and Gary Cooper. I think you know what they do. And the other—subterranean, indispensable, but denied—which can be summed up, let us say, in the tone of Ray Charles. And there has never been in this country any real confrontation between these two realities. . . .

White people are astounded by Birmingham. Black people aren't. White people are endlessly demanding to be reassured that Birmingham is really on Mars. They don't want to believe, still less to act on the belief that what is happening in Birmingham, (and I mean this, and I'm not exaggerating: There are several thousand ways to kill a man; there are several thousand ways to be violent), they don't want to realize that there is not one step, one inch, morally, or actually, there is no distance, between Birmingham and Los Angeles.

Now it is entirely possible that we may all go under. But until that happens, I prefer to believe that since a society is created by men, it can be remade by men. The price for this transformation is high. White people will have to ask themselves precisely why they found it necessary to invent a nigger, because they invented him for reasons, out of necessities of their own. And every white citizen of this country will have to accept the fact that he is not innocent, because those dogs and those hoses,—those crimes —are being committed in your name. Black people will have to do something very hard too. They've done it, some of them, already, which is to allow the white citizen his first awkward steps toward maturity. For we have functioned in this country precisely that way, for a very long time. We were the first psychiatrists in this country. If we can hang on just a little bit longer, all of us, we may make it. We've got to try. But I think that those are the conditions.

WHAT THE NEGRO NEEDS MOST:
A FIRST CLASS CITIZENS' COUNCIL*

John Fischer

What follows may sound offensive to a good many Negroes and to some white people. Nevertheless it needs to be said.

This is a proposal for a new Negro organization—a First Class Citizens' Council. Its purpose is the genuine integration of Negroes into the normal stream of American life.

So far the established Negro organizations—the NAACP, the Urban League, CORE, the Southern Regional Council, and all the rest—have made only limited headway toward this goal. With their ingrained pat-

---

terns of thought and action, they probably can never go much further. Before the Negro community can make its next big forward step, it must find a new kind of leadership, a new type of organization, and a radically different method of attack.

The old organizations have, of course, performed an invaluable service—not only for the Negro, but for all Americans. After two generations of hard fighting, they have finally broken down nearly all the legal barriers which had walled the Negro into a separate world. Much hard fighting is still ahead before desegregation—in schools, jobs, housing, eating places, and public facilities—is finally wiped out; but the decisive battles have been won. At last the law, the full force of the federal government, and the overwhelming weight of public opinion have all come over to the side of racial justice. No matter how stubbornly pockets of resistance in the Deep South (and some Northern cities) may hold out, the result is no longer in question. The rest is a mopping-up operation, like the war in Europe after Bastogne.

So now the American Negro faces an entirely new campaign. It may prove harder than the old one. Certainly it requires different weapons: law suits, sit-ins, and freedom rides—still indispensable in the remaining battles of the old campaign—will not work in the coming one.

For the next inevitable objective is full-scale participation, on easy and equal terms, in the ordinary operations of American society. It will be won only when the average Negro (not just the brilliant exception) is willingly accepted by the average white (not just the self-conscious "liberal") as a reliable neighbor, a good colleague to have in the office or plant, a welcome addition to the local political club, bowling league, trade association and PTA. This obviously will mean the erosion of a lot of white prejudices; but it also demands some big changes in the habits, character, and ambitions of a lot of Negroes.

The aim of the new Council would be to produce those changes. Its slogan: "Let's Make Every Negro a First Class Citizen." Its goal: not merely to win the full rights which belong to every American, but to make sure that these rights are used—that the average Negro is both willing and able to carry the full responsibilities of good citizenship. Once he does, he may be surprised to see how fast white prejudice begins to melt away.

For this prejudice is not altogether baseless—as a few of the braver Negro leaders are now beginning to admit. It cannot be erased just by scolding white people, nor can it be touched by any sort of law or demonstration. It will disappear only when a considerable majority of whites are convinced that they have nothing to fear from close, daily association with Negroes in jobs, schools, and neighborhoods.

The first task of the First Class Citizens' Council, therefore, will be to find honest answers to three questions:

1. What are these white people afraid of? Why do they begin to move out of a neighborhood as soon as any considerable number of Negroes move in? Why are so many desegregated schools becoming "resegregated," as white parents withdraw their children? (In Washington, for example, where desegregation was originally carried out with surprising success and good will, nearly 82 per cent of the students are now Negroes —although the population of the city is only 54 per cent colored. White families with children of school age have either moved to the suburbs in large numbers, or have sent their youngsters to private schools.)

2. How much of this fear is rational, and how much is simply blind, unreasoning prejudice?

3. What can be done to remove the rational, valid reasons for such fear? Once they are gone, the purely irrational suspicions ought to be easier to cope with.

Nobody, so far as I can discover, has yet attempted a serious examination of these questions. White sociologists have shrunk away from them, for fear that they might be suspected of racism, or might give aid and comfort to the white supremacy fanatics of the Deep South. Most Negroes have refused to look at them at all; it is easier—and more popular in the Negro community—to blame everything on white prejudice. (A few Negro leaders, as we shall note in a moment, are exceptions.)

A candid, careful investigation would show (I think) that many white people are afraid—with some reason—of four things:

1. Crime

As the proportion of Negroes in a community increases, the crime rate usually rises sharply. The police chief of the District of Columbia has estimated that Negroes are responsible for 80 per cent of the serious crimes there, although they make up only a little over half the population. In Chicago, when Negroes were 17 per cent of the population, they accounted for 65 per cent of the jail inmates; in Philadelphia, the comparable figures were 21 and 80 per cent; in Detroit, 19 and 58.

A few weeks ago a friend of mine—a middle-aged book editor—had to catch a train at the 125th Street station in Harlem. As he was walking up the stairs inside the station, he was slugged on the back of the head with a blackjack or some similar weapon. While he sprawled semi-conscious on the steps, his assailant snatched his wallet, and then kicked him violently in the face. (If the kick had landed an inch higher, it would have destroyed his right eye.) None of the scores of people in the station, mostly Negroes, made any effort to catch the criminal. None made any effort to help the dazed and bleeding man. As it happens, this editor has always been a quiet, effective fighter for Negro rights. He has never had a trace of racial bias, and has none now. But he may think twice before he catches another night train at 125th Street; and he might feel a little uneasy if he had to live in a neighborhood with a large Negro population. Can you blame him if he wonders whether those people in the station behaved like first-class citizens?

Such crimes—particularly the assault and robbery of taxi drivers—have become so common in Harlem that most New York taxi drivers avoid the area like a battle zone. (This works a real hardship on many law-abiding Negroes, who find it almost impossible to get a cab to stop for them after dark.)

In Washington recently a gang of young Negroes assaulted and robbed a white bus driver. The passengers, who happened to be all Negroes, watched passively—and not one of them was willing to help the police find the thugs.

In many Negro neighborhoods (and a few white ones, too) the bystanders not only refuse to help the police; they help the criminals. During the first six months of last year, 1,171 New York policemen were attacked while trying to make arrests; about a fifth of these were hurt so badly they needed medical attention. Last summer one such incident in Harlem flared into a near-riot, and three hundred policemen had to be called to get it under control. *Jet*, a Negro news weekly blamed this trouble on "politics, poor Negro leadership," and "the street-corner rantings and ravings of a motley crew of soapbox speakers who fancy themselves 'black nationalists.'" It added that local Negro leaders "seemed content to turn their backs on it, hoping the problem will go away."

So long as this remains true, are the fears of the white community entirely illusory?

2. Neighborhood Deterioration

The commonest fear among white families is that their neighborhood will go downhill if many Negroes move in.

Sometimes this fear is plainly unjustified. A number of my Negro friends are as house-proud as anybody I know; one of them has made his home and garden into a town showplace. Nor is this true merely of the relatively wealthy "black bourgeois." A Negro home I visit fairly often is a single room in a slum district, but it always is spotlessly clean, tidy, and comfortable.

Yet this is not always true. A neighborhood where I once lived in Washington is now occupied almost entirely by Negroes; it has indeed gone downhill, swiftly and unmistakably. In part this is due to overcrowding, and to incomes so low that the owners can't afford to keep their places up properly. But it is also partly due to plain old don't-care. Garbage, broken bottles, and old bedsprings accumulate in many a backyard . . . a loose porch board goes unfixed for weeks, though all it needs is one nail and two licks with a hammer . . . broken windowpanes get stuffed with rags. Moreover, the same families that can't find money for a bucket of paint or a pane of glass somehow manage, surprisingly often, to drive fancy cars and buy a fifth of whiskey every weekend.

Similar examples can be cited in almost any American city. Still— nothing about this matter is simple—I know of communities in Atlanta and the San Francisco Bay area which have improved, rather than deteriorated after an influx of Negro families. They prove a basic point: There is nothing inherently bad about Negro occupancy. Given ambition, energetic leadership and a little elbow grease, it can result in neighborhoods as attractive as any. So the job of the First Class Citizens' Council is by no means hopeless; it is just overdue.

3. Civic Apathy

A kindred fear is that Negro newcomers will not pull their weight in the community boat. Few of them seem willing to invest time and effort in the web of civic, political, and voluntary organizations which holds every American community together.

As a precinct captain in a district with a considerable Negro population, I learned at first hand how hard it is to persuade them to register and vote—and harder yet to get them to ring doorbells for either political party. Such indifference is at last beginning to cause some concern among Negro spokesmen. The Michigan Chronicle, a Negro paper in Detroit, recently pointed out that a third of that city's qualified Negro citizens never bothered to register—and that "at least 40 per cent" of those who did register failed to vote. And Louis Lomax, in his notably outspoken book, The Negro Revolt, published this spring, noted that about 200,000 Negroes of voting age live in the Harlem district represented by Congressman Adam Clayton Powell, the most popular and flamboyant Negro politician in the country; yet he normally polls only about 40,000 votes, while his opponents seldom get more than 10,000.

"One reason why Negro leadership organizations think several times before launching highly publicized voter-registration drives," Lomax said, "is that they know Negroes simply will not go to the polls and register."

So, too, with many civic organizations. Negro parents are usually quick to complain (at least in Northern cities) about any covert—or even accidental—segregation in local schools. But how many attend the meetings of their Parent-Teachers Association? How many help collect for the Community Chest or offer to lead a Girl Scout troop?

4. Moral Irresponsibility

White people also are bothered by the casual attitude of many Negroes about sex, and about their family responsibilities.

Such worries are seldom discussed out loud—maybe because so many whites know that their own morals aren't exactly impeccable. But they do have some statistical justification. About 2 per cent of the white babies born each year are bastards; among Negroes the illegitimacy rate is above 20 per cent. And even when they are married, Negro fathers tend to abandon their families with lighthearted frequency. About 8 per cent of the white families with children under eighteen are broken homes; for nonwhites, the comparable figure is 21 per cent.

One result is a heavy burden on the relief rolls, and a growing resentment among white taxpayers; nobody likes to support somebody else's bastards. Another result is that hundreds of thousands of Negro children grow up without a man in the family, to provide discipline and example; which in turn means a steady rise in delinquency. A third is the reluctance of white parents to keep their children in schools with a high proportion of Negroes—not because they are afraid of intermarriage, but because they worry about the habits and attitudes their youngsters might pick up.

Is this blind prejudice? Can a man who won't support his children call himself a first-class citizen?

To all of these complaints, the traditional Negro leaders have a ready answer. The Negro's shortcomings, they argue, are the inevitable consequence of three hundred years of slavery and discrimination. When you hold a man down for that long, he can't spring upright overnight when the pressure is removed. He won't vote because he doesn't really believe that he can have any influence on government. . . . He won't attend civic meetings because he has never been welcomed or listened to—and he is still afraid he will be insulted, or at best ignored. Broken families and promiscuity were forced on the Negro during slavery, and the resulting pattern takes a long time to change.

Crime, so the explanation continues, is largely a result of the Negro's low place on the economic totem poll. "Most Negroes would rather work than steal," as Lomax puts it. "By the same token they would rather steal than starve." And so long as many jobs are closed to them—by their educational handicaps, or by union or employer discrimination—those are the stark alternatives.

Moreover, the "frustration crimes"—dope addiction, drunkenness, sexual assaults, sometimes murder—often are (to quote Lomax again) "rooted in the need to escape from the ugly reality of life in the Negro ghetto." Statistically they are closely correlated with overcrowding, slums, and—perhaps most important—the sense of hopelessness that afflicts so many young Negroes. Feeling that society has stacked its cards against them, they are likely to strike back at society. Especially white society. Much Negro crime, as Lomax points out, "has to do with getting back at white people."

These are valid explanations. For white people, they mean that Negroes need a great deal more help than they have yet had, to overcome the cultural lag that has been imposed upon them. They need—and deserve—the same concentration of money, talent, and organization that we are devoting to underdeveloped people in Asia, Africa, and Latin America. Given the best teachers, the best social workers, special attention to vocational education and job placement, an extra share of understanding and patience, most Negroes will be able to close the cultural gap surprisingly fast. The experimental Higher Horizons program in New York City's schools has already demonstrated how quickly they can move ahead, with a little encouragement and special attention.

For the Negroes, however, these same explanations can be dangerous. It is all too easy to use them as an excuse for despair. And they offer no solutions. So long as the Negro blames his plight entirely on circumstances, history, and the white man, he is going to stay in that plight. He will get out of it only when he begins to change his circumstances, make new history, and shoulder a bigger share of responsibility for the fix he is in.

For example, a Negro minister in a New York suburb recently called on his congregation to picket a dairy, on grounds that it had never hired a Negro deliveryman. The dairy replied that it had never had a Negro applicant.

"I'll have a half-dozen at your office tomorrow morning," the minister said. Not one showed up. The dairy then began a systematic effort to recruit Negro employees; after about six weeks it found one—just one—who was willing to take on the responsibilities of a milk route. A few months later he quit, apparently because the psychological burdens of the job were too much for him.*

Nor is this an isolated instance. For the last five years the National Urban League has been opening up more job opportunities for Negroes in

---

* Nevertheless this story has a happy ending. The dairy refused to accept his resignation, and found another assignment for him inside a processing plant—not a menial job, but one requiring a fairly high degree of technical skill. He has learned to handle it to everybody's satisfaction, and the firm is continuing its efforts to recruit more Negro help.

"white" industries than it can find Negroes to fill. The industry I know best—publishing—has been open to qualified Negroes for many years; a substantial number have risen to positions of considerable responsibility. Many more would be welcome—particularly secretaries, bookkeepers, and computer operators—if qualified applicants could be found. Why they can't is something of a mystery, because the schools in New York and a dozen other big cities are presumably turning out thousands of Negro youngsters with the necessary training.

Maybe the answer lies in a parable frequently told by Dr. Benjamin E. Mays, president of Morehouse College in Atlanta. A zoo lion spent years pacing back and forth in his cage. Then one day somebody left the door of his cage open; but the lion still kept pacing back and forth.

So the job of the First Class Citizens' Council will be to convince American Negroes that the door of their cage is at last open—not all the way yet, but wider than most of them realize. And each one who pushes through that door can help open it a little further for those who lag behind. Or, if he doesn't use his new opportunities well, he can make it harder for the next man to get through the door.

Take the case of five Negro drivers who worked for a taxi company in Williamsburg, Virginia. On the first day of the fishing season, not one of them showed up for work; nor did any of them let the manager know that they planned to take a day off—although they knew he had promised a half-a-dozen customers that he would get them to the airport early that morning. Their irresponsible behavior is not the main point; what is really sad is that nobody in the local Negro community thought it worth mentioning. No Negro newspaper, no minister, no teacher, no official of the NAACP bothered to tell them that they were hurting *all* Negroes. That pan of fish will make at least seven people—the cab manager and his six disappointed passengers—hesitate a little before offering any Negro a job.

For constructive self-criticism is a rare, and much needed, commodity among American Negroes. The Negro press is loaded with criticism of white people—some of it justified, some of it as racist and intemperate as any utterance of Senator James Eastland; but it seldom condemns a Negro politician who takes bribes from a contractor, or a clergyman who makes out notoriously well with his women parishioners. Nobody pickets the Harlem numbers game operators; nobody calls for social ostracism of the relief chiselers whom Lomax describes as "an abomination and an embarrassment."

Almost nobody, that is. Some of the more courageous Negro leaders are at last beginning to speak up—though not yet very loudly or often. The Reverend Martin Luther King has called on his followers "to admit that our standards do often fall short" and to do something about it. "Even the most poverty-stricken among us," he has written, "can purchase a ten-cent bar of soap; even the most uneducated among us can have high morals. . . . By improving our standards here and now we will go a long way toward breaking down the arguments of the segregationist."

Again, Whitney Young, the new executive secretary of the Urban League, is trying to reshape that organization for a new kind of attack on the Negro's problems. He is talking about mobilizing all sorts of community resources—from social workers to churches to the cop on the beat—in a concerted campaign against crime, broken families, and "social disorganization."

Curiously enough, the Black Muslims seem to be more effective than any other Negro organization so far in stimulating a sense of pride and self-reliance. Their doctrine springs from race hatred, and their political program is sheer fantasy; nevertheless, in teaching thrift, hard work, business enterprise, decorous conduct and self-discipline, they can claim some notable accomplishments.

But these are thin beginnings. If a First Class Citizens' Council, or something like it, tackles the job on a really big scale, I suspect that it will be led by new men, uncommitted to the rancors and tactics of the older organizations. Maybe by somebody like Bob Moses, a young man who gave up a bright career in New York to organize Negro voters in Mississippi. He is more like St. Paul than anybody I know; in spite of beatings, prison, and threats of death, he has plugged right ahead on his mission, setting a glowing example of selflessness, austerity, and honor. Maybe the leadership will come from men like Dr. Robert Weaver, who has risen to the highest post in government ever held by a Negro—not by demagoguery, but by long years of dedication to fair play and good housing for everybody, white and Negro alike.

Such men are not content just to demand their rights. They insist on carrying their responsibilities too. That's how you get to be a first-class citizen—as Crispus Attucks knew when he marched to his death in the Boston Massacre. The first man to die in the American revolution, he was a Negro who knew that citizenship is earned, not given. He might well be the Permanent Honorary President of the new Council.

CHAPTER TEN

Foreign Policy: Peace or Victory?

On April 12, 1945, one hour before he died, President Franklin D. Roosevelt dictated a message to Prime Minister Winston Churchill. In part, the message read, "I would minimize the general Soviet problem as much as possible because these problems, in one form or other, seem to arise every day and most of them straighten out . . ." Roosevelt was a man of good will, but Joseph Stalin had other intentions. Things did not "straighten out," and less than one year later Winston Churchill, on March 5, 1946, at Fulton, Missouri, told the free world some harsh facts: "From Stettin in the Baltic to Trieste in the Adriatic an iron curtain has descended across the Continent." The Iron Curtain in Eastern Europe was followed by the Bamboo Curtain in the Far East, and the free world entered the cold- and sometimes hot-war era. For the past eighteen years world peace has been sitting on the powder keg of East-West tension. In Berlin, Korea, Vietnam, Lebanon, and Cuba disaster for the free world has never seemed too far away.

By 1964, "peace" and "victory" have an almost Alice-in-Wonderland quality. Eighteen years of cold war have given these grand words a certain hollow ring. Peace can turn into "appeasement" and victory into "nuclear holocaust" with an almost magic ease. Still, these words can have a mighty impact—for they conjure scenes from yesterday: "the spirit of 1776," Appomattox, Armistice Day, V-E Day, and V-J Day.

But the habit of looking back to yesterday can be a dangerous foundation for building on tomorrow.

Undoubtedly, many Americans look back to 1946 and conclude that the United States was cheated out of the peace that should have consummated the victory of 1945. But whether peace comes from victory in war has become an antiquated question in a nuclear age.

President John F. Kennedy's speech, "A Strategy for Peace," marked the beginning of a new debate on American foreign policy. The significance of the speech is the indication that American foreign policy will no longer assume that nuclear stockpiles assure peace, but rather that lasting peace must come through gradual and mutual accommodation in American and Soviet relations. To that end, he announced a unilateral American nuclear test ban that ultimately led to the signing of U.S.–Soviet ban on atmospheric nuclear testing.

The willingness of the Kennedy Admistration to seek accommodation with the Soviet Union has been the subject of criticism. Senator Barry Goldwater and Senator Henry M. Jackson, one a Republican and the other a Democrat, each have questioned the wisdom of a policy of accommodation. Senator Goldwater has called for a declaration that the aim of American foreign policy is victory in the war against communism. Senator Goldwater sees only defeat for the United States as the alternative to victory. To Senator Jackson, the goal of peace can be achieved not through a policy of inoffensiveness but rather through a tough policy based on superior military strength. Senator Jackson, however, voted with seventy-nine other Senators in favor of the test-ban treaty, in September of 1963; Senator Goldwater voted with eighteen other Senators against the treaty.

The fundamental difference between the Goldwater-Jackson and the Kennedy positions is the question whether a policy of accommodation today can become appeasement and defeat tomorrow. Neither side of the issue advocates war or appeasement, but each side sees war or appeasement as a possible result of its opponent's position.

It would be misleading to conclude that a Kennedy policy of accommodation includes immediate reduction of military strength. A ban on atmospheric testing has not foreshadowed any request by the Kennedy Administration for a reduction in military spending. But there are those who question whether American security can be achieved by continual increases in military expenditures. Senator George McGovern is representative of a growing opinion that military expenditures must be reduced, and the savings invested in social and educational projects to improve the economic and moral fabric of America.

Others question the value of continued foreign-aid expenditures. Critics of foreign aid are wondering just how much benefit the United States has derived since 1946 from the expenditure of approximately $100 billion in foreign aid. Senator Goldwater has called for a halt to the "squandering of our money on unrealistic world-wide aid programs." Representative Otto E. Passman, Democratic chairman of the powerful House appropriations subcommittee on foreign operations, has termed foreign aid an "addiction" of which foreign nations need to be cured. Passman questions whether foreign-aid programs improve American security, and warns of the dangers these programs mean in terms of fiscal soundness. On the other hand, David E. Bell, director of the Agency for International Development, the central foreign-aid agency, defends foreign aid as a "positive contribution to peace."

Peace through accommodation and victory through nuclear strength, disarmament, and foreign aid are all dilemmas in our foreign policy. No avenue seems to promise an easy tomorrow. How much of the policy of accommodation is predicated on the Sino-Soviet conflict? What will the accommodations of today mean in the future if that conflict is resolved to the mutual satisfaction of China and the Soviet Union? Does America receive a dollar in security for a dollar in foreign aid? And if so, must huge foreign-aid programs necessarily become a permanent part of our foreign policy?

A STRATEGY FOR PEACE*

President John F. Kennedy

. . . I have . . . chosen this time and place to discuss a topic on which ignorance too often abounds and the truth is too rarely perceived—and that is the most important topic on earth: peace.

What kind of peace do I mean and what kind of peace do we seek? Not a Pax Americana enforced on the world by American weapons of war. Not the peace of the grave or the security of the slave. I am talking about the genuine peace—the kind of peace that makes life on earth worth living —and the kind that enables men and nations to grow and to hope and build a better life for their children—not merely peace for Americans but peace for all men and women—not merely peace in our time but peace in all time.

I speak of peace because of the new face of war. Total war makes no sense in an age where great powers can maintain large and relatively invulnerable nuclear forces and refuse to surrender without resort to those forces. It makes no sense in an age when a single nuclear weapon contains almost ten times the explosive force delivered by all the Allied air forces in the second world war. It makes no sense in an age when the deadly poisons produced by a nuclear exchange would be carried by wind and water and soil and seed to the far corners of the globe and to generations yet unborn.

---

* Commencement Address, American University, Washington, D.C., June 10, 1963.

Today the expenditure of billions of dollars every year on weapons acquired for the purpose of making sure we never need them is essential to the keeping of peace. But surely the acquisition of such idle stockpiles—which can only destroy and can never create—is not the only, much less the most efficient, means of assuring peace.

I speak of peace, therefore, as the necessary rational end of rational men. I realize the pursuit of peace is not as dramatic as the pursuit of war—and frequently the words of the pursuer fall on deaf ears. But we have no more urgent task.

Some say that it is useless to speak of peace or world law or world disarmament—and that it will be useless until the leaders of the Soviet Union adopt a more enlightened attitude. I hope they do. I believe we can help them do it.

But I also believe that we must re-examine our own attitudes—as individuals and as a nation—for our attitude is as essential as theirs. And every graduate of this school, every thoughtful citizen who despairs of war and wishes to bring peace, should begin by looking inward—by examining his own attitude towards the course of the cold war and toward freedom and peace here at home.

First: Examine our attitude towards peace itself. Too many think it is unreal. But that is a dangerous defeatist belief. It leads to the conclusion that war is inevitable—that mankind is doomed—that we are gripped by forces we cannot control.

We need not accept that view. Our problems are manmade. Therefore, they can be solved by man. And man can be as big as he wants. No problem of human destiny is beyond human beings. Man's reason and spirit have often solved the seemingly unsolvable—and we believe they can do it again.

I am not referring to the absolute, infinite concepts of universal peace and good will of which some fantasies and fanatics dream. I do not deny the value of hopes and dreams but we merely invite discouragement and incredulity by making that our only and immediate goal.

Concrete Actions Needed

Let us focus instead on a more practical, more attainable peace—based not on a sudden revolution in human nature but on a gradual evolution in human institutions—on a series of concrete actions and effective agreement which are in the interests of all concerned.

There is no single, simple key to this peace—no grand or magic formula to be adopted by one or two powers. Genuine peace must be the product of many nations, the sum of many acts. It must be dynamic, not static, changing to meet the challenge of each new generation. For peace is a process—a way of solving problems.

With such a peace, there will still be quarrels and conflicting interests, as there are within families and nations. World peace, like community peace, does not require that each man love his neighbor—it requires only that they live together with mutual tolerance, submitting their disputes to a just and peaceful settlement. And history teaches us that enmities between nations, as between individuals, do not last forever. However fixed our likes and dislikes may seem, the tide of time and events will often bring surprising changes in the relations between nations and neighbors.

So let us persevere. Peace need not be impracticable—and war need not be inevitable. By defining our goal more clearly—by making it seem more manageable and less remote—we can help all people to see it, to draw hope from it, and to move irresistibly towards it.

And second: let us re-examine our attitude towards the Soviet Union. It is discouraging to think that their leaders may actually believe what their propagandists write.

It is discouraging to read a recent authoritative Soviet text on military strategy and find, on page after page, wholly baseless and incredible claims—such as the allegation that

American imperialists circles are preparing to unleash different types of war . . . that there is a very real threat of a preventative war being unleashed by American imperialists against the Soviet Union . . . (and that) the political aims,

and I quote,

of the American imperialists are to enslave economically and politically the European and other capitalist countries . . . (and) to achieve world domination . . . by means of aggressive war.

Truly, as it was written long ago: "The wicked flee when no man pursueth." Yet it is sad to read these Soviet statements—to realize the extent of the gulf between us. But it is also a warning—a warning to the American people not to fall into the same trap as the Soviets, not to see only a distorted and desperate view of the other side, not to see conflict as inevitable, accommodation as impossible and communication as nothing more than an exchange of threats.

No government or social system is so evil that its people must be considered as lacking in virtue. As Americans, we find Communism profoundly repugnant as a negation of personal freedom and dignity. But we can still hail the Russian people for their many achievements—in science and space, in economic and industrial growth, in culture, in acts of courage.

Among the many traits the peoples of our two countries have in common, none is stronger than our mutual abhorrence of war. Almost unique among the major world powers, we have never been at war with each other. And no nation in the history of battle ever suffered more than the Soviet Union in the second world war. At least 20,000,000 lost their lives. Countless millions of homes and families were burned or sacked. A third of the nation's territory, including two-thirds of its industrial base, was turned into a wasteland—a loss equivalent to the destruction of this country east of Chicago.

Today, should total war ever break out again—no matter how—our two countries will be the primary targets. It is an ironic but accurate fact that the two strongest powers are the two in the most danger of devastation. All we have built, all we have worked for, would be destroyed in the first 24 hours. And even in the cold war—which brings burdens and dangers to so many countries, including this nation's closest allies—our two countries bear the heaviest burdens. For we are both devoting massive sums of money to weapons that could be better devoted to combat ignorance, poverty and disease.

We are both caught up in a vicious and dangerous cycle with suspicion on one side breeding suspicion on the other, and new weapons begetting counter-weapons.

In short, both the United States and its allies, and the Soviet Union and its allies, have a mutually deep interest in a just and genuine peace and in halting the arms race. Agreements to this end are in the interests of the Soviet Union as well as ours—and even the most hostile nations can be relied upon to accept and keep those treaty obligations and only those treaty obligations, which are in their own interest.

So, let us not be blind to our differences—but let us also direct attention to our common interests and the means by which those differences can be resolved. And if we cannot end now our differences, at least we can help make the world safe for diversity. For, in the final analysis, our most basic common link is that we all inhabit this small planet. We all breathe the same air. We all cherish our children's future. And we are all mortal.

Third: Let us re-examine our attitude towards the cold war, remembering we are not engaged in a debate, seeking to pile up debating points.

We are not here distributing blame or pointing the finger of judgment. We must deal with the world as it is, and not as it might have been had the history of the last eighteen years been different.

We must, therefore, persevere in the search for peace in the hope that constructive changes within the Communist bloc might bring within reach solutions which now seem beyond us. We must conduct our affairs in such a way that it becomes in the Communists' interest to agree on a genuine peace. And above all, while defending our own vital interests, nuclear powers must avert those confrontations which bring an adversary to a choice of either a humiliating retreat or a nuclear war. To adopt that kind of course in the nuclear age would be evidence only of the bankruptcy of our policy—or of a collective death-wish for the world.

To secure these ends, America's weapons are non-provocative, carefully controlled, designed to deter and capable of selective use. Our military forces are committed to peace and disciplined in self-restraint. Our diplomats are instructed to avoid unnecessary irritants and purely rhetorical hostility.

For we can seek a relaxation of tensions without relaxing our guard. And, for our part, we do not need to use threats to prove that we are resolute. We do not need to jam foreign broadcasts out of fear our faith will be eroded. We are unwilling to impose our system on any unwilling people—but we are willing and able to engage in peaceful competition with any people on earth.

Meanwhile, we seek to strengthen the United Nations, to help solve its financial problems, to make it a more effective instrument for peace, to develop it into a genuine world security system—a system capable of resolving disputes on the basis of law, of insuring the security of the large and the small, and of creating conditions under which arms can finally be abolished.

At the same time we seek to keep peace inside the non-Communist world, where many nations, all of them our friends, are divided over issues which weaken Western unity, which invite Communist intervention or which threaten to erupt into war.

Our efforts in West New Guinea, in the Congo, in the Middle East and the Indian subcontinent have been persistent and patient despite criticism from both sides. We have also tried to set an example for others—by seeking to adjust small but significant differences with our own closest neighbors in Mexico and Canada.

Speaking of other nations, I wish to make one point clear. We are bound to many nations by alliances. These alliances exist because our concern and theirs substantially overlap. Our commitment to defend Western Europe and West Berlin, for example, stands undiminished because of the identity of our vital interests. The United States will make no deal with the Soviet Union at the expense of other nations and other peoples, not merely because they are our partners, but also because their interests and ours converge.

Our interests converge, however, not only in defending the frontiers of freedom, but in pursuing the paths of peace.

It is our hope—and the purpose of allied policies—to convince the Soviet Union that she, too, should let each nation choose its own future, so long as that choice does not interfere with the choices of others. The Communist drive to impose their political and economic system on others is the primary cause of world tension today. For there can be no doubt that, if all nations could refrain from interfering in the self-determination of others, the peace would be much more assured.

This will require a new effort to achieve world law—a new context for world discussions. It will require increased understanding between the Soviets and ourselves. And increased understanding will require increased contact and communication.

One step in this direction is the proposed arrangement for a direct line between Moscow and Washington, to avoid on each side the dangerous delays, misunderstanding, and misreadings of the other's actions which might occur in a time of crisis.

We have also been talking in Geneva about other first-step measures of arms control, designed to limit the intensity of the arms race and reduce the risks of accidental war.

Our primary long-range interest in Geneva, however, is general and complete disarmament—designed to take place by stages, permitting parallel political developments to build the new institutions of peace which would take the place of arms. The pursuit of disarmament has been an effort of this Government since the 1920's. It has been urgently sought by the past three Administrations. And however dim the prospects are today, we intend to continue this effort—to continue it in order that all countries, including our own, can better grasp what the problems and the possibilities of disarmament are.

The only major area of these negotiations where the end is in sight— yet where a fresh start is badly needed—is in a treaty to outlaw nuclear tests. The conclusion of such a treaty—so near and yet so far—would check the spiraling arms race in one of its most dangerous areas. It would place the nuclear powers in a position to deal more effectively with one of the greatest hazards which man faces in 1963—the further spread of nuclear weapons. It would increase our security—it would decrease the prospects of war.

Surely this goal is sufficiently important to require our steady pursuit, yielding neither to the temptation to give up the whole effort nor the temptation to give up our insistence on vital and responsible safeguards.

I am taking this opportunity, therefore, to announce two important decisions in this regard:

First: Chairman Khrushchev, Prime Minister Macmillan and I have agreed that high-level discussions will shortly begin in Moscow towards early agreement on a comprehensive test ban treaty. Our hopes must be tempered with the caution of history—but with our hopes go the hopes of all mankind.

Second: To make clear our good faith and solemn convictions on the matter, I now declare that the United States does not propose to conduct nuclear tests in the atmosphere so long as other states do not do so. We will not be the first to resume. Such a declaration is no substitute for a formal binding treaty—but I hope it will help us achieve one. Nor would such a treaty be a substitute for disarmament—but I hope it will help us achieve it.

Finally, my fellow Americans, let us examine our attitude towards peace and freedom here at home. The quality and spirit of our own society must justify and support our efforts abroad. We must show it in the dedication of our own lives—as many of you who are graduating today will have an opportunity to do, by serving without pay in the Peace Corps abroad or in the proposed National Service Corps here at home.

Peace and Freedom Related

But wherever we are, we must all, in our daily lives, live up to the age-old faith that peace and freedom walk together. In too many of our cities today, the peace is not secure because freedom is incomplete.

It is the responsibility of the executive branch at all levels of government—local, state and national—to provide and protect that freedom for all of our citizens by all means within our authority. It is the responsibility of the legislative branch at all levels, wherever the authority is not now adequate, to make it adequate. And it is the responsibility of all citizens in all sections of this country to respect the rights of others and respect the law of the land.

All this is not unrelated to world peace. "When a man's ways please the Lord," the scriptures tell us, "he maketh even his enemies to be at peace with him." And is not peace, in the last analysis, basically a matter of human rights—the right to breathe air as nature provided it—the right of future generations to a healthy existence?

While we proceed to safeguard our national interests, let us also safeguard human interests. And the elimination of war and arms is clearly in the interest of both.

No treaty, however much it may be to the advantage of all, however tightly it may be worded, can provide absolute security against the risks of deception and evasion. But it can—if it is sufficiently in the interests of its signers—offer far more security and far fewer risks than an unabated, uncontrolled, unpredictable arms race.

The United States, as the world knows, will never start a war. We do not want a war. We do not now expect a war. This generation of Americans has already had enough—more than enough—of war and hate and oppression. We shall be prepared if others want it. We shall be alert to try to stop it. But we shall also do our part to build a world of peace where the weak are safe and the strong are just.

We are not helpless before that task or hopeless of its success. Confident and unafraid, we labor on—not toward a strategy of annihilation but toward a strategy of peace. Thank you.

WHY NOT VICTORY?*

Senator Barry Goldwater

. . . I have been challenged to explain what victory in the Communist War means, how we could achieve it, and what we could do with it after we won it. This challenge, astounding as it is, comes from the Chairman of the Senate Foreign Relations Committee—Senator J. William Fulbright of Arkansas—who reflects in his statements a policy line now being promoted within the top ranks of the Kennedy administration. Senator Fulbright, and I am sorry to say some others in positions of influence today, believes that victory in the Communist War is impossible, that we must co-exist with an alien ideological power which is using every device at its command to overwhelm us, and that one of the means toward co-existence is "aggressive compromise."

. . . I believe it is important for the reader to understand how the exchange between Senator Fulbright and myself evolved. It began on June 29 of last year when the Foreign Relations Committee Chairman delivered a speech to the Senate entitled, "Some Reflections Upon Recent Events and Continuing Problems." These remarks were hailed in a certain segment of the press as a major foreign-policy declaration. Now since these "reflections" contained so many arguments for doing nothing in the Communist War but waste more and more money in the name of social reform for other nations, I felt impelled to reply. I did this in a Senate speech on July 14. I challenged the Foreign Relations Chairman to explain why his approach to the Communist War, which boils down to more and more foreign aid, has not yielded results after the expenditure of nearly a hundred billion dollars. I challenged his assertion that a successful American action in Cuba would result in alienating Latin America, Asia, and Africa. I challenged his assertion that communism ninety miles off our southern coast was not "intolerable" to the American

---

* Reprinted by permission from *Why Not Victory?* MacFadden-Bartell Corp., New York, 1962. Condensed.

people. I challenged his declaration that the erection of missile bases by the Communists in Cuba would not increase the danger to our national existence. And I also said that this nation needs an official declaration stating that our aim in the Communist War is victory.

Now in his response to this, Senator Fulbright ignored my question concerning the wisdom of pursuing a costly and ineffective foreign policy. He ignored quite a few other things in commenting briefly on the Senate Floor on July 24 on what he referred to as "certain themes" contained in my remarks. He was excessively bemused with one of my phrases—"total victory." He seemed to think there was something funny about it. He referred to total victory as a "stirring term with a romantic ring." He ridiculed it as something that "quickens the blood like a clarion call to arms." I suggest that ridicule is a curious attitude for an American to take when discussing victory in a struggle that means survival. It is even more curious when that American holds the influential office of Chairman of the Senate Foreign Relations Committee—and I say this whether he is referring to "total victory" or just plain "victory." There are many details of our conduct in the Communist War which invite scoffing and ridicule, but the subject of our *winning* in this desperate struggle is definitely not one of them.

The Senator from Arkansas says he does not know what victory would mean—as he puts it—"in this age of ideological conflict and nuclear weapons." Perhaps we are meant to believe that victory for the forces of freedom in the world takes on a different meaning because ideology is a factor and weapons are more powerful. If Senator Fulbright finds difficulty in understanding what victory would mean perhaps he should spend a little thought on the question of what defeat—*the only alternative to victory*—would mean. This is a frightening thought—*what would defeat mean?* But, it is one which must be considered—and considered seriously —if our national policy is anything but victory.

This is a conflict where one side or the other must win, and no amount of wishful thinking can make it otherwise. On this question, the decision is out of our hands. The rules for the conflict have been laid down by the Soviet Union through a massive design aimed at destruction of the United States and domination of the world. Against the Communist strategy as it is being pushed today, there can be no middle alternative between *a policy aimed at victory or one that would permit defeat.* There is no cozy twilight zone such as Senator Fulbright envisions where the *status quo* is maintained. We know this from what has happened to the world since the end of World War II. We have continued to delude ourselves with something called "peaceful co-existence" while communism has kept right on gobbling up one country after another. Hundreds of millions of the world's people have fallen under the yoke of communism while we have followed a useless policy of spend and drift. Now we are told that this is the only feasible approach; that we can't hope for victory; that we can't risk a war; that we couldn't cope with victory if we won it. I say this is the most dangerous kind of sheer nonsense.

If there is doubt as to what victory in the Communist War means, let me say that it means the opposite of defeat; it means freedom instead of slavery; it means the right of every man to worship God; of nations to determine their own destiny free of force and coercion. Victory in the Communist War means the sum total of all the hopes of free men throughout the world. It means human dignity, freedom of choice, the right to work. And it means peace with honor for men who prize liberty and do not fear death.

Can victory be achieved without a nuclear war? My vociferous critics would like us to believe that there can be no Communist War victory without the destruction of civilization. This is precisely what the Communists would like us to believe. Their whole line of attack, through propaganda and adroit economic, political, and military moves, is directed toward making us think in terms of fear. They want to make sure that we believe the risk is too great to employ our strength. Their purpose is intimidation and it is working too well.

Indeed, a decisive victory over the Communists is possible. It won't be easy because we have lost too much valuable time and too many golden opportunities. But it can be done with the proper integrated strategy—a strategy that *aims at victory;* that retains our economic strength; that incorporates the principles of political, military, economic, and psychological strength in meeting Communist challenges and in presenting some challenges of our own. Those who argue against any use of strength, against any military risk, against any unilateral action fail to understand that political victory in the Communist War is the only way to avoid a strictly military solution of the East-West crisis. It involves some risk, but experience shows us that this risk is greatly overexaggerated. Every time we have stood up to the Communists they have backed down. Our trouble is we have not stood up to them enough.

Despite the arguments of Communists and left-wing propagandists who want us to believe that the present ideological struggle will inevitably lead to a shooting war, just the reverse is true. A shooting war can only be avoided by *winning the Communist War.* And unless we win this struggle, we will be an easy push-over for the Khrushchevs, the Castros, and the Mao Tse-tungs when they decide the time is ripe to shift their strategy into a shooting phase.

Senator Fulbright has joined the ranks of those who would paralyze the foreign policy of this nation by advancing the alternatives that either you accommodate the Soviet Union—or you fight a nuclear war. These are the alternatives which are stressed every time the Communists seek to advance their position. The essential weakness of this reasoning lies in accepting the enemy's terms—that the only alternative to self-destruction is to yield. First, we yield on one issue—unimportant, it appears, in context of such a horrible alternative as nuclear war. Then on a second and a third and a fourth, ad infinitum. So what is finally left to us except the same terrible dilemma we were confronted with on that first day when the enemy said: Yield or die?

If we could finally satisfy the enemy's appetite by giving him one city or one country or one territory, who among us, Democrat or Republican, liberal or conservative, would not be tempted to say: Let them, in the name of peace and freedom for the rest of the world, let them, once and for all, have their way and be done with it. But this is not possible. We are dealing with an enemy whose appetite is insatiable, whose creed demands slavery for everyone, Americans included. The more we give in to that enemy, the more he wants; and the more we give in to him, the more he is encouraged to demand.

My opponents adroitly try to make it appear that I am in favor of nuclear war, that I would make war the prime instrument of our policy. I can't imagine what makes them think that. No one values life more than do I. Would I take satisfaction from exchanging my pleasant life, my family, my freedom, for a nuclear graveyard? Certainly not. But that does not mean that I am prepared to assure the enemy that, under *no* circumstances, will we *ever* consider war. If we are not prepared, under any circumstances, ever to fight a nuclear war, we might just as well do as the pacifists and the collaborationists propose—dump our entire arsenal into the ocean.

But my critics have proposed no such venture in national suicide. They want us to save our bombs. Only they apparently want us to act as though we did not have them—because the mere thought of having them terrifies those who are dedicated to the principle of co-existence. Thus, we are supposed to eliminate our possession of nuclear weapons from our consciousness in discussing the formulation of American foreign policy.

If victory is not our official aim, then there would appear to be no point in bringing all our arguments—be they military, economic, political, or psychological—to bear on the side of freedom. But can we be sure that if we completely eliminate the possible use of nuclear weapons the Communists will follow suit? Can we risk our future and the future of mankind on exclusive emphasis on conventional rather than ultimate weapons? Can we make any assumptions that would diminish our strength —in any field—when dealing with the Communists? Merely to ask the questions is to answer them. We can assume *nothing* where the Communist leaders are concerned. We can trust *nothing* that the Communist leaders say. We can accept *nothing* that the Communist leaders sign as a conclusive guarantee.

The Communist plan of world conquest makes the element of time a vital factor. Time is running out on the West while it is working in favor of international communism—at least under our present policy. I would remind you the policy we are following today is the same one which we have followed—with a few exceptions—since the end of World War II. It is the policy of spending in the hope of gaining allies. It is the policy which has permitted the Communists to gain in almost every area of the world while the cause of freedom has been losing.

I want to emphasize this time factor particularly in the light of what Senator Fulbright sees as our objective. He says that "total victory" is a process. And he defines that process as one *"of civilizing international relations and of bringing them gradually under a world-wide regime of law and order and peaceful procedures for the redress of legitimate grievances."*

If this is our objective, what is our hope of achieving it? This just says that the United States should work for the establishment of some kind of international super-state whose members would behave in a civilized and peaceful way toward each other. At the very least this would take several centuries. And we have no assurance that the time will *ever* come when all other states will want to behave peacefully toward each other. The lessons of history are all against it. There have always been men and states that would not hesitate to use arms to advance their national policies and defend their special interests.

A world without arms, a world living peacefully and adjusting its grievances in a global regime of law and order is more than an objective. It is a glorious dream, a kind of utopia. Even if it were practical, such an objective has not direct application to the urgent problems which beset the world today. We haven't the time for implementing dreams right now. We must deal with reality, the ever-present threat of Communist tyranny which is *not* going to submit to the kind of civilizing Senator Fulbright envisions.

Suppose there is a big fire in your neighborhood. What do you think about first? You think of saving your house from destruction and your family from death. And if the flames have already enveloped your garden fence, do you lose time planning to build a dream house next year or next decade in a nonexistent fire-proof city in a theoretical country? Of course, you don't. You go to work fighting the flames to save the house you've already got in the city and country—no matter what their imperfections— where you live now.

This is the way it is today with our country and with the world. There is a fire, and its Communist flames are threatening to destroy the American way of life. Not next year, or in the next decade, or in a future century, but right now—today. These ugly Red flames are already brushing our shores and they continue to rage unchecked.

This is no time for an American foreign-policy objective designed to erect an impractical international dream city of the future. Our objective must be the practical means of dousing the fire and smothering the flames of international communism.

So what can we do? Our job, first and foremost, is to persuade the enemy that we would rather follow the world to Kingdom Come than consign it to Hell under communism. Having made that clear, we must seize opportunities as they arise to protect freedom and demonstrate our strengths. Many such opportunities have arisen in the past, a few of which we have used to good advantage. For example, we were told by the weak of heart and the peddlers of despair that unless we yielded Quemoy and Matsu, the islands off the Chinese coast, to the Communists, a terrible war would result. The Eisenhower administration said, in effect, very well, if the Communist world chooses to go to war to occupy these islands, then that's the way it will have to be. But the Communist world did not so choose, and Quemoy and Matsu are free today. And they will be free tomorrow and just as long as our resolution lasts.

This sequence of events was repeated in Lebanon. We sent in Marines there against the trembling advice of those who fear any display of determination and strength. And Lebanon is free today. We acted from strength, too, when threatened Berlin was saved by our airlift in 1948, and at least half of Berlin remains free today. In Korea, we responded in June of 1950 with courage and a commitment but we allowed the fear-mongers among us to whittle that initial commitment to victory down to an acceptance of a humiliating stalemate.

On the other hand, our resolve was not strong enough in Cuba to back our intent with the strength required. The result is that Cuba languishes in chains while a Communist dictator thumbs his nose at the United States and plays the enemy's game to the hilt. And when my critics worry lest we alienate the rest of Latin America by taking affirmative action in Cuba, I am sure Castro guffaws. Much of Latin America has already been alienated by the timidity and ineffectiveness of our American policy. The Latins cannot understand why a world power, such as the United States, allows a two-bit Kremlin stooge to spit in our eye. And they wonder what source of support we could possibly be to them when communism pushes its expansion program throughout the Western Hemisphere. They see us weak and baffled in an area of vital concern, not only to them but to our own existence.

Must we surrender Laos, too? Is that the fixed conviction of Senator

Fulbright when he worries lest we commit American soldiers to a jungle war? Are there not Free Chinese, South Vietnamese, South Koreans, Filipinos, and Japanese who would fight if the United States gave them backing? Have we ever asked them?

When Senator Fulbright questions what we would do with victory if we won it, he implies that any doubt or difficulty on this score becomes, per se, an argument against winning. He asks whether we would occupy Russia and China and launch a program to re-educate the Russians and the Chinese in the ways of democracy. The answer to this is simply "no." We would not have to occupy China and Russia because the vast majority of the people in both of these countries are not Communists. They will, with proper guidance, take care of their own freedom once they are released from the iron grip of Communist dictatorship. But even if this weren't true, the mere fact that victory would pose problems is not reason to submit to slavery. . . .

In the final analysis the choice is not yield or fight a nuclear war. It is: *win, or fight a nuclear war.* For a nuclear war we shall certainly have to fight, from whatever beleaguered outpost we are reduced to occupying, if we continue to yield, piece by piece, all over the world. Finally in desperation, we would see the horrible alternatives clearly in view—a violent act of nuclear aggression or surrender. Our only hope is to proclaim victory as our aim and then to press boldly and unremittingly on all fronts— always *prepared* to fight and making sure the Communists always know we are prepared to fight.

And, in laying that groundwork, there are a number of immediate steps we should take to re-orient our policy for maximum United States effectiveness in the Communist War. They include the following:

1. We must stop believing that our primary objective must be to humor the public opinion of neutral or uncommitted nations rather than to defend our strategic interests, cooperate closely with our allies, and advance our positions of strength. This we must do the more readily because much of this so-called opinion which entrances our co-existence proponents is fabricated by the Communists to our detriment. We must realize that we have no proper method by which we can judge what public opinion really is throughout the world.

2. We must stop lying to ourselves and our friends about disarmament. We must stop advancing the cause of the Soviet Union by playing along with this great Communist-inspired deception. We must abandon the illusion that the Soviets, in their disarmament policies, are interested in furthering peace rather than baiting a trap for us. Their objective is to contrive *our* unilateral disarmament while they continue to arm themselves secretly as fast as they can.

It is not "dialectics" but schizophrenia when we increase our military budget by 15 percent and the Soviets theirs by 33 percent while, at the same time, we proclaim that disarmament is our highest goal and a practical method of solving the present conflict. The American people can stand the truth, but they cannot prosper under an official policy of self-deception.

3. We must not again abandon nuclear testing. This is the worst and most transparent trap into which the United States has fallen during the course of the Cold War. A ban does nothing but serve the Soviet Union to improve its nuclear weapons by clandestine testing, to stop our own advances in offensive and defensive nuclear technology and, ultimately, lead to a situation where we wake up confronted with superior Soviet weapons.

4. We must stop negotiating about things that are non-negotiable, such as the rights of our allies, compromises of our security, treaties like the test ban which can be neither controlled nor enforced. We must not deceive ourselves and our friends into believing that nuclear weapons and modern technology can be negotiated out of existence.

5. We must stop helping communism, whether by trade, political concessions, technical disclosures, soft talk in the United Nations, recognition of Outer Mongolia, pilgrimages to Moscow, or support for revolutionaries of the Castro type.

6. We must avoid economic collapse by scaling down extravagant and useless domestic programs, and halt the squandering of our money on unrealistic world-wide aid programs.

In this mortal struggle there is no substitute for victory. The way of strength is not an easy way. It is a hard course requiring determination and difficult decisions involving considerable risk. But it is the way of peace, not war, of freedom, not slavery. It must be the way of all Americans, Republicans and Democrats alike, the way of all free people with the will to remain free.

NEW PERSPECTIVES ON DISARMAMENT*

Senator George McGovern

Mr. President, a single warhead from the American or Russian stockpile if exploded over a great city would instantly transform it into a raging fireball 3 miles in diameter with a direct heat and blast capable of burning human flesh and collapsing buildings 25 miles from its center. Above a smoking crater a mile wide and several blocks deep, a gigantic, poisonous radioactive cloud would rise 20 or 25 miles to rain down torturous death on millions of human beings not fortunate enough to be incinerated quickly in the initial firestorm.

In spite of this grim prospect, the accumulation of more and more devastating weapons continues. The great powers are spending over $100 billion yearly on arms—each side justifying its investment in the name of defense. Yet, modern science supports the ancient Biblical wisdom, "there is no place to hide."

. . . Every patriotic citizen desires that his country be prepared to defend itself against attack. Even the most ardent economizers—men who vote with zeal to cut funds for education, conservation and health—are quick to shout "Aye" for more billions for arms.

I share the conviction that America ought to have a defense force which is second to none, and fully adequate to meet any need.

But, Mr. President, has the time not come to question the assumption that we are adding to defense and security by adding more and more to the nuclear stockpile? I suggest that we need to examine carefully the assumptions on which our military budget rests. . . .

Have we remembered that the defense of a great nation depends not only upon the quality of its arms, important as that is, but also on the quality of its economic, political, and moral fabric?

Have we considered the impact upon these other sources of strength of our vast military investment?

Is there a point of diminishing returns in the race for security through arms?

Have we made the wisest possible allocation of our material and human resources to insure maximum security?

---

* From "New Perspectives on American Security." Condensed. 109 *Congressional Record*, 13198 (August 2, 1963). Mr. McGovern is a Democratic Senator from South Dakota.

Are we building national strength by creating a higher pile of nuclear bombs and adding to our overkill capacity while failing to match our millions of idle, untrained youth with the Nation's needs for constructive economic growth?

And most important of all, are we following a blueprint for peace or racing toward annihilation?

For this fiscal year, we are asked to approve a Department of Defense budget of $53.6 billion, plus additional billions for the Atomic Energy Commission and the space program. That is well over half of our entire Federal budget. It represents more than the combined cost of all the social and economic programs of the New Deal period from 1933 through 1940.

. . . I suggest the following propositions:

First. The United States now has a stockpile of nuclear weapons in excess of any conceivable need.

Second. Bringing the arms race under control involves risks less dangerous than the proliferation of nuclear warheads and the acceleration of the arms race.

Third. Present levels of military spending and military foreign aid are distorting our economy, wasting our human resources, and restricting our leadership in the world.

Fourth. Diverting some of our present and proposed military spending to constructive investments both at home and abroad will produce a stronger and more effective America, a more secure America, and will improve the quality of our lives and strengthen the foundations of peace.

The unprecedented condition of today's strategic military power is this: neither the United States nor the U.S.S.R. can prevent the other from wielding a society-destroying blow, regardless of who attacks first. Offensive military power has been made so varied and strong that all conceivable defensive systems can be overwhelmed or bypassed by the power of offensive nuclear weapons.

The Russians do not have a nuclear capacity equal to ours, but our superiority is largely a meaningless concept in view of their relative parity. In the days when warfare was limited to rifles and cannons and tanks and conventional aircraft, the side with the most weapons and soldiers had a great military advantage. But in today's age, when a nuclear exchange of a few minutes' duration means instant death and indescribable devastation to both sides, what consolation is there to the dazed survivors to know that there remains under the poisoned skies somewhere in the rubble some unused overkill capacity?

It might be argued by some that our excessive nuclear spending serves an indirect purpose in that it forces the Soviets to strain their less affluent economy to match our effort. But the Russians, from all indications, seem to be avoiding construction of highly sophisticated weapons beyond what they regard as enough to destroy the United States in the event of war.

During the late 1950's when the Soviets could have built hundreds of the latest types of long-range bombers they constructed less than 200 as against our more than 1,600. There is no indication that they intend to try to narrow this gap. At the present time, while we have a capability of a thousand ICBM's—perhaps considerably more—and are building many more, the Russians have built only a minor fraction of that number. Indications are that they will improve and replace rather than greatly increase the number of their missiles.

The question is whether the United States can afford the vast "overkill" capacity which seems to underlie much of our military budget.

My own conviction is that we cannot afford this policy of adding to overkill capacity economically, politically, or morally and that if we persist in following it we will weaken our Nation both at home and abroad.

It may be argued that the economy of many of our communities has become so intertwined with military spending that an arms cut of several billion dollars which I have proposed would result in a painful economic dislocation.

A closer look at our present level of arms spending will show that it is not an unmixed blessing now as a stimulus to our economy.

First of all, we have distorted our economy in allocating such a high percentage of our highly trained manpower, research, and technology to weapons production at the expense of our other industry. Japan and our West European Allies have all modernized their civilian industrial plant at a much higher rate than the United States, largely because of our concentration on arms production. This has added to our civilian production costs, decreased our efficiency, undercut our competitive position in international trade, and aggravated the balance-of-payments problem.

American machine tool production was once the envy of the world, but today we have slipped to fourth or fifth rank among the nations. Our best scientific and technical competence is going into arms, not to the modernization of our civilian plant.

Many U.S. industries are losing their capacity to compete not only in world trade but also in the United States. The concentration of capital and technical skill in arms production is a basic cause of our declining competitive ability.

As matters now stand, the U.S. Government is financing 65 percent of all research and development, and most of that is for military purposes. In Germany, by contrast, 85 percent of research is privately financed, and nearly all of it is being used to modernize civilian industries which compete with ours. Those who view military spending as an unmixed blessing to our economy should take a look at the gleaming up-to-date civilian plants in Germany, Belgium, Holland, Italy, and Japan—plants that are surpassing our own neglected civilian production in both quality and low-cost operation. Where will this kind of imbalance leave us in the toughening competition of international trade?

The U.S. economy is jeopardized further by the flow of our gold overseas and the undermining of the dollar as a unit of international exchange. Today, we have a favorable trade balance, but because of our military investments overseas and the flight of investment capital we are suffering an unfavorable balance of payments. Heavy arms spending has aggravated a U.S. fiscal situation that has led many American investors to seek more attractive oversea outlets for their capital.

Our traditionally strong currency has been a powerful instrument in American economic and political leadership in the world. But the strain imposed on our gold reserves as a result of heavy military commitments abroad and excessive arms spending at home is a threat to our international position. . . .

When a major percentage of the public resources of our society is devoted to the accumulation of devastating weapons of war, the spirit of democracy suffers. When our laboratories and our universities and our scientists and our youth are caught up in war preparations, the spirit of free man is hampered.

We need to remind ourselves that we have sources of strength, of prestige, and international leadership based on other than nuclear bombs.

The United States must be prepared to lead that contest into areas that draw on our true sources of greatness—politics, economics, and morality. There is a growing indication that the course we follow may play a major part in determining the course which our adversaries take for good or ill.

We have millions of idle youth who could be employed in existing job vacancies if only they had sufficient training and education. A sizable proportion of these are Negroes and their idleness is at the base of the explosive civil rights crisis now convulsing the Nation. What better use could we make of some of our excess military spending than to divert it to an expanded program of vocational and technical training?

Our civil rights problems require for their solution a major expansion of employment opportunity. The economically depressed regions of the country require fresh capital and technical talent. Both these basic problems of economic development require sizable productive investment.

We have an urgent need for more classrooms, laboratories, libraries, and capable teachers.

We have millions of citizens, particularly among our older people, who need more adequate hospital and nursing home care.

Some of our present defense installations might in the future be converted into vocational schools, community colleges, or health centers.

We have rivers and streams to be saved from pollution and waste—a task calling for considerable engineering and technical manpower.

We have a growing number of farm youth who can no longer make an adequate living on the farm whose lives would be enriched by an expanded rural area development effort.

And for years to come there will be hungry, afflicted people abroad who look to us for help. As the former director of our Nation's food for peace program, I came to a keen realization that most of the people of the world are undernourished rural families who are trying to scratch an existence from the soil by incredibly primitive methods.

We have arrived at the point in history where we indeed "glower at one another from atop competing stacks of hydrogen bombs." And if the present trend continues, in a few short years, a half dozen, and then a dozen, new powers will climb atop their hydrogen stockpiles to glower at their frightened neighbors.

There are powerful options of peace as well as options of war. Still alive in the world is a faith that can move mountains if we will only seize upon it. From our own heritage the philosophy of Jefferson and Lincoln speaks with a voice that is more effectively heard in Asia, Africa, and Latin America than any number of nuclear explosions or moon shots. A conscientious effort on our part to eliminate excessive nuclear stockpiling will give that voice of peace and reason an even clearer tone. I pray that our country will in every possible way use its unique power and influence on the side of peace. . . .

MISCONCEPTIONS ABOUT FOREIGN POLICY*

Senator Henry M. Jackson

The longer I work at the problems of national security, the more I come to share Jefferson's view that a person "is less remote from the truth who believes nothing, than he who believes what is wrong." Or, as Josh Billings has said: "It isn't ignorance that causes so much trouble; it's what people know that isn't so."

---

* © 1963 by The New York Times Company. Reprinted by permission. Mr. Jackson is a Democratic Senator from Washington, a member of the Armed Services Committee, and chairman of the Committee on Interior and Insular Affairs. He is a former chairman of the Democratic National Committee.

It is harder to deal with error than with ignorance. Error, after all, is a child of our minds and we love it as our very own. Error is more often than not rooted in myths and wishful thinking. A nation may have great power and yet exercise it ineffectively, particularly if its people are careless of the facts and rest their judgments on misconceptions.

As Walter Lippmann once said: "A man may have the finest automobile, be the best driver, have perfect vision and a heart of gold. But if he tries to find his way around Paris with a map of Chicago and around Hanoi with a map of Oakland, Calif., he just will not arrive where he set out to go."

If today's assumptions are false and our estimates are too misleading, America will take the wrong turns and end up in the wrong place.

The Sino-Soviet Quarrel

We confront complex issues, and understandably many of us hope for simple answers. So it is not surprising that convenient but false assumptions work their way into some people's thinking. It is useful to examine the credibility of certain assumptions about international affairs held by considerable numbers of people.

(1) There is the widespread assumption that the Chinese-Soviet quarrel reduces the Communist threat to the West.

A Vietnamese might be permitted some doubts. Or a Nehru.

I believe that the truth may be exactly contrary to the reassuring words.

Khrushchev thinks our day has passed. Khrushchev and Mao are not quarreling about whether to bury us. They are quarreling about how. It may be that Mr. Mao plans a 12-foot grave and Mr. Khrushchev a six-foot one. In any event, they both seem to have in mind a cemetery.

The Moscow-Peking dispute is being played for very high stakes. The leadership of world Communism is involved. So is the fate of men who see themselves as the locomotives of history. Khrushchev and Mao each desperately desires to show that his policy for liquidating the West is best. Each needs victories. The consequences for us may well be a period of rising tensions and dangers. At any rate this possibility weighs as much as the opposite one.

In these days, Khrushchev's tactics must be tailored to take into account his troubles with Mao. This does not mean his objective of world supremacy has changed.

Khrushchev just told the Chinese: "The struggle for peace, for peaceful coexistence, is organically bound up with the revolutionary struggle against imperialism. It weakens the front of imperialism, isolates its more aggressive circles from the masses of the people and helps in the struggle for national liberation."

Khrushchev has been a very adept and resourceful tactician. It is well to remember that where Stalin was obvious in his maneuvers, Khrushchev is devious. We have been exposed to his smiling face and his pounding shoe; we have seen him export doves of peace one month and nuclear missiles the next. The point is that whether Khrushchev is the jovial back-slapper at a cocktail party or is launched on a harangue at the Berlin Wall, he is the same dangerous man. He can turn it on and off again in short order. We can expect that Khrushchev will continue to twist and turn, thaw and freeze, agree and disagree—in pursuit of his ultimate aim, which he openly admits is to bury us.

And there is both a lesson of history and a warning for the future in Russia's sudden signing of a nonagression pact with Hitler.

(2) There is the widespread assumption that we can win our way with the Russians with a policy of inoffensiveness.

This is a fallacy held by many good and decent people who let their hearts prevail over their heads. We have all heard arguments that amount to nothing more than "if we trust the Communists, they will trust us." We are told that the United States should take unilateral initiatives to reduce our strength to set a "good example" and quiet Soviet suspicions.

It is not convincing to say that we won't know whether this policy will work until we try. There are some experiments that are best left undone.

Just consider India's experience. No state has tried harder than India to find security by a deliberate policy of inoffensiveness. India has had to learn the hard way, as have others, including ourselves, that expansionist states do not respect weakness. I am sure Mr. Nehru does not relish this on-the-job training program, but it may save others from a similar schooling.

Peace Is The Objective

As Reinhold Niebuhr has said: "If the democratic nations fail, their failure must be partly attributed to the faulty strategy of idealists who have too many illusions when they face realists who have too little con-science."

Almost all Americans are members of the peace movement in the sense that they want peace. The debate needs to receive our most thoughtful, honest, tough-minded attention. But certainly, the weight of responsible opinion lies with preparedness combined with restraint—what Teddy Roosevelt meant when he said we should talk softly and carry a big stick.

The only way to bargain successfully with expansionist states is to make bargaining attractive to them.

(3) There is the widespread assumption that the arms race is leading straight to catastrophe.

A familiar line of this argument goes this way: Arms races have always led to war; the world is engaged in an arms race; therefore, we are heading for a nuclear holocaust.

Hollow Argument

This argument rings hollow. It was not an arms race that led to World War II. On the contrary, it was the failure of the Western democracies to prepare for war that led to its outbreak in 1939. It was Chamberlain's failure to recognize the danger of a demagogue like Hitler, bent on aggression, that led to Munich. This is the reason Winston Churchill has called the Second World War "The unnecessary war."

As I read history, international peace and security depend not on a balance of power but on a certain imbalance of power favorable to the defenders of peace—in which the strength of the peace-keeper is greater than that of the peace-upsetter.

An expansionist nation will never, of course, be satisfied with this state of affairs. And precisely for this reason, disarmament or arms control is a difficult objective to achieve. As I see it, a would-be aggressor will not settle for an arms control agreement that freezes him in a position of inferior power. On the other hand, an agressor's objectives are served by an agreement which would permit him to acquire superiority by stealth.

As for the second premise: What arms race are people talking about? The United States is not engaged in an arms race. We could, if we wanted to, build more weapons and build them faster. But our goal is not an unlimited build-up. Our goal—and we should be perfectly clear about it and frank to acknowledge it—is to create and maintain, in cooperation with our allies, a relationship of forces favorable to peace. The real road to catastrophe would be to permit an unfavorable relationship of forces to arise.

Nuclear Test Ban

I believe that this is an understandable position—and that our public statements about defense and about arms control or disarmament should be put in this perspective. Too often, however, high officials speak as though a nuclear test-ban were mankind's last best hope, or as though the choice we face is between one more concession and catastrophe.

(4) There is the widespread assumption that a test ban will halt the spread of nuclear weapons.

For those who have not mastered Anglo-Saxon, "spread" is a six-letter word meaning proliferation.

It is utterly unrealistic to take the position that a test-ban agreement will stop the spread of nuclear weapons. We need to think clearly and straightforwardly about the test-ban issue. Unfortunately, there has been some loose thinking, about this subject, which arouses such strong emotions.

The public lacks expert knowledge of the problems of inspection. "Decoupling" does not conjure up the same image for John Q. Public that it does for, say, Edward Teller. But the public does not lack common sense. It knows that de Gaulle has refused to participate in the Geneva disarmament talks and that Mao has not been invited.

It knows that the Chinese will be exploding a nuclear device at almost any time—this year or possibly early next year, and that Peking has been quick to say it will not be bound by the test ban. It knows that de Gaulle has said France will not sign the test-ban agreement and will proceed with an independent nuclear program.

All of us, I am sure, regret that 10 years hence, as President Kennedy recently told us, there may be a sizable number of nuclear powers, each capable of touching off actions with irreparable consequences. I wish this were not the prospect. Efforts to limit the spread of nuclear weapons deserve our serious attention. But an agreement along the lines worked out in Moscow will not stop a non-signatory country which desires to become a nuclear power and is able and determined to invest substantial resources to do so.

(5) *There is the widespread assumption that a test-ban agreement will necessarily lead to growing East-West confidence and reduced tensions.*

Danger to Morale

Obviously, we would hope a test-ban agreement would be a first step toward decreasing world tension. But obviously, too, we cannot count on it, and unless we view the outlook in proper perspective we run the risk of a dangerous drop in public confidence and morale through the disappointment of exaggerated expectations.

For example, what would be the reaction to the knowledge that Communist China is conducting extensive nuclear tests—or to the strong suspicion that the Soviet Union might be cheating—or to a growing apprehension that the Soviets might abrogate the agreement without warning?

A test ban must not be merchandized like cosmetics—with claims that cannot be met. Government officials are not salesmen, but stewards.

The Senate will ratify a test-ban agreement that proves, after careful study by the appropriate committees, to be in the national interest.

But before reaching such a determination, the Senate, to fulfill its Constitutional obligations, must look at any agreement with the greatest care, to make sure that the possible gains are not overshadowed by the risks that are inevitably run.

The prevention of fallout from tests is a clear benefit from any test-ban agreement that works. But that benefit must be weighed against the risk of compromising our ability to prevent a nuclear war.

I deeply believe that in national security matters we should act according to a scale of national priorities that puts first things first and second things second. What is of first importance is to protect our military deterrent—to maintain a position where our power and our will to use it are understood both by our adversaries and our allies. Why has the Russian position changed—if it has? A good deal of credit must be given to the power we have maintained. If our deterrent ever ceases to be credible, the Communist bear will be on the loose.

(6) There is the widespread assumption that our superiority in conventional forces was the decisive factor last October in the near-collision over Cuba.

This is, of course, wrong, as ought to be apparent.

I have strongly supported the strengthening of our conventional forces. This is one of the major accomplishments of this Administration. Our forces are better balanced than they were and better prepared to meet the contingencies they may face.

No Mumbo-Jumbo

But the decisive factor last October was will—the evidence that the United States was prepared to take whatever risks were necessary to obtain satisfaction of its demands. It may be that we did not demand enough—but that is another question. We got most of what we asked for. And the reason was that Khrushchev became convinced that our will was firm.

His reply to Communist Chinese criticism was as free of mumbo-jumbo as a statement could be. He said, "The paper tiger has nuclear teeth." And, as Bernard Brodie of the Rand Corporation recently observed, when Khrushchev found that we were not as tolerant as he had supposed, he rushed to get the missiles out, "apparently unimpeded with any worries about 'humiliation.'" He was clearly less worried about his face than his future.

It is important to be very clear about all this, for if conventional superiority was the decisive factor in Cuba, what defends Berlin? The answer is that the security of Berlin also depends on our will. I, for one, would not wish to convince Mr. Khrushchev that our conventional superiority was decisive in Cuba. Or so to convince our European Allies.

The Communists, by virtue of their geographic position, can deploy their forces to achieve conventional superiority at most points along their long boundaries. What deters them is fear that they might start something bigger than they are prepared to risk.

We need strong conventional forces; there is no argument about that. But it would be a tragic error to encourage the Communists to believe that they will meet only these forces so long as they restrict themselves to aggression with conventional means.

(7) There is the widespread assumption that our national policies should be more flexible.

I do not know when "flexibility" became accepted as an unqualified virtue. It is a virtue in a tire or in a skyscraper—in moderation. Beyond a point it becomes softness in the former and wobbling in the latter. And who wants a wobbly skyscraper, or a soft tire?

Flexibility is also a virtue in foreign policy—if it goes as far as resiliency but not so far as a wavering in will. The Bay of Pigs seems to have involved some wavering, the Cuban missile crisis of last fall some resiliency. I am in favor of resiliency—which my dictionary defines as "the capability of a strained body to recover its size and shape after deformation, especially when the strain is caused by compressive stresses." We are bound to suffer some compressive stresses here and there and we want the capability to bounce back, firm in purpose and resolve.

Referring to the Founding Fathers, Abraham Lincoln once said:

"They were pillars of the Temple of Liberty; and now that they have crumbled away that temple must fall unless we, their descendants, supply their places with other pillars, hewn from the solid quarry of sober reason."

We must be vigilant, then, to make certain we are not misled by false assumptions. It is urgent, too, that we in Government should be very careful what we ask the public to believe. Our national situation is too precarious to justify a nonchalant attitude toward the truth.

I believe, the American people, if they have the facts, are able to distinguish nonsense at a hundred paces. They do not expect infallibility in their Government officials; indeed, they wisely suspect anyone who claims it. They welcome candor, and they can take it.

A POSITIVE CONTRIBUTION TO PEACE*

David E. Bell

Since I joined the Agency for International Development [A.I.D.] last December, I have had the opportunity to see the United States foreign-aid program in action in countries as widely different, and as distant from each other, as Korea and Ecuador, Vietnam and Venezuela, Pakistan and Chile.

I have also traveled and spoken in many parts of the United States. The questions I have been asked in San Francisco, New York, Little Rock and other cities, as well as those asked by Congressional committees, seem to reflect the main concerns held by American taxpayers about our economic and military assistance to other countries.

If I understand them correctly, the American people are asking four principal questions about our foreign aid programs:

Has our economic and military assistance been getting us anywhere; is it worth the cost?

Is foreign aid a major cause of the United States' balance-of-payments deficit?

Should not the other well-to-do countries carry more of the burden of helping the underdeveloped countries?

Can we not operate our foreign-aid programs more efficiently?

The following answers to these questions have grown from my own observations in Washington and in underdeveloped countries around the world.

Is Foreign Aid Achieving Worthwhile Results?

Although the merits of the Marshall Plan were vigorously disputed at the time it was undertaken, there is no disagreement today that our economic assistance to Europe and our parallel help to postwar Japan were highly successful.

SOME AID HAS ENDED. Our economic aid to those countries ended years ago. The Western European countries and Japan today are thriving economies, themselves contributing between $2 and $3 billion each year in foreign aid to the underdeveloped countries of Asia, Africa, and Latin America.

Nor is there serious dispute over the value of our military aid to Europe and Japan, which has continued longer. This has helped to build defense forces of great significance to us, forces which would not exist but for our help.

But aid to Western Europe and Japan is essentially past. Our present military assistance to these countries is simply the winding up of commitments made some years ago.

Over the last 10 years our foreign aid has been increasingly concentrated in the underdeveloped countries of Asia, Africa and Latin America. What can we show for results?

There are many spectacular gains in human terms. United States aid— skills, equipment, chemicals—has been largely responsible for great advances in the worldwide war on malaria. For example, in 1953 India suffered one million deaths from a total of 75 million malaria cases, but in 1962 reported fewer than 2,000 cases of malaria all told. In 1950, there were 1.2 million cases of malaria on the island of Taiwan; in 1961, only 61. There were 12,000 deaths in 1950—none in 1961.

Foreign aid is attacking illiteracy. In Nigeria, American university teams financed through A.I.D. funds in the last three years have trained 150 instructors who, in turn, have passed on their training to 5,000 teachers. In Latin America, 18,000 classrooms have been built or are under construction with United States help. Four million textbooks are being distributed.

FOOD IS USED. Foreign aid is feeding hungry people. The United States Food for Peace program, administered jointly by the Department of Agriculture, A.I.D. and the President's Food-for-Peace director, Mr. Richard Reuter, is now benefiting more than 90 million people around the world.

Under one aspect of this program, surplus food that would otherwise lie in storage at a cost to United States taxpayers is being used for part-payment of wages for reforestation and for school, hospital and housing construction in many countries.

Under another, the United States in the next school year will be providing ingredients for a hot hunch for approximately one-third of the school children of Latin America—for most of them their only hot meal each day.

Foreign aid is helping people build decent places in which to live. In Chile, several thousand people have built their own houses with materials financed by the United States. In Peru, a little more than a year ago, a desert area 11 miles north of Lima was an arid waste. Today 1,500 families are living there in a satellite city, complete with schools, shopping center and water and sewage facilities, financed by a United States loan under the Alliance for Progress.

Illustrations of this type could be cited in great numbers, but it would be a mistake to think that, by themselves, they measure the success or failure of the foreign-aid program.

For the United States is aiming at something more than an improvement in the material welfare of the less developed nations—important as that is. We want to see them stand on their own feet, independent of our help or anyone else's.

We believe that the fundamental security of the United States rests on the successful establishment of independent, self-supporting countries around the world, countries that are prepared to join in defending their own freedom against Communist—or any other—aggression. It is this concept of United States security interests that has guided our foreign policy consistently since the end of World War II.

The test of the foreign-aid program, therefore, is not merely in numbers of children fed, schools built and business firms established. It is whether the countries we are helping are enlarging their resources of skill and capital, and relying increasingly on their own resources and less on our gifts and "soft" loans to achieve economic development and, where necessary, military strength.

Assessing results against this standard, two kinds of evidence can be cited.

One is statistical. The A.I.D. recently analyzed the economic growth of the 41 countries that have received substantial amounts of economic assistance from the United States since 1945. (This includes Europe and Japan. "Substantial" aid was defined as $300 million or more for a country, or at least $30 per capita for some of the smaller countries.)

MORE EVIDENCE. It was found that 33 of the 41 countries had rates of economic growth of at least 1.5 per cent per capita for at least five years. These gains are encouraging but we should not overlook the fact that our standard, arbitrarily chosen, is a modest one and that several countries did not reach it.

A second type of evidence is the progress toward economic independence that has been achieved. Since economic aid was ended some years ago for the 14 Western European nations and Japan, it has also been terminated for two more countries—Spain and Lebanon. Technical assistance (though not capital assistance) has been ended in Greece and Israel.

In several countries, progress has been so satisfactory that we are making definite plans to terminate economic aid in the next two to five years.

These include Greece, Israel, free China (Taiwan), Mexico, Venezuela and the Philippines.

With luck, several other countries could join this group.

It should be noted that, after economic aid on "soft" terms has been ended, these countries will be able to borrow from the Export-Import Bank, which charges an interest rate high enough to cover all costs—currently about 5¾ per cent. We will no doubt also wish to continue for some time longer military assistance to some of these countries—such as Greece and free China—which will be sustaining military forces larger than they could support by themselves.

Some of these countries are already beginning to provide technical assistance to other countries, thus following the same transitional route from recipient to donor countries previously followed by the European countries and Japan.

In recognition of the increased economic strength of these transitional countries, we have already "hardened" our loan terms to some of them. The most recent loans to Greece and to free China, for example, were at 3½ per cent interest and 20-year maturities, rather than the ¾ per cent, 40-year terms, which are used for countries with less immediately favorable economic prospects.

MANY MAKE PROGRESS. A number of other countries are making solid economic progress although they are not yet near the end of their need for outside aid. India and Pakistan are examples, as are Nigeria and Turkey.

In these countries the annual growth in output is substantial—higher than the rates of population growth—and the competence of the society to mobilize and manage resources, through public and private institutions, is growing steadily. These countries are on the right road, and in dollar terms, the bulk of our economic aid today is going to them.

But we also seek to advance the United States interest in situations where circumstances are not so favorable. Some countries are plainly not doing all they could do for themselves. We have no wish to leave them with only the Communist bloc to turn to for support. But we have no intention of providing assistance that would let them avoid solving their own problems.

Increasingly, we are working with such cases on a contingent basis, standing ready to help them when they undertake—and stick to—the hard measures necessary to help themselves.

Then there are countries in which military security is of first priority at present—Korea, Vietnam and Laos are examples. Here the first objective is to achieve some degree of internal security and stability and on that base to build toward economic independence.

These situations can be painful, risky, and costly, as witness Vietnam today. But it would be fatal to our objectives to give up the struggle. The great successes we have had since 1945—Western Europe, Greece and Turkey, Japan, Korea, free China—were achieved precisely because we did not give up when the going got tough.

Therefore, I believe it a fair assessment that U.S. foreign aid has achieved a great deal that is of fundamental importance to our national interests: Many countries have "graduated" from the need for aid; a number more can be expected to join them soon. Others are making strong and steady progress.

At the same time, we should recognize that there are countries, most conspicuously in Southeast Asia and in Latin America, where the Communist threat is grave and immediate and where we are not making nearly as much progress as we should like.

Is Foreign Aid a Major Cause
of the Balance-of-Payments Deficit?

This question can be answered categorically: Under present policies, the United States programs of economic and military assistance are not major contributors to the deficit.

Ten years ago, under different policies, foreign-aid dollars were spent abroad in large part. Beginning in 1959, however, under the Eisenhower Administration, those earlier policies began to be radically changed. To-day's policies result in the commitment of more than 90 per cent of all assistance to United States-produced goods and services.

In these circumstances a cut of $1 billion in appropriations for foreign assistance would slice something under $100 million from the deficit in the balance of payments but something over $900 million from United States export of good and services.

Even if surplus agricultural commodities, military equipment, and Export-Import Bank loans were omitted from these calculations, leaving only the "soft" loans and grants commonly called economic aid, the proportions would change only slightly—from 90 per cent of U.S.-produced goods and services to 80 per cent. The main point would remain valid: An appropriation cut intended to reduce the balance-of-payments deficit would in fact mainly reduce United States exports.

It is sometimes argued that foreign aid, whether or not it is tied to United States procurement, has an adverse effect on the balance of payments because it makes goods and services available to other countries that might otherwise be bought with their own funds. The evidence shows, however, that United States assistance helps countries add to their regular imports, rather than substitute for them.

Commercial imports from the United States have grown, and the United States share of the local market has improved, in countries assisted by our economic aid programs. (The only exceptions are in some countries in Latin America where the normal foreign-exchange earnings have dropped sharply for reasons having nothing to do with our aid program.)

The long-run benefits to us from successful aid programs can be very great. United States exports to Europe, for example, doubled between 1953 and 1962; our exports to Japan tripled between 1953 and 1962. Cutting foreign aid in a largely futile effort to trim our payments deficit would seem to be plainly unwise, even in the narrowest sense.

Should Other Nations Share More of the Load?

On inspection, this question turns out to be rather complicated to analyze, although in summary my response is: Yes, other advanced nations should do more to help the less developed countries.

Contrary to popular opinion, the burden of foreign aid to the United States has declined over the past 15 years. As a share of the gross national product, direct economic and military assistance has dropped from 2 per cent at the start of the Marshall Plan to about seven-tenths of one per cent. As a share of the Federal budget foreign aid declined from 11.5 per cent in 1948 to 4.1 per cent in 1963.

PARTICIPATION LIMITED. In recent years, Western Europe and Japan have doubled the amount of their economic aid, from $1.2 billion in 1956 to $2.4 billion in 1962. In 1962, of total governmental economic aid from all the advanced countries, the United States provided about 60 per cent, and the other countries about 40 per cent. This was approximately the same proportion as the ratio of the United States national product to the national product of all the other countries. (There are, indeed, three or four countries which are putting a larger share of their national product into foreign aid than we are.)

In some 40 countries, including most of those in Africa, United States participation is quite limited. The bulk of the outside help for many of these nations comes from some other country—France or the United Kingdom, in most instances.

Recognizing all this, however, there are important respects in which we believe other countries can and should do more. We feel, for example, that there are several countries which, in view of their economic strength, balance-of-payments positions, and trade and security interests, ought to increase their aid programs substantially.

A second point—our major concern at present—relates to the terms on which other advanced countries provide that part of their aid which is in

the form of loans. In 1962, the average terms of all United States eco-
nomic-aid loans were 2.6 per cent interest and 30 years' maturity. The
average of all other countries was about 5 per cent interest and 19 years'
maturity.

AGREEMENT ON TERMS. There had been some considerable softening by
some countries prior to this agreement, and there has been some additional change since. The United Kingdom, for example, has cut the effective rate of interest on aid loans nearly in half.

Nevertheless, the United States Government believes that there is a
considerable distance still to go before there will be what we would
consider an equitable sharing of foreign-aid costs among the advanced
countries.

Can We Not Operate Our Aid Programs More Efficiently?

The effort we are making to persuade the other developed nations to
assume more responsibility is a part of our continuing endeavor to make
economic assistance increasingly effective, to speed the day when we can
retire from the foreign-aid business.

One way in which this is being done is through a policy of careful se-
lectivity. We are stressing aid to those countries where the United States
interest is most urgent, which are in a position to make the best use of
our help, and where other donors cannot supply all the aid needed. As a
result, of the $2.2 billion committed to 82 countries by A.I.D. in fiscal 1963,
four-fifths went to only 20 countries. (Military assistance is even more
concentrated.)

Another way in which we seek to obtain maximum results is through
stressing self-help measures. As we know from our experience under the
Marshall Plan, the most important ingredient for achieving economic
progress is what a country does for itself. If it asks its people to make
major sacrifices, undertakes necessary reforms, and follows sound budget
and fiscal policies, then—and only then—can outside help have large and
lasting effects.

The corollary is a readiness on our part to hold back some of the funds
made available for foreign aid if potential recipients do not do all we
think they should to help themselves.

The result of such a policy was evident in the fiscal year just ended.
Largely because some of the recipient countries did not meet our criteria for self-help and reform we left uncommitted on June 30, 1963, over
$100 million of available loan funds (and requested that much less in
new funds for the next fiscal year).

Let me close with one important qualification. It would be a mistake to think that our aid efforts will automatically make friends for us. In Harlan Cleveland's famous phrase, we are seeking "not popularity or gratitude, but respect and results."

The object of foreign aid is to help create a community of free and independent nations. If we are sincere about independence, we plainly should not expect the countries we are aiding to become satellites. We want them to be strong, not servile.

For the great majority of the people in the world, regardless of what some transitory leaders may say or do, the United States is the standard-bearer of world peace, prosperity, humanitarianism and freedom in the competition with Communism. They look to us for help against aggression and the poverty of centuries. Our response must be more than words of concern. There must be deeds to back them up.

I would not wish to overstate the importance of our assistance to the underdeveloped nations. Foreign aid is a limited instrument. It is only one of the means for carrying out the foreign policy of the United States, along with military activities, information programs, diplomatic negotiation, participation in the United Nations and the Organization of American States.

Recognizing these limitations, however, I believe that of all the implements employed by the United States in its international relations, none offers a better hope for making a positive contribution to peace and building a better world for ourselves and our children.

I AM OPPOSED TO FOREIGN AID*

Representative Otto E. Passman

Secretary of State Rusk saw fit recently to accuse Members of Congress and others who favor substantial reductions in this country's spending for foreign aid of "cooperating with global Communist strategy." It is regrettable that the Secretary made such an intemperate and groundless statement but, no matter what his real opinions are, the remarks tie right in with the unrealistic point of view held by many overidealistic people in the Executive branch of Government regarding the vast and complex world-wide foreign-aid program.

I am one of those the Secretary was talking about. I am opposed to foreign aid; it has been, in my opinion, one of the greatest foreign-policy failures in history. But, as a realist, I recognize that it is, however distasteful, a political "fact of life" today.

Our foreign aid is the basis of such foreign policy as we have. Over the past 16 years, Washington administrations have made long-term "moral" commitments that involve our country's good faith and that must, as a matter of course, be fulfilled. Even if the executive were to decree a fundamental shift in foreign-aid policy—surely an unlikely possibility—considerable time would be required to carry out the change. Nations all over the world have come to expect largess from us. They would need time to make substantial adjustments—time to cure themselves of what has become literally an "addiction" to foreign aid.

Such is the "political fact" of foreign aid. In view of that fact, my work as chairman of the House Subcommittee on Foreign Operations Appropriations is not to end the program at one stroke but rather to help "contain" it, to encourage common sense in its policies and operations and to curb as much as possible its waste and mismanagement.

However, this necessarily limited effort in no way alters my personal belief that the whole program is wrong. I believe it is wrong for four main reasons:

First, it has undermined the dollar. In one form or another, United States foreign aid has gone to 104 countries, at a cost since the end of World War II of $120 billion, if we include the interest on the money we have borrowed to give away. The impact of all this on our own fiscal position becomes obvious if we consider how the program works.

When nations are credited with foreign-aid dollars against which they can place orders for goods and services, the invoices for these goods and services are sent to the United States Treasury for payment—from the taxpayers' till—rather than to the government which receives the shipment. In normal commercial practice, when the United States sells a nation goods or services, we receive something in return—dollars, gold, or goods and services. Under our foreign-aid program, however, it is a one-way deal—the goods or services go out, the United States Treasury pays the bill, and the United States receives nothing of a tangible commercial nature in return.

So great has been America's outpouring of wealth through foreign aid that many of the recipient nations have accumulated dollars far in excess of their needs. Consequently, they demand gold in exchange for the dollars, and in the past 10 years our gold reserves have been reduced from more than $23 billion to less than $16 billion. Over the same period, other "free world" countries increased their gold holdings from $13 billion to nearly $25 billion and their short-term dollar credits from less than $11 billion to $25 billion. For these dollar credits, those countries can demand gold, and if such a demand should come, the United States could not meet it.

This is the condition that is fundamentally at the root of our dangerous balance-of-payments situation. And, substantially as a result of our fiscally irresponsible action, the annual budget deficits increase, and the public debt—already exceeding by $24 billion the combined public debts of all other nations of the world—continues to rise at an alarming rate. Some day the debt must either be repaid, or repudiated through inflation.

My second criticism is that foreign aid has made the dollar a symbol of international charity. It has inculcated in less-favored nations the belief that the United States is morally responsible for bringing the whole world up to our standards of living and freedom by using our taxpayers' money.

The fact is, the majority of the aid-recipient countries do not, and will not, tax their own people at rates even remotely close to the United States rates to assist in bringing about the improved standards which we say we are trying to help them attain. Our aid is treated rather generally by recipients as a substitute for internal initiative and effort and in many cases it cannot be effectively utilized.

In the third place, the aid program has become not only an added tax on our producers, but also a subsidy to our foreign competitors. While rapidly depleting our own wealth and resources, it has been a primary reason for our increasingly noncompetitive position in world markets. Largely because of our wasteful giving, our prices have become so high that we cannot now compete successfully in world trade without the Federal Government's subsidizing our exports by as much as 30 per cent.

Finally, despite our tremendous aid expenditures and commitments, our world position remains a precarious one. Within a relatively brief span of years, our country became great, free and respected, in large measure because we had a firm but fair foreign policy based substantially upon trade. Today, through foreign aid, we have substituted "dollar diplomacy," a foreign policy that is a new concept among the family of nations—a weak policy, bordering on appeasement. We have been dissipating our resources in the hope that we shall acquire friends, yet there is little evidence that we have done so.

These are some of the general failings of the foreign-aid program as I see them—and I consider them serious enough to call the whole program into question. But, as I have said, it is politically impossible to abolish it now. Therefore, I believe we should recognize and attempt to remedy as many as possible of the faults of the present operation.

Cited briefly, here are a few of the more readily evident shortcomings:

1. There has not been adequate advance planning, in the form of firm

technical and financial arrangements, and we have failed to reach definite understandings with recipient countries on just what projects are essential. As a result, too many projects have been undertaken in individual countries, and assistance has been dispersed over too wide an area. Quantities of material have been delivered that are greater than the recipient countries need or can use.

2. In several countries, the official exchange rates used by the United States Government have substantially overvalued the local currencies. The use of such rates has unduly increased the dollar cost of our aid; and also, in some of the countries, the use of these unrealistic exchange rates has resulted in windfall profits to importers and provided incentives for speculation and irregular practices.

3. There has been a lack of qualified personnel and an oversupply of unqualified or poorly qualified personnel.

4. In the military-aid program, the objectives have not been sufficiently clarified so as to distinguish between forces which are justifiable on the basis of military roles and missions and those which are equipped and maintained for other than military reasons.

5. We have acceded to too many requests for "prestige projects." Many nations, including those that are relatively newly independent, seek status by building huge dams, steel mills, superhighways and national airlines, all financed by the United States taxpayer. We have placed entirely too much emphasis on meeting the personal desires of foreign political leaders for such prestige-builders.

Without delay, our spending for foreign aid—in all of its categories—ought to be drastically curtailed. The time is here to start on the task of gradually phasing out the foreign-aid program as a whole. Meanwhile, we should try, by tightening up the loose administration, cutting down on over-staffing and eliminating as many as possible of the impractical and overidealistic plans and projects, to reduce substantially the number of good American dollars that are wasted.

CHAPTER ELEVEN

Defense: Nuclear Stalemate v.
Nuclear Superiority

"Certainly it seems now that nothing could have been more obvious to the people of the earlier twentieth century than the rapidity with which war was becoming impossible. And as certainly they did not see it. They did not see it until the atomic bombs burst in their fumbling hands."—H. G. Wells, *The World Set Free*

H. G. Wells's Carolinum bomb was first-rate science fiction. But the eerie thing about his book is that he wrote it in 1913! Wells would be at home—although surely not at peace—in the inner sanctums of the Pentagon in the 1960s. Few laymen today, however, are comfortable in the world of Pentagonese, of counterforce and overkill, of mutual deterrence and GRIT—graduated and reciprocated initiative in tension-reduction. The modern farmer is willing to discuss the economics of government price supports, and the businessman government controls of collective bargaining. But they shy away from any discussion of defense strategy. Defense strategy in the nuclear age seems to be so sophisticated that it is best left to the generals. And yet, one is reminded of Clemenceau's warning, "War is too important to be left to generals."

If for no other reason, the layman should be concerned about American defense strategy because of its staggering cost. For the fiscal year 1964, the Kennedy administration requested the Congress to appropriate over $53 billion—approximately 56 percent of all federal spending and roughly 10 percent of the gross national product. At the close of World War II, defense spending had reached $90 billion, then dropped to $10 billion in 1947. By 1953, the Korean crisis had brought spending up to $50 billion, and then it dropped again. The last Eisenhower budget for the fiscal year 1961 called for $40 billion in defense spending. The 1964 request for $54 billion, the highest since 1945, would represent an increase of over 30 percent in the past three years.

What accounts for this sudden rise in defense spending? The testimony of Secretary of Defense Robert McNamara and General Maxwell Taylor, Chairman of the Joint Chiefs of Staff, offers a partial explanation. The Kennedy administration has adopted a form of the "balanced deterrent," described in the Arthur I. Waskow article. The balanced deterrent calls for continued expenditures for nuclear forces, but—and this is where the new expenses are important—it also calls for strength in conventional forces, the forces necessary to fight brush-fire warfare in areas such as Korea or Vietnam. Thus, since 1961, Army and Navy appropriations have increased more than $5 billion while Air Force appropriations have remained at approximately the same level. Although the testimony of General Curtis LeMay, Chief of Staff of the Air Force, is not entirely clear on the issue of conventional forces, his statement regarding the failure of the United States to use effectively its nuclear superiority in the Korean crisis tends to question the necessity of such forces.

The McNamara, Taylor, and LeMay testimony also reveals some of the current division of opinion regarding defense strategy. During 1963, it was widely rumored that President Kennedy was in disagreement with some of the military chiefs, particularly Air Force officers, on the issue of "overkill." The overkill thesis holds that since the United States presently has the retaliatory nuclear capacity to destroy the Soviet Union many times over, it is therefore wasteful to continue to increase our overkill strength. President Kennedy was reputed to share this view, and to believe that the United States was entering an era of "mutual deterrence" with the Soviet Union. Some of his opponents have attempted to equate this with a "no win" or "stalemate" policy.

All of the defense-appropriations testimony must be read against the background of administrative cuts in Air Force requests, particularly the decision not to develop the Skybolt missile, and the decision to phase out the manned-bomber system. The latter decision resulted in an administrative policy against the RS-70 bomber.

The Air Force prefers a policy of nuclear superiority. In practice, this policy has amounted to strong reliance on nuclear bombers and missiles—described by one of its advocates as "more bang for the buck." This superiority would be used to keep the peace by threatening the Soviet Union with nuclear war should the Soviet Union disturb the peace—"it means bombs on Moscow," as Congressman Mahon (D-Tex.) phrases it. This policy was incorporated into the Dulles foreign policy in the Eisenhower years and was generally called "massive retaliation." Some scholars have questioned such a policy. Charles Osgood recently asked, "How much real defense is there in mutual fear?"

Perhaps all of the verbal fencing in the testimony about "stalemate," "no win," and "overkill" is merely an indication of congressional frustration. Congressmen Ford (R-Mich.), Laird (R-Wis.), and Whitten (D-Miss.) all seemed to be alarmed at not being able to pinpoint American defense strategy. If mutual deterrence means that the massive-retaliation policy is no longer viable, does it follow that American policy is beginning a trend toward new solutions to cold-war problems? Do mutual deterrence and the recent nuclear test-ban treaty mean that we are approaching what Arthur Waskow called "disarmament-plus"? Does this mean that the United States is writing off Eastern Europe?

An increase of 30 percent in defense spending in three years is hardly an indication that the United States is approaching peace along the lines described by Mr. Waskow. Nonetheless, an analysis of the testimony given by defense experts before congressional committees in 1963 does indicate that American defense strategy is becoming more complex, less single-, or some would say, simple-minded. If congressmen find current strategy a frustrating exercise, they should take comfort at least in being the beneficiaries of all those "off the record" exchanges.

NUCLEAR BALANCE AND
CONVENTIONAL WEAPONS*

Mr. Mahon. We shall resume the hearing. . . .

I have the feeling that a big war will be averted if we remain strong and if we can find ways to make it clear to our opponents that, regardless of the costs or the hazards, we will maintain our position in the world.

Effect of Conventional Weapons
Buildup on Nuclear Deterrent

Back in 1953 and following the end of hostilities in the Korean war, our Government became thoroughly disenchanted with conventional war and more or less conventional weapons. The then Secretary of Defense, Mr. Wilson, a great industrialist, talked about "more bang for the buck." The general implication was that we did not propose to become involved again in a Korean-type war, which turned out to be in some ways indecisive, and that we wanted the whole wide world to know that people who played fast and loose with the United States might very probably

---

* House of Representatives, Committee on Appropriations. *Hearings,* condensed, Department of Defense Appropriations for 1964, Part 1, Government Printing Office.

be confronted with atomic weapons in sufficient quantity to achieve our national objectives.

We are doing more and more to improve our conventional weapons and our weapons for special operations in guerrilla warfare and counterinsurgency. No one should say, in my opinion, that we are starting too early to modernize our conventional forces. What I am concerned about here is the impact of this situation on our world and the influence it may have on our policies.

Could it be that by this modification of course of policy that we are taking some steps that might encourage a nuclear war by indicating too strongly a reliance upon conventional weapons? . . .

Secretary McNAMARA. As evidence of my very strong belief that an increase in our conventional forces, taking place, as it is today, at a time when we are not only maintaining but increasing our nuclear forces, in no way detracts from the deterrent, I cite the Soviet Union. I do not place any less credence on their deterrent because they have maintained their conventional forces and, as a matter of fact, reversed a plan to reduce those forces.

Military Power of United States
Compared with that of U.S.S.R.

Mr. MAHON. How do you size up the overall military power of the United States in relation to that of the Soviet Union? I do not mean that you should go into an exhaustive discussion, but what is your general feeling about this matter?

Secretary McNAMARA. On balance, in conjunction with the military forces of our allies, I believe the power of this Nation is superior to that of the Soviet Union. There can be no doubt but that our nuclear forces exceed in number, quality, and effectiveness the nuclear forces of the Soviet Union.

Mr. MAHON. Do you mean to imply at all in your statement before us that you recognize the existence at this time of a nuclear stalemate between the United States and the Soviet Union?

Secretary McNAMARA. No; I at no place used the word stalemate. I have said, and I believe it is true, that the Soviet nuclear forces, particularly their strategic forces, are increasing in size, that as they increase they will become increasingly capable of achieving severe damage by an attack on the United States.

Mr. MAHON. . . . A nuclear weapon is a terror weapon to some very considerable extent unless it is very small. The greater the yield of the weapon, the greater the terror.

Would it be fair to assume that a nation with a 100-megaton nuclear weapon can confront an opponent, in some respects, with a greater deterrent than a nation that lacks this awesome weapon in its arsenal? Bear in mind that in the background of my thinking is the fact that we have no weapons of this magnitude, and, as far as I know, we do not plan to have any. . . .

Secretary McNamara. Mr. Chairman, I do not personally hold to the view that the greater the yield of the weapon the greater the terror. I think that a more proper standard of evaluating the degree of terror associated with a potential threat is the magnitude of destruction which that threat can bring about. The facts are that a given yield under most circumstances will bring about more destruction if launched in a series of warheads rather than concentrated in a single warhead. . . .

General Taylor. It seems to me the more balanced approach to our requirements, whereby we provide amply for the strategic deterrent, for conventional forces and for this new factor, counterinsurgency forces, gives much greater strength to our national posture. Our negotiators—our President, our Secretary of State—can do many things, backed by this kind of flexible force, which they never could have done in the days when massive retaliation was virtually the sole military response.

Mr. Mahon. I would like to shift this discussion a bit.

As we all know, there is a tremendous push in progress to reduce taxes, to modify the tax structure, and to undertake to stimulate economic growth, more employment.

I will admit my theories of economics are quite homespun and I could not hold my own in the forum with the theorists on this subject.

The reason I make this observation is that . . . the pressures are going to be tremendous for a reduction in appropriations, both in certain fields of nondefense expenditures and in certain fields of defense appropriations.

Secretary McNamara. I think it is . . . interesting to point out that the budgets submitted to me by the military departments totaled $67 billion, and that I reduced those estimates approximately $13 billion to achieve the budget we are requesting—$53.7 billion in new obligational authority, and which presently lies before the Congress. This reduction of $13 billion was made without reducing the force requirements below the levels I believe are necessary to serve as a proper foundation to our foreign policy.

I have heard it said by certain Members of Congress, and by others, that $3 billion could be removed from the defense budget. I would be very pleased if the Congress could recommend to us areas in which the budget could be cut by a sum such as $3 billion without so reducing our force levels as to endanger our Nation. I know of no such areas.

My problem has been to prevent appropriations exceeding those which we have recommended. There have been tremendous pressures, for example, to appropriate funds for programs that I do not believe add to our national security; pressures to increase the budgets for Reserve and Guard forces above those required to support our contingency war plans; pressures to appropriate funds for such missile systems as SKYBOLT which we do not require to achieve the appropriate level of nuclear deterrence; pressures to carry out development of aircraft programs such as the RS-70, which are not necessary to our national security; pressures to add to the funds for such development projects as DYNA-SOAR beyond the limits which we can properly and effectively spend.

Mr. MAHON. Mr. Secretary, in your statement you discuss the dangers of nuclear war and you seem to imply that you reject the theory we would be able to strike all targets in the Soviet Union and destroy them in one attack.

You speak of a discriminating exchange in which we would seek to strike only military targets and then you use the phrase "strike these targets in a controlled and deliberate way," and so forth.

My feeling is in the event of nuclear war the emotionalism would be so high and the degree of hysteria in some quarters would be so great and the stakes would be so tremendous that if you begin to drop atomic weapons from airplanes or through utilization of intercontinental ballistic missiles, you are in a situation where no holds are barred and you would not have the advantage of this refinement of reacting in a deliberate and planned way.

It seems to me it would be all or nothing at that stage.

Secretary McNAMARA. With respect to your . . . point relating to a controlled response, I personally believe that it is extremely unlikely that in the event of a nuclear strike by the Soviet Union against this country they would do anything other than to strike all of our Nation with all of their power in the very first strike. However, I have stated on page 31 that—

The most likely possibility is that we would have to strike back after absorbing the first blow. This means we have to build and maintain a second strike force. Such a force should have sufficient flexibility to permit a choice of strategies, particularly an ability to: (1) Strike back decisively at the entire Soviet target system simultaneously, or (2) strike back first at the Soviet bomber bases, missile sites and other military installations associated with their long-range nuclear forces to reduce the power of any follow-on attack—and then if necessary, strike back at the Soviet urban and industrial complex in a controlled and deliberate way.

Mr. MAHON. With respect to the question of overkill or unnecessary excess of nuclear capability on our part, am I to assume that we are not trying to plan to be able to hit all targets and to kill all nuclear weapon sites that might exist?

Will you clarify for me just what the pros and cons are of this situation and what we are trying to do?

Secretary McNamara. Mr. Chairman, we do not believe it possible by utilization of the force we are recommending, or by a force two, three, or several times larger than the force we are recommending, to destroy, or kill all the Soviet nuclear capability. A portion of it is today, and almost certainly in the future will be, deployed at sea, under the sea, in locations that we cannot expect to detect certainly, and we cannot expect therefore, with any high probability, to kill.

(Discussion off the record.) . . .

Mr. Mahon. I recognize fully that it is not wise to underestimate the capability of an opponent. Where does the testimony which you have just given us tie in with this theory about our overkill capability in nuclear weapons about which we have heard so much?

Secretary McNamara. I don't think I have personally advanced that theory. Without commenting on the theory of overkill I don't want to leave you with a misimpression of what I have said.

I have said simply that given the force we have today I believe that that force can survive a Soviet attack with sufficient power to destroy the Soviet Union. I mean that in any normal sense of the word "destroy." It can be destroyed as a civilized nation of the 20th century, by destroying its industrial capacity, by destroying its military power, and by destroying a high percentage of its population.

Similarly I also believe that this cannot be accomplished without the probability of severe damage to our Nation, severe damage resulting from the launch against our Nation even under favorable circumstances of warheads in number on the order of that which I have outlined to you. . . .

Mr. Mahon. General Taylor, do you agree that we do not have and do not plan to have an overkill capability in the field of nuclear weapons?

General Taylor. I think we now have something which did not exist in former years when I came here as Chief of Staff; namely, a measure of sufficiency, a rationale for developing this force. Behind these figures are endless files of computations which crank in various assumptions on missile performance. I am sure there are probably errors in those assumptions as would be true of any assumptions about future systems about which we have no very detailed knowledge.

I have great confidence in the approach which has been developed. I would say it comes up now with something which makes sense and has a justification in terms of a rational approach to the problem.

Mr. FORD. I don't think you answered the question.

General TAYLOR. Have I misunderstood you, Mr. Chairman?

Mr. MAHON. Are you saying you do not believe we have an overkill capability in nuclear weapons? That was my interpretation of your answer.

General TAYLOR. (Off the record.)

Mr. FORD. Mr. Secretary, on page 27 of the prepared statement, you make this comment:

More armaments, whether offensive or defensive, cannot solve this dilemma. We are approaching an era when it will become increasingly improbable that either side could destroy a sufficiently large portion of the other's strategic nuclear force, either by surprise or otherwise, to preclude a devastating retaliatory blow.

As I read that statement I come to the inevitable conclusion that you are saying that at some point we, the United States, will reach a point of mutual deterrence, a nuclear standoff, or a nuclear stalemate with the Soviet Union. Is that correct?

Secretary McNAMARA. No, that is not what I have said.

I believe, to characterize what I described by a particular noun, even with one adjective in front of it, may lead to misunderstanding. Particularly I think the terms "nuclear standoff," "nuclear stalemate" may mislead individuals into believing that our military program does not provide for the maintenance of our nuclear superiority measured in terms of quantity of nuclear power and therefore I prefer to describe the situation as I have in the sentence you quoted:

We are approaching an era when it will become increasingly improbable that either side could destroy a sufficiently large portion of the other's strategic nuclear force, either by surprise or otherwise, to preclude a devastating retaliatory blow.

Mr. FORD. The next sentence, following the one I quoted, reads as follows:

This may result in mutual deterrence, but it is still a grim prospect.

It certainly has led many people to come to the conclusion that we, under the programs submitted to Congress, will be reaching a period of nuclear standoff, nuclear stalemate.

Can you differentiate between mutual deterrence and the other two phrases?

When do we reach this period of mutual deterrence which is a "grim prospect"?

Secretary McNAMARA. I think the date on which we reach it is difficult to pinpoint with any accuracy because in part deterrence is a frame of mind.

Mr. FORD. Why must we assume that this is going to come to pass?

Secretary McNAMARA. Well, I have not assumed it. I have said, "We are approaching an era when it will become increasingly improbable." I do not assume it is coming to pass. I believe we are approaching that era.

Mr. FORD. Why do we have to approach that era? Are we so unimaginative, lacking in skill and diligence, to permit this to be upon us relatively soon?

Secretary McNAMARA. I do not believe we are either unimaginative or lacking in skill, but I do believe that a careful assessment of the probable increases in the Soviet nuclear power as estimated by the experienced intelligence evaluators in our Government indicate that power will increase in such ways, particularly in such types, that there will not be a possibility for us to build a force that can destroy that power to such a degree that there will not remain elements so large as to cause severe damage to our Nation in retaliation for our destructive effort directed against that power.

Mr. FORD. . . . I refuse to believe—and I think this has been the traditional attitude of the America people—that we must concede that we cannot be sufficient militarily, that we must accept a position that is a grim prospect. I have never known us to assume that or to believe that or to concede that in the past. . . .

Mr. WHITTEN. If the gentleman will yield, . . . after years on this committee it strikes me that we have no plan to win, and this present question and answer further indicate that some plateau, where there is a mutual standoff at the cost of 60 percent of the governmental income, seems to be about the most that anybody militarily is planning for or hoping for, unless it be the moral transformation of mankind. . . .

Secretary McNAMARA. Mr. Chairman, may I respond to Mr. Whitten's statement. . . . I personally believe—and I believe that the passage of time will support my conclusion—that this Nation can support the current level of military expenditures indefinitely. I hope it will not be necessary to continue the current level of military expenditures indefinitely, but there is no doubt whatsoever in my mind that our Nation has the economic strength to support such level indefinitely.

Mr. FORD. Everything you have said in the last 5 or 10 minutes leads me to the absolute conclusion that after 1968, under the plans and programs that must follow from your comments, the manned aircraft will have little or no part in the strategic retaliatory force.

Secretary McNamara. . . . Perhaps this is a useful point, if you wish, to discuss the term "manned bomber" versus "missile." Much confusion has been caused, I think, by the implications associated with the term "manned bomber." It is assumed that a manned bomber system is not a missile system. I think that is an inappropriate assumption when applied to the future. Basically, we have two variables, each of which has basically two alternatives. One is the form of launcher. It may be either fixed or mobile. The other is the form of energy applied to the delivery of the warhead. It may be either gravity or some form of power. To date, the manned bomber has been associated with a weapon which depends upon gravity to reach its target. It seems almost certain that as the years go by a manned aircraft will not be able to depend upon moving directly over the target, where gravity becomes effective, to deliver the warhead against the target. Therefore the aircraft will have to stand off from the target some distance and depend upon some other form of energy, some powered trajectory, for the delivery of the warhead to the target. A powered trajectory by definition is a missile. It simply means, therefore, that manned strategic systems of the future will be missile systems. They may be missile systems that are launched from mobile airborne platforms, but they will nonetheless be missile systems.

Mr. Laird. I think in the area of policy there are certain questions which we in Congress should have a better understanding of and should become familiar with. I am not sure in my own mind what the objectives of our present defense policy are. What is the overall objective? Is it to deter war, to avoid war, to destroy communism, to coexist peacefully, or what?

I am not sure in my own mind what our objective is in this cold war. In all past wars, whether hot or cold, we have had an overriding objective to win, to defeat the enemy. Sometimes it seems to me that when we talk about our present strategy—and I am not limiting this to the last 2 years or the last 4 years—it seems to me that we place major emphasis in our strategy to avoid war. Is that the case or not?

Secretary McNamara. I do not believe it is. I think that, quite clearly in the case of the Cuban crisis of last October, we acted in a way we hoped would avoid war but certainly we exposed ourselves to the risk of war.

As to our objective, I think it is quite clear—it is to me—that it is to advance the cause of freedom throughout the world and to do this in a way that protects our own national security, which means we are not prepared to destroy our Nation in the process of attempting to advance freedom elsewhere in the world.

Mr. LAIRD. In a Saturday Evening Post interview that you had with Mr. Alsop the impression was given—and this may not be correct—that we were in a position of an almost stalemate with the Soviet Union. . . .

You talked in your interview about a more "stable balance of terror." This is a quotation attributed to you from the Post article. Perhaps it is incorrect. I am not sure. It would seem to me from reading that particular paragraph in which you refer to "balance of terror" that the implication is that strategy of the United States does not include the objective of eventual defeat of the Communists in this cold war challenge with which we are faced. If nuclear power were near a stalemate, or a balance of terror, however you want to describe it, I am not sure what kind of policy we would then pursue as compared to the policy we are presently pursuing.

Secretary McNAMARA. I do not believe I said, and I certainly did not wish to imply, that our objective does not include eventual defeat of the Communists. Quite the contrary. Our objective is the defeat of the Communists. I do not believe we can achieve that victory by engaging in strategic nuclear war. I think that kind of stalemate will become increasingly more controlling with the passage of time. . . .

I think that was specifically the point at issue in the article. Implicitly the question was, "Can we achieve defeat of the Communists by engaging in strategic nuclear war? You have said we have superior nuclear forces measured in terms of numbers. Can we not use those superior nuclear forces to achieve defeat of the Communists?"

My answer is, I do not believe we can achieve defeat of communism by engaging in strategic nuclear war. There are some who do believe that. I do not. I think it is very dangerous, as a matter of fact, for any significant number of our people to believe we can achieve defeat of communism by engaging in strategic nuclear war.

Mr. LAIRD. But at the same time, Mr. Secretary, if we are forced to engage in that kind of an activity we must mention our present superior position in order to win? Are we not in that position?

Secretary McNAMARA. No, sir; I do not believe we are, not in the normal sense of the word "win," because in my opinion there would be so much severe damage done to this country that our way of life would change, and change in an undesirable direction. Therefore, I would say we had not won. In another sense of the word "win" we would win. We would win in the sense that their way of life would change more than ours because we would destroy a greater percentage of their industrial potential and probably destroy a greater percentage of their population than they destroyed of ours. By "ours" I am speaking of the United States. I suspect that in terms of facilities the amount of industrial destruction in the West would exceed that of the Soviet Union. This is so because you would have to add to the destruction in the United States the probable destruction of Western Europe. My personal opinion is—and I think you should hear from General Taylor on this subject because it is so important —we cannot win a nuclear war, a strategic nuclear war in the normal meaning of the word "win." I think you should hear from General Taylor.

General TAYLOR. I can only add that throughout history men have waged war presumably because they felt that at its conclusion their country would be in a better position than had they not waged war. In other words, they acted in accordance with the old Clausewitzian theory that war is the pursuit of national policy objectives by forceful means. The kind of war we are talking about is not that kind of war at all.

I quite agree with the Secretary, that when you talk about "winning" a general nuclear war it is usually in a sense I do not understand. The losses on both sides would reduce these two world powers to secondary or tertiary powers. Certainly in a general nuclear war we would lose many of those things which have been thought worth fighting for in the wars of the past.

NUCLEAR SUPERIORITY AND OVERKILL*

Mr. MAHON. In the overall, how do you, today, compare the strength of the United States, militarily, with the military strength of the Soviet Union? I realize the Soviet Union has a larger land force, more divisions, et cetera, but, in the overall, how do you compare the strength of these two countries, particularly in reference to any conflict that might arise between the two countries?

General LEMAY. I do not think there is any doubt but what we have superior military power to Russia. I think the best proof is the Cuban situation, where they backed down in the face of our will to use our military force.

---

* House of Representatives, Committee on Appropriations. *Hearings*, condensed, Department of Defense Appropriations for 1964, Part 2, Government Printing Office.

Mr. MAHON. Do you support the theory that we are now in what could be called a period of mutual deterrence?

General LeMay. No, sir; I do not believe that at all.

Mr. MAHON. When you answer the question what is your interpretation of "mutual deterrence"?

General LeMay. As for a definition, I quote what I believe other people say when they talk about mutual deterrence, and that is, each of the adversaries possesses enough nuclear weapons to inflict unacceptable damage on each other; therefore, they will not be used. This is what they call "mutual deterrence." It may exist for a short period of time, but it will change from day to day. In other words, the threat against you may change from time to time; in fact, it will change from time to time. You may get intelligence information on one day that could change the whole picture. . . .

Mr. MAHON. Under conditions existing today, would it be fair to say that the United States would not want to go to war with the Soviet Union for, among other reasons, the reason that we would sustain heavy casualties, and the Soviet Union would not want to go to war with the United States for the reason that the Soviet Union would sustain even heavier and more unacceptable losses; is that a fair statement or not?

General LeMay. Frankly that is not a military decision to be made, Mr. Chairman. That one will have to be made by the President.

I would think that under normal methods for a war getting underway, or any reasonable assumptions you might want to make, we would surely win such a war with Russia if one could call coming out on the top side of a modern war as winning it. No one actually wins a modern war. I think we would survive as a viable nation and I doubt if the Russians would. That is the situation now.

(Discussion off the record.) . . .

Instability of Mutual Deterrence

Mr. MAHON. You might have mutual deterrence and still have a war, could you not?

General LeMay. No; I do not think you can have mutual deterrence and still have a war because the very definition that we have just agreed upon was that both sides knowingly had sufficient offensive capability to inflict damage on the other side that would be unacceptable; in other words, each would come out of a war with much less than he went in and no one is going to want that. . . .

Mr. MAHON. Do you consider that we are in any sense of the word seeking to equate our military strength with that of the Soviet Union and that we would consider having as our goal the maintenance of strength equivalent only to that of the Soviet Union, or is it our policy to have strength superior to that of the Soviet Union, today and for the future?

Secretary ZUCKERT. I would state our policy as an answer to you, and that is our purpose is to have enough strength so that the Soviets will be deterred for fear of the damage that would result to them even if they make the first move as we would likely assume they would. I think that is our policy.

(Discussion off the record.)

Mr. MAHON. Is any responsible person in the Department of Defense, to your knowledge, advocating that we recede from our position of military superiority and accept the position of military parity? This is a matter of the greatest importance. I would like to know what your answer is.

Secretary ZUCKERT. I know of no one, sir. . . .

Mr. MAHON. . . . It seems to me that our philosophy of 5 years ago was: If you move into Berlin, it means bombs on Moscow. Is this our position now, in your opinion?

General LeMAY. . . . As long as we maintain a clear strategic superiority, I don't think the time will come when we will have to go to war with Russia. I definitely don't believe that we should ever indicate that we would be willing to keep a war between our country and Russia on a conventional weapons basis. We should indicate that we will use whatever forces and weapons we consider necessary for our defense.

Change in Overall Military Strategy

Mr. FORD. . . . Has there been any revision in our overall military strategy on a broader basis?

General LeMAY. I think there has been a change to some extent, yes. The present administration is building more conventional strength into our Armed Forces than we have had heretofore. This is the basic change, I think.

Mr. FORD. When Secretary McNamara was before the committee, at page 226 of the original transcript, Secretary McNamara said this:

I think General Taylor has raised a very important point. Whether nuclear superiority ever gave us what I would call a universal deterrent against all forms of Soviet political and military aggression, I believe is open to question. As General Taylor suggested, even at a time when our nuclear superiority was so great as to represent a monopoly, it did not deter Communist aggression in various parts of the world, as is illustrated by the Communist invasion of Korea, as is illustrated by the Communist pressure on Berlin in 1958, and as is illustrated by the series of other aggressive acts, political and military, by the Communists during the decade of the fifties.

Before asking you a question, I would like to say, in my opinion, he is comparing apples and oranges in the two illustrations that he gave.

General LeMay. Not necessarily. Certainly, for example, we had the conventional forces to go in and take care of the missiles in Cuba or any other conventional Russian forces that were there.

Our strategic superiority gave us the option of whether we would go or not. The choice was made that it was not necessary to go because the Russians removed the missiles.

As far as strategic superiority not preventing limited wars, it did not prevent the limited war in Korea because we did not exercise it like we did in Cuba. In Korea we did not say there will be no limited war. We just said there will be no general war or we will use our nuclear weapons. I think if we had said there will be no limited war or there will be no war in Korea or we will use the nuclear weapons, there would not have been any. . . .

Mr. Ford. So, in the case of Korea, it was not a lack of strategic power but a failure to make the decision that we would use it.

General LeMay. I would term it a failure to announce the policy of using it for preventing that type of conflict.

Mr. Ford. Mr. McNamara's second illustration was Communist pressure on Berlin in 1958. It is my recollection that at the time the threat was made by Mr. Khrushchev in 1958, former President Eisenhower made the statement—I think the quotation is correct—"We will never use ground forces in Europe." There was never any change in the status in Berlin in 1958, was there?

General LeMay. No.

Mr. Ford. We had a threat. The formidable statement was made by President Eisenhower, and the status was not changed in Berlin. . . . There was this unsettled condition in the Middle East. President Eisenhower sent Army troops which were airlifted by the Air Force from Germany to Lebanon, and we sent Marine and perhaps Army forces by sea and air from the United States. The inference, if not a specific statement, was that we would use our nuclear forces if there was any expansion of the trouble. Is that a correct statement?

General LeMay. I think that was clearly understood. I think this is another classic example of what you can do if you have strategic superiority and then are able to exploit any situation with your conventional forces without interference. Without nuclear and strategic superiority, I do not think we would have dared go into Lebanon.

Mr. FLOOD. What are you suggesting? The logical conclusion of your premise is that any time we have an argument in the plaza with some Latin republic we do not like, we say, "We are going to use nuclear weapons. You had better stop that street riot in Lima."

General LeMAY. No, sir; I do not say that at all. It just seems odd to me to think that you can stop a big war with nuclear weapons, but something less than that you cannot.

Mr. FLOOD. This does not follow, Q.E.D. On your first premise, you and I have no quarrel. But it does not follow necessarily from that premise that if you have trouble on the border someplace or in the provinces someplace, you trot out your great, big, powerful nuclear force and say, "If you don't stop that, we have strategic might and power and we will have a nuclear war." Is that what you want to do?

General LeMAY. No; that is not what I said at all.

Mr. FLOOD. What did you say?

General LeMAY. I said if you have the power to stop a big war, certainly that same power ought to be capable of stopping a small war.

Mr. FLOOD. Then if we want to stop the trouble that is going on in Vietnam by half-past 9 tonight or in the next half hour, all we have to do is announce: "If you Reds do not get out of South Vietnam by half-past 10 tonight, we are going to strike at Cambodia, we are going to strike at North Korea, and we are going to strike at North Vietnam, where you are getting your supplies and munitions and aid." Is that what we are supposed to say? You can stop it?

General LeMAY. (Off the record.)

Mr. FLOOD. Oh, yes. No doubt about that. Do you want to do that?

General LeMAY. Once a war starts and we are attacked, as in the case of Korea, where we were in there fighting, I think that could have been stopped by the threat of using nuclear weapons.

Mr. FLOOD. Now we are getting you backed into a corner. We can agree with that. There are certain demarcating lines, all things being relative, even in your thinking about this, I would hope.

General LeMAY. Certainly. I certainly do not want to settle every little border dispute around the world by threatening to use nuclear weapons.

Mr. FLOOD. If I had not asked you, that is just where the record left you.

General LeMay. This is certainly not what I intended, and I do not think I said that, Mr. Flood.

Flexibility of Manned Bomber

Mr. Mahon. It has been argued that you are given additional flexibility in strategic planning if you have the long-range bomber. I think that we would all have to agree that there is additional flexibility in a mix of weapons as compared with a single weapon. I would like to direct your attention solely to this element of flexibility. It is said that the bombers can take off, they can approach the target, they can stand off just far enough that they can withdraw if necessary, but if they have to move in they can move in.

On the other hand it is said that the missile when once launched cannot be recalled, but the missile goes faster than the bomber and can be launched at a later time under certain circumstances. To what extent is this important?

General LeMay. Well, once you are committed to war—in other words, you are fighting—there are tasks that can be performed by the missile better than the bomber. On the other hand, there are tasks that can be performed by the bomber better than the missile. All of our war gaming has indicated that the most efficient campaign can be fought with a mixture of the two, so you can use the strong points of each of the weapon systems and get a net result greater than the sum of each one of them if you use them separately.

However, to my mind, the big advantage of the manned system over the missile system comes before you get into war. We do not know how the next war is going to come about, if we have one. With a missile you only have two choices: you are either on the button and you are at war, or you are off the button and you are at peace. It is pretty hard to show your will to resist with just missiles. All you can do is say, "I am going to press a button if you do this."

Mr. Flood. . . . You are talking about manned vehicles, manned planes, manned bombers, the RS-70's. As a matter of fact, the RS-70 is a standoff weapon. We are going to use missiles, perhaps not the SKYBOLT, but you do not propose with the RS-70's to drop any bombs. No one has asked you that, but I do not think that you will.

General LeMay. No.

Mr. Flood. So no matter how manned your bomber is, you are not going to look down on a target, you are not going to drop a bomb on a target. You have a standoff weapon with missiles; is that not what you have?

General LeMay. Not exactly.

Mr. Flood. Either you have or you do not.

General LeMay. Let me explain. You are actually going to look at your target through your radar, but you are not going to fly over it and drop a bomb on it, depending on gravity to take the weapon to the target. It is standoff in the sense that the bomber stands off from the immediate target; it must nevertheless penetrate enemy territory to do this.

Mr. Ford. I detect a tendency on the part of some people to accept the philosophy that mutual deterrence or nuclear stalemate is inevitable?

General LeMay. No, I do not accept that philosophy at all. I think it is a dangerous philosophy to say, well, a stalemate is going to exist, we cannot do anything about it; therefore, we do nothing. If we accept mutual deterrence, this will, I think, inevitably lead to defeat. In other words, if we stop trying, we certainly are not going to succeed in defending ourselves.

Mr. Mahon. General LeMay, when you were commander of the Strategic Air Command, you could have, of course, incinerated the Soviet Union with that arm of United States power. Some argue that we had overkill capabilities at that time and that we continue to have overkill capability. . . .

General LeMay. . . . As for having overkill, the Joint Chiefs just went out and reviewed the war plan of SAC and the atomic portions of the theater commanders, the other commanders', plans.

(Statement off the record.)

So I do not think we have an overkill. Too many people are adding up the weapons and assuming that every one of them is delivered on target and, therefore, we destroy everything. . . .

If we could be assured that we could deliver all of our weapons on target, then I would be willing to say we have got enough right now.

Mr. Mahon. If you could deliver one-third of them on target, would that probably be reasonably adequate or not?

General LeMay. Can you guarantee me that in any future war I will deliver one-third of them?

Mr. Mahon. No.

General LeMay. I cannot, either. What is the opposition going to be doing and how many are going to be destroyed on the ground before we ever get off? How is the fight going on during the delivery phase? What defenses have they got? Things of that sort.

This is going to be a war the same as wars in the past. You have to defeat the enemy forces. There are many variables here.

Mr. MAHON. In other words, you do not feel that we now have too much capability in strategic weapons and you do not feel that we have programed for overcapability in strategic weapons?

General LeMAY. That is correct.

THE LIMITS OF DEFENSE*

Arthur I. Waskow

Until recently in our national history, Americans believed that when wars were thrust upon us, the United States could win them, or, at the very least, could successfully defend its basic interests. But since 1945 we have discovered limits to our own defense. The impact of the atomic bomb and its successors has persuaded many makers of military policy that a modern war could not be won, and that in such a war defense of American interests might well be impossible.

If victory and defense were both outmoded, policy makers asked themselves, what goal could there be for American military power? They decided that our military power must be so disposed as to prevent wars from beginning. The new goal is deterrence.

Adopting deterrence as the key to policy has, however, opened the door to a vigorous debate over how deterrence should be carried out. Some thinkers argue that comparatively controlled wars are still acceptable possibilities. These might range from a thermonuclear attack on military targets instead of people down to a small-scale rebellion in some nation on the periphery of American interest and alliance. For such lesser wars, defense is, therefore, still important, according to this group of thinkers. Others disbelieve that any thermonuclear war can be a controlled or limited war, and insist that defense applies only to nonthermonuclear, or only to nonatomic, wars.

The debates over deterrence are also concerned with how best to preserve both life and liberty. Americans, as Patrick Henry once pointed out, should hold liberty more dear than life and be ready to die to protect liberty. But a nation of corpses is not free. Today life and liberty are opposite sides of a coin. Deterrence must protect them both. That means

---

* Condensed from *The Limits of Defense* by Arthur I. Waskow. Copyright © 1961, 1962 by Doubleday & Company, Inc. Used by permission of the author and publisher. Mr. Waskow is a staff member of the Institute for Policy Analysis.

it must prevent war, prevent our conquest by foreign tyranny, and prevent our surrendering liberty to homegrown tyranny in a mistaken belief that such a surrender would protect liberty.

Both domestically and internationally, the technological and political heat and pressure of the twentieth century have welded together the means the American people use and the ends they hold. Only a defense made up of peaceful acts can protect the peace, since warlike acts, even done only in self-defense, are so highly threatening as to start a spiral of more warlike acts. Only a defense based on continuing democratic decisions can protect democracy, since the time span of thermonuclear weapons rules out appeal to the people or their representatives even on the most basic issues of life and death.

The Counterforce Theory of Deterrence

One theory of deterrence argues that it is still possible to fight a counterforce thermonuclear war against the enemy's military forces. Much of the population, and with it the fabric of society, of the warring powers would be allowed to remain intact.

Counterforce theorists argue that if such a war were fought, American society could face the prospect of survival and renewal, regarding it as unappetizing but acceptable. They admit, however, that damage to the United States would be unprecedently great, and therefore they sometimes refer to prevailing, rather than winning, in such a war. "Prevailing" essentially means the bare defense of vital American interests.

This theory is most strongly and widely held by officers in the Air Force, though some officers in the other services accept it. The Air Force has possessed atomic weapons much longer than the other services. Its theorists have become habituated to the concept of atomic warfare and skilled in its potentialities. They react to the Soviet thermonuclear capability not by deciding that thermonuclear war is too dangerous for the United States to consider, but by working out a refinement of thermonuclear war which they hope will not be too dangerous. The Air Force has constructed various models of what several possible wars might be like. The dominant characteristic of these models is that they require intense self-control from both sides in such wars, self-control based on a coldly rationalistic analysis of self-interest.

The Air Force suggests that war is most likely to start through the Soviet bloc's launching a major atomic strike at the United States, which would knock out as much as possible of the American atomic striking force. With what was left of its atomic forces, the United States would have to return the blow. The major decision would be whether to retaliate against Communist cities or forces. But an attack against cities would leave enemy atomic forces intact for a second blow, and this blow would come against American cities in revenge for the annihilation of Communist cities. Since American cities cannot be adequately protected against H-bomb attack, such a return blow would destroy American society. For that reason, the Air Force would aim the American retaliatory attack at Soviet atomic missile and bomber bases, hoping to smash as much as possible of the Soviet thermonuclear capabilitiy without destroying Soviet society. . . .

This belief in self-control leads counterforce theorists to their second major point, that American society would not be absolutely destroyed by such a war. These theorists estimate that up to thirty million Americans might die, but they believe that after absorbing the first blow, the United States (and Communist governments also) would continue to act by carefully rational calculations, in an attempt to minimize destruction. They believe it likely that neither side would try to destroy the other's capital and government, since each side would want to have the other's authorities intact, able to negotiate or surrender.

What basic requirements would our weapons systems have to meet in order to be able to fight a second-strike counterforce war? American thermonuclear weapons would have to be made relatively invulnerable in order to survive the first enemy attack, and be powerful and numerous enough to destroy enemy atomic forces that would be similarly protected. The American population would have to be separated from American forces, so that it would sustain as little damage as possible. This separation could be accomplished partly by physical distance between cities and missile or airplane bases, but people in the cities would also have to be protected against radioactive fallout.

The Air Force can also imagine a second kind of war, one beginning with a major Communist attack upon some area less crucial to American defense than the United States itself—for example, an invasion of western Europe, or a take-over of West Berlin, or even a Communist revolution in a strategic Latin American country. In such cases, the Air Force argues, the United States should threaten to use its thermonuclear power in order to make the Communists back down, and then strike first to punish them if they refuse. The American threat or attack could be scaled according to the size of the Communist provocation—perhaps ten Soviet cities as punishment for invading western Europe; perhaps a single city for capturing Berlin. . . .

In this counterforce-plus war, as well as in pure counterforce theory, the crucial belief is that H-bomb wars can still be made to follow the nineteenth-century rules: Wars can be won. Predominant fighting force is necessary to win the war. Fighting forces can be kept distinct from the nation. The nation can with self-control use the fighting forces to thrust and parry, as a duelist can use his sword.

Objections to Counterforce Theory

That a thermonuclear war would actually be fought in the fashion counterforce theorists suggest seems impossible. The key factor, the separation of atomic forces and the population, is most doubtful.

A close look at the present deployment of Air Force missiles shows that in practice our forces, including anti-aircraft installations, have not been separated from our people and probably could not be. Nor does separation through civil defense seem workable. Evacuations to blast shelters would actually encourage the enemy to attack pre-emptively.

The proponents of fallout shelters assume a two-week stay and never explain why an enemy confronted with a defense based on this assumption should restrict himself to a two-week war when he could easily nullify the shelters by reserving some weapons to fire at the end of two weeks. A difficult and expensive program of civil defense can be rendered useless as an element in counterforce strategy by relatively easy and inexpensive actions on the part of the enemy.

For other reasons as well, the enemy will be tempted to increase the power of his attack. As our missiles are made harder to find and destroy, the Soviets might decide to take no chances on distinguishing forces from population, but, instead, to attack at one stroke the whole of American society, both forces and population, using high-burst pattern bombing across the whole American continent or extremely dirty radioactive H-bombs. The suggestion that trying to build a sophisticated counterforce system would merely bring about an increase in violence should not be surprising. Certainly the history of twentieth-century wars is that, as either side diffuses its armed might more effectively, the other side's reaction is to raise the ante. . . .

The second premise of the counterforce theorists is the belief that rational control over the fighting of a thermonuclear war will be possible after that war has begun. But rational control must rest on extremely effective communications, and communications would surely be one of the first casualties of a thermonuclear war. There will be extreme difficulty even in assessing the damage caused by the first exchange of strikes. Any American government that is still functioning after the attack will have to give orders without knowing its own surviving defenses, the power left to its own striking force, or the targets still requiring destruction in the enemy's territory. . . .

The most serious doubts of all are cast on counterforce theory by the likelihood that, far from deterring war, it would actually tend to bring war on. Counterforce strategy would almost inevitably reward the nation that struck first. The nation to absorb the first strike would have great difficulty in finding enough weapons to outweigh the enemy's strength. When a crisis begins, each side will try to discern that moment at which the enemy intends to fire, and each side will try to anticipate that moment. And each nation will realize that the other is trying to do this. With the pressure so enormous and the stakes so high, there can be little doubt that each side would be forced to try to fire first, pre-empting the other's attack.

Finally, counterforce theory would endanger our liberty because it would require an endless arms race. We would try to discover and build new weapons that could destroy the enemy's forces, and he would be accelerating his own arms program in the attempt to keep up with our improvements. We would be building more and deeper shelters in a desperate race to keep ahead of his new weapons. In constantly increasing taxes, in constantly proliferating controls over raw materials and labor, in constantly harsher attacks upon minority dissent, in constantly more severe restrictions on publication of government information, the costs of counterforce strategy would mount forever. Free enterprise and free speech would probably be early victims.

The Theory of the Balanced Deterrent

The second major theory of deterrence is built on the belief that any thermonuclear war may easily become a total thermonuclear war, and that all thermonuclear wars must therefore be prevented. Supporters of this view have concluded that to win or to lose any thermonuclear war is inconceivable, and any such war will end in the destruction of American society.

These theorists believe in deterring war by making it absolutely clear to all the world that war could not possibly have any result but disaster. They propose to do this by deliberately increasing the terror of war to the nth power, by deliberately aiming our H-bombs at the cities of Communist nations. Their hope is that the result of making thermonuclear wars irremediably disastrous will be the elimination of all but limited wars fought with tactical atomic weapons or with conventional weapons. They believe that such wars can be won if American and Western capabilities for fighting them are strengthened.

Because this program requires the creation of a thermonuclear deterrent on the one hand and of a limited-war capability on the other, it is often called the "balanced deterrent." The theory of the balanced deterrent appeals especially to the officers of the older services, the Army and

Navy. In those two services a strong attempt has been made to keep war within the limits of traditional military and naval tactics.

Theorists of the balanced deterrent first examine how to deter thermonuclear war as completely as possible. They conclude that if both the United States and its chief enemies have great masses of citizens open to atomic attack—in a sense, being held as hostages—and that if on both sides the atomic forces to mount an attack are themselves invulnerable and are powerful enough to destroy enemy cities but not the protected enemy forces, the attack will never be mounted. The theory is that any nation which struck first under such circumstances would be condemning its own people, its economy, its government, its very existence to death. For its attack would not be able to destroy its enemy's invulnerable atomic force, and the enemy would then strike back at civilians.

The Navy believes that the invulnerable deterrent is to be found in its Polaris submarine, driven by atomic motors and armed with thermonuclear missiles capable of destroying cities but not hardened missile sites. The argument runs that the Polaris can cruise the oceans in secrecy, ready to strike but with every incentive not to do so unless the United States is struck first. Always at sea, the Polaris would avoid attracting an attack against the continental United States. For an attack would have no purpose if it left the Polaris still capable of striking.

To deter or answer provocations less than all-out war, balanced-deterrent theorists look to modernized tactical forces able to fight limited wars, ranging from the scale of World War II down to a Laotian-style infiltration. In limited wars, the Army and Navy would use foot soldiers on the spot and the fleet to support them. But four important factors compel modernization of these old-style warriors: the numerical advantage in population of the Sino-Soviet bloc over the United States and its military allies; the totalitarian organization of the Communist states, which permits them to conscript greater proportions of their men and resources for military uses; the far-flung frontier from which Communist tactical attack might come at any moment; and the development of a new Communist tactic of combined infiltration, subversion, and guerrilla warfare.

The Army and Navy feel that these four factors require increases in the mobility and numbers of Western tactical forces. They demand an airlift capability that could transport infantrymen to any part of the world in sizable force within hours. They urge that sizable fleets, floating off the shores of critical areas, be ready to deposit American Marines on land at a moment's notice. They believe that every attempt should be made to increase the numbers of allied soldiers available to integrated Western commands. This last requirement has emphasized the need for building a strong German army and for increasing military aid to nations on the Communist periphery that cannot afford to support large armies.

Recent Communist successes in areas like northern Laos have persuaded some theorists of the balanced deterrent that a new component is needed for our limited-war arsenal: commando fighters and specialists in infiltration, to combat internal subversion and revolution.

The one matter on which the theorists of the balanced deterrent disagree is the question of increased firepower for tactical forces. Some believe that the West will find it extremely difficult, despite added mobility and increased military aid, to catch up with the Sino-Soviet bloc in the number of available soldiers. They therefore insist that the West's presumed technological superiority must fill the gap, and that atomic or chemical or biological weapons must be placed in the hands of Western armies to be used against hordes of Sino-Soviet invaders.

Other balanced-deterrent theorists believe that atomic, chemical, and biological weapons would spread tactical war into general war. These men argue that the only observable limits are defined by the so-called conventional weapons, that once war goes beyond this limit, there is no way of stopping either side from employing still more powerful weapons, including the H-bomb.

Theorists of the balanced deterrent believe that their system would prevent thermonuclear war and make possible American victory in old-fashioned wars.

Objections to Balanced Deterrence

The doubt is whether any weapon can be made permanently invulnerable, as the balanced deterrent requires. In fact, even now the Polaris is probably vulnerable. The range of its missiles is so short and many Communist cities are so far from navigable oceans that to be capable of hitting them, the Polaris submarine must circle quite close to Communist coasts, within easy range of enemy planes. To launch its missiles, the submarine must release enormous and easily detected bursts of energy. The firing of just one of its missiles may immediately alert enemy aircraft to the position of the Polaris submarine and cause it to be destroyed before it releases more than a few of its sixteen missiles.

Refinements of the Polaris may, of course, add to its range and to its ability for self-concealment. But there will undoubtedly also be refinements in ways of detecting and attacking submarines. The same problem would apply to other supposedly invulnerable weapons. The invulnerable deterrent cannot stand still, it cannot halt the arms race. . . .

The other element of the balanced deterrent, tactical readiness, is also open to severe criticism. High firepower in terms of atomic, chemical, or biological weapons is clearly capable of leading to a thermonuclear war. To defend Europe by firing tactical nuclear weapons the size of the Hiroshima bomb at invading armies would leave little of Europe to defend, and Europeans would be certain to demand that the war be ended by using thermonuclear weapons against the enemy.

Those who have proposed paramilitary, or guerrilla, warfare by the West have been extremely naive in their understanding of guerrilla warfare. Those theorists who emphasize the role of paramilitary forces seem to think that American commandos can operate as guerrillas in other countries in the same way that North Vietnamese Communists act as guerrillas in South Vietnam. Successful guerrillas are not merely underground soldiers in an alien land. They need the support of the population and get it by demanding, or pretending to demand, social and economic reforms that would benefit the population around them. If the United States is prepared, with huge amounts of economic aid, to support social revolution even against Western business and political associates in the local governments, it is not necessary to send commando fighters. If we refuse to support basic social changes, sending commandos will not stop Communist guerrillas, because our commandos will not get popular support.

The military-aid aspect of balanced-deterrent strategy has tended to prevent the United States from supporting the needed social changes in many underdeveloped countries. Armies aided by the West, since they use up, for noneconomic purposes, whatever wealth might be available for economic development, ally themselves with the status quo of poverty and ignorance. Armies built on this basis can only try to hold down the violence born of desperation. When their holding action fails, the Communists benefit from the identification of the West with the repressive army.

Tactical readiness leads to a dilemma. Depending on increased firepower, and therefore on tactical nuclear weapons, makes too easy the expansion of the conflict in area and its increase in violence. But not depending on increased firepower would force the West in underdeveloped areas into either a useless attempt at quasi guerrilla warfare or a self-stultifying attempt at arming Asian, African, and Latin American ruling groups. The dilemma leads on the one hand to thermonuclear war, and on the other hand to the continued Communization of the uncommitted world.

In the very short run, the balanced deterrent would undoubtedly be safer than a counterforce strategy, but it would only be useful as a way of getting the time to move to new solutions.

The Mix: Strategies Confounded

Another theory is that the existence of potentially unstable and unpredictable situations may guarantee actual stability. If a would-be aggressor does not know what might happen, he will stay his hand and nothing will happen. On this belief there has been constructed the theory of the "Mix," calling for the simultaneous existence, side by side, of all the weapons and strategies involved in both the counterforce and balanced-deterrent theories, all of them available for use in order to confound prediction.

Support for the Mix is closely connected with particular interests inside the Defense Department. Officers connected with the Joint Chiefs of Staff and the central Department of Defense, in trying to understand and reconcile the conflicting claims of Air Force, Army, and Navy strategists, often come to the conclusion that all the services are right and that all their strategies and weapons deserve support.

In addition, some officers in each of the particular services actually believe in either one pure theory or the other, but think they must support the Mix in practice. They fear they would hurt themselves, their own careers, and their own ideas by demanding exclusive support for their own position. Many officers, therefore, publicly support the Mix while working to incorporate into it as much of their own program as they dare.

Like any mixture, this compromise strategy can be made up of varying proportions of the ingredients. Although the Mix has for many years been the actual makeup of our defense, its composition is probably changing. The Kennedy Administration is emphasizing the balanced-deterrent component of the Mix by stressing Polaris production and tactical readiness. The Kennedy Administration is also, however, stressing one element of counterforce theory—civil defense.

Objections to the Mix

Insofar as the Mix actually preserves both counterforce and balanced-deterrent theories, the objections which apply to each of them separately apply to them in the mixture. The Mix, however, is not merely a mixture of the two pure deterrent theories but is actually a chemical compound in which the best aspects of both disappear. They disappear because an enemy would view the American military system as a whole. He would doubt that a balanced-deterrent policy or a counterforce policy had been clearly adopted if weapons systems alien to one of these were continued.

For example, the chief advantage claimed for the balanced deterrent is that it would slow down reactions during a crisis and make surprise attack unlikely. But if, alongside weapons intended for city-busting, second-strike use, the United States were to build counterforce weapons that might be used pre-emptively, the enemy would fear surprise attack and himself consider pre-empting. Conversely, if, next to counterforce weapons, we insist on building weapons that can only be used effectively against the civilian population rather than forces, we will make impossible the development of a war according to counterforce theories. Once the enemy fears we will go in for city busting, the most rational course is to attack our capital, leadership, people, economy, and industry, as well as our striking force.

Confusion between the two strategies would also arise if a major civil defense shelter program were to be built alongside the second-strike deterrent. The theory of the invulnerable deterrent works, if at all, only if populations are vulnerable. If the United States were to start building blast shelters, the Soviets might fear such shelters would free our hand for a punitive first strike against their cities. Building fallout shelters in cities would seem to an enemy to fit into counterforce strategy, and the fear of pre-emptive attack might disturb him. Either blast or fallout shelters would contribute greatly to the instability that the invulnerable deterrent is supposed to alleviate.

For all the reasons suggested, the counterforce or the balanced-deterrent theory must be pure to be in the least effective. A choice would have to be made between them for either to be believable. It is conceivable that the Mix might for a time freeze the world in its tracks, making every state fearful of the slightest move. But when one nation did finally act, the results might well be extremely dangerous. A rapid series of jumps from one war level to another would be extremely easy under Mix conditions, because all sizes and types of weapons would be available to whatever side was losing any particular conflict.

Escalator to Oblivion

The Mix is a disguise behind which adherents of counterforce and balanced-deterrent strategy continue to battle. The Mix blurs any understanding of the two pure theories, and also hides the fact that they are actually not alternatives but merely alternate steps on a rising escalator of destructive capacity.

This escalator to oblivion is powered by the pursuit of research in new military technology. The first step on the escalator is a period of high instability, tied to a counterforce strategy. Then, as one side or the other catches up in the techniques of making its weapons invulnerable, there would be a second period of moderate stability, and the dominance of balanced-deterrent strategies. During this period, continuing research would tend to nullify weapons invulnerability, increase the power of the weapons, and make the population less vulnerable. When one side or the other had achieved a breakthrough in one of these techniques, a new period of extremely high instability would result, and again the counterforce theorists would dominate. But in the third period, the destructiveness of the weapons, the hostilities of the peoples, the speed of reaction would all have been heightened.

On every step of the escalator, an intense political crisis could dissolve all rationality. Fearful of unprecedented catastrophe in the offing, men and nations may react so unpredictably that deterrence would disappear when most needed. . . .

All the theories claim to provide a deterrent that is either stable or rational. But the stability claimed by balanced-deterrent theorists and the rationality claimed by counterforce theorists are true only on a superficial level. Short-run stability would lead to long-run increases in the chances of war. None of the three theories meets the requirement that deterrence work in a crisis, that it eliminate the need for trusting the enemy, that it preserve liberty in the United States and advance it in the world, and that it allow us to take the initiative. We need a new and more workable deterrent.

A Workable Deterrent

A workable deterrent must operate in three ways: It must make extremely likely the punishment of any preparations to use violence on the international scene. It must make available to every nation many avenues of obtaining the desired national goals through other than violent means. And it must make it practically impossible for those who do resort to actual violence to obtain any rewards, to achieve any of their goals by doing so.

The first requisite, that of making punishment sure, has been from ancient times the function of the police and the courts. But the basic assumption of the police force as deterrent does not exist in international relations. In international life there is no agreement as to who are the cops and who the robbers. That agreement could be based on totally excluding violence from the range of techniques available to the various nations in their conflicts with each other. The abolition of violence would be enforced by police. Where the clash of individual and group interests can find other outlets, there need be no resort to violence. Where such avenues are closed—where the economic system will not give people bread, or where the political system will not permit them a hearing, or where the prestige arrangements afford them no chance at dignity—men will appeal to the sword. We must make such adjustments in the international field that no nation need feel that its progress is impossible.

This means that ways of protecting and expanding the area of liberty must be developed that do not depend on the use of violence. In our arsenal must be dozens of techniques, some open and some secret, some gently appealing to the best in men and others toughly attacking evil men and ideas when they appear, speeches where possible and bribes where necessary. The only technique to be excluded is the possibility of using violence. Meanwhile, other nations will possess the same wide range of techniques and the same absolute prohibition on violence. Fighting for freedom in a disarmed world will require brains and stamina, but free men can fight without guns.

We know that even in societies with effective laws, a vigilant police, and many nonviolent avenues of action, criminals are not always deterred. Crime is sometimes attempted when would-be criminals expect great rewards if they succeed. Where the would-be criminal sees that even success will not bring him any rewards, he will not risk the criminal act. The safecracker who knows for sure that the safe is empty will not take the chance of capture in order to crack it. We must work out a way of making sure that in the international field no one who takes up arms can profit. Such an arrangement would act as an ultimate deterrent, the final plus in the whole system of Disarmament-Plus. . . .

Fighting for Freedom in a Disarmed World

In a disarmed world, all the energies and imagination of free men could be directed in new and unexpected campaigns for liberty. In an all-out economic competition with the Communists, the ability developed throughout the West in the fast-and-loose mixed economy of private, semipublic, and public enterprise should be a great advantage. In our own past, our flexibility under new conditions gave birth to family-owned department stores, General Motors, the Tennessee Valley Authority, farm cooperatives, the regulated public utility, chain groceries, the Federal Reserve banks, labor-union pension funds, city-owned transit systems, and a multitude of other economic forms and techniques. That flexibility is precisely the quality needed for effective competition with the Communists' centralized economic system under the new conditions in Africa, Asia, and Latin America.

Freed from the burden of arms expenditures, the Western economies—far more advanced than even the most highly productive Communist states—could be turned to demonstrating the economic progress possible under private and mixed enterprise. The United States now spends over $45 billion for its military establishment. Those billions, some of them returned to private hands by way of tax cuts and some channeled into desperately needed public improvements, could wipe out the pockets of ugliness and poverty that remain in our own society and stimulate inventive private enterprise to new adventures. Part of the money, along with funds from western Europe and Japan, could supply capital for the dams, roads, and schools necessary to help hungry nations achieve scientific agriculture and industrialization.

In a disarmed world, the West and the United States could make vigorous use of international exchange of persons, an able press and radio, and educational aid to make available to the underdeveloped countries the ideas and the skills by which free societies operate. Subtle and flexible use of political, economic, and public-information techniques upon the present Communist states might well encourage either their liberation from below or their liberalization from above. In all these ways, the West and the United States could promote the extension of liberty in areas where it either does not now exist or exists only precariously. The suppression by dictatorial regimes of people who wish to be free would become much more difficult, and at the same time the desire and need of governments to suppress freedom for external reasons would be much lessened.

Advancing freedom would not be simple. All the brains and toughness available in the Western world would be needed in order to, let us say, free Hungary from dictatorship by nonviolent means or reduce the influence of the Communist Party in Indonesia. Undoubtedly, in a disarmed world the Communist states would be trying to sell their own ideas and system of government, but we start ahead in this race, for we want only to help others to make their own free choice.

Competition in the spheres of ideas and economics could be paralleled in many other fields. For example, the exploration of space, under careful controls to prevent space technology from being turned to military ends, could provide a major challenge to all nations and societies. Economically and psychologically, the human voyage into space calls forth all the best qualities of the war spirit without war's dangers to mankind. Space exploration requires the same kind of nonproductive expenditure that military systems demand, and for countries that can afford it, this may be a positive good. Yet the hardware produced is not destructive of human life. The astronaut, like the soldier, is required to face danger, to abandon comfort, to undergo discipline; yet the psychology of space will not demand the surrender of our liberty. No more perfect challenge could be imagined for the energies, talents, and courage that now go into the stultifying profession of improving war.

For Disarmament-Plus to be established as a workable deterrent, it is absolutely necessary that the West and the Communists come to a clear understanding that international violence alone should be prohibited, and that all other techniques would be freely used in all-out competition. . . .

INDEX OF AUTHORS